D0934211

From Sarah to Sydney

From Sarah to Sydney

The Woman Behind All-of-a-Kind Family

June Cummins

WITH ALEXANDRA DUNIETZ

Yale

UNIVERSITY PRESS

New Haven and London

Yale University Press books may be purchased in quantity for educational, business, or
promotional use. For information, please e-mail sales.press@yale.edu (U.S. office) or
sales@yaleup.co.uk (U.K. office).

Set in Bulmer type by IDS Infotech Ltd.
Printed in the United States of America.

ISBN 978-0-300-24355-0 (hardcover : alk. paper)
Library of Congress Control Number: 2020947837
A catalogue record for this book is available from the British Library.

This paper meets the requirements of ANSI/NISO Z39.48-1992 (Permanence of Paper).

10 9 8 7 6 5 4 3 2 1

Contents

Acknowledgments

THROUGHOUT HER LIFE, June Cummins was ever gracious in expressing her appreciation for others. As the result of my wife's untimely death from ALS, it is left to me to recognize the people who helped make this book a reality. Although June and I often discussed her work, I regret that I do not know the names of all those she would have acknowledged. My omissions do not diminish June's gratitude.

As a professor of children's literature at San Diego State University in the late 1990s, June began research into the life and work of Sydney Taylor. She contacted Taylor's daughter, Jo Marshall, and they arranged to meet in the summer of 2002. Interested in June's proposed biography, Jo opened her New Jersey home to June where a trove of Taylor's papers and other effects were kept in the basement. Each summer for the next decade, Jo and her partner, Mary-Carol Mason, welcomed June to study Taylor's collected diaries, letters, scrapbooks, notes, and manuscripts. Without Jo's commitment to and belief in June, this book would not have been possible. Those documents allowed the deep and comprehensive look into Taylor's life that forms the core of the book. Thanks also to Susan Baker and Judy Magid for their insights and for providing access to their mothers' memoirs, and to the many other generous family members and friends whose interviews provided significant, colorful information about Taylor.

At the end of 2015 when June had become too ill to return to work at SDSU, she devoted herself to working on the book full time. By the following summer, her disease had advanced to where she could no longer type, but she could give dictation with the use of an eye-tracking communication device. At that point June asked Alix Dunietz if she might help. As a scholar and a friend, Alix became hooked and came to our house for a few hours most days to work with June, rapidly moving from typist to research assistant and then collaborator. As a result of Alix's devotion, June was able to finish a draft of the book before her death in early 2018. Alix has since then completed the editing and helped prepare the manuscript for publication. My family and I cannot sufficiently express our gratitude for her role in bringing June's work to the world.

June's research trips always included a stop in New York, where she was aided by staff of many institutions, including Ettie Goldwasser, librarian at the YIVO Institute for Jewish Research; Peter Filardo, the Tamiment Archivist at the New York University library; Bibi DrePaul and Charles Oswalt at Morris High School; Esther Zito and Bill Tatton at P.S. 188 on the Lower East Side; and Laura Tosi, librarian at the Bronx County Historical Society. In New York, June was enthusiastically hosted by Naomi and Steven Toder. Naomi also tracked down research materials and brought New York expertise to the book. Thank you also to the staff of the Center for Jewish History, the Little Red Schoolhouse, the Kerlan Collection at the University of Minnesota, and the Veterans History Project Collection at the Library of Congress, especially Megan Harris. The research for this book was greatly aided by the resources of the Northwestern University library, where June was provided borrowing privileges. We are grateful to Susan Addelston and all the Cejwin Camps alumni whose interviews were crucial to understanding that phase of Taylor's life and who remain steadfast in their enthusiasm for this project. Paul Zelinsky was of particular help to Alix in visualizing the Lower East Side of a century ago.

Friend and fellow scholar David Chinitz was always ready to discuss with June matters of biography, scholarship, and life in academia. Later, he provided valuable feedback to Alix in revising the initial draft. With her expertise in the world of books and great kindness, Susan Cohen at Writers' House was an invaluable supporter. Reidar Hahn's photographic talents were vital to preparing the digital images. The professional skills of Sarah Miller and Heather Gold, the book's editors at Yale, and their staffs brought the book to fruition.

Many other people supported June's work along the way. For almost two decades, June commuted between her Chicago home and San Diego because, as she often said, her professorship at SDSU gave her the opportunity to work "in a community of scholars." We are grateful to her colleagues at the university, and especially those in Children's Literature—Jerry Griswold, the late Alida Allison, Joseph Thomas, and Phillip Serrato—for building that community in which she was respected and cherished. Thanks also to the department chairs—Carey Wall, Sherry Little, Joanna Brooks, and Mike Borgstrom—who allowed June a teaching schedule that maintained life-work balance. Mary Garcia always made sure that June's professional life ran as smoothly as possible and was a dear friend as well. June's students at SDSU continually inspired her. Many of them were immigrants or the first in their families to attend college. The story of Taylor's earlier immigrant generation spoke to them and encouraged them to bring fresh ideas to the classroom.

Beyond SDSU, June was active throughout her career in the Children's Literature Association. At the annual ChLA meetings, she met good friends and enjoyed the excitement of the exchange of ideas. Thanks go to all of June's ChLA friends for their support of June and her work, first among them Michelle Martin, June's conference roommate and confidant through the years.

This book could not have been completed without the skill and dedication of the doctors and staff at Northwestern Memorial Hospital and June's caregivers who made it possible for her to work nearly every day for the last two years of her life, especially Paulette Booth, Jasmine Booth, and Lissette Livera. We are also grateful for the assistance of Ileane Mindel and the Les Turner ALS Foundation.

June had champions in her parents, Arthur Cummins and the late Eilene Cummins, and in her sisters, Jackie Dimont and Yvonne Venger. Our sons, Jacob, Noah, and Ethan, share June's love of literature, and as they grew up they too were invested in the insights of her research. Their love, and that of Jacob's wife, Arielle, sustained June throughout the process of writing the book and through her illness.

Finally, thank you to all the Sydney Taylor fans whom June met through the years: your enthusiasm and encouragement remain an inspiration.

Jonathan Lewis
November 2019

From Sarah to Sydney

Introduction

"WHO ARE YOU?" That was a question frequently asked by fans of the *All-of-a-Kind Family* series of books in letters to the author, Sydney Taylor. Readers wanted to know which of the five sisters the author might have been— Ella, Henny, Sarah, Charlotte, or Gertie. Sometimes they hazarded a guess, wrong as often as not. Because Sydney was an ambiguous name, readers also asked whether the author was a man or a woman. Most thought that a woman must have written the books, but some fans addressed their letters to "Mr. Taylor." The third persistent question was whether the stories were true. Children related their own experiences of losing a library book or disliking household chores, spoke of grandmothers who had grown up on the Lower East Side in New York, and confided their own hopes of becoming writers. Seeing themselves in the *All-of-a-Kind* stories, they *wanted* everything to be true.

As a professor of children's literature, I became interested in Sydney Brenner Taylor as a scholarly subject when I decided to include her most famous book, *All-of-a-Kind Family,* in a course syllabus. I was surprised to discover that no scholarship about Taylor or her books had been published, aside from entries in reference series. I remembered reading Taylor's books repeatedly as a child and knew that many others also deeply enjoyed and reread them. My curiosity piqued, I began to dig. The more I learned, the more I wanted to know, and the more surprised I was that so little had been written about her. Those questions her fans asked opened windows on her complex personality: Who was this woman? What was her family like? Why did she have a name of ambiguous gender? How authentic were the experiences she related of a Jewish immigrant past?

As I pursued my research, I gradually realized that Taylor was a transformational figure not only in American children's literature but in

American Jewish life as well. When *All-of-a-Kind Family* debuted in 1951, it was perceived as groundbreaking, the first book from a mainstream publisher to feature Jewish children and reach a sizable general audience. Immediately praised and highly successful, that book and its four sequels, published over the next twenty-five years, introduced millions of Americans to Judaism, forging a bridge through literature that moved Jewish characters and themes from the margins of children's book publishing—and American culture at large—into the national arena, enlarging the public's understanding and increasing its acceptance of American Jews.[1]

All-of-a-Kind Family is still in print and can be found on the shelves of public and school libraries and in bookstores across America. To this day, Taylor's books participate in the national conversation about Jewish culture and identity. They link Jews to non-Jews, as well as contemporary Jews to those of previous generations. The millions of people who read her books as children stand as witnesses to the vital importance of children's books in the transmission of Jewish culture and the preservation of ethnic heritage.

Understanding why the series had such an impact requires knowledge of the historical and cultural environment in which its author grew up and of the circumstances that shaped its publication. This biography not only recounts the life of a daughter of immigrants who achieved artistic and cultural success, but also shows how it belongs to the history of Jewish identity in America and of ethnic diversity in children's books. Taylor lived a life replete with experiences both ephemeral and enduring that were typical for millions of immigrants and their children. In many ways, her life was ordinary. She was educated, worked, married, had a child, and remained close to her family all her life, most of which was spent in New York City. What sets her life apart is that it was so thoroughly documented, and more important, that in her classic series, Taylor transformed her experiences into critically acclaimed literature. Born at the beginning of the century and starting to publish exactly at its midpoint, Taylor both reflected and shaped American Jewish national identity through her writing for children. In doing so, she bridged a cultural divide and made Judaism interesting, familiar, and knowable across the country.

Taylor's semi-autobiographical books exemplified complicated issues of identity because their author's life was rich with the possibilities of being a Jew in America. The eponymous family of the series includes five sisters, each two years apart, dressed alike by their fastidious mother and looking all the same, all-of-a-kind. Sydney Taylor was, in fact, the third of the five sisters, known in the books as Sarah. The other four sisters all had names that are the same in the books and in their real lives, but the real-life Sarah changed her name to Sydney at age fourteen.

Taylor's conscious desire to change her name at this young age was emblematic of three intertwined issues: Jewish identity, artistic identity, and sexual identity. Much later in her life, Taylor claimed that she changed her name when she joined an acting troupe in her early twenties, but her diaries reveal that she changed it significantly earlier. Letters she received as a teenager show that her friends and relatives tried hard to address her by Sydney, or Sid or Syd, but sometimes, not surprisingly, slipped and referred to her as Sarah. This confusion of names and the identities attached to them persisted throughout Taylor's life and even past her death, as children continued to send fan letters to "Mr. Taylor."

Taylor's decision to change her name emerged from her idealistic plans to make a mark on society. She was determined to be different, a self-made American woman. In terms of artistic identity, at the time Taylor made the change, she also began keeping a diary and was imagining and inaugurating herself as an author. As she became an actress, a dancer, and a writer, she kept the name she chose as a teenager for her developing artistry. In terms of sexual identity, the gender of Sydney is ambiguous, as demonstrated by the initial confusion of the woman who became her editor, as well as by the mistakes of children writing fan letters. Taylor liked to be mistaken for a boy, and her own daughter experimented with lesbianism as early as age twelve. Taylor seemingly both encouraged and rejected her daughter's lesbianism, suggesting a lifelong conflict with sexual identity, of which her name change was emblematic.

The name change expressed a hunger for change and self-transformation typical of second-generation Americans. The child of Jewish immigrants who came to the United States at the turn of the last century, Taylor was born and grew up in New York City. She was shaped by her mother's attachment to German culture and her father's artistic skills and absorbed the ferocious work ethic of both parents. Like thousands of Jewish children, she attended public schools on the Lower East Side and in the Bronx, started working while still a teenager, and participated in the leisure and cultural activities of her peers. She also belonged to a socialist youth group—an activity shared by many Jewish teens in New York during this time—and attended a socialist summer camp. While engaged in political activities, Sydney Brenner met and married another child of immigrants, Ralph Schneider, equally ambitious and equally determined to forge an identity for himself.

In her twenties, Taylor's path started to veer from politics to the arts, inspired by personal inclination and her husband's interests in dance and music. She performed with an experimental acting company and then became a dancer, joining Martha Graham's dance troupe. Nonetheless, her interests in politics and the arts were not disconnected. Most of the young women dancing with Graham were progressive Jews, the daughters of immigrants—and Taylor's socialist politics persisted in some form throughout her life.

Taylor's left-leaning politics exerted an influence on her writing for children, and other aspects of her life colored her portrayal of childhood on the Lower East Side. Contextual research on a variety of subjects—such as progressive education, the New Woman, socialism, Jewish assimilation—that influenced Taylor's life and books allows us to assess her impact more clearly. It elucidates the deep connections between the books and American Jewish experiences and demonstrates how influential Taylor was in the development of national Jewish identity.

In addition to being a successful writer, "Aunt Syd" worked for more than forty years at Camp Cejwin in Port Jervis, New York, one of the oldest Jewish culture camps, where she served as resident playwright, theater director, and dance instructor for young campers. Remembered today as a beloved staff member, she was an instrumental figure in an institution that enriched Judaism for thousands of children. As Jonathan Krasner, a prizewinning historian of Jews in America, wrote: "It was at Cejwin and its early imitators where Jewish education 'as participation in Jewish life in all its aspects' was pioneered and arguably reached its apex."[2]

Taylor herself pioneered an embrace of "Jewish life in all its aspects" by meticulously describing many Jewish holidays, observances, and customs to both non-Jewish readers and assimilated Jews who had little or no previous knowledge of the culture. At the same time, Taylor depicted the normal, quotidian experiences that any young reader would find familiar: losing a library book, getting sick or lost, buying candy, or learning to tell time. Blending the unusual and the ordinary with humor, wit, and affectionate rendering of character, Taylor made her readers aware of Judaism as something worth knowing and not strange. Adult readers, both Jewish and non-Jewish, who remember reading Taylor's books always exclaim with passion that they "loved" them and frequently say they enjoyed learning about Jewish customs from them.

Sydney Taylor's books occupy an important place in the dialogue specifically of Jewish identity and generally of ethnically diverse children's literature. But there was a period when Taylor's writing career stalled and her choices for dramatic material at Cejwin were questioned. Her heartwarming stories may have been beloved by readers, but in the 1960s and '70s publishers and critics questioned their market and pedagogical value. Looking at that difficult period in Taylor's life allows us to trace how adults have negotiated social change through the construction of reading material for children. Because children's books are often concerned with the development of identity and are influential in inculcating cultural norms, evolving editorial responses to Taylor's work offer clues to societal change on a fundamental level. The story of the woman who wrote what she knew, bridged cultural and generational divides, and brought awareness of Judaism to the American public through literature opens a path to understanding how American identity is formed.

Author's Note

Because of its various permutations during the author's lifetime, Sydney Taylor's name presents a challenge. In this biography, the writer is referred to as "Taylor." When material from her books and from her sister Charlotte's memoir "Touched with Fire" is used, she appears as "Sarah" or "Sara," depending on the usage in those sources.

Silent corrections in the quotations from letters and diaries were made for common errors in spelling and grammar. The exception is the idiosyncratic style of Morris and Cilly Brenner's correspondence. To keep their voices, their letters have been copied as written.

The books are referred to in abbreviated form: *All-of-a-Kind Family* (*AKF*), *More All-of-a-Kind Family* (*More*), *All-of-a-Kind Family Uptown* (*Uptown*), *All-of-a-Kind Family Downtown* (*Downtown*), *Ella of All-of-a-Kind Family* (*Ella*). Page numbers refer to the original Follett editions, and for ease of use they have been included in the body of the text rather than in the endnotes.

Family Background in the Old Country

1880–1900

O N E D A Y I N B R E M E N, Germany, in around 1893, a pert ten-year-old girl looked out the window of her family home and saw a funny-looking man walking down the street toward her house. She thought, "Was für ein hässlicher Mann!" ("What a horrible man!").[1] It may have been his beard, or the unfashionable clothes indicating that he was from the country, or perhaps he wore *peyes*, the sidelocks that some observant Jewish men wear, though that was not the custom in her own family—but something about the man made her recoil. She was a cultured young woman, physically well developed for her age, who dressed in contemporary German fashion and attended school. A city girl, she laughed at the country bumpkin walking down her street. Little did she know, at that moment, that she would later marry this man and move to America with him.

At seventeen, the man Cecilia Marowitz saw, Morris Brenner, was seven years her senior. He had come to Bremen to join his older brothers and to find a job. With Bremen undergoing rapid economic expansion over the preceding decade, immigrants like Morris made up 40 percent of its population.[2] Had he stayed in his small town in the Austro-Hungarian Empire—Wisnicz, in the province of Bochnia, near Krakow—the only job available to him would have been in a brush factory, crafting brushes with pig bristles. In addition to supporting himself, he had to earn enough money to help pay for the dowries of his sisters back in Wisnicz, an obligation that brothers were expected to fulfill in shtetl culture.[3] After Morris arrived in Bremen, he joined one of the few industries open to the Jews of the town—the junk business.

Related to the garment and textile industries long associated with Jews, the junk business involved collecting used clothing, discarded materials, and unwanted household objects and then sorting, bundling, and reselling them. In effect, it was recycling. There is a traditional Jewish folktale, redacted by many authors, which tells the story of a tailor, or child, making something from nothing. In Phoebe Gilman's picture book version of the story, a little boy does not want to let go of his baby blanket but allows his grandfather, a tailor, to cut it down bit by bit and recycle it into a jacket. As the boy grows, the piece of cloth shrinks as it is repurposed in various ways, until it is big enough only to cover a button, which is then lost. The final "something" that the child makes from "nothing" is the story itself, the tale of the many lives of his blanket.[4] And *this* story, too, the story of the life of Sydney Taylor, is a text about texts, another story of a writer, and another story that begins in recycling.

Readers of the *All-of-a-Kind* series know that Papa's occupation is the junk business. Those familiar with Jewish immigrant history could probably draw a connection between the junk businesses Jews were allowed to own in late nineteenth-century Germany and the industry that they would be instrumental in founding and developing in the United States—namely, the garment industry, or as older Jews would call it, "the *schmatte* business." *Schmatte* is the Yiddish word for rags, and rags are what Morris Brenner dealt in, both in life and in fiction. His daughter Sarah Brenner, who would grow up to be Sydney Taylor, was also in the schmatte business, if the physical material of the pages of the book are considered a kind of rag, and the mental material of the story a recycling of the scraps of her history. The meeting of Morris and Cecilia in Bremen was the first haphazard event of a series that would lead to the publication of Taylor's books for children, almost sixty years later.

Cecilia, known throughout her life as Cilly, spoke German, but she was not born in Germany; she came with her family from a part of Poland then under Russian control when she was about two years old.[5] The story of this, her first immigration, was the stuff of fairy tales. After her family left their small town near Warsaw, they stopped for a time in Krakow while waiting for their connecting train to Bremen.[6] Cilly's two older brothers, Samuel and Morris, were charged with watching their toddler sister while the parents, Israel and Yetchin Marowitz, took a walk with their infant son, Herman. The two older boys went sightseeing with Cilly, but somehow misplaced her.

When the loss was discovered, the entire family desperately began searching for their baby. They turned to a Jewish agency in Krakow, one of several that existed to help Jewish immigrants moving from city to city. The agency took care of them, contacting people about the lost girl, taking out ads, and helping the family post signs in carriages (*droschkes*). A whole week passed with no sign of Cilly.

In the end, it was the signs in the droschkes that produced results. A cabdriver approached the family with Cilly in his arms. He had found the child in the city, and since he and his wife were childless and wanted a baby, he took her. They kept Cilly until the man noticed a sign in a droschke and realized her family was searching for her. He felt he had no choice but to return the ceaselessly crying child to her parents, who were delighted and relieved to have their daughter with them once again.

Cilly nearly slipped away from her family, but another daughter was deliberately left behind. That daughter, Minnie, who would be known by Taylor and her sisters only as "Tanta" ("Auntie"), lived with her mother's sister-in-law.[7] The aunt had taken Tanta—who was no more than two at the time—to her home when Cilly's mother had a miscarriage, before Cilly was born. While Tanta stayed with these childless relatives, her mother recovered from the miscarriage, became pregnant with Cilly and gave birth to her, and then suffered another miscarriage. After she had her next child, a son named Herman, the father, an aspiring merchant, decided to leave their small town and move to a big city so he could earn a living. He and his wife wanted to take their daughter with them to Germany, but the aunt begged to keep the girl, pointing out that the Marowitzes had four children while she had none. Cilly's parents agreed to leave Tanta behind. In both cases of their daughters' disappearances, a couple's childlessness played a part in the story, as it does in so many fairy tales. For the little lost Cilly, the cabdriver's kindheartedness and her family's diligence resulted in a happy ending. For Tanta, however, her fairy-tale beginning as a child lent to another family took a darker turn. As the rest of her family prospered in Bremen, Tanta was deprived of an education and treated as an unpaid servant, forced to do housework for her childless aunt and uncle.

In the meantime, Cilly and her brothers enjoyed the life their father created in Bremen. The city was something of a boomtown at the end of the nineteenth century. Situated on the Weser River in the northern part of Germany, it became a major port city, developing from a relatively sleepy town where most people worked in the clothing industry into an industrial center that attracted many people from other parts of Germany and Europe, such that by 1905, the majority of its residents had come from somewhere else. Additionally, thousands of Europeans moved through Bremen on their way overseas, most often to America.[8] A worldly, ambitious man, Israel Marowitz set up several businesses, including one in jewelry and other luxury goods, and flourished in his bustling new home. Cilly was sent to school and given fine clothing and other possessions.

By the 1890s, the Marowitz family had become comfortably middle class, like the majority of German Jews at that time. Seeking to be as respectably German as possible, in a bid to increase acceptance and diminish anti-Semitism, many Jews adopted the values of the *Bildungsbürger*—that is, a member of the educated middle classes.[9] The state of *Bildung*, roughly translated as "education" and "culture," "appealed to Jews," writes historian Marion Kaplan, "because it could transcend differences of religion or nationality through the development of the individual personality."[10] The values connoted by *Bildung* included "a cultured, well-bred personality, an autonomous person of refined manners, aesthetic appreciation, politeness and gentility."[11] Jews thus actively participated in cultural activities such as going to the theater and opera; they sought education more than other groups in Germany, including German nationals; and they invested much energy and attention in the furnishing and decorating of their homes.

Cilly was very much a product of this German Jewish bourgeoisie. She attended school like other Jewish girls, who were generally more educated than non-Jewish girls.[12] Her daughters long remembered her love of Shakespeare, whose works she studied in German translation. Raised in a culture where great emphasis was placed on refinement and gentility, Cilly wore fine clothes and studied feminine arts such as penmanship and singing. Hence, when Morris Brenner appeared before her, she immediately sensed the difference between her, a bourgeois German Jewish girl, and him, one of the lower-class *Ostjuden*, or Eastern European Jews.

Morris's children heard fewer stories about his family than about their mother's, but they gleaned enough to be touched by their father's poverty and impressed by his intelligence and artistic creativity. Family lore said that his parents were originally from Hungary, and that both their fathers, his grandfathers, had been rabbis.[13] The youngest of eleven children, Morris (Moshe) went to religious school (*cheder*), where he learned Hebrew and studied the Torah. As adults, his children surmised that he attended a secular school as well, because he knew some basic mathematics and could read and write Polish. Ella Kornweitz née Brenner—his oldest daughter and the eponymous heroine of *Ella of All-of-a-Kind Family*—recalled that her father helped her with her algebra homework when she struggled with it in high school. He did not tell his children much about his school days, either what he learned or whether he liked going to school. Before he was thirteen, he was already working in the local brush factory.

Ella remembered a number of stories about her father's childhood poverty that affected her deeply. When she asked him what kind of candy he had enjoyed, expecting him to mention an Old World equivalent of jellybeans or lemon drops, her father chuckled ruefully. He said he would take a few lima beans from the soup pot and slip them in his pocket to eat later as "candy." After she heard that story, Ella could never eat lima beans again without thinking sadly of her father's childhood privations. She remembered feeling guilty because she and her sisters did not want to eat the beans in their soup, while her father had eaten them as a treat. She learned to think of beans as a delicacy, and could always see in her mind's eye her papa digging around in a dirty pocket for "candy"—a lima bean.[14]

Morris retained more memories of his mother than of his father because of his father's job as an itinerant peddler. Joseph Brenner left Wisnicz after Passover and did not return until Rosh Hashanah. Three weeks later, after Sukkos, he was on the road again, not returning to his family before Purim—often to learn that another baby was on the way. If he was having a good season, he might make it home for the holidays of Shavuos or Chanukah, but the family could not count on those visits. It was Morris's mother who stayed in Wisnicz, scraping together money by working in a bakery and finding other temporary work.

Although the need to work weighed on all the family members, time for other activities was carved out of the busy days. From an early age, Morris showed signs of artistic ability. At six, he displayed an aptitude for carving when he shaped a large stone into a kind of tombstone and carved his own epitaph on it. A little later, he fashioned his own violin with a cigar box, complete with horsehair bow. When he became a bar mitzvah, Morris followed the custom of the boys of Wisnicz in choosing to do something special to commemorate the experience and to demonstrate the importance of his religion: he made a *mizrach* in the form of a papercut, an intricate, many-layered image created from the simple materials of butcher paper and vegetable dyes.[15]

It took Morris four years to complete his papercut. As described in the catalogue of an exhibition of Jewish art, it "combines two elements of two types of documents: the mizrah, meaning 'east,' a drawing or tapestry symbolizing hopes for the restoration of the Temple in Jerusalem, which is hung on the east wall of a house to indicate the direction of prayer; and the *shivviti,* from the phrase 'Shivviti Adonai l'negdi tamid' (I have set the Lord always before me. Psalm 16:8), frequently found on the bimah in a synagogue."[16] The piece contains fantastical plants and animals, signs of the zodiac, Kabbalistic terminology, and long sections of the Song of Songs and Psalms in Hebrew. The double-headed eagle, which dominates the center of the picture, conveyed a double meaning: the eagle was both a religious symbol from Jewish sacred texts and, in the double-headed form, a political symbol of patriotism, referring to "the royal crest of Austro-Hungarian Emperor Franz Joseph, who was known for his goodwill toward Jews."[17]

When he was seventeen, the five-foot-tall Morris left Wisnicz to find a better job and a better life. In this way, he resembled thousands of other Jewish young men from Eastern Europe and Russia who left their homes, primarily for economic reasons.[18] Morris chose Bremen because his older brothers, Schloimon and Hyam-Yonkel, had gone there earlier. The brothers lived in the other half of the building in which Cecilia Marowitz's family lived, and were later joined by yet another brother, Nathan. The brothers were part of a larger trend that deeply affected German Jewish society. In the late nineteenth century, the Jewish population in Germany had been declining relative to the non-Jewish population; thus, Jews made up a smaller percentage of the nation even though the absolute number of German Jews was increasing slightly. It was the influx of immigrants from the east that prevented the decline from being even more marked.[19]

Over the next few years, Morris flourished. Young and ambitious, he climbed into the lower middle class as he worked for Cilly's parents, who ran a used clothing and furniture business on the ground floor of their home. It was a successful enterprise, and Morris benefited from their prosperity. His

Morris Brenner papercut (Courtesy of Susan Baker)

particular task was to go around the town with a dogcart to collect used clothing. He sold this clothing to Cilly's mother, and he began to set aside his earnings so that he could ask Cilly to marry him.

For it did not take long before Morris and Cilly fell in love, not much longer than it took for Morris to shed his sidelocks and religious clothing. He never became assimilated, but his transformation during those first years after he left Wisnicz, though common, was radical. He became a city boy, self-assured and dapper. By the time Cilly was in her mid-teens, she wanted to marry Morris, but Morris first had to return to Wisnicz with enough money for the dowries of his unmarried sisters. Morris and Cilly's courtship dragged out, and Cilly grew frustrated. At the same time, she wanted Morris to be well established financially, so that she could continue to live in a home as comfortable as that of her parents.

Israel Marowitz had done well in Bremen. As a businessman, he was a success, but as a family man he might have done better, as far as his wife was concerned. Having lived for several years in the household of an uncle whom she, though traditionally pious in many ways, considered almost fanatical, Yetchin had been glad to marry this dashing teenager when she was eighteen. Two years her junior, Marowitz was already a promising merchant, and his grandchildren repeatedly described him as a "man of the world." That was true on more than one level. Most obviously, as a traveling salesman he saw much more of the world—albeit the relatively small world of Germany—than his housebound wife did. On another level, he was worldly and charming. Derby hat perched jauntily on his head, he always had a cigar in his mouth and often a woman by his side.

The distance between Marowitz's worldliness and Yetchin's religiosity caused problems for their marriage, for her adherence to the rules of Orthodox Judaism reportedly caused friction between them. A hundred years later, the Brenner sisters repeated what they had heard about the strict religious prohibition against having sex for at least two weeks out of every month being at the root of the sexual distance between husband and wife, driving their grandfather into the arms of other women.[20] It must be remembered, however, that Yetchin bore six children and suffered several miscarriages. The couple clearly had sexual relations, but according to family lore Yetchin considered this a duty and not a pleasure.

The granddaughters concluded that there must have been sexual incompatibility because Marowitz had a long-term mistress, whom he met through his business. She was a *sartirfrau,* one of the women who used to sort and grade the woolens collected in the used clothing and recycling trade. This woman eventually moved into his family's home and lived with him, his children, and his wife. Yetchin obviously put up with the arrangement, since it was happening under her roof, but there is no record, oral or written, that explains how she felt about it. Her children, including Cilly, grew attached to the mistress, who was affable and lovely. The children referred to her as the *machshaifeh* (the witch), an epithet that referred to her enchanting personality. As Ella explained later, "Mama said you couldn't help but like her. She had something magical about her. You couldn't hate that woman no matter what she did to you."

When Marowitz and his mistress went on business trips together, Yetchin would sometimes send a child to join them. On one of these occasions, when Cilly had gone to her father, she was sleeping in a room adjoining the one shared by her father and his mistress. During the night, she heard the two of them laughing and carousing. Cilly considered this activity to be sinful. When she grew up and had her own children, Cilly told her daughter Charlotte this story, explaining that the incident embarrassed her and may have been responsible for why she herself was "turned off" (as her daughters put it) from sex for most of her adult life. Her children saw her as having inherited the "Puritanical" views toward sex that her mother, Yetchin, expressed, although Yetchin of course would not have used that term.

Unsanctioned sexual behavior in the Marowitz family did not occur only between Marowitz and his mistress. Even though his behavior was outside the rules of Orthodox Jewish family life, by having both a wife and a mistress Marowitz was still acting within the range of what was—and still often is—considered normal adult male behavior. Elsewhere in his household, however, others were engaging in sexual behavior that most would see as far more unconventional and even morally repugnant.

When Cilly was in her early teens, she caught a glimpse of her brother Morris and her sister Tanta in an embrace, and she knew it was not the sort of embrace siblings should share. When she realized what she was witnessing, her "eyes nearly popped out of her face."[21] She looked over to her mother, who was in bed, having recently given birth, but her mother just shook her head and turned her face to the wall. Cilly knew then that her mother was aware of the incestuous relationship, and she was upset not only by the relationship but also by her mother's apparent decision not to intervene. As her daughters described it, this was more *tsuris* (trouble) Cilly had to carry around with her throughout her life.

The affair between the siblings began when the two older brothers in the family went to fetch Tanta from Poland. She had been living with her aunt and uncle for years, but when Tanta turned sixteen Yetchin insisted on having her back in her own family, so arrangements were made for the older boys to travel to Krakow and bring her to Bremen. When Morris laid eyes on his sister, whom he had not seen in years, he was smitten. She had platinum-blonde hair and lovely blue eyes. Morris was only two or three years older than Tanta. The two had not grown up together, and their instant and mutual attraction would have been understandable and natural had they not been siblings. Youthful ardor overtook moral taboos, and the two became lovers. Cilly's children found out about the incestuous relationship from their uncle Herman, who presented it to them not as something to celebrate or gossip about but as a terrible family secret. As adults, the Brenner children realized the far-reaching implications of the incest, and Ella said that it destroyed her aunt and uncle's lives.

Tanta's life was difficult from the beginning, starting with being left behind when her family moved to Germany, and in the intervening years before she rejoined them when she was treated as a servant. She could cook and clean, but she could neither read nor write, and her family's efforts to educate her came too late.[22] When she was reunited with her family, she was extremely resentful. She saw that her younger sister Cilly was accomplished and educated. Not only was she attending a private school, but Cilly also worked in the family business as a bookkeeper, helping to keep the voluminous records required by the government. She had beautiful handwriting and a lovely singing voice. Ella recalled that her aunt never overcame her envy. As sympathetic as Ella was toward the difficulties Tanta experienced, she did not seem to fully comprehend how much forces beyond Tanta's control were responsible for her aunt's lifelong unhappiness: abandonment, forced servitude, lack of education and opportunities, and neglect.

Now Cilly, used to being the only daughter in a sea of brothers, had an older sister. Another sister, Frieda, was born about thirteen years after Cilly, but for many years Cilly had been the only girl in the family. Tanta and Cilly remained close, at least in terms of physical proximity, for the rest of their lives, but Ella remarked on the lack of sisterly feeling between them.[23] Despite this emotional distance and Tanta's ongoing resentment, Tanta became a tremendous help to her sister. Through all of Cilly's years as a mother and her struggles adjusting to life in New York City, Tanta stood by her and was like a second mother to the Brenner children. Even as adults, they spoke of Tanta with affection, but it is telling that they never referred to her by her given name. Ella said that for much of her life she did not even know what it was. Other aunts were called Tanta Olga or Tanta Frieda, but Tanta was just Tanta.[24]

Unusual or deviant sexuality never surfaces in the books and plays that Sydney Taylor wrote for children. But Tanta as a character does. She is one of the only relatives outside the Brenner nuclear family who recurs as a character in the series, appearing in three of the five books (*AKF, Downtown, Ella*), while *Downtown* is dedicated "To Tanta—always there when needed."

Extramarital affairs and incest are far apart on the range of sexual behavior that falls outside social conventions, yet the Brenner family accepted both to some extent. Marowitz's mistress shared the family home, and Morris and Tanta were not cast out but, it seems, were tacitly allowed to have their relationship, at least for a while. This acceptance, or at least acknowledgment, of sexuality that pushed the boundaries of traditional family structure reappeared in subsequent generations.

Against this background, Cilly and Morris Brenner proceeded with a normal, almost routine courtship, its only obstacle being Morris's financial obligation to his sisters. Eventually Cilly grew tired of waiting for Morris to propose and took steps to make him act more quickly, flirting with a young non-Jewish man who was enamored of her. Her daughters assumed that she could not have been serious about this potential relationship, though intermarriage in Bremen did happen. Cilly had attended a school where she and one other girl were the only Jews. She had non-Jewish friends, and it was possible she could have fallen in love with a non-Jewish boy. However, family lore does not suggest anything more serious than a brief dalliance between Cilly and this gentile beau. In any case, her attempt to spur Morris into action by exciting his jealousy failed. Morris still did not propose.

Cilly's next plan was more drastic. Since jealousy proved ineffective in making Morris declare himself, perhaps absence would work. Cilly decided to go to America. It was not that unusual for single women to cross the ocean, and German Jewish women had been doing it for some time. They sometimes left with men they were engaged to, and sometimes they left in order to find a man to marry in the New World. That may have been the pretense under which Cilly left in the hopes of inspiring Morris to act.

Cilly's one Jewish friend, the only other Jewish student at her school, was a relative of her uncle Hyam-Yonkel's wife. This young woman had already immigrated to America, and Cilly decided to follow her, aided by some money from her father. As much as she hoped to encourage a proposal from Morris, Cilly also thought she would make her fortune in America. When she arrived, she learned right away that immigrants were more likely to struggle with poverty than to strike it rich. Like hundreds of thousands of Jewish immigrants, she first settled on the Lower East Side of Manhattan, in the neighborhood of Sheriff Street and Rivington Street, which the Jewish immigrants pronounced "Re-VINK-ton." Following a common trajectory, Cilly first boarded in a tenement apartment with earlier immigrants—in her case, with Hyam-Yonkel's wife's family. Most of the residents of these tenements had boarders, often relatives fresh off the boat. Conditions were so crowded that two shifts of people frequently lived in one tenement: the day-shift people slept at night and vacated the house during the day, while the night-shift people did the opposite. As soon as a bed became empty, someone else would come to fill it for the next shift.

Cilly soon found a job with a wealthy family much farther uptown, on Central Park West. The family wanted a *fräulein,* a young German woman, to care for their son. Cilly was well educated and spoke German beautifully, both characteristics considered desirable in a nanny. Such traits were also in increasingly short supply.

In the "Old Country," Jewish women had always worked.[25] Cilly herself worked for her family's business, keeping the books in her elegant handwriting. To girls like Cilly, though, including those far less well off than she, domestic service was considered far from the first choice for employment. To be sure, being a nanny is not the same as scrubbing floors and emptying chamber pots. Still, Jewish women disdained the idea of living in someone else's house to work for them, as Cilly would be doing. Historian Susan A. Glenn writes that for Jewish women in Europe, "whatever material comforts and security were afforded to domestics, the benefits scarcely compensated for

the humiliation associated with servitude. It impl[ied] a loss of independence
and an acknowledgement of inferiority."[26] That attitude persisted in America.
By the end of the nineteenth century, it was clear that wealthy, uptown families would be disappointed in their search for Jewish immigrant household
help, and Jewish working girls were never identified with domestic service in
the same way as immigrant women from other countries.[27]

Thus Cilly took an unusual step in becoming a domestic worker, and
her quick move out of the Lower East Side into a much wealthier area of New
York was also unusual.[28] By taking the job, Cilly was able to escape the over-
stuffed tenements, but she soon realized that the situation was not ideal. Her
charge proved to be an undisciplined, difficult child, and Cilly could not
stand how he took advantage of his parents' permissiveness. When she finally
confronted them about their son's behavior, the parents dismissed her complaints, which made Cilly even more insistent. In response, the boy's mother
slapped Cilly's face and turned her out of the house, not even paying Cilly
her wages.

Cilly's next job was again that of a *fräulein* for a young boy, this time on
crowded, tumultuous Hester Street. The work proceeded smoothly, until
one fateful day. Unable to sleep due to bug bites that caused itching all over
her body, Cilly determined to identify the source of her misery. It turned out
to be bedbugs, and in a feverish attempt to ease her torment, she began to
clean her sleeping area. She was aghast at the filth under her bed, crawled
right under it to clean, and lost track of her five-year-old charge, who ran out
into the street to play. Informed by the neighbors that her son was unat-
tended, the boy's mother found her son playing alone in the middle of the
road, then rushed into the building calling for the *fräulein,* only to discover a
pair of legs sticking out from under the bed. She pulled Cilly out, "slammed
her good and hard," and cursed her.[29] Once again, Cilly was fired on the spot,
turned out of the house, and not given the money that was owed her. At this
point she found work in a factory, which allowed her to earn enough money
to pay for her board and buy a few small luxuries. Her life gained some stability and regularity—until the day she received a shocking letter from her Morris back in Germany.

Unbeknown to Cilly, Hyam-Yonkel's wife, Tanta Rivka, who wanted
Morris to marry her own niece, had set in motion a scheme to break his commitment to Cilly. Illiterate, Tanta Rivka forced her husband to write letters in

her sister's name filled with falsehoods about Cilly, claiming that she was dating all kinds of men and had become what Ella delicately called "a fallen woman." Hyam-Yonkel then mailed the letters to Rivka's sister in America, who mailed them back to her sister in Bremen as if they had originated with her. The American stamps disguised their origin and lent credence to the accusations. When Rivka received the fake letters, she showed them to her brother-in-law Morris, who was devastated. He wrote Cilly to tell her it was over between them, and Cilly was of course shocked and grief-stricken.

Back in Bremen, one of Morris's brothers took a look at the letters and ridiculed Morris for not realizing they were falsified. Ella surmised that Cilly and Morris must have reconciled, because after about seven months in America, Cilly decided to return home and resume being Morris's girlfriend. Cilly had to ask her father for money because she did not have enough for the fare. Once Cilly returned, Tanta teased her about coming back with a "fortune," which amounted to one rabbit-fur cape.

After more reverses and misunderstandings, Cilly and Morris finally became engaged. Morris took his fiancée to Wisnicz, to show her off and to take care of some paperwork in his village. Cilly later shared with her daughters her vivid memories of the visit. She wore a beautiful green taffeta dress that set off her lovely strawberry-blonde hair. Morris hired a droschke and paraded Cilly around Wisnicz. All the townspeople came out to see the couple drive by, reacting as if Cilly were royalty, and some stood on their rooftops to see the German girl. A well-dressed young woman from Germany, Cilly was the embodiment of elegance to the inhabitants of this rural Polish village.[30]

During this visit, Cilly awoke one night and was dismayed to find her future father-in-law polishing her shoes. She felt that he should not be doing such a lowly job and tried to take the shoes away from him. But he took the position that she was such an important person, he must polish her shoes. The act illustrated to Cilly the high regard in which her fiancé's family held her. Cilly also became friendly with Mina Brenner née Riegelhaupt, the wife of Morris's brother Nathan, and the two women continued to correspond until Mina's murder in the Holocaust. Morris and Cilly still had to negotiate German bureaucracy, which threw obstacles in their way related to birth and marriage certificates. They finally married in August of 1899.

Morris and Cilly established a junk business of their own, but continued to have trouble with German authorities in Bremen. In their campaigns against Polish Jews, government bureaucrats harassed Morris so much that he decided to set up shop in a different German city, Magdeburg. To make this move, he had to give up his business in Bremen, suffering a significant financial loss. His situation remained insecure, and soon became downright dangerous. Morris faced trumped-up charges of dealing in stolen goods and was jailed for six weeks. When his case went to trial, Cilly's meticulous records and the judge's doubts about police corruption—the detective in charge of the case reportedly pressured Cilly to sleep with him—led to dismissal.

On July 14, 1900, Ella was born. The legal papers confirming her birth labeled Ella a *lästige Ausländerin* (unwanted alien) because her father had not been born in Germany. The perceived slight infuriated Morris. Having been hounded from one city to another and falsely accused of a crime, he announced that this was the last straw. He decided to move to America. Israel Marowitz pleaded with Morris to leave Cilly and Ella in Germany with him until Morris established himself in America, but Morris would not be separated from his wife, who felt she had no choice but to comply with his wishes.

Uncle Hyam-Yonkel decided to accompany Morris, as did Cilly's brother, also named Morris. Thus, the Brenners' departure broke up the Marowitz home. To a certain extent, it had disintegrated already. Cilly's mother, Yetchin, had long ago given up taking care of her youngest children, Herman, Joe, and Frieda, in effect handing them over to the care of her husband's mistress. Ella related that her grandmother felt she did not have enough money to look after the children properly. By all accounts, the Marowitz children were happy living with their father's mistress; she was, after all, a likable person.

The family was now broken up to such an extent that caring for Yetchin became a problem. She refused to return to her family in Poland lest they learn of her shame. Tanta seemed the natural choice to stay as her mother's companion, but she bristled under the command that she take care of the ailing woman. In the end, she agreed to accompany Yetchin to Wisnicz, where they lived with Morris Brenner's family. Yetchin soon died, and Tanta began her own journey west. Lacking the wherewithal to buy a ticket to America, Tanta moved first to London, where she was shocked by the poverty of Whitechapel; there she made enough money to reach her preferred destination, America, to be with her brother Morris.

The family was not the only thing falling apart in Cilly's life. Morris wanted to arrive in America with enough money to live on until he established himself, so he auctioned off almost all his little family's possessions in order to avoid shipping costs and secure some cash. Although she was allowed to keep her jewelry, Cilly was devastated by the loss of her elegant furniture. Home furnishings were very much a symbol of the bourgeois German respectability of which Cilly was so proud.[31] Cilly felt that the buyers at the auction conspired to keep the prices unfairly low. She stood in the street with tears running down her face, watching her gorgeous furniture sold for a song. She never forgot this grief and often told her daughters of her devastation.

Because Morris wanted to save every penny, the Brenner party traveled in steerage, the harsh conditions of which are well documented.[32] As soon as the ship left the shore, Cilly was seasick. She crawled into her bunk, where she stayed until the last days of the voyage, which would have taken between thirteen and twenty days. Cilly was in no position to care for fifteen-month old Ella, who was starting to walk and run, and Morris was tending to his wife. The uncles were supposed to keep an eye on the little girl but were not always up to the job. Uncle Hyam-Yonkel always loved to tell the story of seeing baby Ella, who had slipped under some railings on deck, about to topple overboard and grabbing her by the long gown that babies wore in those days to save her from a watery death.

Cilly began to feel better a day or so before the voyage ended. She befriended an officer on the ship and engaged in a mild flirtation, which may have helped her when she encountered her first difficulty upon disembarking the ship. As she was going through customs inspection, her boxes of jewelry aroused the suspicion of the immigration officials, who wondered why a passenger in steerage carried such expensive-looking items. Cilly was subjected to a strip-search—a female official even probed her vagina, looking for stolen jewelry. Cilly was humiliated but eventually convinced the officials that her jewels were gifts from her husband. She always believed that the officer she had been friendly with on board the ship had helped persuade the immigration officials of her integrity. Thus Cilly made her second entrance to America, one colored by humiliation and accusation but rescued by a helping hand.

While Cilly remembered this arrival with mortification, Morris was so moved by the sight of the Statue of Liberty and by the promise of the words he knew were written on its base that his first act after leaving customs was to inquire of strangers how he could become a citizen of the United States. Before finding the home of his aunt and uncle, where he and Cilly planned to stay temporarily, Morris located the office where he could get the papers to start the process of acquiring citizenship. The devotion Morris felt that day for his new land stayed with him the rest of his life. His daughters remembered him as extremely patriotic. Morris hung an American flag out for every holiday, and he wrote a prizewinning article for the Jewish daily newspaper *Forverts,* describing his love for his adopted country.[33]

The difference between Morris and Cilly's memories of their arrival together in America foreshadowed the many conflicts the husband and wife weathered throughout the early years of their marriage, both with each other and with the challenging environment in which they landed. These immigrants, possessing some skills and much ambition, had uprooted themselves from family and tradition. They had to learn to be parents to their own rapidly growing family, at times suffering terrible poverty and even worse calamities. Difficult years lay ahead of them—the very years Taylor depicted as loving, charming, and relatively carefree in her children's books. But even though Taylor omitted some of the enormous trials experienced by her parents, she was not dishonest, only intentionally selective, in her portrayal of this young family's transition to becoming Americans.

Sarah's Childhood on the Lower East Side

1901–1910

WHEN MORRIS AND CILLY stepped off the boat in 1901, they joined a huge movement. That year alone, 58,000 Jews from Eastern Europe landed on American soil.[1] In the period from 1880 to 1920, more than 2 million Jews immigrated to the United States, creating a massive demographic shift.[2] Whereas about 75 percent of the world's 7.7 million Jews lived in Eastern Europe in 1880, and only 3 percent in the United States, by 1920, 23 percent of world Jewry lived in America. Of those immigrant Jews, almost all entered through New York Harbor, and more than any other immigrant group, they stayed in New York. Specifically, they made their home in the small patch of land known as the Lower East Side. When the Brenners arrived, that neighborhood was one of the world's most densely populated spots, with 1,000 residents per acre, surpassed only by Bombay and Calcutta.[3]

Not surprisingly, the Brenners did not find ideal conditions on the Lower East Side, with so many people with few resources packed together. Crammed into tenement housing, Jews lived in homes that were hard to keep clean, lacked hot water and bathrooms save for one toilet down the hall, and crawled with vermin. Lighting, drainage, and ventilation were poor. Often a dozen people or more lived in two rooms. Out in the street, the odor of animal excrement permeated the air, and saloons and brothels were found side by side with markets and general stores.

Morris and Cilly's first stop was the home of his maternal aunt and her husband, the Timbergs. Mr. Timberg ran a barbershop on the ground floor of their building, and every afternoon he closed the store to give violin lessons to his son Herman—later of vaudeville fame. Two of the other

Timberg children were also musically talented and had successful artistic careers.[4] This home was located on 2nd Street near Avenue C, considered a respectable locale. The Brenners' stay there was short, for they soon moved to an inferior dwelling on 5th Street. It had a front room where two boarders lived, Cilly's brother Morris Marowitz and Morris Brenner's brother Hyam-Yonkel. Morris, Cilly, and Ella shared a cramped bedroom in the back.

At this time, baby Ella was fifteen months old. Cilly kept nursing her toddler to prevent another pregnancy. Relying on nursing as a method of birth control often fails, but in Cilly's case it seemed to work, as she continued to "nurse clean" and did not conceive. She did, however, become ill with jaundice, or "de gelsa" (the yellow disease) as she called it, and a doctor was summoned. He impressed upon her how dangerous it was for her to nurse when she was so ill. Frightened by his admonition, Cilly stopped nursing; she quickly became pregnant.

Cilly was sick not only with jaundice but also with longing. She begged Morris to return to Germany, and Morris agreed that they would when her health improved. Cilly later told her children that he never had any intention of going back, and she was angry when she got better and realized she had been deceived. When she recounted this story to her daughter Charlotte, portraying her yearning for repatriation as an illness, she may not have realized she was describing the onset of a mental condition that would worsen over the next few years. For Cilly was entering a rocky time, with pressures that weighed more heavily on her as each new child arrived. While the family increased in size, its finances did not grow commensurately, and Cilly continued to pine for Germany—which to her meant not only a return to her family and a country she loved, but also a return to a financial status that disappeared the day the sham auctioneers took away her beautiful furniture.

When Henrietta, the second child, was born, she was named for Cilly's mother, Yetchin. The night of her birth proved another dreadful time for Cilly. First, a charity doctor arrived to deliver the baby. This unscrupulous man proceeded to molest Cilly while tending to her during childbirth. She did not know what made her weep more—her labor pains or her anger at the doctor's violation. Henrietta was finally born after a difficult labor, and Morris and Cilly went to sleep.

Sometime during the night, a burglar entered through the tiny bedroom window. He crawled right over Morris and Cilly, who were so exhausted that they did not wake. The burglar stole watches and money from the uncles sleeping in the front room. Morris would later tease Henrietta—Henny—by calling the night of her birth and the invasion of the burglar "a bad omen." Every time the rambunctious Henny misbehaved, her father referred back to that incident, jokingly, but obviously never forgetting the calamity that befell them the night she was born.

Shortly thereafter, the family moved across the street. They now lived in a fourth-floor apartment in a building with a high stoop, and Cilly carried her large baby carriage up and down the stairs and stoop whenever she went out or came home. The carriage was special to Cilly because her father bought it for her when Ella was born, and it was one of the only things she was allowed to take with her from Germany. With quality ivory-colored leather, it was, as Ella later described it, a "showpiece." Cilly was proud of it, but struggled to haul it, along with the baby, pillows, groceries, and other domestic burdens, up the stoop and then the four flights of stairs every day. Cilly would have two more children while living in this fourth-floor apartment; she carried that carriage up and down the stairs for years.

It was in this apartment at 708 East 5th Street that Sarah Brenner was born on October 30, 1904. Other than what is conveyed on her birth certificate, nothing specific is known about Sarah's birth. One can imagine, however, the tremendous strain Cilly felt as she struggled to take care of three children, the oldest of whom was only four; cater to the constant stream of relatives who boarded with them; deal with near penury; and haul that carriage up and down the steps. A little over two years later, on January 23, 1907, she gave birth to her fourth child, Charlotte.[5]

Morris Brenner had saved enough money to start his own business, without having to draw on the funds he had brought from Germany and deposited in the bank. Since arriving in the United States, he had lost his initial investment in a candy store near the Lenox Assembly Hall, and his subsequent six-month apprenticeship in a sweatshop, where he learned to sew sleeves on men's suits, was unpaid labor. He decided to return to work he knew and open a junk shop. He saw himself as a businessman, not a factory worker. But a junk *shop* in America was quite different than the junk *business* had been in Germany. In Bremen, the junk business was more respectable, more of a second-hand trading business. In America, the junk business was dirtier, scruffier, and less profitable. Ella preserved painful memories all her life of crying as her father set out on cold days behind his pushcart with its bells, watching him wind woolen cloth and newspaper around his feet before struggling into the big boots that never stayed dry in the slush.

When Morris moved his family yet again, to 17 Avenue D near 3rd Street, he kept what was now a rag business at 79 Avenue D. He decided to specialize in woolen waste, buying rags from peddlers, grading them by fabric type and color, and then selling the bales of rags to middlemen, who sold them as shoddy to factories, where they were reprocessed into cheap yarn for the production of inexpensive clothing. Morris subscribed to a trade magazine for the woolens business, which he diligently read both for its content and in order to improve his English.

The family's new home was a three-room flat on the second floor of a two-story house. Because it was in the attic, the kitchen in the new apartment had a sloping ceiling, but the other two rooms were airy and relatively spacious. The room that remained seared in the children's memories was the communal bathroom. For the two families in the building, the only bathroom was on the ground floor, way back in the hall, behind the stairs. It was next to a coal bin infested with rats, and when residents used the bathroom, they could hear the noise of the vermin. Neighborhood children teased the sisters by telling them that water rats could crawl up the toilet while they were using it, which only added to their terror. Charlotte recalled having to be careful because the coal in the bin could soil one's clothes. No matter how persistently Cilly tried to keep it clean, the toilet remained dirty and frightening.

On the first floor of the building was a landing that opened into a small yard. Above the landing was a large skylight installed to provide light for the first-floor apartment. By crawling over the windowsill, or out through the kitchen window, one could gain access to the little yard, which was surrounded on three sides by the walls of the adjacent buildings. In this space, Morris annually built the family's sukkah, the symbolic booth that Jews erect during the holiday of Sukkos. The entrance to the roof was a trapdoor that was propped open in the summer. It was in the ceiling of the large second-story hall, which contained a closet where Cilly's brother, Uncle Joe, used to store his things. He also used to lock Henny up in it whenever she misbehaved. He was the disciplinarian, and Cilly, with her hands full, let her brother handle punishments however he thought best. Ella hated him and felt sorry for poor Henny, who was often locked in that closet.

Shortly after their move to Avenue D and 3rd Street, Cilly found she was pregnant again and tried to induce a miscarriage. Although Ella was barely seven years old, she was dimly aware of what her unhappy mother was attempting to do. She saw her mother jump on and off tables, washtubs, and other "crazy" things. But nothing worked. Gertrude, the fifth child of the family, was born in the spring of 1908; she was named after her father's sister Gittel, who had died young. Ella remembered that the difficult birth took a long time and that a midwife rather than a doctor attended her mother. Gertie was sickly at the beginning and remained frail and delicate throughout her life. Tanta, who had helped Cilly during previous confinements, was not around this time, and Cilly fell ill herself.

When his wife began coughing up blood, Morris sent her to stay in the country for her health. But when the other guests in the boardinghouse heard her coughing and saw the blood, they threatened to leave, worried that she had brought a dread disease with her from the city—namely, tuberculosis, one of the leading causes of death on the Lower East Side at that time. Cilly actually had pneumonia, another killer. Nevertheless, she was forced to return to the city, as miserable as ever.

Back on the Lower East Side, poverty and ill health haunted the growing family. Cilly's distress did not abate. She was physically weak, still dealing with the pneumonia that caused her to cough up blood, and she became increasingly depressed, often making threatening comments about "taking the gas." By this she meant she would kill herself by putting her mouth on the gas pipe attached to a meter that hung from the ceiling, as in many other Lower East Side homes.[6] Ella vividly remembered the day her mother tried to carry through on the threat and how it was only the prompt action of her father, who happened to be working nearby, that saved her. As Cilly recovered from her suicide attempt, Tanta came to help the family, and Morris was solicitous in his efforts to make things up to his wife. Sometime later, when the summer ended and Tanta went back to work, the family employed a servant.[7] She was a good worker and a kind woman, and the family desperately needed her assistance. But Tanta drove the servant away by making derogatory remarks within her hearing and laughing at her. After the servant left, Morris failed to find another one, and it was Tanta who moved in with the family and did the work of running the household.

Cilly's health improved, but Gertrude came down with dysentery so severe that Cilly and Morris took her to a baby hospital, where the prognosis

Cilly and Morris with the five sisters: Ella, Sarah, Gertie, Charlotte, and Henny, 1909 (Courtesy of Judy Magid)

was dire. Leaving their baby in the hospital, the Brenners, who had no telephone, had to give the nuns the phone number of a local saloon so they could be reached when Gertie's anticipated death occurred. Gertie recovered, but when she was about a year old, she developed convulsions that were somehow related to a stomach ailment. Ella remembered that it was during this time that Gertie's eyes became crossed. All of the older sisters' early memories of Gertie were of her being ill.

In 1910, Morris was just emerging from financial difficulties, which had started in the economic crisis of 1907. He had lost half the money he put into his new business. It took three years, but by 1910 trade was picking up and the family's finances were less strained. At this point, Cilly declared that she would not live in their apartment any longer. Living in an upstairs apartment with five children, plus Uncle Joe, and having no bathroom—no toilet, no bathtub— had become untenable. Their landlady promised to make a bathroom, to pull out a wall in order to make the bedroom larger for the four sisters, and to in-

Sarah (left) and Gertie (Unless noted otherwise, photos are from the private collection of Jo Taylor Marshall and are used with her permission)

clude a window that looked outside. The new bathroom was fully equipped with a toilet and a tub, the new bedroom was larger, with space for two beds, and a new boiler provided hot water.

At the end of that year, however, Cilly again began insisting that they move. Despite the improvements, she wanted a larger apartment. The landlady now offered her own apartment to the Brenners. At first Cilly refused, because the landlady's apartment did not have a toilet. The landlady praised the beautiful, large rooms and the skylight, and agreed to put in a bathroom and a toilet. She pointed out to Cilly how impressive her new furniture would look in the spacious living room. Uncle Joe's employer was a prosperous man whose wife had died after only ten months of marriage. Upon the employer's wife's death, Cilly had been able to buy his fancy furniture, including a piano and a Turkish carpet—all for $100.

In the landlady's former apartment with the new, lovely furniture, the Brenner children rose in their friends' estimation, a fact Cilly mentioned many years later in a letter to Taylor.[8] Absorbing the compliments of her friends, Ella felt she must be privileged. The apartment also boasted a coal stove, a large gas range, and a big boiler. The whole family took baths every

Tuesday and Friday, so even in the summer the stove was kept hot for the bathwater. And because Uncle Joe married right before the move and rented his own place, for the first time the family had no boarder.

From Ella's perspective, these "good" years were only a small part of her childhood. In the audiotapes she made with her sister Charlotte when the two women were older and recalling their youth, the memories she recounts most vividly are of impoverishment and of her struggles as a teenager and young woman trying to pursue a career. But it was this apartment, with its front room and elegant furniture, that Sydney Taylor would describe in her books set on the Lower East Side—three of the five books she published about the All-of-a-Kind Family—and so it is this home that came to represent the family to millions of readers.

In the first book of the series, *All-of-a-Kind Family,* the narrator makes clear that the family is not rich and has to be careful with money. In the opening chapter, the character Sarah is distraught because she lent her library book to a friend who claimed to have returned it to her, but Sarah cannot find it.[9] The loss of the library book is presented as a problem equally of a lack of responsibility and a lack of money in the little lecture Mama delivers to Sarah:

> I'm afraid the library will expect you to pay for it. And it's only right. . . . You borrowed the book and that makes you responsible. The library lets you borrow the book and you're not supposed to lend it to anybody else. I know you wanted to be kind to Tillie, but if Tillie wants to read a library book, then she should take out her own. I wish I could help you pay for this, but you know, Sarah, there's no money for such things. (*AKF* 15)

With this speech, Mama not only intertwines the importance of responsibility and money, but also establishes a set of priorities she wants to impart to her daughters. Friends are important, but they are not as important as adherence to regulations, responsible behavior, and civic duty. Mama's priorities are often an issue in the series, and this is the first clue that her priorities may not be the same as those of other people. Mama is set apart from others in many ways, and the narrator of the books always arranges these comparisons so that Mama comes across as correct and often as superior.

The focus then shifts away from Mama as the girls leave the house and go to the library. There they encounter the new, young, attractive librarian who helps Sarah solve her problem and who will become important to the plot of the book. Even though the librarian is described in glowing terms and quickly becomes an object of adoration of Sarah and her sisters, there is no sense that she is to be compared to Mama. The librarian's high status must be sealed with Mama's approval, which will eventually come.

Readers often cite the next chapter, "Dusting Is Fun," as the episode they most remember when asked what they recall about the *All-of-a-Kind* books. Here, Taylor moves from lessons about responsibility and civics, and from excursions to the outside, public world, to withdrawal into the private, domestic space of the family's front room. The privacy of the room is emphasized as Mama sends in one sister at a time to take her turn at dusting. At the beginning of the chapter, Mama notices that the girls hate this job, and as a result, she comes up with a plan. The next day she hides ten colorful buttons in hard-to-see spots around the front room and tells each girl that when it is her turn to dust, she, Mama, will know how thoroughly the job was done by the number of buttons the girl finds. Now the sisters clamor to be the one to dust that day, wanting to try the game, and Sarah is chosen—it was her turn, after all. Sarah goes into the front room and closes the door.

The next six pages—the majority of the chapter—recount Sarah's quest as she moves from object to object in the room, dusting each one and searching for the buttons. The ostensible purpose of the detailed description of her activity is to relate the fun of looking for and finding the buttons. Yet as Taylor describes Sarah's progress around the room, she also describes in detail the various things that make the front room special. These include a large table, a second table, five chairs, a big fruit bowl, a family photo album, a thick red and green carpet, a piano with several knickknacks on it, a mantel with a china shepherd and shepherdess, lace-curtained windows, doilies, a tall mirror, large seashells, and white-painted woodwork around the windows, door, and baseboard. All of the items Sarah dusts speak to the family's *class*. The previous chapter established that the family does not have much money, but the elegant, even luxurious, objects in the front room demonstrate that someone cares about having lovely things, the kinds of things that cost money and require care to maintain.

In a book series that Taylor's books are sometimes compared to, the *Little House on the Prairie* novels by Laura Ingalls Wilder, a china shepherdess plays a similar role. Whenever the pioneer family is able to settle in a new residence, Laura's mother sets out the china shepherdess to signal that the house, though perhaps rough, has become a home for her family. Even more so, the china shepherdess represents civilization, symbolizing not only Mama's role in the Ingalls family as the person who makes sure her girls are well mannered and refined, but also the Ingallses' role in bringing order and cultivation to the prairie, or at least their belief that this is what they are doing. The shepherdess that Mama displays in *All-of-a-Kind Family* shares the same purpose of making a house a home, and to a certain extent she also serves the purpose of identifying the family as civilized and refined in a place, the Lower East Side, that is described at the beginning of the next chapter as "not pretty," as having a river that smells of "fish, ships, and garbage" (34).

Mama's china shepherdess also distinguishes her family as more refined than the neighbors. That point is reinforced in a variety of ways. The most obvious is when the narrator overtly compares Mama to other women in the neighborhood: "The children were very proud of Mama. Most of the other Jewish women in the neighborhood had such bumpy shapes. Their bodies looked like mattresses tied about in the middle. But not Mama. She was tall and slim and held herself proudly. Her face was proud, too" (65). Physically, Mama's superiority is in both shape and height. The word *proud* comes up three times in the paragraph as the narrator subtly connects Mama's pride to the control and maintenance of her appearance.[10]

At other times, Mama's superiority is alluded to without being spelled out. At the end of "Dusting Is Fun," when Mama's plan to get her daughters to dust has proved an obvious success, the narrator concludes, "The grumbling didn't stop completely, but it was not nearly so loud or so often. And in the meantime, the children were taught to be the best little housekeepers in the whole world" (33). Even as the girls' housekeeping abilities are praised, the word *taught* maintains, subtly, the presence of the mother who teaches them to be so clean and orderly.

A third way that Mama's superiority is suggested, and in this case an additional way her superiority is linked to cleanliness, comes up both in the novels and in Charlotte Brenner Himber's autobiography, "Touched with Fire." In this case, it is the sisters' clothing that is described. The prolonged attention to what the girls wear serves more than one purpose. On one hand, it explains the title of the book and series, "All-of-a-Kind," as all the girls wear the same outfit. On another, it establishes Mama's skills as a seamstress and her high standards. The lengthy description of the sisters' clothing is presented from the point of view of the Library Lady when she first meets them:

> Had she been able to peek under those dresses, she would have understood why they billowed out in such a manner. Underneath there were *three* petticoats, a woolly, flannel one first, a simple cotton one next, with both of these topped by a fancy muslin garment which was starched to a scratchy crispness. In order to save money, Mama made those petticoats herself. Still further underneath was long woolen underwear, over which were pulled heavy knitted woolen stockings, making thin legs look like well-stuffed frankfurters. How the girls hated those stockings! They itched so! *And they never wore out!* Mama knitted them herself on long needles and she could always reknit the holes the children made. (23)

With her emphasis on the unusual number and durability of the children's clothing and her inclusion of the phrase "fancy muslin garment . . . starched to a scratchy crispness," Taylor signals Mama's specialness. Taken together, numerous details about the family—the comparison of Mama's physical self to that of the other women, the description of the elegant front room, the label of "the best little housekeepers in the whole world," and Mama's role in her daughters' public dress—lead to the conclusion that Mama expected her children to claim a superior position in their neighborhood.

In her autobiography, Charlotte Brenner describes the girls' clothing similarly, but makes clearer how it set their mother apart. She also remembers that their clothes were better than those of other children, although her focus is on how the clothes were *made* differently. When Charlotte recounts her first day at school, she describes the clothing of the other first-grade girls: "Of those who wore pinafores, none had the ample starched needlework wings of ruffles on the shoulders such as Mama had their dressmaker sew for her girls. Nor did they have the silky percale sashes tied in huge bows in the back. Mama was proud of those pinafores and laundered them stiffly on Mondays. Lottie felt a little superior to the girls with their skimpy pinafores."[11]

It is Charlotte who tells how the term "all-of-a-kind family" was coined. In her memoir, she writes that a group of Chinese women visited the school the sisters attended. Called to the principal's office with some other students, the Brenner girls made an impression: "They all wore the same starched snow-white pinafores, with the white embroidered ruffles standing out like angels' wings on their shoulders." Charlotte then switched to the perspective of the principal: " 'My, I see you all wear the same hair ribbons too.' She admired the bows and Ella looked proud, for it was her chore each morning to make them, and she always took great pains to see that they stood up and billowed. Other children's bows always lay limp and flat on their heads." The principal singled out the sisters for their exemplary appearance: "You can see . . . they are clean and well behaved right here in New York's East Side. And these are perfect little ladies; you should meet their mother, a fine gentlewoman." At that moment, one of the visitors said, "They're all of a kind—an all-of-a-kind family."[12]

Charlotte, like Taylor, associated their refined, elaborate clothing with their mother, although she also credits Ella. Furthermore, she learned from the principal's treatment of the Chinese visitors that what had embarrassed her about her mother was not a cause for shame:

> The Chinese women spoke English with an accent. Charlotte was surprised that such important people who were treated with deep respect by a lofty school principal spoke with an accent. She had been ashamed of her mother's German accent. To add to her delight she understood that their family had been singled out for this demonstration. Cleanliness, cleanliness, that was the whole magic. Always, she resolved, she must remember that with cleanliness you can lick the world.[13]

Here, Charlotte glides from the topic of embarrassing accents to the seemingly unrelated realization that cleanliness will get you anywhere. In fact, the word that links these two topics together is *German*. For Mama's German accent is not unrelated to her emphasis on cleanliness, stereotypic though that association seems to be.

Charlotte connects another feature of the family's dynamics to her mother's German-ness: her mother's love for and favoritism of her middle daughter, Sarah.

Sara had shiny blonde braids and soft blue eyes. Not strong, she was a quiet child and kept her clothes clean. All the others said Sara was Mama's "pet," so the nickname they gave her was "liebling" (beloved one). It was true, Mama did seem to favor Sara, because she was quiet and good, and never needed to be scolded. But more than that, Sara reminded her of her revered native land. She looked exactly like the little German "Graetchen" of her own school girl days. Her bright presence among the dark-haired, dark-eyed masses in the ghetto fed the dream in Mama's bosom that she would someday be back among the trees and flowers, where dust didn't gather daily on her glistening bric-a-brac and satiny mahogany furniture.[14]

Charlotte was well aware that her mother preferred German-ness, and Taylor, too, in her writing as a grown woman, recognized that her mother's distinctive discipline in dress and housekeeping was tied to Cilly's German identity.[15]

According to the historian Marion Kaplan, German Jewish women wanted to be part of the German bourgeoisie and were successful at combining both German and Jewish values in order to achieve that social status. This combination of national and religious values resulted in mothers cultivating certain behavioral traits in their children: "Mothers helped children absorb bourgeois norms, training them to keep their voices down, their clothing neat, their manners perfect."[16] In the Germany of the 1890s, middle-class German Jewish housewives exemplified the notion that "it was the housewife's 'unselfish love' for husband and children, the production of homey-ness, as evidenced by her cozy, clean home and tidy, orderly offspring, which was praised as an example of morality itself."[17] Thus, the five little girls in their matching clothes strike the Library Lady as a "step-and-stairs family," a term that evokes not only the similarity of each girl to the others but the orderliness of their sizes and ages (*AKF* 18). The illustration on the same page shows the five girls lined up in front of the library desk with the Library Lady on the other side of the counter. The girls appear regimented in their matching clothes—almost a uniform—and their evenly descending sizes depicting their ages.

Kaplan also discusses how German Jewish women of the imperial era were careful to hide any indication that they were not as well off as their

bourgeois friends and neighbors. As she explains, "Families often sur-
mounted formidable income limitations to attain emblems of bourgeois status. Strategies included the use of lending libraries, the careful mending of
worn clothing, the purchase of standing-room-only tickets in theaters, and
housewives' hidden housework in lieu of servants or alongside their one
maid-of-all-work."[18] Three out of four of those strategies are at work in the
first few pages of *All-of-a-Kind-Family*. But this book is set in early twentieth-
century New York City, not in nineteenth-century Germany. Taylor absorbed
her mother's values and included them in her written work for children.
With the understanding that her mother came from a time and place in which
it was important not just to appear to be of a certain class but to exemplify the
values of that class, such as refinement and culture, it becomes easier to see
why Taylor wanted to express simultaneously that her fictional (but also autobiographical) family was poor and yet of another class than the people they
lived among. Unbeknown to her readers, Taylor was walking a delicate tightrope, trying to do two things at once: show that her family was middle-class
in behavior and standards, but also demonstrate that its members had the financial constraints of people of a lower class.

In addition to promoting cleanliness, refinement, and order, German
Jewish women were intent on inculcating in their children the habits of duty,
obedience, thrift, industriousness, and respect.[19] The adoption of those values and their incorporation into existing Jewish traditions resulted in a set of
beliefs and mores particular to Jews at this time. Through German Jewish
immigration to the United States, those values came to be identified with
American Jewish culture. Having arrived earlier than the masses of Russian
and Eastern European Jewish immigrants, German Jews in America provided a model of success for later immigrants, exemplifying a desirable social
pattern. Although Cilly arrived in the later wave of Jewish immigrants, her
identification as a German Jew allowed her to see herself and her family as a
cut above from the moment she stepped off the boat.

In addition to its roots in German bourgeois culture, ideals of housekeeping among immigrant Jewish women derived from their religion. Jewish
tradition emphasizes that women are responsible for the maintenance of the
home and for making the food and cleaning the house—especially for the
weekly Sabbath meals, which begin with Friday night dinner and last through
Saturday. These significant meals are observed with tablecloths and china

and silver of better quality than those used during the week. The food, like-wise, is specially prepared to be in keeping with the day's holiness.[20]

Taylor uses the Sabbath to introduce the family's Judaism in *All-of-a-Kind Family,* a third of the way through the book. The chapter "The Sab-bath" begins on page 63, and the word *Jewish* does not come up until page 65, in the paragraph discussed above, where Mama is compared favorably to the other Jewish women in the neighborhood. Before she introduces the word *Jewish,* Taylor uses the words *Yiddish* (when describing the language of the proprietor of the nearby grocery store, Mr. Basch) and *Sabbath,* lead-ing her readers gently to the realization that these girls are different because they are Jews. In the opening sentence of "The Sabbath," Taylor indirectly signals difference by stating, "The Sabbath begins Friday evening at dusk and for two days Mama was busy with her preparations" (*AKF* 63). If readers have not yet picked up that the All-of-a-Kind sisters are Jewish—and many of them in the 1950s did not, as shown in letters they sent to Taylor—it was here that they would begin to realize something is different.

Before signaling that the Sabbath of the chapter's title is a Jewish event, Taylor specifies its importance in terms of housework. She begins the chap-ter by explaining the labor involved in getting ready for the Sabbath:

> On Fridays, she cleaned, cooked, and baked. On Thursdays, she shopped. Sabbath meals had to be the best of the whole week so it was most important that she shop carefully. Every Thursday afternoon, Mama went to Rivington Street market where prices were lower than in her neighborhood stores. (63)

This description serves several functions. In addition to distinguishing the family's Sabbath as different from the mainstream American Sabbath, it re-minds readers that the family has to be frugal because they are not wealthy. It also explains that the Sabbath is not only different from the rest of the week; it is superior to it. Most of all, it emphasizes the amount of work involved in the preparation of the special day.

Although Taylor never alludes to her mother's suicide attempt in the *All-of-a-Kind* books and also does not ever disclose that her mother was depressed or even unhappy, she does explain how hard her mother worked.[21] In the first book of the series, Taylor alludes often to Mama's cleaning and cooking. Things become especially difficult when most of the sisters come down with scarlet fever right before Passover. In the chapter titled "Mama Has Her Hands Full," Taylor describes the amount of work involved in preparing for Passover:

> But, oh dear me! thought Mama. Less than a week and so much had to be done to get ready. Throughout the Festival of Passover, which lasts eight days, no bread or leavened foods may be eaten. In the days just before Passover, Jewish people thoroughly clean their homes to remove all traces of such leaven. Even the pots, pans, and dishes have to be changed. Every religious Jewish household has so much kitchenware that it looks like a store. The family must have two sets of dishes for everyday use: one for dairy products and the other for all meat foods; as well as two sets for Passover, to say nothing of special dishes for company use. (114–15)

Taylor weaves this lengthy description of Jewish kitchen habits—enfolding features of Passover into general practices of keeping kosher—as well as a paragraph about the history of Passover, into the developing tale of Sarah's illness and the visit of the family doctor, Dr. Fuchs. Those passages augment the points made earlier, in the chapter on the Sabbath, about how much work and preparation Jewish observance involves. In "The Sabbath" and another earlier chapter, "Purim Play," Jewish practice is presented as requiring some effort, but the work is not described as unduly onerous. In "Mama Has Her Hands Full," however, Taylor begins to describe its effect on Mama. When Dr. Fuchs tells Mama that Sarah has scarlet fever and hints that her sisters may also have it, Taylor is candid about Mama's reaction: " 'Scarlet fever!' Mama's heart sank. That meant quarantine and isolation. It meant special diets, probably leavened foods, and they were coming into the Passover holidays. How would she manage it? But none of this dismay was noticeable in either her voice or manner. She seemed calm as always as she lined the children up for their examinations" (115).

This is as close as Taylor ever comes to conveying the tremendous pressure on her mother and how overwhelmed she often felt. When they looked back on their childhood, Ella and Charlotte gave a fuller description of Cilly's reaction to the stress in her life. To the delight of many readers, *All-of-a-Kind Family* ends with the birth of baby Charlie, and fans repeatedly wondered if Mama would have even more babies. In Ella's telling, Cilly's attempts to induce a miscarriage before Gertie's birth actually took a more extreme form when she discovered she was expecting again in 1912, the period during which the book is set. Pregnant after a weekend at Rockaway Beach, Cilly "was in a terrible state" and sought an abortion, an illegal procedure. On the scheduled day, however, the doctor failed to show up at the house. Ella remembers being extremely anxious, knowing that women who tried to give themselves abortions often died, and she feared what drastic measures her mother would take.[22] As it turned out, Cilly carried the child to term, and Irving—called Charlie in the books—was born.[23]

Charlotte omits that drama, but she does present much more detail about the layout of the family apartment than does Taylor. In her autobiography, it becomes clear that the front room that is so important in the novel is not in fact a separate room. In keeping with Ella's description of the large room in the apartment with the skylight, Charlotte explains that a room over thirty feet long is divided into a kitchen area, a sleeping area, and an area called "the front room" at the far end. There are two fireplaces in the long room, "both completely enclosed by heavy sheets of embossed metal, painted the color of the walls."[24] The source of heat in the long room was the kitchen stove, behind which Charlotte and her sisters would undress before sprinting to the icy sleeping area where they would get into bed and "shiver and shake under the crisp cold sheets."

Charlotte's memory of those wild dashes prompts her to remark on her mother's parenting style and methods of discipline. She explains how Mama, when she "was in a good mood," would sometimes wrap heated irons in towels for the girls to take into bed with them. But other times she would not heat the irons, instead telling the girls it was "better for them to let their own bodies warm the sheets." Charlotte links this attitude directly to her mother's background, explaining that "Mama had a rough German upbringing, and she practiced the same discipline fiercely with her children, in all sincerity believing this was the wise way to raise them." Their father, on the other hand, was raised differently and would often disagree with and contravene Mama's techniques, for example by heating the irons himself and bringing them to the girls' beds.

One particularly dramatic scene in "Touched with Fire" involves an iron that Papa had heated too hot and a new white porcelain sink.[25] The landlord had recently installed the sink to replace a rusted metal one, and Mama cherished the new sink "as much as she cherished her Dresden figurines, her delicately hand painted vases, her sterling hollowware, the curved mahogany whatnot, and several other precious treasures she had rescued and brought to this country from their beautiful home in Bremen." She was shocked when she heard the sink crack as Papa dropped the hot iron into it and ran cold water. When Mama realized what had happened, she "put her hands through her hair and shook her head from side to side and screamed." She scolded them for wanting the warm irons, then turned to Papa and upbraided him.

This incident put Papa over the edge, for he "finally lost his patience and, equally distressed, raised a big, male voice to the strange, wild bark." Papa then made a speech, cataloging all the things he felt Mama cared too much about:

> He was tired, he said, of her always putting things first before anything else. Tired of the way she woke the children every morning, polishing and polishing the iron stove, with its loose clanking hinges and movable shutters banging away so early each morning, tired of the daily scrubbing of the huge kitchen floor, that had to be protected from the children's shoes all day with newspapers— papers that were taken up again only in time for the next day's scrubbing. Tired of the smell of furniture polish all over the house, and the greasy feeling of the elegant mahogany chair arms. Tired, tired, tired. He lifted up a heavy kitchen chair and dropped it vehemently back to the ground so it fell over with a thump.

The children huddled in their beds while this was going on, anxious because Papa did not usually get so upset and angrily demonstrative. Soon, their parents were silent, and then the children heard a strange sound that they deciphered as their mother crying. When they heard Papa whispering "soothing endearments," Henny snuck out of bed to spy on her parents, returning to her sisters with an amazing report: " 'He's kissing her!' she whispered, her eyes glowing with the wicked discovery. 'She's sitting on his lap, and he's kissing her, right on the cheek!' "

This vividly remembered scene demonstrates how rare it was for the children to see intimacy between their parents, while the term "wicked discovery" hints again at the commingling of shame and delight the girls were learning to associate with romantic or sexual pleasure. It also signifies that the girls saw the differences between their parents as being not just a matter of personality but of cultural, indeed national, background. Mama's refinement, her lovely things, and her obsessive cleaning and privileging of things over people are all identified with her "German upbringing."

As discussed earlier, this rift between the parents' backgrounds was one that Jews in Europe experienced when Cilly and Morris lived there, and it was also experienced by American Jews. For the most part, German Jews had arrived in the United States in the mid-nineteenth century, about two generations before the Russian and Eastern European Jews. By the late nineteenth century, German Jews were well established in America, many having been successful financially and socially. They had rapidly assimilated, giving up many traditional Jewish practices and beliefs, such as keeping kosher. Large numbers affiliated with the Reform Jewish movement, a less stringent form of Judaism that consciously tried to be more like Christianity (by having organs in synagogues and conducting religious services in English, for example) in order for its followers to fit into mainstream society. They were thoroughly "Americanized," and many of these bourgeois American Jews were discomfited by the Eastern European and Russian Jews who arrived between 1880 and 1920. The newcomers were, by and large, less educated, less stylish, less refined, and often less clean, and they embarrassed the German Jews who, at the same time, felt a responsibility toward and kinship with their brethren from "the Old Country."[26] In Taylor's fiction, the tension is not explicitly addressed, and the differences between her two parents' personalities are not described as differences of nationalities. Yet Taylor distinguishes her mother from other Jewish women, and our knowledge of the family story reveals that Mama's difference was related to her German heritage.

As the heirs of both the Eastern European and German traditions, the Brenner sisters thus negotiated not only the tensions between the two, but also the complications introduced by America. Memoirs, diaries, and novels all portray the family in the process of adapting their religious, as well as their ethnic, identities to the New World. Mama lit four candles to welcome the Sabbath on Friday nights, and Papa collected the leftover wax for use in his shop.[27] Papa wore a yarmulke on his head even at night; he attended shul (the synagogue) and rested on the Sabbath, but he prayed alone in the kitchen with his tefillin (phylacteries) and tallit (prayer shawl) during the week in order to save time. In her memoir, Charlotte describes her and Ella's anxiety when the family moves to the Bronx. Ella worries what people at the synagogue where she works will say about her living in a building owned by a gentile, and Charlotte thinks that "it would be a little scary to see a man working on Saturdays" while her father displays his Sabbath observance. The thought of living near people who wear gold crosses around their necks also makes her uncomfortable. In response, Papa "deliver[s] a sermon, like a rabbi: 'A Jew can be a Jew anywhere. What difference does it make, about the religion of the landlord?' "[28]

What Charlotte did not say was that her and her sister's unspoken anxiety was about assimilation. When his junk business became more successful after World War I, Papa postponed his early morning Sabbath routine of going to synagogue and instead rose early to pray at home.

> Then he dressed in his good suit and carried on his contacts with the recyclers.
>
> The morning over, he returned, changed his clothes, and joined the family for their Sabbath dinner.
>
> "God will forgive me for saying my Sabbath prayers at home; He knows I'm doing it to take care of my family."[29]

After dinner, he took a nap, "the cherished repose of the Sabbath, as God had ordered." Religious nonobservance was justified in Papa's own mind by the paramount values of family and self-sufficiency, and he permitted his daughters to live that contradiction as well.

Papa's children accepted the sincerity of his belief and were conscious that he trained them to follow the rules "that were not too difficult for them."[30] He gave the children a one-cent allowance each day, but if they saved it all week, he gave them a dime, the extra three cents being the equivalent of interest in a bank, as well as an extra penny "to spend on Saturdays to compensate for denial." Sarah stood out by saving her Saturday penny for Sunday, "because she was unwilling to handle money on the Sabbath," while after breakfast on Saturday her sisters went to the candy store, "all dressed up in their Sabbath finery."[31] Charlotte thus artfully draws a lexical distinction between the Sabbath—a sacred day honored by traditional regulations, including the refusal to engage in monetary transactions and the wearing of choice clothing— and Saturday—a secular day on which candy can be bought.

The Brenners were representative of Jewish immigrant life in improvising traditional culture and also in enrolling their children in extracurricular programs that had as their mission the preservation of that culture, even as the instruction the children received contradicted what was practiced at home. Before the Brenners moved to the Bronx, all the girls attended Sunday School. Sarah underwent a period of religious enthusiasm after she enrolled in a Hebrew language course held on Sunday afternoons at the synagogue, where she picked up "the strict orthodox rules that even her own parents no longer followed." Not only did she not touch money on the Sabbath, but she also scolded her mother for allowing a non-Jewish peddler to start the coal stove fire on Saturday morning because it might tempt her to cook, and waited six hours after a meat meal before eating dairy, consequently forgoing the family's Sabbath mid-afternoon treat of coffee cake and cheesecake with raisins. When it came to food, Mama was the authority, and in this case she took Sarah's punctiliousness in stride: "It was a nuisance, but Mama expected it wouldn't last. The children were always getting into and out of phases."[32] No distinction is made between irritating habits of childhood, such as climbing up on tables, and trying to form a religious identity. Both were phases that passed with maturity.

THREE

Gateways to a Wider World

1910–1916

MOVING FROM PERSONAL FAMILY history to broader trends in society, it becomes increasingly clear that the tension between German and Eastern European traditions shaped many of the institutions Taylor interacted with in her childhood on the Lower East Side. Three of those institutions are the public school, the Henry Street Settlement House, and the New York Public Library, which provided a framework for the child Sarah and the adult Sydney. Taylor wrote about all three in her books, and after she became a popular author, speaking engagements at schools and libraries in the New York area and across the country dominated her fall and winter schedules.

German Jews in New York City turned to educational and social welfare institutions to help newly arrived Eastern European Jews find acceptance through a process of assimilation. Their motives derived from a mix of progressive reformism, Jewish traditions of charity, and anxiety about the status of Jews in America. They wanted to modernize and Americanize the new immigrants, and saw public schools as the place to accomplish their goals.[1] Jewish children had the highest rate of school attendance of any ethnic group in the city, although most left school between the sixth and seventh grades.[2] Taylor and her sisters attended school until at least the eighth grade, and during the years depicted in the *All-of-a-Kind* books they spent most of their week at school.

Yet school receives relatively little attention in the series. In the first book, school is where the older sisters go to and return from each day, but events there remain offstage. In each of the other four books of the series, one chapter is set at school, with one of the sisters singled out as the main character.[3] It may be that Taylor avoided school settings because grade stratification allowed depiction of only one sister at a time. By contrast, in the library, the settlement house, and most of all in streets and stores, the girls could interact freely. Sometimes the children appear together in performances, most often in a play or pageant directed by Ella, but even the scenes that take place on stages and in auditoriums are set not at schools but rather at synagogues and community centers. One would not conclude from a superficial reading of Taylor's books that school played a huge role in the lives of immigrant children of the Lower East Side.

Taylor attended P.S. 188, opened in 1903, which the *New York Times* reported was "the largest public school in the world."[4] Located at 442 East Houston Street, P.S. 188 still functions as an elementary school, and it is a huge building even by today's standards. Built of brick and standing five stories high, the structure is imposing. Its original entry area, since reconfigured, ushered students into a vast, empty hall with marble floors. The space was breathtaking, and it impressed upon students not just the importance but also the *sanctity* of education.

An auditorium on the second floor reinforced that perspective. Set in a recessed area enclosed on three sides by white walls adorned with plaster friezes, the stage area of the room was raised slightly higher than the floor. The designs in the plaster were purely decorative, with looping wreaths and garlands of flowers. They covered the upper half of the walls; the bottom half was paneled with dark, elegant wood. At the back of the enclosed area was a window, originally made of colorful stained glass. Light poured from the back of the stage, bathing a speaker in multiple colors, lending any school authority a numinous appearance. The two structural elements taken together—the entry of the building, with its vast open space and marble floor, and the stage that functioned almost as a pulpit—suggest that the school was designed to impart to the children a sense that school was sacred, a place deserving of their respect and reverence.

In fact, the morning assembly at these Lower East Side schools in the early twentieth century did seem much like a religious service, with its formal march into the assembly room, singing of a patriotic song such as "The Star-Spangled Banner," flag salute, and reading from the Bible.[5] Often, the Lord's Prayer was recited. As the historian Stephan Brumberg describes it, "The Assembly resembled a morning prayer service as one might encounter in a

Protestant chapel with its tone of moral uplift, ritualization of activities, and choral song (radically different from a morning service in a synagogue)."[6] In an effort to Americanize immigrant children, the board of education inspired devotion toward school and also made school like church.

As clear as it may seem to historians that ritualization, morning assemblies, school curriculum, and the school calendar were Protestant in nature, a woman who attended one of these schools in the early 1900s described the experience differently when recalling the morning assembly: "[It] was all done in precision, real Germanic. There was a great big beautiful looking platform, there was a grand piano and a big desk where the principal stood up, all carpeted. And—I can see it yet—very elegant."[7]

This woman, who did not know the Brenner family, could have been describing the Brenner home. If the Brenners were exceptional in their German-ness in this place and time, and the schools were enforcing a culture and elegance that was seen at least by some as "Germanic," it would seem that the Brenner girls would perform especially well at school. Indeed, as we have seen, they were singled out when the Chinese visitors came, and for other visitors thereafter, because of the superiority of their clothing and behavior. Charlotte relates, "There were to be many such experiences during the years that they attended P.S. 188 on the East Side. Every time some foreign official, missionary, royalty, researcher, social worker, visited that section of the country and decided to 'do' the schools they wound up examining the all-of-a-kind family."[8]

Charlotte also describes at length her participation in a public tableau in front of thousands of people. She tells a poignant story of being chosen as a second-grader out of all the children in her school, fitted repeatedly for a red, white, and blue dress and hat, taken in this dress on a long train ride during which she developed motion sickness and vomited, and then being forced to stand for hours on display, holding the hand of a tall girl wearing a white gown and a silver crown who was playing the role of "Justice." As she stood for what seemed an eternity with one hand in Justice's and the other held aloft, bearing an American flag, Charlotte was at first elated, then tired, and finally in pain. To her great consternation, she ended up urinating while standing in this costume because no one provided her with a break or a way to signal that she had to go to the bathroom.

During this entire episode—the selection process, the rehearsals, the fittings, and finally the performance—Charlotte had no idea what role she was playing. The next day, Ella showed Charlotte a newspaper with her picture in it. Ella read aloud, "The part of *Miss America* was chosen after examining over five thousand school children on the lower East Side. It was played by Charlotte Brenner, who is in the second grade of P.S. 188." Charlotte was not impressed with this description and worried instead that people had noticed that she had urinated. She asked Ella, "Is that all?" and Ella exclaimed, "All? For God's sake, isn't that enough? Do you realize how important you were? You're famous! Here, let's save this." Ella cut the picture out of the newspaper and the girls pasted it in the family album. In her telling, Charlotte's feelings about her role remain mixed, and are only partly assuaged because "the whole family was enjoying it, and if Mama could look so pleased it had been worth all the tension and distress."[9]

That incident illustrates the constellation of associations that so tightly connected the Brenner family to the Americanization imposed by educational authorities on immigrant children. The Brenner sisters were repeatedly trotted out to represent the best of the school's assimilation goals when dignitaries visited the school. The fact that German-bred girls (the Brenner children learned German as their first language and spoke it with their parents throughout their childhoods, although they spoke English to each other) were singled out to represent America is not a coincidence.[10] What the school officials interpreted in the Brenner girls as Americanization was actually the result of their mother's German background, standards, and aesthetics. The sisters were seen as more refined, better dressed, with better breeding than the other children. Their mother was commended for this superiority. But the school officials did not mention to their guests that this mother was German-speaking.

It was also German Jews who created the institutions of which the primary aims were to Americanize the beneficiaries through assimilation and modernization. German Jewish leaders included wealthy individuals such as Jacob Schiff, Felix Warburg, Daniel Guggenheim, and Cyrus Adler, whose names grace renowned public institutions to this day, and educational reformers such as Julia Richman.[11] Those establishment Jews worked closely with the board of education in New York City, overlapping ideologically and personally. For example, prominent banker and philanthropist Felix Warburg, an immigrant from Germany and son-in-law of Jacob Schiff, was twice a member of the board and was a friend of Superintendent William H. Maxwell, who strongly advocated assimilation for immigrants. An American-born Jew of German heritage, Julia Richman rose in the ranks from teacher to principal to become ultimately the first woman district superintendent of schools in New York City, administering the district that included the Lower East Side. Her Jewish and pedagogic interests were intertwined throughout her life, as she served on both the board of education and the Board of the Educational Alliance, a Jewish educational organization.[12]

Two goals shared by the board of education and the establishment Jews were that the immigrants should learn cleanliness and hygiene and that they should adopt English as their primary language. Immigrants at this time were seen as dirty, and conditions on the Lower East Side, with its crowded tenements, lack of running water, insufficient toilets, and coal-burning stoves, made it a dirty place even if individuals tried to keep themselves clean. In 1903, the board adopted curricula that included not just standard academic courses such as English, mathematics, and history, but also a mandatory class in "hygiene."[13] P.S. 188 had an entire "Health and Hygiene Room" devoted to instruction in housekeeping and cleanliness.[14] In such classrooms, children learned table manners, the preparation of American foods, and methods to keep a spotless home.

Along with cleanliness, the board of education and the establishment Jews wanted immigrants to learn English. Russian and Eastern European Jews who came to New York City at the turn of the last century could often speak the language of the countries in which they were born, and most of the men could at least read Hebrew, but Yiddish was the dominant language. It was spoken all over the East Side, and the Hebrew letters of signs in Yiddish punctuated the windows of many shops. Taylor includes some Yiddish words in her books, usually providing parenthetical translations when she has a character use them. For example, when the sisters and their mother go shopping on Rivington Street, they encounter a peddler selling chickpeas. Taylor renders the peddler's speech: " 'Arbis! Shaynick, guttinke arbislach! Keuf meine heise arbis!' (Chick peas. Fine, nice chick peas. Buy my hot chick peas!)" (AKF 75). Henny, characteristically, mimics the peddler, repeating his words in Yiddish and causing her sisters to laugh uproariously.

But Taylor makes it clear that these girls do not themselves customarily speak Yiddish. When the family steps into the street, Taylor explains, "Only one tongue was spoken here—Yiddish. It was like a foreign land right in the midst of America. In this foreign land, it was Mama's children who were the foreigners since they alone conversed in an alien tongue—English" (*AKF* 72). To the extent that she describes the language spoken by adults on the Lower East Side streets, Taylor was accurate. Yet she occludes the truth in three ways. The first is that the language that separated the Brenners from the other East Side Jews was not English but German. The second is that the Brenners valued facility in numerous languages, even though the paramount goal was to become English-speaking Americans. Foreigners came to Papa's shop "learning to speak English and be Americans. Papa would speak to them partly in German, in Polish, in Yiddish, in Russian, even in Italian."[15] When the fictional Brenner girls make fun of greenhorn Lena's English, Mama scolds them impatiently: " 'Do you know she can speak several languages? Russian, Polish, Jewish. Any of you speak Polish as poorly as you seem to think Lena speaks English?' " (*More* 71). Last, virtually all the children in this area were rapidly learning English at school and in the streets, and, however ungrammatical, it was their preferred language.[16] Yiddish became a source of embarrassment for many schoolchildren, who often feared that they would be mistaken for inexperienced newcomers if heard speaking it.[17]

It is unclear how well the Brenner children knew Yiddish, aside from words they picked up from shopkeepers or vendors in the street. Although their mother spoke German, and German was the language of their household, their father grew up speaking Yiddish, as did virtually all Polish Jews of the time. No record remains of whether Mama insisted that Yiddish not be spoken or if Papa simply elected not to teach it to his children. The names he and his wife chose for their daughters were mostly derived from German, not Yiddish: Ella, Charlotte, Henrietta, and Gertrude. Only Sarah was given a name that bore any hint of ethnicity, coming as it did from the Hebrew Bible.

The subject of the sisters' names is complicated, however, by the school records kept at P.S. 188. Three of the names are immediately recognizable: Ella, Charlotte, and Gertrude. The other two are somewhat different. On the record for the child born September 28, 1902, known in real life and in Taylor's books as Henny, someone has written "Brenner, Yetta." Above the word Yetta, the unknown scribe added the name Henrietta. On the back of the card, where the "Physical Record" is located, the name written is "Yetta Brenner." What is surprising is the name Yetta, for no other document refers to Henny this way, although her sisters knew that she was named for their maternal grandmother,

Yetchin Marowitz. Still more surprising is the name written on the card for the girl born October 30, 1904. Instead of Sarah, the card says "Brenner, Sadie." On the back of the card, the name is repeated: "Sadie Brenner." Sadie was an English nickname commonly given to Jewish girls in families where Yiddish was spoken, and may have been used by school administrators to distinguish Sarah Brenner from other Sarahs in the school. Yet in no other document, no letter, no diary entry, no scrap of paper, is Taylor referred to by this name.

The discovery that Sarah was known as "Sadie" at least on her elementary school record adds another layer to the riddle of Sydney Taylor's name— a name that was to go through several permutations, each referring to a different aspect of her personality and personal history. While the conscious change from Sarah to Sydney arguably involved at least some attempt at assimilation (and upon her marriage she further adopted the name Schneider, which her husband's family later changed to Taylor), buried beneath "Sydney Taylor," a name that obscures ethnic and gender connections, is "Sadie Brenner," a vividly Jewish feminine name. Deep within the most German-looking of the Brenner sisters, underneath the layers of Americanization that Taylor experienced, is the little Jewish girl who grew up to translate Judaism for young American readers.

Although only four chapters are set in schools in the various books, each provides insight into the multifaceted importance of educational institutions to the Brenner household, touching on authority, discipline, ethics, and personal responsibility. As mentioned above, the first book has no chapter that takes place in school. In *More All-of-a-Kind Family*, the first chapter with a school setting involves Gertie and is titled "A Timely Errand." When the teacher asks if any of the children can tell time, Gertie raises her hand, but actually she cannot read a clock. Taylor creates a conversation between Gertie and her conscience, which she writes in the format of the script of a play, the two characters being "Gertie" and "Conscience." The conscience chides Gertie for pretending to be able to tell time and asks why she did it, and Gertie explains she does not know why and had not realized that if she raised her hand, the teacher would ask her to go find out what time it was. The conscience suggests that Gertie tell the truth, but Gertie refuses, saying, "And have the whole class know! I can't. I just can't." The conscience has the last words: "You'll be sorry, you'll see. You'll get pimples all over your tongue 'cause you told a lie!" (50). Gertie must go out into the hall and stare at the big clock, "a great round monster high on the wall," until she can ask the time from an older student passing by. The bulk of the chapter concerns Gertie's anxiety, both about having to go out in the hall every day and wait until someone comes along who can tell her the time and about sprouting pimples on her tongue for lying.

When asked, Charlotte tries to teach Gertie how to tell time, but Gertie has trouble learning, and she does not dare tell Charlotte why she must know, afraid that Charlotte will not be her friend anymore if she finds out that Gertie lied. Finally, Gertie figures it out herself in school. She is excited and happy but feels she had better check with someone whether she is right. Suddenly, she hears a voice:

> "Would you like to know the time?" a gentle voice asked.
>
> Gertie jumped, startled. There standing beside her was just the most important person in the whole school—Miss Phillips, the principal! Gertie's voice shook. "Is it—is it—ten minutes after eleven?" she stammered.
>
> "That's right," Miss Phillips answered with a smile. "That's very good for such a little girl."
>
> "Oh, yes, I can tell time! I can really and truly tell time! Miss Phillips, don't you think this is the loveliest clock in the whole world?" Gertie laughed all over herself. Without waiting for a reply, she whizzed down the hall, leaving Miss Phillips staring after her in puzzled amazement. (54)

This encounter with the school principal does more than portray Gertie's growth and happiness. A female school principal would not seem unusual to children today, but she would have been a rare sight in the early 1900s. Miss Phillips is, however, representative of the type of woman all the sisters would have seen as teachers in their elementary schools.[18] Most of the teachers in these schools were women. Few were Jewish, although a relatively high percentage of grade school teachers on the Lower East Side were. Whatever her background, the teacher was perceived as very much the American, and her role, whether students realized it or not, was to Americanize her students.[19] Miss Phillips, with her trim body, neatly tucked in shirtwaist, straight black necktie, and reading glasses, as her illustration reveals, looks nothing like the neighborhood women Mama is contrasted against in *All-of-a-Kind*

Family. As Taylor describes her, she exemplifies the kind of authority figure the Jewish children encountered throughout their years of public school, the very embodiment of the beneficent, authoritative, respectable schoolteacher.

Gertie receives the highest praise she could possibly earn outside of her home at this point in her life—the principal saying she is "very good"—by learning to make sense of the clock, learning that time is orderly, rule-bound, and comprehensible, as everything in life should be. Those are exactly the lessons the Jewish establishment and the board of education wanted immigrant children to learn, and this is precisely where educators and social leaders wanted the children to learn them. Gertie's conversation with the principal, while seemingly fleeting and inconsequential, actually captures much of the significance of the public school encounter of the Jewish girl of this place and time. By learning to tell time from the huge clock in the long hallway, Gertie has mastered a measure of the orderliness and routine created by clocks and has received praise from an exemplary American, one who is powerful, but kind, and female.

Surprisingly, Henny, who is almost proud of being the least academic of the sisters, is the star of two of the four chapters set in schools. True to her character, she is not an exemplary student. In fact, she is a disruptive troublemaker. In "On the Wrong Side of the Bed," Henny is having a hard time even before school starts. She spills cocoa all over her pinafore, squeezes her baby brother Charlie too tightly, causing him to cry, and cannot find her history book, which suggests that she did not do her history homework. By the time she gets to school, Henny has already been scolded several times. Once in the classroom, Henny is bored and hot. Taylor suggests that it is the school's regulated atmosphere that rubs Henny the wrong way: "Henny heaved a big sigh. How dull it was in the classroom! She was sick of sitting up straight with her hands behind her back while Miss Corbett's voice went on and on about geography. Henny's eyes darted restlessly over the room" (*Downtown* 103).

Henny, unlike her more compliant sisters, opts to fight the system by disrupting it. She surreptitiously emits a high, squeaking sound. When she sees her teacher's annoyed but mystified reaction and hears her classmates' "delighted titters," she repeats the noise, hiding behind the "protecting back" of her friend Fanny, who gets pulled into Henny's mischievous behavior (104). Henny squeaks a few more times. " 'Teacher, there must be a mouse in the room!' yelled Fanny in mock alarm, jumping up from her seat. 'There it goes!' Henny shouted and began scrambling under the desks for the imaginary little visitor. Now from under the desks the squeaks came—louder and squeakier" (105).

Of course, Miss Corbett can now determine who is responsible for the squeaks and havoc, and she speaks sternly to Henny: "Miss Corbett glared at her. 'Henrietta,' she exclaimed, 'you've tried my patience long enough! Now you march yourself right down to Miss Phillips' office this minute!' " The other students respond in whispers. " 'She has to go to the principal's office!' 'I'd be scared to death if it was me!' 'Maybe they'll throw her out of school!' " Henny "flounc[es]" out of the room insouciantly, but inwardly she is "quaking with fright." She engages in a little self-talk: "Aw, what are you scared of, she kept steeling herself. All Miss Phillips will do is give you a lecture or put you in a baby class for a day or so. Bravely she entered the principal's office" (106). With words like *quaking, steeling,* and *bravely,* Taylor conveys that Henny views Miss Phillips as a formidable authority figure.

Readers who recall that Miss Phillips is the principal who spoke so kindly to Gertie in an earlier book can anticipate that she will not be overly harsh with Henny. Indeed, when Miss Phillips enters the room behind a seated Henny, she says, "So much gold in the hair! What a pity there's so little in the heart!" With this comment, Taylor switches the perspective from Henny to Miss Phillips, allowing the reader to see how an adult views Henny. "Miss Phillips studied Henny's stubborn little face. No use trying to talk to the child now, she decided." She writes a note and gives it to Henny. " 'Henrietta . . . you will give this note to your mother. I've asked her to come see me tomorrow.' Her face softened. 'You may go back to your classroom now' " (107).

Henny is dismissed from the principal's office, but she does not escape punishment. Her teacher makes her stay after class and write the words "I'll never make noises in class again" on the blackboard one hundred times. Taylor dwells on Henny's physical discomfort and emotional turmoil: "Henny wrote and wrote and wrote. Her arm began to ache and the lines became more and more wavery. But all the time, the anger inside her bubbled and boiled. This was just too much. Nobody likes me, she thought to herself glumly" (108). The accompanying illustration shows Henny with her arm outstretched to write and her face set in disgruntlement. On the blackboard, the viewer can see the sentence repeated over and over. Here is the dark side of regulation and order—the uniformity and repetition of the words on the blackboard are used to discipline the child and teach her a lesson.

In her anger, Henny decides to hide in a barrel outside after she leaves the school, and she inadvertently falls asleep in it. As afternoon becomes evening and evening wears into night, the family members become concerned about Henny's failure to appear, so they set out to look for her. Finally, Henny hears voices calling for her. At first, she is overjoyed: "Just think of it, exulted Henny, all this fuss about me! Now that I've gone, I bet they're awfully sorry. Well it serves them right!" (113). Fear and cold soon set in, however, and Henny returns home to discover her family in disarray, one sister in tears, and neighbors suggesting they call the hospital and fire department. After she walks in, Papa's first reaction is to go for the strap hanging on the kitchen wall, but a look from Mama makes him stop. Eating the food Mama puts out for her, Henny blithely works into the conversation, "By the way, Ma . . . I think the principal wants to see you tomorrow. She gave me an invitation." The chapter ends with this line: "That night Mama and Henny had a long, long talk" (116).

In this chapter, Taylor uses Henny as a foil for her better-behaved sisters, giving readers the opportunity to see them as unique individuals. Furthermore, in showing that disruptive behavior has consequences, she places the different modes of punishment into a hierarchy. At the bottom is Papa's "Old World," physical punishment, his inclination to beat Henny. That method is abandoned. In the middle are Miss Corbett's punishments, which include sending Henny to the principal's office and having her write a sentence one hundred times on the board. Those methods are deemed acceptable but not necessarily effective. Henny leaves the classroom after her writing exercise angry and in no way reformed. Highest in the hierarchy are the note Miss Phillips sends home to Mama, and by implication, the meeting she will have with her student's mother, and the talk Henny has with Mama. Progressive, modern parenting and leadership techniques are privileged, and the school supersedes the disciplinary style of at least one parent. One could argue that the school influences the gentler, modernized style of discipline that Mama uses with Henny—that of the "talk." For that is what Miss Phillips, the genteel, refined, American principal, models. In this moment Taylor demonstrates, through her fiction, the function of the public schools in Americanizing immigrant families.

The second chapter that features Henny in school occurs in *Ella of All-of-a-Kind Family* and takes place when Henny is attending high school in the Bronx. While all the scenes of this chapter, "Election in the Balance," are set in school, it is not about sitting in class, and teachers and administrators go almost unmentioned. Instead, the chapter focuses on Henny's decision to be the first girl to run for student council and the rollicking debate that takes place between the candidates, so that episode will be addressed in the next chapter, in the context of Taylor's feminism and progressive politics.

"The History Prize," the school chapter from *All-of-a-Kind Family Uptown,* is about Sarah. The chapter's title hints at the difference between this chapter and the others set in school, as well as the difference between Sarah and her sisters. Gertie's and Henny's school chapters were not about course content. Taylor mentions that Miss Corbett goes "on and on about geography," but Henny has no interest in the lesson. In contrast, Sarah's school chapter is all about a subject, history, and Sarah's desire to excel. It opens: "Sarah had studied hard. Her head felt crammed full of history—dates, names, and places. All year her work in class had won praise from Miss Brady. Even her classmates kept assuring her, 'You'll surely win the prize!' " (146).

Taylor quickly establishes that Sarah is not only studious but also competitive and anxious about her work. The chapter focuses on assignments, tests, grades, and in particular, the final exam. Sarah knows she must get the best grade in the class on this exam in order to be chosen to receive the History Prize. She is worried about her rival Dorothy Miller, who responds to Sarah's whispered admission that she is scared as they enter the classroom for the final exam with the boast "I'm not! I know my work!" (147). Taylor describes Sarah's thoughts and feelings as she takes the exam and mentions the content of a question Sarah is not sure she answered correctly, about the French and Indian War.

Sarah is so nervous about the test that her mother intervenes. "At home, Sarah talked of nothing else, till Mama finally said, with some concern, 'Listen, Sarah, I've told you over and over, you've got to understand that winning is not the most important thing. What is important is that a person should do the very best he can, whether he wins a prize or not. You did that. So even if you don't win, we'll all be just as proud of you.' " Taylor then leaves a blank line, indicating the weight and importance of Mama's words, but not displaying Sarah's reaction to them. Instead, she switches to a discussion of Sarah's graduation dress, which the young graduate is making herself: "For the whole year, during sewing periods in school, Sarah and her classmates had worked on their graduation dresses. They were made entirely by hand, and every stitch had to be perfect" (148).

Sarah Brenner in her graduation dress, 1918

In fact, the real Sarah Brenner did make her own graduation dress, and it is stored among the things kept in her daughter's basement, with a note that reads, "Syd's graduation dress from elementary school, 1916 [*sic*]. Handmade by Syd." Taylor describes the dress in detail in her book: "It was made of white nainsook, high waisted and full skirted, with little rosebuds trimming the neck and tiny puffed sleeves" (148). The dress obviously meant a great deal to Taylor when she made it and for the rest of her life, for she kept it as long as she lived.

Knowing that Taylor made her own graduation dress does not, of course, prove that everything else in the chapter "The History Prize" is also true. The competition for the prize may not have taken place, and Taylor may not have performed the recitation mentioned in the chapter. However, extant written sources, namely Charlotte's memoir and Taylor's books, do indicate that Sarah was a serious student, and even though Charlotte also liked school and liked to write, Sarah was probably, among her sisters, the most dedicated to her classes and the most anxious about her grades.

Significant to the issues raised in this chapter is Sarah's relationship to her teachers and principal. She does not have a personal encounter with the principal the way Gertie did, but she has a much more developed relationship with her teacher than either Gertie or Henny do with theirs. Miss Brady encourages and compliments her before graduation night, and after Sarah fails to win the History Prize, to her pain and sadness, the teacher tries to console her without playing favorites: "Close by the stairs [Sarah] bumped into Miss Brady. 'Good luck, Sarah.' Miss Brady took hold of Sarah's hand. She said nothing more, but her eyes studied the young girl's face. Sarah struggled hard to keep from crying. 'Good-by,' she mumbled, pulling her hand away and rushing down the stairs. Tears blinded her eyes." (151). Miss Brady's concern is evident, but Sarah can focus only on the anguish of her loss. At home, no one dares mention the prize, instead complimenting Sarah on her recitation and appearance, and Sarah goes to bed so she can be alone as soon as possible.

The next day a parcel arrives, addressed to Sarah and lacking a return address. The sisters assume it is a graduation present and urge Sarah to open it quickly. She works too slowly for Henny, who snatches a kitchen knife to cut the packing cord and then tears away the wrapping. Taylor stretches out the moments leading up to the discovery of the box's contents, heightening the mystery and excitement: "There was lots of straw and paper first, then underneath, carefully folded in tissue paper, lay a handsome black leatherbound book with gleaming gilt-edged pages. 'Why it's a dictionary!' cried Sarah. 'Did you ever see anything so beautiful?' " (152).

The dictionary is the "handsomest" the girls have ever seen, full of "pages and pages of bright colored pictures" that illustrate costumes, precious stones, flowers, flags, strange animals and "many, many other fascinating things." Sarah is revitalized and thinks the book will be helpful for her in high school. She wonders who sent it.

As her fingers caressed the soft leather binding, a little card fell out.
Sarah opened it and immediately recognized the bold handwriting:
> To Sarah,
>
> For the joy and pleasure she gave to her teacher by her
> outstanding work in history.
>
> Lillian Brady
>
> P.S. See page 1176 for the correct answer on the French
> and Indian War.

Sarah hugged the book to her. "Oh!" she gasped, and tears sprang
to her eyes. Only this time they were tears of joy. (152)

In this scene, the relationship between teacher and pupil transcends
the classroom. Miss Brady has reached out to Sarah both intellectually and
affectionately. The words *joy* and *pleasure* are not used lightly, and they are
explicitly tied to Sarah's intellectual ability. While they convey praise for
Sarah's acumen, they also convey that she is likable as a person, indicating
that Miss Brady experienced more than pride at her student's academic gifts.
When Sarah cries tears of "joy," that word connects her to Miss Brady and
conveys an intimacy between them. Miss Brady has found an appropriate
way to express that she likes Sarah very much and to wish her a successful
future. Sarah understands these messages, and the implication is that the
teacher's approbation and love are more important than the History Prize.

Through the connection Taylor makes between Miss Brady and Sarah,
the figure of the teacher develops from the role model she was to hundreds of
thousands of immigrant children to friend. That the child who emerges as worthy of being a teacher's friend is Sarah is in perfect keeping with what is known
about this Brenner sister, who is the most refined, most presentable, and most
studious of them all. Charlotte describes Sarah as their mother's favorite, and
now in *Uptown*, the fictional child becomes the teacher's favorite. Charlotte
surmises that Mama prefers Sarah because she is the most German of her
daughters. Miss Brady may prefer Sarah for similar reasons—that she is quiet
and good and never needs scolding. But for Miss Brady, it would be Sarah's
exemplary American-ness, not German-ness, that made her special.

The second institution depicted in *All-of-a-Kind Family* that was developed
by German Jews was the Henry Street Settlement House, a fixture of the

Lower East Side. It was founded and for many years directed by Lillian Wald, a German Jewish woman from Rochester, New York. After moving to New York City in 1890 and training to become a nurse, Wald studied at the Women's Medical College in lower Manhattan, where she became acutely aware of the need to provide better health care to the immigrant population.[20] Wald, whose family had assimilated in nineteenth-century Germany and included members who had intermarried, was, according to biographer Marjorie Feld, always ambivalent about her Jewish identity. Early in her career, she affiliated with the Social Gospel movement, in which Protestant leaders in England and the United States urged their followers to combine faith with good works, particularly by addressing the social problems created by industrialization and urbanization.[21] And she attended nursing school at a time when almost all nurses were Christian. Despite her distance from, even distaste for Judaism, Wald dedicated her life to helping the Eastern European Jewish immigrants who populated the Lower East Side. Between 1893, when she founded the Henry Street Settlement House with the financial help of the German Jewish philanthropist Jacob Schiff, and her retirement in 1933, Wald directed the settlement house and lived in it most of the time.[22]

Neither Taylor nor her sisters ever mention Wald, but Taylor gives the Henry Street Settlement House a prominent role in the (chronologically) third book of the series, *All-of-a-Kind Family Downtown*. *Downtown* was published, however, as the fourth book in the series, in 1972, fourteen years after *All-of-a-Kind Family Uptown*, which is set in 1917 (*Uptown* 119)—making for some chronological confusion.[23] As it turns out, Taylor actually wrote *All-of-a-Kind Family Downtown* just after she wrote the first book: set in 1915, it was supposed to have been the second book in the series. She submitted it for publication in either 1952 or 1953, but it was rejected. In an interview in 1972, Taylor offered her opinion about the rejection: "Perhaps the time was not right for it. We are far more ready today for descriptions of some of the stark realities of life on the Lower East Side which, only a short time ago, publishers were not quite as willing to accept in a child's book."[24] From the later vantage point, when the darker *Downtown* finally was published, Taylor saw the wisdom in her editor's earlier preference for more cheerful books about the family, but at the time, the rejection hurt.

Indeed, *Downtown* does depict aspects of the Lower East Side that were glossed over in the first book, including poverty, filth, disease, and hunger—all of which affect a child not related to the main characters, an Italian boy named Guido. Guido is the only non-Jewish child in the entire series whose problems shape a determinative plot line. In the first book, the family friend Charlie and the "Library Lady" Kathy are important characters, but they are not central to the plot. They do serve important narrative roles, for they tie the rather episodic chapters together with their repeated appearances, and their reunion in the family's sukkah provides a romantic climax that would be difficult to achieve with a purely episodic structure. Grace Healy, Ella's friend in *Uptown* and *Ella*, is from an Irish family, but again her role in driving the plot is minimal. In *Downtown*, Guido also provides narrative structure as a recurring, mysterious, and sympathetic character, but he does more. He brings out traits in core characters, namely Ella and Mama, that would not be as apparent without his presence. Those traits are highly connected to the activities and goals of another important non-Jewish character, Miss Carey, the visiting nurse from the Henry Street Settlement House.

Miss Carey embodies both the activity and personality of the typical visiting nurse, as described by Lillian Wald in her book *The House on Henry Street* (1915). Early in her account, Wald describes how she moved from teaching a homemaking course in the settlement house out into the streets, initiating the ever-expanding role of visiting nurse, although she did not yet use that term. She describes how this change of events occurred:

> From the schoolroom where I had been giving a lesson . . . a little girl led me one drizzling March morning. She had told me of her sick mother, and . . . led me over broken roadways,—there was no asphalt, although its use was well established in other parts of the city,—over dirty mattresses and heaps of refuse . . . between tall, reeking houses whose laden fire-escapes, useless for their appointed purpose, bulged with household goods of every description. . . . Through Hester and Division streets we went to the end of Ludlow; past odorous fish-stands, for the streets were a market-place, unregulated, unsupervised, unclean; past evil-smelling, uncovered garbage-cans . . . the child led me on through a tenement hallway, across a court where open and unscreened closets were promiscuously used by men and women, up into a rear tenement, by slimy steps whose accumulated dirt was aug-

mented that day by the mud of the streets, and finally into the sickroom.[25]

In *Downtown*, Ella is similarly taken to the poorer sections of the Lower East Side when she runs into Guido in the street. He is "staggering under the weight of two large bundles," which turn out to be clothing from a garment factory that he had brought home so that his mother could "finish" them—" 'You know—sewing on pockets and buttons and things like that' " (85). Guido explains that his mother is too sick to work in the factory anymore, so he brings the work to her, then returns the finished garments to the factory, although this time he is bringing back unfinished work because she is now too ill to sew even at home.

Ella insists on helping Guido with his bundles and accompanies him on his walk to the factory. He is reluctant at first to accept her help, explaining that the factory is located in the Bowery. Ella says she does not mind and takes one of the bundles. During their walk, Guido admits that he is having a hard time coping. He and his mother have no relatives or friends who can help.

When Ella returns home that evening, she describes Guido's dire situation to her family. She recounts how Guido stopped attending school because of his mother and notes that they have no support in the community. Papa suggests that Mama go to Guido and his mother, and Mama gets right to work, putting together a package of food. Ella sets off with her mother on her second walk that day to a poor section of the Lower East Side, and again Taylor focuses specifically on the walk, as Wald did in her book. While the two of them are still in the Brenners' neighborhood, Taylor describes the urban environment as peaceful and pleasant, with the lamplighter lighting the gas mantles and adults sitting on stoops chatting, while children play in the gutters. But the language changes as Ella and Mama get closer to Guido's home:

> They had not gone far when Ella said, "It's somewheres on this block."[26] A moment later she pointed to a house next door to a stable. "This is it."
>
> The stable doors were open and from its interior, there poured forth such a strong overpowering horsey smell, Ella had to hold her nose.

They entered a long, narrow hall. Walking past the stairs . . . Ella pushed open the back door which led into a gloomy, littered yard. At the far end was a second building. "A yard house," Mama remarked.

Above them, flickering rays of light skipped from the open windows onto washlines full of clothes, that crisscrossed from one building to the other. Several cats were rummaging in the open pails and boxes. From a pipe which ran up the side of the house, rusty-colored water dripped and settled into a dark brown puddle.

They crossed over the cracked slate walk to the rear building. Inside the hallway was so dark, they had to grope for the staircase. Up and up they climbed. From behind closed doors, they could hear a baby wailing, loud voices speaking in a foreign tongue, and an occasional snatch of song.

At last they came to the top floor. "Five flights!" gasped Mama, as they stopped to catch their breath. (94)

Once Mama and Ella find the room, Guido admits them. "In the darkness they could make out a small, shabby room almost bare of furnishings. In one corner, on a cot, lay a thin, motionless figure."

Taylor employs many of the same techniques Wald does in describing these odysseys from cleaner to dirtier sections of the Lower East Side. Both writers focus on the signs of domestic life that are perhaps inappropriately located outside. In Wald's description, it is the mattresses on the street and the household furniture on the fire escapes, while in Taylor's case it is the clothes on the wash lines, which by implication would include undergarments. Both authors also focus on putrid smells and sights. Wald is straightforward in describing the privies that adults "promiscuously used," while Taylor more delicately discusses the stable with its door open, "pour[ing] forth such a strong overpowering horsey smell." In both books, the authors associate the poor not just with insufficient space but also with the squalor that resulted from densely packed quarters. Both authors describe going up the stairs and arriving at the sickroom where a woman lies in bed, suffering.

Most important, both authors emphasize the work of people serving as beneficent helpers of the poor and the sick. Wald explains that she saw the role of the visiting nurse as more than just a medical helper: "From the root of the old gospel another branch has grown, a realization that the call to the nurse is not only for the bedside care of the sick, but to help in seeking out the deep-lying basic causes of illness and misery, that in the future there may be less sickness to nurse and to cure."[27] In other words, Wald hopes the nurse will not only make society better, but also figure out why it suffers. What she describes is not just a nurse—it is also a social worker, and her task of "seeking out the deep-lying basic causes" places her in the field of sociology. By having Mama and Ella emulate the work of the visiting nurse, Taylor positions her characters, too, as social workers, and by having the All-of-a-Kind sisters frequently interact with Guido at the settlement house, Taylor emphasizes the importance of effective social welfare institutions.[28]

At the memorial service held at Carnegie Hall after Wald died, one speaker, Dr. C. E. A. Winslow of Yale University, spoke about Wald and her role in public health. No one, he said, thought of Wald "primarily as a nurse, or as a social worker, or a pioneer in public health, or a citizen or a stateswoman. . . . She was all of these things, but she was more than all of these things."[29] By investing Mama and Ella with Wald-like qualities and activities, Taylor endows her characters with the same assets—they are not just helpers but stateswomen who improve society. Wald herself saw the young people living on the Lower East Side in 1915 as positive agents of change. She wrote, "New York City is richer for the contributions made to its civic and educational life by the young people who grew up in and with the settlements, and who are not infrequently ready crusaders in social causes."[30] The impact of these early experiments in social work was not confined to Taylor's memories of childhood, for they ended up playing a role in her politics as a young woman and in her daughter's choice of career many years later.

The third institution shaped by German Jews that has an important presence in the *All-of-a-Kind* series is the Hamilton Fish Park Branch Library. When Taylor became a celebrity among librarians for her positive portrayal of Kathy the Library Lady and for championing public libraries in her speeches and school visits, she identified the Hamilton Fish Park Branch on Houston Street as the "beloved library" of her childhood.[31] The Beaux-Arts building Taylor frequented as a child housed the library until it was destroyed to make way for FDR Drive, when the library was reopened elsewhere on Houston

Street. The original structure was funded by Andrew Carnegie, designed by Carrère & Hastings, and opened on February 26, 1909. Taylor's description of the library accords with photos of the structure: "A branch of the New York Public Library was only a few blocks from their home; soon the familiar brown building came into view. Through the high door and up the staircase they went" (*AKF* 16). The "high door" and the "staircase" indicate a large, stately, multilevel structure. In a later book, Taylor confirms that the books for adults are housed downstairs, and the children's room is upstairs.[32]

The Brenner sisters took trips to other libraries as well, sometimes in search of German books for their mother. Another imposing library built around the same time as Hamilton Fish Park and located not far away was the Seward Park Branch, designed by the "white-shoe firm" of Babb, Cook & Welch. Historian Jenna Weissman Joselit points out that the architects

> displayed a degree of sensitivity that historians only rarely grant the well-to-do; they sought to design a structure that, while typifying "all that a library stands for," would not be "too incongruous for its surroundings." . . . What was called for, and eventually built, was "a building of simple, yet dignified type." . . . The interior of the Seward Park Branch, no less than its exterior, also reflected a concern for the needs of the local residents who, both at work and home, were "packed away like sardines" in exceedingly close quarters. In contrast to the Lower East Side's congestion, and its gray, scowling presence, the Seward Park Library was light, airy, and spacious.[33]

The contrast that Joselit describes between the library and the surrounding structures is one that Taylor made many years later in her speeches to librarians. She recalled in glowing detail how spacious and bright the rooms were, with windows that overlooked a park. On the third floor was a study room open to older children: "They didn't come just for reference books. There was so little room in their own homes, they came here to do their homework. Here it was peaceful and quiet. There were comfortable chairs and tables and good lighting."[34]

While the branch public libraries in the neighborhood were generally not staffed by German Jews (as the Settlement House was, in the form of

Lillian Wald), the Seward Park Branch was conceived of and ultimately funded by the Aguilar Free Library Society, a philanthropic organization whose board of trustees consisted of prosperous, socially prominent Jews, many of German extraction, almost all of whom were affiliated with institutions and organizations determined to Americanize the Russian and Eastern European immigrants who populated the Lower East Side. They saw libraries as a path to this Americanization. One of the major donors to the Aguilar Free Library Society was Jacob Schiff, whose influence in bringing German Jewish values to the Lower East Side touched all three of the institutions discussed in this chapter—the school, the settlement house, and the library.

Branch libraries offered English language classes, educational lectures, and assembly halls for community activities. In New York Public Library archives and throughout the pages of contemporaneous publications such as the *New York Times,* there is ample evidence that libraries were seen as agents of acculturation, with close attention paid to language and hygiene. Tensions about the library's role in the absorption of immigrants were reflected in debates concerning what sorts of books and periodicals libraries should have in their holdings—and in what languages. A major point of contention was whether the library's holdings should contain books written in Yiddish.

Joselit demonstrates how the Americanization project of the public libraries became intertwined with a civilizing mission. She opens her article about Jews and the New York Public Library with anecdotes illustrating the social benefits of the Seward Park Branch, which offered an alternative to saloons and the streets.[35] To get into the children's room, children had to display clean hands, and before they were allowed to receive a library card, they had to read and sign a paragraph that began, "I promise to keep this book clean."

The branch libraries could be noisy and crowded. Taylor later recalled that as many as seventy-five children attended Saturday story hour. In a lecture in 1951, she remembered the stories being told rather than read, and said, "Many of us got our first introductions to the delightful story book characters like Aladdin and Sinbad, and Loki and Thor and so on, right at these storytelling sessions."[36] Despite the noise and crowds, the librarians imposed structure both physically, by having children line up to have their hands inspected or to borrow books, and procedurally, through the check-out and book-return systems. In other words, the public libraries, significantly funded by the German Jewish philanthropists, were agents not just of Americanization but also of the values of the German Jews, such as cleanliness and order, which had become synonymous with American values.

The importance of the library to the *All-of-a-Kind* series is established in several ways at the beginning of the first book. The title page includes a picture of the girls coming down the library steps, each of them (except Gertie, who was too young to check out library books) clutching a book. The first chapter is titled "The Library Lady," and the first sentences link Sarah to the library. As discussed above, the main issue in this first chapter of the series is that Sarah has lost a library book. The climax and resolution of the chapter are provided by the Library Lady, who devises a solution to the pressing problem. Thus Taylor establishes not only the importance of the library to the series but the particular importance of Sarah as well. The library is the primary setting of the chapter, and Sarah is its main character. The values of the library will be borne out in Sarah in this book and throughout the series, for both Sarah and the library, as a place of learning, of acculturation, of literature, and of civilization, embody the values that Taylor emphasized as a writer.

In the next book in the series, *More AKF*, Taylor situates another important set of scenes in the library. The chapter title "Secret in the Bookstack" again refers to the library, but attention shifts from Sarah and responsibility to Ella and romance. As if to remind her readers that Sarah should be identified with the library, near the beginning of the chapter Sarah is mentioned once: "Sarah hugged her library book. 'Don't you just love Friday afternoons?'" (19). But once the girls get to their destination, Ella emerges as the main character. She has a new interest in the library—she has seen a young man there who attracts her.[37] The intrigue of the chapter is how that young man, Jules, finds a way to signal his interest to Ella. After he observes Henny and Ella hiding a book in the stacks so they can find it when they return the following week (as they have reached the limit of books they can check out that week), Jules tucks a note in the book with the expectation that Ella will find it when she retrieves the book.

Two relevant topics come up in this chapter. The first is that Henny has the idea to hide the book they want in the "foreign section," because "people who read foreign books don't even know English, so they won't bother with it. It'll still be there when we come back next Friday. See?" (23). Later, Taylor reveals that the "foreign section" in which Henny hid the book was the "German shelf." Whether in homage to the language her family spoke or to lend an air of high romance to the chapter, Taylor chooses German to be the language to which the Brenner sisters gravitate.[38]

Second, Taylor explicitly raises the issue of rules, as she did in the chapter "The Library Lady." Again, it is the librarian who is concerned with rules, and again the librarian bends them. When Miss Martin, the librarian introduced earlier in the chapter, finds the English-language book on the German-language shelf, the note catches her eye and she reads it. Realizing it is for Ella and written by Jules, who she thinks is "such a nice boy," she wavers. "Well, it's against the rules, but—. Carefully she put the note back and replaced the book where she had found it. Better a broken rule than a broken heart, she said to herself, with a little laugh" (24).

Thus the library represents rules and order, while the librarian is human and sensitive and realizes when a rule can be bent to help a patron—in both this and the earlier case, a Brenner sister. With this repetition, Taylor emphasizes both the importance of rules and the value of flexibility. Throughout the books set on the Lower East Side, Taylor conveys that message many ways, not only through librarians but also through teachers, a social worker, a principal, and parents. Careful to show that rules exist and that they matter, Taylor also teaches that adults who care for children must be adaptable when the needs of the child require it. In this way, Taylor may have been "prettying" up the behavior of adults in the same way she beautifies the Lower East Side. By making Mama warmer than she really was, describing the Brenner home as grander than it really was, and making teachers and librarians friendlier than they really were, Taylor was able to show her readers what it was like to be Jewish on the Lower East Side in the early 1900s in a way that her readers could accept and comprehend, and at the same time to see that place and that time as desirable.

Taylor employed the same sort of strategies as she accomplished the double inculcation of German Jewish and American values with her books. Obscuring the years of poverty and hunger (which she fully acknowledged in speeches she gave as a successful author), almost completely hiding her mother's sadness and desperation, and downplaying family strife (but not dismissing it—she does depict tension among the sisters and between the parents and their daughters), Taylor portrayed a close-knit, loving Jewish family that was also, largely due to the influence of the mother, focused on cleanliness, proper behavior, refined possessions such as clothing and furniture, responsibility, social welfare, and orderly habits. By emphasizing the neighborhood institutions of the school, the settlement house, and the public library, Taylor simultaneously emphasized the values of those who created and supported those institutions—German Jews. Such an emphasis was natural to Taylor, herself of German Jewish heritage. The introduction of Jews to millions of American readers was an introduction to a specific kind of Jewry that through certain public institutions—and through Taylor's books—came to define all American Jews to many.

FOUR

Sarah Becomes Sydney

1916–1920

IN 1915, PAPA RELUCTANTLY resolved to leave the junk business and, with his brother-in-law Joe Marowitz, open an embroidery shop at 127 Fifth Avenue, between 19th and 20th Streets. Cilly had long been ashamed of the junk business and kept urging her husband to rise in the world with an enterprise that was cleaner and of a higher social status, which would help his daughters make good matches. He had a health scare about this time, and finally agreed to start the new business, although it meant forgoing an opportunity to capitalize on the booming wool trade during World War I. The partner who urged him to stay in woolens made a fortune during the war, while Morris lost half his savings during his first year in business with Joe.[1] About the only positive memory the family retained of the failed venture was the store's unrivaled view of the Preparedness Parade on May 13, 1916. On that fair spring day, they looked down on "the greatest civilian marching demonstration in the history of the world" as close to 145,000 men and women in civilian dress showed support for strengthening American defenses in readiness for what looked like inevitable involvement in World War I.[2] The marchers took close to twelve hours to march up from the Battery and along Fifth Avenue, which was decorated with hundreds of fluttering flags. The reviewing stand was at Madison Square Park, only five blocks from the store, and windows up and down the avenue were at a premium.

During the summer of 1916, a devastating polio epidemic swept through New York, sickening some nine thousand people and killing about a fifth of the afflicted. Morris responded by taking two rooms for his family in Rockaway Beach. Readers of the *All-of-a-Kind* books will recall the vivid description of the epidemic in *More*. Frightened friends and neighbors flee the city, and when Uncle Hyman's lively fiancée Lena is crippled three days before their wedding, Papa insists that his family leave for the clean air of Rockaway Beach ("Epidemic in the City"). While the children are delighted to have their first family vacation, Mama reminds them of the financial burden their father is assuming in order to keep them safe. She also mentions the personal toll it will take, for Papa must stay alone in the city all week in order to keep working and will join them only on the weekend. In real life, all the children joined their mother at the beach except Ella, who kept house for her father in the city and came out to the seaside with him every weekend. The Brenners were hardly alone in this move, for a complex network of relatives and friends, some of whom knew Morris Brenner and his brothers from Wisnicz, lived in the same boarding house or elsewhere in town, sharing meals and leisure excursions.[3]

The next significant change in the Brenners' lives was a move to the Bronx in the fall of 1916 to live near Uncle Joe and his wife, Tanta Fannie. The Brenners moved to an apartment on the second floor of 927 East 169th Street, paying $26 a month, which was only $2 more than their rent on the Lower East Side. It is hard to overstate the effect that the development of the New York subway system had on demographic patterns in the city. Families could move to more spacious neighborhoods with newer apartments and bucolic parks while continuing to work at their previous places of employment and patronize familiar shops on the Lower East Side. Cilly insisted that the move was right for the family, even though Morris had to commute to work each day. He extricated himself from the embroidery business after a year, taking a significant financial loss, and returned to the woolen trade, with a shop on Avenue D and 7th Street in Manhattan. His brother-in-law Morris Marowitz joined him, while feckless Uncle Joe went into a resale business. Morris Brenner gradually recovered financially, only to be hit by the economic slump of 1920–21, caused by the transition back to a peacetime economy.

The move and financial uncertainty affected the children, primarily in their schooling. Ella had already been taken out of high school and forced to train as a bookkeeper. Morris's financial troubles meant that the family needed another wage earner, whatever the personal cost to his eldest daughter. According to Taylor's school record from P.S. 188 on the Lower East Side, her last day there was October 31, 1916, one day after she turned twelve. The record cards of Taylor and her two younger sisters show that they transferred to

P.S. 20, the Charles James Fox School on 167th Street, only a few blocks from their apartment. At the time of her transfer, Sarah's class level was listed as 7a. She graduated from P.S. 20 in the spring of 1918 and went on to attend Morris High School.[4]

Henny's card also has the notations "removal" and "Brx 20" written after the same date. However, she returned to P.S. 188 on November 9, apparently to complete a math class, and she commuted there through February 6, 1917. Similarly, when Ella resumed her studies in public school after taking clerical classes, rather than attending high school in the Bronx she returned to Washington Irving High School, which was in its relatively new home on Irving Place between East 16th and 17th Streets in Manhattan.[5] With all the coming and going, domestic routines endured. When the children came home from school, they were given hot tea and fresh crusty rolls with butter and were free to meet with their friends in the neighborhood unless chores and homework intervened.

It is from this period that actual physical objects from Taylor's youth began to be preserved, and they provide substance to her literary reimagining of her past. The first item that Taylor is known to have created herself is the dress she made for her elementary school graduation. The dress is the rare remaining artifact of Taylor's childhood, and it is one of the only objects in existence that prove that something discussed in Taylor's books is true. No evidence exists, for example, that Taylor actually received a dictionary from a history teacher in elementary school. From the dress, however, the real person behind Sarah—Sydney Taylor—recycled the events of making the dress into the story she incorporates into her children's book. This dress is the first evidence of Sarah's creative powers, proved here through tailoring and later developed in writing.

The first written document still in existence that belonged to Sarah Brenner was her graduation autograph book. During the celebratory time of graduation, her autograph book was filled with the signatures and good wishes of her classmates and family members. Bound in genuine leather, the book has an aura of importance and planned longevity. Girls wrote most of the autographs, and of the dozens of names that pepper the pages, none show up later in Taylor's diaries and letters except for her sisters. Signed at a time when names reflected ethnicity or nationality more precisely than they might today, the book—containing such names as Mary McKenna, Irene A. Kilgalon, Mai

R. McCall, Ruth Schwartz, and Ethel Kaufman—suggests a student body consisting largely of Irish and Jewish students. In this respect, the autograph book confirms one aspect of the *All-of-a-Kind* books set in the Bronx: unlike in the stories set in the Lower East Side, the friends of the Brenners in these later books have Irish names and are obviously Christian. Ella's closest friend, for example, is named Grace Healy. Whether or not Ella actually had an Irish best friend cannot be determined, but that the Brenner family began to mix with non-Jews, particularly the Irish, is borne out in the signatures in Taylor's autograph books.

Entries written by friends and acquaintances tended to be short and banal, often including little rhymes and cautionary platitudes. For example, a girl named Eleanor Grant wrote, "To Sarah / Love many / Trust few / Paddle your own canoe." Dorothy Alexander was even more blunt, with "Hold your friends by holding your tongue." Sweeter comments address love and friendship, with wishes for a good life. One of the few with a reference to location states, "May your life be as bright / as Luna Park at night. / Your loving classmate, Lillian Kardo."[6]

Taylor's older sisters took it upon themselves to write longer and more thoughtful comments. Henny wrote down what appear to be lyrics to a song or lines of a poem (the words do not seem to be her own) titled "Smile." It is a long exposition on the importance of keeping a smile. At the end of the passage, Henny signed with "lovingly, your sister, Henrietta." After her signature, she wrote emphatically, "Not seem—BE!" This rendering of the common Latin phrase, *Esse quam videri* ("To be, rather than to seem"), which has frequently been used as a motto by schools and other organizations, is itself unexceptional; it is the emphasis provided by the capitalization of the word *BE* and the exclamation point that convey Henny's forceful and upbeat personality. Henny calls on her sister to live life to the fullest, an appropriate gesture to make in an autograph book and one that may hint at a certain passivity that Henny perceives in Sarah.

Ella wrote what amounts to a letter, full of advice for her younger sister. On the left-facing page, she wrote, "If at first you don't succeed—try, try again." On the right-facing page is the body of the letter:

'Tis true, dear sister, that the simple little proverb written on this page is old—and to some, it has almost become meaningless. Let it not be so with you. Till now, you have had very little to contend with. "Life," till now—did not call for any responsibilities from you. You are only beginning—you cannot expect "Success to run ahead of you." "Failure" may confront you time and again—but do not let it discourage you ever—. It is "Failure" at first—"Success" afterwards—which gives you "Experience"—and—"Experience" teaches one how to live.

Always remember no matter how keen the "defeat"—with your head up—chin in—defiance pictured in your eyes—face "defeat" and say "If at first *I* don't Succeed—I'll try—try—again."

Ella signs this letter, "Lovingly, Ella." Clearly, Taylor's two older sisters considered it entirely appropriate to lecture their younger sibling when signing her autograph book. Both sisters indicate that Sarah should be more optimistic, cheery, and perseverant. The platitudinous advice hints at the teenage Taylor's personality and outlook.

Charlotte was the last sister to sign Taylor's autograph book. In 1918, Gertrude would have been ten and presumably old enough to write, but her name does not appear. Charlotte's entry is markedly shorter than her sisters', and much like the conventional sayings penned by the many other, nonrelated signers: "Good Gooder Goodest. Learn to correct this and succeed in life. Your true sister Charlotte Brenner."

World War I loomed over Taylor's middle school years. It also hastened her family's detachment from their European roots. When the United States entered the war, anti-German feeling intensified and the children insisted that their mother finally learn English.[7] She took classes and became a reader of serious English literature, but her writing always remained idiosyncratic, heavily influenced by German grammar and spelling. Although she became more fluent in speaking English than Morris, she spoke it with a heavy accent throughout her life.[8] She gradually let her children know how difficult it had been to be a Jew in Germany—less for her with her fair hair and blue eyes than for their father, with his darker features. And yet "for years she had suffered the agony of a mixed loyalty."[9] To her, Germany represented material comfort, financial security, order, and familial and neighborhood affection, with anti-Semitic incidents fading into half-forgotten memories of ignorant classmates and strangers. Morris had no love for the land they had left behind and he demanded that Cilly's handwoven tapestries of the Kaiser and the Kaiserin, which she had received as a wedding present, be thrown out on the street, where he led the neighborhood children in pelting them with stones.

The family's ties to relatives in the Old World also weakened. Their distance from the shtetl was put in stark relief when they heard about the death of Morris's father. Joseph Brenner died during the war at age eighty-seven, but Morris did not learn about it until several years after his death, at which point he sat in mourning for the one day required by Jewish law.[10] According to Ella, the family learned that during the war Cossacks commandeered her grandfather's house, where the old man lived alone. They reportedly mistreated him, forcing him to work for them and provide their meals. The Brenners' youngest child, Jerry, born in October 1919, was named for his grandfather Joseph and was called Joey as a child.

Jerry's birth followed a heartbreaking event even closer to home: the death of baby Ralph. It was a tragedy covered with a cloak of silence. From Charlotte's memoir, it can be inferred that this second son was born in late 1916 and died in 1918.[11] Ralph was walking and talking, but still in diapers and drinking from a bottle, when one autumn day he cut his finger on a piece of glass. Cilly took him to a druggist at the local pharmacy, but a neighbor woman berated her for not taking him to a doctor. Thinking customs in the Bronx were fancier than what she knew on the Lower East Side, Cilly gave in to the pressure, despite the added expense. Eleven-year-old Charlotte, who accompanied her mother to the doctor's office, heard her mother screaming that the doctor had killed the baby by using too much chloroform. In her autobiography, Charlotte says that Cilly took to her bed for a week, consumed by grief, then got up "and quietly resumed her tasks." Charlotte's daughter, Susan Baker, however, was told that Cilly made another suicide attempt at this time, and other family members said she never got over the boy's death, keeping his photograph on her dresser until the day she died. When Ella and Charlotte recorded their memories as adults, the episode evaporates into barely a murmur: "Oh, that was when Baby Ralphie . . ."— and nothing more.

Taylor skirted the issue of her brother's death in the chapter "Follow the Leader" in *Ella,* when Charlie has a life-threatening accident and is hospitalized.[12] He hovers between life and death for a week, during which time

Mama and Papa are models of comfort and religious faith, although anguish seeps through their every word. On the evening that news reaches the family that the little boy is out of danger, Mama takes Ella aside and tells her that she is expecting another baby, to the delight of her oldest daughter.

> "I wasn't sure how you'd take the news." Mama looked away. She seemed to be talking to the wall. "Here Ella is, a grown woman, practically engaged to be married, and her mother's going to have a baby! Will she be embarrassed?"
> "Embarrassed! Oh Mama! I'll be so happy and proud."

Mama is relieved by Ella's reaction and continues:

> "Papa and I, we knew it meant another mouth to feed, and that we were not young anymore. But when Charlie was so sick, when we were afraid we might lose him, how very precious each child seemed to us then. I wondered all along, was this God's way of granting me another child? If God in his infinite wisdom saw fit to take our son away from us, was he perhaps giving us another son in his stead?"

The real-life Ella noted that her sister revised dates in the Brenner history to make better stories. Taylor also revised this family trauma. Sorrow over a child's death becomes the shadow of a loss, without the actual child—baby Ralph—ever appearing. The grief is resolved both in the book and in real life through Mama's last pregnancy, which she announces by turning to the wall, her strong feelings once again restrained by the undemonstrative nature that all her children acknowledged and regretted.[13]

Little of the family's sorrow appears in Taylor's correspondence, which she began to collect in 1919.[14] A great saver of letters, Taylor began filing her correspondence in two big box binders, one labeled "A–L" and the other "M–Z." In these binders, she filed letters by the last name of the writer. She did not, however, make copies of the handwritten letters that she wrote (later in her life she kept carbons of the hundreds of letters she typed), so the letters from 1919 and through the 1930s offer only one side of her written conversations.

Most of Taylor's correspondents in 1919 were teenage girls on vacation, who wrote gossipy, breezy letters. The one issue that emerges as noteworthy is that the letter writers referred to her variously as Sarah and Sid, so apparently that summer was when Taylor changed her name and instructed her friends to call her Sydney, which they tried to do, inconsistently. Two girls, Dorothy and Rose, corresponded with Taylor beginning in June 1919. In the first of Dorothy's three letters, she began with "Dear Sid, (Sarah)," an address that aptly reflects her confusion about Taylor's name change. The later two letters use only Sarah. Similarly, Rose addressed her as Sarah on July 16, but referred to her as Sid on August 4.

Anna Kornweitz, whose brother eventually married Ella, also shifted between Sarah and Syd. In salutations and closings, Anna often used endearments such as "kiddo," "kiddy," "dearest beloved," "snookums," and "thweetie," and then addressed Taylor by name in the middle of the letters. In a letter from August 6, for example, Anna opened with, "My own and Dearest Beloved," but a few lines down wrote, "Darling Sarah, tell me you received the letter previous to this one and take a load off my neck." A letter of August 14 was addressed to "Dear Sarah," yet Anna used the name Sidney in the body of the letter, as she did in the next letter, dated August 15.

What this small collection of correspondence from the summer of 1919 shows is that Taylor's later version of her name change was a fiction. Once she became famous and had to address the public's curiosity about her name, she told her fans that she chose Syd because she was working in the theater and felt—or was told—that Sarah was old-fashioned. In a letter to one such fan, she explained:

> When I was considerably younger, I used to belong to a theatre group and then to a concert dance group. In those days they thought the name of Sarah very unglamorous for the theatre so it was changed legally to Sydney. Now I feel the name of Sarah to be much more beautiful; actually in the original Hebrew it means Princess. But it's too late to change back so I still keep the name Sydney.[15]

Taylor used some version of this explanation in dozens of letters, often explaining to her young readers that she was a woman despite the confusing

Sarah Brenner, 1920s

name Sydney.[16] It made a good story, but it was not true. To more intimate friends, Taylor stated later in life that she changed her name in high school because Sarah did not suit her aspirations of becoming a writer. She wanted to be different and make a mark.

The first extant document written in Taylor's own hand was the diary she began while a student at Morris High School. She marked the occasion and her beginnings as a writer with these words on the title page: "My Thought Book / Sarah R. Brenner / Begun August 1919." This was one of the last times she referred to herself as Sarah, as it turned out. Also, she did not refer to her project as a diary or a journal but instead as a "thought book." Indeed, it was far from a daily record of her activities; sometimes several months elapsed between entries, while other times she wrote more frequently. But over the course of the next fourteen years she poured her thoughts into these books, not consistently in terms of frequency but quite consistently in terms of introspective content.[17]

The opening words in what would turn out to be many years of journal keeping are, "I have decided to adopt you dear thought book so's I could have someone to tell my thoughts to and these I could never, never as long as I live tell to any living person. You see you're dead and dead men tell no tales." Taylor immediately engages both life and death in this first entry. Her description of the diary as *dead* is remarkable, a far cry from characterizations made by many diary keepers who feel passionately that their diaries are their living companions, addressing them in the second person and calling them by pet names. In fact, Taylor also employs such practices, first referring to the diary in the second person ("you") and then affectionately calling it "dear." Her first words in the journal position her among myriad other young women or older girls who kept diaries, but the abrupt shift to calling the diary "dead" is unusual. One senses that Taylor did think of her thought book as dear and as lively—and that her description of it as "dead" later in the paragraph was meant in specific contrast to the word *living* in the previous sentence. In other words, Taylor was already thinking carefully about her choice and arrangement of words.

Some of Taylor's acquaintances knew about the thought book and connected it to her incipient vocation as a writer. Anna Kornweitz wrote Taylor several letters in August 1919, while Taylor was vacationing in Rockaway and Anna was stuck in the city working in an office. In her letters, Anna laments the drudgery of working in the city and wishes she could join her friend at the seaside. She also mentions Taylor's diary, referring to it the way Taylor does, as her "thought book": "Listen Syd, about the thought book, how are you progressing? I would have one but if I were to write a lot of thoughts that I don't express, I would fill the book up in less than a day. I think about so many things during the day that I would love to tell *someone*."[18] Anna's remarks make it clear that Taylor did not keep her diary's existence completely private, and Anna's question reveals that she knew its importance to her friend. The contrast Anna draws between herself and her friend in terms of the impracticability of her keeping such a book suggests that she saw Taylor as different—as someone who, unlike her, was selective about recording her thoughts, and who found a notebook a more suitable confidant than another person.

The entries Taylor wrote between 1919 and 1923 focused on school, work, and leisure activities. Taylor first mentions school in the third entry of the diary, written on January 19, 1920, many months after she enrolled at Morris High. Still standing today, the stately building is an aesthetically pleasing structure built in the collegiate gothic style. It looks like an urban castle and occupies an entire block. Opened in 1897, it was first named the Mixed High School, then Peter Cooper High School, and in 1902 Morris High School, in honor of the Bronx landowner Gouverneur Morris, a framer of the U.S. Constitution.[19]

From the beginning, Morris High School was dedicated to progressive ideals. It was called the Mixed High School because it enrolled both male and female students, the first high school in the New York City public school system to do so. The fact that Morris High was coeducational was not inconsequential to Taylor. She participated in many activities and gained leadership roles that had that much more meaning because she participated along with and was elected by both boys and girls.

The contents of the January entry show how much Taylor's education occupied her. Still addressing her thought book in the second person, Taylor wrote, "Though I haven't written for months, I have not forgotten you. School, business school, and those manuscripts have filled up all my spare time beautifully. It is pretty nearly the finish of this term now and when I last wrote, the term hadn't yet begun. I have been struggling with geometry and will have to start struggling all over again next term."[20] To this entry Taylor clipped a composition she wrote on September 15, 1919, noting: "This is the story of our fishing expedition / Written for school, but never used." She preserved this earliest extant example of her story writing among her papers, although she never submitted it for English 213.

The composition is slight, but it displays Taylor's early literary experimentation. The opening paragraph of "Fisherman's Luck" describes setting and emotion: "It was a wonderful morning, a morning that somehow or other caused every heart, heavy with sadness, to throw off its weight and become light with a happy lightheartedness, a morning for irrepressible youth, a morning that made you want to sing for joy! It was in fact, a perfect July morning!" This opening paragraph again shows how Taylor relied on repetition for artistic effect. In her first diary entry, she repeated the words *living* and *dead;* here, she repeats *morning,* and *light,* demonstrating awareness of strategies to unify ideas in a paragraph.

Throughout the story, Taylor displays other signs of a budding writer who relies on techniques she has seen used by published authors. She employs subtly extended metaphors and phrases that one would not normally encounter in conversational speech. Similarly, she refers to her own inward thoughts in heightened language, even when the subject is simply a dropped fishing line: "I inwardly cursed myself in language very unsuitable for a young lady for losing a 5-year-old line." Taylor was learning her craft through imitation, consciously writing in a way that she perceived authors wrote.

The only one of Taylor's high school report cards to survive dates to the second half of her sophomore year. It lists all the classes available to second-year students in one section, and then discusses Taylor specifically in another. Morris High offered many classes designed to support girls in office-based careers, including bookkeeping, stenography, and typewriting. Instead of taking those classes in her final semester, Taylor took English, French (she passed her New York State Regents exam), algebra, biology, drawing, music, and physical training.[21] Today—and for most of the twentieth century—such a schedule of courses would be considered college preparatory. Taylor's diaries reveal that she also studied Spanish at some point and was interested in literature enough to join an extracurricular literary club. Taylor saw high school as a place to gain intellectual and artistic cultivation rather than vocational training.

In addition to classroom lessons, high school afforded Taylor opportunities for leadership and creativity unavailable in the workplace or at home. As the first coeducational high school in the five boroughs of New York City, Morris offered a unique experience in providing leadership roles for girls that enabled them to vote in class and club meetings and to preside over peers of both sexes.[22] From photographs in the *Morris Annual,* it is clear that many girls belonged to the wide variety of school clubs, which ran the gamut from mandolin to athletics.

In the 1920 edition of the yearbook, sophomore Sarah Brenner is listed as a member of the Alacris Literary and Debating Club, and the page indicates that she served as club secretary from February to June 1920. The mission of this literary society was to create "a sound taste for good reading by intimate study of the famous authors. We have sought in all cases to find the concrete elements of literary value."[23] Despite the formal name of the club, the brief mission statement indicates the members were more interested in discussing literature than in debating.

The Alacris was one of five literary clubs at Morris High School included in the 1920 yearbook. Another was the Journeyman Club, which "in spite of its masculine name, is composed only of girls who are interested in the study of parliamentary law who hope to further the participation of girls in all school activities; and who hope, finally, by a thorough study of the ever-growing number of women, to better fit themselves for the leadership which shall be demanded of the future."[24] The Journeyman-Fio Club paragraph in the 1921 yearbook begins, "Are you a feminist? Then you should be interested in the Journeyman-Fio Club."[25] Female membership and leadership were thus actively encouraged at Morris.

Taylor took advantage of those opportunities; on February 19, 1920, she wrote jubilantly:

> I am so happy that I've stopped in the midst of my lessons to write this—I'm president of the Spanish Club and Miss Carnahan is so dear to me! I'm so excited that it's affecting my writing. I want to dance a jig or stand on my head or do something. I'm positively going crazy.
>
> Sid Brenner if you don't come down to earth this very minute; I'm have to pull you down.
>
> It is 10 P M & I have finished only my geometry so so long.

She then signed this entry with "Syd," in quotation marks, as if she was writing a letter to herself. This was the first time in the thought book that Taylor referred to herself in the third person and "signed" the entry, a practice she continued to follow. Also noteworthy is that Taylor spelled her name two different ways. She was still working out how she wanted the world to refer to her and understand her.

The diary entry reveals that high school gave Taylor access to new facets of identity previously unavailable to girls. Setting aside elite institutions, attending high school as a matter of course was relatively new to the majority of young people in 1920, and even more so for girls. Once enrolled, girls had the novel opportunity to run for elective office; being elected by both boys and girls to preside over the entire student body could happen only at a co-educational high school. But the entry addresses more than just jubilation over an election victory. Mingled with the excitement of having achieved the position is Taylor's devotion to the teacher who served as head of the Spanish faculty, Grace Carnahan.[26] The two issues—becoming president of the club and feeling so strongly about the teacher—are intertwined.

The next entry in the diary, dated March 2, relates similar news. It begins: "Well, I'm in! Do you notice how plainly I am writing. I'm trying to come down to earth. So I'm really 4th Term Representative. I can't believe it." Election as class representative in the Morris Organization was more of an achievement than leading the Spanish Club. The Morris Organization appears to have been the largest student group in the school and was the equivalent of a student council of today. The paragraphs describing the Morris Organization—or M.O. as it is called both in the yearbook and among the students—attest to its members' sense of importance, however tongue-in-cheek: "With the ending of the Great War, the Morris Organization was confronted with the same problems as devastated Europe, and, in fact, the entire civilized world found itself in—namely—Reconstruction. Due to that great spirit which has been one of the characteristics of Morris Students, we have been able to accomplish a great deal in a remarkably short time."[27] Like similar organizations, the M.O. oversaw literary, art, and athletic contests, theatrical shows, "Field Day," and other forms of entertainment. The extensive list of officers for each term (September–January and February–June) as recorded in the school yearbook include a president, vice-president, secretary, treasurer, assistant treasurer, and eight term representatives. As her diary indicates, Taylor is listed as the fourth term representative during the second semester.

What Taylor does not say in the diary is that she appears to be the only female in the entire group of twenty-six officers. On the September–January list, several term reps give only their first initials along with their last names, so it is possible some are female. But the name Sarah Brenner is listed in its entirety, and Sarah is the only female name in either of the lists. Underscoring the maleness of the organization, the photograph of the executive officers on the bottom half of the same page shows four young men sitting on a bench.

Taylor transformed her experiences with school elections in *Ella of All-of-a-Kind Family*. The chapter "Election in the Balance" opens with a group of girls, including Henny, chatting over lunch in the cafeteria about the upcoming election. Rose delivers the first spoken sentence: "Election for term representative to the General Organization is just a week away. Who's getting your vote?" (29). In this fictionalized account, Taylor took both the name of the elected position and the school's student body organization from her own experience, while making Henny the girl in high school, not Sarah. In real life, Henny never went to high school, but Taylor had good reason to make her sister the subject of this chapter about elections instead of herself. A reader familiar with any of the previous *All-of-a-Kind* books would already know that Henny is rambunctious and a bit of a troublemaker. Even if *Ella* was the first of the books readers encountered, they would quickly realize that she is a rabble-rouser. Rose explains:

> "There are three candidates this time—Calvin Spencer . . ."
> "Oh, the good-looking one with curly hair and beautiful eyes," Hannah gushed.
> "Yes," agreed Henny, "but he's awfully stuck on himself. Thinks he's God's gift to women."
> "Still you've got to admit he's great fun in class," Betty said. "He's always coming up with some wisecrack."
> Henny dismissed Calvin with a flip of her hand. "Aw, he's just a big show-off. Who are the other two?"
> "Jack Berger, the bean pole with the long nose—and Dennis Reilly. You know, the one whose ears stick out."
> "Yeh," Henny grinned, "one look at him and you can tell which way the wind blows."
> The girls burst into hysterics. (29–30)

Outspoken and brash, Henny sets herself apart from the other girls who "gush" and who form the audience to her verbal antics. Henny's bravado and iconoclasm are reinforced when the conversation becomes more serious in the next sentence:

> "Not much of a choice," Jenny remarked. "Not that it matters which one gets elected. It would still be a boy."
> Rae nodded. "And with a boy representative to the General Organization, most of the activities and programs are always planned for boys."

"So why don't we get a girl to run for a change?" Henny suggested.

"A girl!" the others chorused.

"Sure. Why not? Why does it always have to be a boy?" Henny looked around at the startled faces. "What's the matter? Don't you think a girl could handle the job?"

"I guess she could," Bessie considered. "It's just that we never thought of it before."

"I'm with you, Henny," Rose cried. "I think it's a great idea! Let's try. Even if we don't win, at least they'll realize girls have some rights after all."

Henny is not the first girl in the conversation to bring up the gender imbalance, but she is the one to come up with a radical solution, that a girl should run for office. She continues to stir the pot when she tells her friends that a girl who ran for this election would have a good chance of winning because the boys would have their votes split three ways. Henny assumes that the boys will vote for male candidates while the girls will vote for the one female candidate—in other words, the students will vote according to their sex.

Henny convinces her friends that a girl should run for office, and the friends convince Henny that she should be their candidate. Henny is at first surprised that she has been chosen and asks, "Why me?" (30). As the girls start to enumerate Henny's winning qualities, they emphasize her debating skills. They also point out that Henny is "marvelous in gym." In addition to arguing that Henny would be a good candidate, the girls try to sell her on the idea by explaining the perks she would get: " 'As term representative,' Jenny tempted, 'you'll get to arrange the athletic events. You'll have to go out with the teams every time they play some other high school. Think of all the boys you'll get to meet!' " Ultimately convinced, Henny "felt a heady excitement at the challenge. 'Okay, I'll do it! she declared' " (31).

The rest of the chapter concerns the campaign and the war between the sexes that it instigates. Taylor does not describe in her diary the campaign she undertook when she ran for president of the Spanish Club or for fourth term rep. In *Ella*, however, she goes into quite a bit of detail, and a strong feminist agenda emerges. The girls challenge the boys to a debate, but the boys treat the campaign "as some kind of joke" (32). One boy yells, "The charge of the Suffragette Brigade," and another jeers, "That's just what we need around here, a girl rep . . . Instead of a basketball game, she could organize a sewing bee" (33). When the girls work harder in their campaign efforts, the boys step up the hostilities.

> As election day neared, the boys began to play rough. They defaced the girls' signs with scribbles and daubs of paint. They handed out leaflets with statements like "How about it boys? Do you want to join a cooking class?" Posters Henny's campaigners pinned up in the morning were found lying crumpled and torn on the floor by midday. Even the attractive poster outside their homeroom door was not spared. The pretty girl's face on it was disfigured by a large black walrus moustache. Underneath someone had penned, "Henrietta, the Suffragette." (33)

Henny prepares for the debate seriously, yet under her air of confidence she is anxious when the day arrives. At the scheduled time, she is on the stage, ready to go, but the boys do not arrive. The students in the packed auditorium get restless, and just when the teacher says the boys will have to lose by default, they suddenly appear—but not as boys. Instead, they are "dressed in regulation girls' gym bloomers, navy blue and puffed-out pleats! At a signal, they linked arms and came marching down the center aisle with Calvin holding aloft a poster proclaiming in big black letters, 'We are the fighting Suffragettes!' Up the steps of the stage they stomped, grimacing and tittering in silly-girl fashion." Dressed in the bloomers, the boys each attempt a handstand, "their skinny legs projected comically from the bulky bloomers as they teetered unsteadily on their hands. It sent waves of laughter bouncing from wall to wall" (35).

Not to be outdone, Henny runs backstage and changes into her gym bloomers and rushes back, striding past the boys who are throwing kisses to the audience. "She put two fingers to her lips and blew a loud, piercing whistle. Instantly, the audience quieted down, wondering what was going to happen next" (35). Henny shouts to the audience, " 'This was supposed to be a debate. But if this is the only kind of argument my opponents can come up with, then let 'em try this!' Whereupon she executed three perfect cartwheels across the stage floor. Then going into a handstand, she gracefully flipped over backward, landing quietly and smoothly upright on her feet. Arms outstretched, she curtsied gracefully. A roar of approval rose from the audience" (37). One boy tries to counter Henny's success by attempting cartwheels, but he is clumsy and knocks over a chair, causing all the boys on the stage to fall into a tangled heap. Now the audience laughs at them rather than with them. As if to emphasize the importance of this escapade, an illustration shows Henny in a handstand while the three bloomer-dressed boys react negatively in the background.

Henny wins the election, and the boys sheepishly apologize for their behavior, calling themselves fools. The chapter ends with Henny having the last word: " 'Well,' Henny said with a bright smile, 'it proves they're good sports after all' " (38). Here, Henny flips the gender balance just as the boys had tried to do when they donned girls' bloomers and attempted their antics on stage. The boys acted like girls then; now Henny adopts the tone and vocabulary of boys by calling them "good sports." She equalizes the playing field with that statement, implying that the boys treated her the way they would treat other boys when losing an athletic game.

Pervading the chapter is an awareness of women's suffrage. When Taylor was writing in her diary about winning two school elections, women were on the cusp of obtaining the vote through the Nineteenth Amendment to the U.S. Constitution, which was passed by Congress on June 4, 1919, and ratified on August 18, 1920. There is no doubt women's suffrage was a topic of debate all around New York City and at Taylor's high school throughout that year. Taylor does not mention women's suffrage, the Nineteenth Amendment, or the right to vote in her diaries, but the books she wrote years later and her sister's memoir showed her family members and friends as aware of the movement and the change to the Constitution at that time. These events also allowed her to address the feminist movement of the 1970s—*Ella* was published in 1978—in terms safely embedded in the past.

In "Election in the Balance," Papa protests when he hears Henny will be running for president of the General Organization. "At home everyone was amused over Henny's running for office, except possibly Papa. 'Listen to her! A regular suffragette already! Next thing you know, she'll be marching in a parade and carrying a sign like all those crazy women!' " (31–32). Not only Henny but also Ella and Mama begin arguing with him:

"They're not crazy, Papa," Henny retorted.

Papa shook his head doubtfully. "I feel sorry for our country. What's going to happen when the women start taking over?"

"It might even be better," Mama returned mildly.

Papa clapped a hand to his head in mock horror. "Mama, you too?"

"Why not? Mama's a woman," Ella said, "Equal rights for women. It's coming, Papa. You can't stop it. Pretty soon the Suffrage Amendment is going to be submitted to the states. I bet by next year, women will have the right to vote."

Papa looked around at his family. "Charlie, with six suffragettes surrounding us, you and I don't stand a chance." His voice sounded woebegone, but his eyes were twinkling. (32)

At school, the boys bring up women's suffrage as a way to deride and insult Henny and her campaign. The implication that Henny is being mannish by running for election is completely in keeping with the zeitgeist of the time, in which suffragettes were seen as gender-bending or just plain masculine. At the end of the chapter, the girls berate the boys with a speech about how the war effort required that women work; now that they have held jobs, Rose claims, "you can't send us back to the kitchen!" Hannah adds, "That's right . . . When women get the right to vote, they'll run for public office, too!" In response, Calvin growls, "What do you girls want? A female president?" Rose responds, "Give us one reason why not?" (38). The boys change the subject, promising to "argue" about this topic another time.

Another theme undergirds the chapter—one not entirely disassociated from suffrage but not exactly the same. That more hidden theme is the New Woman, a cultural phenomenon in full bloom in the 1910s. That label was applied to young women who exhibited, through their clothing and activities, an emboldened modernity and nascent feminism. The iconic image of the New Woman was that of a young woman riding a bicycle, wearing short skirts, and smoking a cigarette. The bicycle hinted at mobility, the short skirt at emerging sexuality, and the cigarette at a daring independence. Pictures of the New Woman in the visual media and written depictions in both low and high literature presented her as stridently modern, rebellious, and gender-bending. Casting aside voluminous petticoats for bloomers, careening through towns and parks on bicycles, entering the workforce in ever greater numbers, and becoming more and more educated, New Women were objects of derision, as well as sources of both fear and admiration. Juxtaposed to Victorian women characterized by fragility, submissiveness, dependence, and domesticity, New Women sought freedom, health, movement, advancement, and worldliness. It is not just equity that drives Henny's friends to encourage her to run for student office. Over her protests, they enumerate her good qualities, all of which fit the model of the New Woman. She is active, articulate, and ambitious, and her friends see her as a leader.

Although media and literary characterizations were often exaggerated, the reality was that millions of young women were indeed becoming more independent. As they attended high school and poured into the workplace, girls were gaining education, some financial security, mobility, and opportunities to hold leadership roles.[28] In high school, Taylor's independent leadership proved to be her most public New Womanly trait, but this aspect of her nascent feminism and progressivism did not come easily to her. She expressed elation when she was elected, but even at the beginning of her new position as class representative, her success was diluted by critical reactions from others and complications that arose when she asserted her opinions.

In her diary entry of March 2, 1920, Taylor recounts that a male opponent immediately contested the vote. While she describes herself as replying saucily to the disgruntled loser, it was her defense by another male student that proved effective. In subsequent diary entries, Taylor discovers that her exercise of authority is not always met with approval. On March 5, after having criticized some Alacris members for dividing into cliques, she writes, "I am in the depths of despair. Why did I do it? Why, why, why???" As she quickly explains, the act that made her despondent was outspokenness: "In short, why did I speak my mind to the Alacrists? . . . I regret it, regret it. I spoke too bluntly and too hastily. I shouldn't have." The language should not be dismissed as the histrionic effusions of a teenager, for Taylor's discomfiture shows how a young woman in a position of leadership might feel that speaking forthrightly about her beliefs verged on the unseemly.

Although Taylor and her classmates were not necessarily aware of the impact of broad social change on their daily lives, some of Taylor's unease stemmed from the evolving cultural discussion that expressed fear of emerging female roles and of the figure of the New Woman. As women experimented with independence in cultural, political, educational, and economic spheres, their historical position as charming adornments to the masculine world and mothers devoted to domesticity seemed precarious.[29] Certainly the pushback Taylor felt when she assumed leadership positions in her school did not arise specifically from fears on the part of her male classmates that she would not be a good mother, but just as certainly, anxiety about women's changing roles was prevalent.

Subsequent entries demonstrate that the negative emotions connected to directing the Alacris Club did not abate: "I'm feeling unnecessary. I almost always feel so after the Alacris."[30] Later in that March entry, Taylor describes how her leadership position affects her: "I wish I were just plain little Syd without dozens of offices on my shoulders. You see, I think I'm making enemies now. I wonder if I am though. When I really think of it—after all, I doubt whether I would be happy without these offices." Taylor's diary during these months reveals her awareness of the ongoing difficulty as well as the desirability of ascending to positions of authority. Her writing captures the mixed feelings that society itself was experiencing about women's changing roles.

Interspersed with commentary on leadership and expressions of self-doubt is commentary on Taylor's romantic interests. By far her greatest preoccupation was boys. In these years before she met the man she would eventually marry, Taylor had intense involvements with several young men. Three whose given names appeared frequently in the early diaries were Milton, Julius, and Nat. Taylor's relationships with those boys and her writings about them seem in many ways typical of the experiences and ruminations of a female adolescent at any time during the twentieth century, but closer scrutiny reveals that Taylor was both a product of her time and an exceptional young woman. It is through her statements about her relationships that the nascent thoughtfulness of a budding artist and intellectual flickers. Taylor wove together common feelings of rejection, confusion, jealousy, and elation that adolescents regularly experience in courtship with her sophisticated and in some ways advanced analyses of the changing roles of women and of sexual identity.

In her entry for June 16, 1920, Taylor appears to have gotten past the feelings of social rejection and despair she described in March. She begins by saying, "I feel so curious, like a different girl ever since it happened. I'll begin from the beginning." What happened was her first kiss. Describing a surprise party she helped organize, Taylor focuses on a boy she has never seen before, Irving Weinberg: "He is tall, dark hair, light-complected, rather strong face. It so happened that we were partners." Taylor's friend Anna is also at the party, and when Taylor and Irving are seated together, Anna tells him that Taylor has not yet been kissed by a boy: "He was then determined that he was to get a kiss that very night. I laughed at him, little thinking what would occur."

Anna's role throughout the party seems to be ensuring that girls and boys play with physical intimacy: "The boys had been mumbling kissing games all evening. Anna and I had a little talk and finally reached the conclusion that in order to make the party a success, we would have to suit the whim of the boys. I had to promise that I would enter the game." Anna is clearly the one encouraging the sexual play, and Taylor makes clear her lack of interest and her discomfort, claiming that she somehow "evaded" the bottle in the first game of "Spin the Bottle," and again "evaded" a kiss in the second game of "This or That." When it was Taylor's turn to call "this or that," a boy came in, Taylor "slapped his face"—slapping being part of the game—and just then Irving entered the room.[31]

Taylor records no reaction from the boy who received a slap instead of a kiss. Instead, she throws her attention to Irving, who claimed it was his turn as the other boy left the room. Then followed a conversation so thrilling that Taylor wrote it out like a playscript.

> I R V I N G —"Well, what are you supposed to do?"
>
> S Y D —"Nothing."
>
> I R V I N G —"Nothing?"
>
> S Y D —"Unless you want me to slap your face. I slapped the other boys."
>
> I R V I N G —"Well, slap me then."
>
> S Y D —"Hard?"
>
> I R V I N G —"Yes hard."
>
> I did.
>
> I R V I N G —"You call that hard?"
>
> S Y D —"No."

IRVING —"Come on," he coaxed me, no—I cannot say coaxed because there is some compelling force in him which makes you do the thing he wants you to. "Come on." I can just picture him as he said it. I yielded. He kissed me full on the lips. I cannot explain the conflicting emotions which had possession of me. It seemed as if the old Syd had vanished, and a new one had taken her place.

This was not the first time since she was elected to office that Taylor juxtaposes a new self to an old self. Recall that on March 12 she had written that she wished she "were just plain little Syd without dozens of offices on my shoulders," implicitly defining herself as a new version of a person she used to be. Normal adolescent awareness of changes in the self is distinguished in Taylor's case by her artistic consideration of the changes in her diaries. Now she slips into the mode of dramatist, as she relates an intense encounter in the format of a script. She actively constructs herself throughout her diaries, and in this particular case she transparently constructs her sexuality.

The vague underpinnings of sadomasochism in Taylor's encounter with Irving are expressed with little fanfare. In fact, slapping was a regular feature in certain kissing games that involved a choice of action on the part of a player; depending on how players felt about the person they were paired with, they would administer either a slap or a kiss. These teenagers in 1920 had learned that slapping is a form of flirting and a substitute for intimate physical interaction. Irving is seen as compelling not just because he commands Taylor to slap him harder, but because he implies, by saying she has not hurt him, that he is stronger and more powerful than she, an imbalance of power that Taylor clearly perceives.

Taylor's conflicting feelings stem from the combination of pleasure and resentment that she experiences in her weaker situation. The script continues:

SYD —"Why did you kiss me on the lips?"

IRVING —"Why not there?"

SYD —"Oh, because—" I could not explain how I regarded a kiss on the lips as something almost sacred.

IRVING —"Where then, should I have done it?"

SYD —"Oh, anywhere."

IRVING —"There's no harm in it. You kiss me where you wanted me to." Again he said, "Come on."

Faced with this invitation, Taylor again finds the language of power and confusion useful: "I don't know what happened but that same compelling force was holding full sway over me. I kissed him on the cheek. Then ashamed, I left the room." When she was issuing slaps and telling boys what to do, Taylor experienced no shame. It is when she is invited to make the move of kissing that it creeps in. Its effect is so strong that she must flee.

A bit later in the evening, Irving tries to equalize the power between the two of them, holding out his hand for a friendly handshake. Taylor grasps it, and the tension between them eases: "For the rest of the evening I was outwardly very serious, but inwardly thrilling with joy." When the party guests take leave of each other, Irving suggests that he and Taylor see each other again, speaking "in that manner of force and assurance." Taylor agrees, and brings the story to a close as Irving "squeezed my hand in silence and it was a few moments before he let go."

Although Irving seems to have the upper hand in this final conversation, the earlier exchange in which mutual respect was established still flavors the atmosphere, which is not described with confusion or conflict. When Taylor gets home and begins to "picture the whole scene," she comes to a conclusion about the event. The last line of the entry reads, "Don't you think that action of his was—well, just great?"

In her study of working women's pursuit of leisure in early twentieth-century New York City, Kathy Peiss primarily examines public venues, but her argument that "young women experimented with new cultural forms that articulated gender in terms of sexual expressiveness and social interaction with men, linking heterosexual culture to a sense of modernity, individuality, and personal style" certainly applies to the private party Taylor attended.[32] Kissing games involved sexual expressiveness, especially in a game like "Spin the Bottle," where the kissing takes place in the view of all the other party guests. Even when players were required to leave the main room for the privacy of another space in a game like "This or That," everyone knew that the goal of the departure was to increase sexual behavior. Peiss's point—that this sexual expressiveness and heterosexual interaction increased women's individuality in the goal of self-creation—can be seen in Taylor's diaries, where Taylor's self-creation extends to changing her name and consciously writing her life.

Irving Weinberg appears in only one more entry, written on September 6, a week before school is to start, when he stands her up for a date. Taylor mentions his unreliability, but shifts to another topic, one that arouses a more emphatic reaction:

It's Labor-day. I've been working all summer. One short week before school opens—and I don't even know whether I'm going back or not.

I want to go back!

I want to go back!

I *must* go back! I've been looking forward to becoming a pupil of Morris once more.

It's twilight. I can scarcely see, but I do not want to light the gas. I like the darkness. Somehow it is comforting in my present mood. Twilight, the most beautiful hour of the day—It doesn't appear so now. I do not see it through rose-colored glasses now. I feel too disappointed in myself—in everybody, too blue. It has been a nasty day and my mood corresponds to it.

I cannot write any longer. I'm going to cry—cry hard—till I'll be myself again.

As it turns out, Taylor did not return to high school the next week. Her education did not end, but the part that took place in a school that teenagers attended during the day in a building built for that purpose was over.

FIVE

Romance and the New Woman

1920–1923

TAYLOR WAS NOT UNUSUAL in leaving high school without graduating. In fact, the two years she did attend were already an advance over the amount of time girls of the previous generation spent in school.[1] At the turn of the century, even though high schools began popping up all over the United States, the path to a high school diploma was not universally taken. Increasing numbers of teenagers attended some high school, but the majority did not go at all.[2] Although Taylor attended Morris High for only two years and did not graduate, her short stay should not be seen as a failure on her part. Graduation from high school was not a requirement for future financial or social success. The fact that Taylor attended some high school put her in the vanguard of a tremendous social change. Her attendance through her sophomore year may be in part ascribed to her Jewish background. Compared with other immigrants or children of immigrants, Jewish girls had higher attendance rates in high school not only in New York but in urban areas across the country, although graduation rates remained low.[3]

Like most young people who left school, Taylor did so in order to work. As craft-based labor declined in the early twentieth century and office-based jobs increased, employers wanted to hire people with office skills, such as typing and using an adding machine. High schools thus became the training ground for office workers. Yet while girls needed more education than eighth grade afforded them, they did not need more than what tenth grade provided, and certainly not what a college education offered. "As education became more closely tied to work," the historian Melissa Klapper writes, "limits on women's work translated to limits on working-class girls' education."[4]

Taylor knew nothing about the statistics of her peer group, but she did pay attention to the education of her sisters. Ella had been taken out of school in 1916 in order to take clerical classes and work, but she rebelled. She learned to type, then insisted on returning to Washington Irving High School to earn her remaining credits, pass her exams, and graduate in 1918. Giving piano lessons all over the city at fifty cents a lesson, she earned enough money to appease her father. School administrators and several teachers went out of their way to accommodate her, helping her make up classes she had missed and allowing her to continue with vocal performances and lessons.

After graduation, Ella had an opportunity to attend Columbia Teachers College at no cost, which her parents made her turn down so that she could pursue a career on the stage—a decision she resented all her life and blamed on her mother's frustrated ambitions to be a singer. Her parents' generation was skeptical about education for their daughters, especially since girls could earn respectable salaries in offices, but Ella saw education as a stepping-stone to the career she really wanted, which was to graduate from college and become a teacher.[5] When her dreams of the stage slipped away, Ella sewed in a factory and kept books in a bank, until she married Joe Kornweitz in 1920.

Henny was never considered academic material and left school as soon as she could, also marrying young. Younger sister Charlotte achieved the highest educational level, graduating from Hunter College. It remained a point of pride with her that she had paid her own way by writing for various publications and doing secretarial work. Gertie did not go to college, and neither did the two boys. Irving chose not to, and joined his father in the woolen grading business upon graduating from high school; Jerry, not considered college material by the family, eventually joined his brother and father after attending Staubmuller Textile High School in Manhattan.

By October 18, 1920, Taylor was much more cheerful and decisive: "I could not help but smile as I wrote the date. Did I ever dream things would be as they are now a year ago,—even 2 months ago. I never went back to school. I'm still working or was—at least till last Saturday. I have no job now. I'm looking for one." Taylor acknowledges with her smile that she made the right decision in leaving school. That entry is the last she wrote until June 1, 1921. On that day, Taylor records her approval of the family's move to Borough Park, "a most beautiful spot." She called 976 57th Street home at

Ella and Joe Kornweitz's wedding

least until 1927, at which point she returned to Manhattan, where she lived for the rest of her life.

The last paragraph of this short entry brings up the subject of work and conveys even more decisiveness than did the entry from the previous October: "I'm still working, but have never regretted the decision I made when I gave my money to Dad and told him I was not going back. I'm happier by far—this way—feeling self-supporting." She signs the entry with "Syd." Here the decision not to return to school, which Taylor now claims to have initiated, is seen as not only economic but also family related. Klapper explains that Jewish parents wanted their daughters to be educated, but they also had to negotiate their own economic needs with their growing daughters' ability to earn income.[6] Although Taylor initially expressed distress over the wrenching decision to leave school, she came to feel over the course of the year that she had made the decision on her own, and that it was made in the best interests of her family. She directed no anger or disappointment toward any specific family member during this process.

Based on the diary entries alone, Taylor seemed reconciled to the decision after a few months, but Charlotte's memoir tells a different story. In describing her father's plan to run an embroidery store, Charlotte writes that the family discussion turned to their hopes if the business succeeded: "Sara voiced a latent dream in her gentle way. 'Mama, if the new business goes all right, will I be able to go to college?' " Papa became angry and made an impassioned speech: " '*College? A girl* go to college? And me with two sons I'll have to educate?' Now he was on familiar ground. 'There you go getting American ideas, to educate a girl so that she'll be too smart to attract a husband. If I stayed in the junk business there would be no talk of college.' "[7] After the embroidery store fails and Papa returns to his junk shop, Mama tries again to gain his approval for Sarah's college education, but Papa remains adamantly opposed. Tanta also thinks higher education is wasted on girls, whose main purpose should be to find a good husband and raise a family.

Only two years younger than Sarah, Charlotte presents herself in her memoir as more determined to continue her education after high school than her gentle sister. To her apparent surprise, while having coffee and cake with guests Papa states enthusiastically that she should take advantage of the free education offered at Hunter College, admission to which was made possible by her excellent grades. Even before Charlotte learns that he supports her choice, he brags to his guest that his daughter will be an "American college girl," and seems to take credit for the decision.[8]

Even if Charlotte exaggerated for dramatic purposes, she was close to the mark about her sister's disappointment. Many years later, writing to her parents about her determination to send her daughter to college so that she will have a future, Taylor reveals the effort it took to see her father's decision in a positive light: "I'm beginning to believe that the greatest spur to ambition is denial. When I think back to how we wept because we were taken out of school—and how today—children are offered every opportunity—and spurn them."[9] Looking for a silver lining, the adult Taylor's interpretation of her needing to leave school was that by depriving her of a college education, Papa

drove her to educate herself and become financially self-sufficient, but it was
not a situation she chose to impose on her own child.

Taylor attended business school at night both during and after high
school in order to learn skills such as typing and bookkeeping. When the family moved to Brooklyn in the early spring of 1921, she continued to attend night
school, which, when combined with a full-time job, made for a heavy load. In
October 1922 she writes: " 'Tis late. I cannot write tonight, for I am tired.
Work in the day-time and school in the nighttime does tire one so." Again,
Taylor's obligations do not lead to criticism of her family or questioning of her
decision to leave high school.

Just as decisions about leaving school rarely resulted in ruptures in the
family, young women did not see the end of formal schooling as the end of
their liberal arts education.[10] Taylor's ongoing education took place not in
ivy-covered buildings on green quads, but in the streets, offices, concert halls,
movie theaters, dance clubs, night schools, and subways of New York City.
After leaving Morris, Taylor frequently mentions activities such as attending
and discussing plays, lectures, and musical performances. Every event leads
to conversations with her peers and essays in her diaries. Going with her
girlfriends to hear Rabbi Stephen S. Wise (1874–1949) deliver a talk titled
"The Eternal Quest" at Carnegie Hall, for example, inspires her to consider
and write about her own views of immortality and the soul.[11]

Taylor and her friends sought to be intellectuals outside academia.
When she listened to ragtime, she noted that it was because she was too restless to appreciate "good" music, and she and her friends clearly distinguished
between popular and classical works of literature and music. They did not
dismiss the need for entertainment, but they did not confuse that with the
need to grapple with big ideas. Rather than seeing the lack of a high school
diploma as an impediment to her intellectual development, it makes more
sense to realize how much the two years she spent at Morris contributed to it.

More formally, Taylor attended classes at the Rand School of Social
Science. Founded in 1906 by New York socialists, primarily German and
Eastern European Jews, and named after its benefactress Carrie Rand, a
wealthy widow with socialist sympathies, the school reached out to people
like Taylor and her friends. Its goal was to create a working class educated in
social and political science, and thereby prepared to lead the class struggle.
Director and theater educator Martha Schmoyer LoMonaco writes that in its

home in "The People's House" at 7 East 15th Street in New York City, "the school maintained a library, bookstore, and cafeteria, as well as a theatre which regularly housed dramatic, dance, and musical performances."[12] It offered classes on social and political science, although those on literature, art, and music enjoyed greater popularity.

Perhaps more than any other activity, reading was essential to Taylor's self-education. In her diaries, Taylor describes the books she reads and the ensuing discussions with her friends about them. When she left high school, her taste ran to Edgar Allan Poe and Bret Harte, and *Wuthering Heights* was a book she recommended to a younger woman. Soon she was reading modernist novels, such as Leonid Nikolayevich Andreyev's *The Red Laugh,* Romain Rolland's *Jean-Christophe,* August Strindberg's *Married,* and Walter de la Mare's *Memoirs of a Midget.* Her writings at this time mention some thirty novels that she read and at least another dozen that her sisters and friends brought to her attention. The young people compared each other's characters to those of fictional heroes, lent each other books, and gave books as gifts, with the women evaluating potential boyfriends by how well-read they were.

Ownership of books was essential to Taylor's happiness. In a letter to her sister Charlotte written on December 20, 1923, Taylor complains that her "meager purse" has reduced her to asking her sister to check books out of the library for her. She follows that with a long meditation on why she prefers her own books to the "public books." She explains it is because she has "no right" to mark up library books and because of the "delight" one feels in owning something that one immensely likes. She talks with "pride" of her "small collection of books," which she never wearies of reading and rereading—"or even in lonely gazing at them!" Later on, she notes that she bought *Ethan Frome* for $1.49, which she admits was a lot of money for her. Taylor reveals through her letters and diaries how much she valued cultural objects and activities by recording how and why she allocated her modest funds.

When she resumed her diary-keeping in June 1921, Taylor had completed the transition to being a full-time working woman. By the time of this June 20 entry, she was employed at the Nantoon Company, an embroidery and needlework business at 303 Fifth Avenue in Manhattan, whose owners were from Nantungchow (now Nantong), China. Taylor does not often mention her work at the company in her diaries, but the letters she received—and decided to keep—from co-workers and her employers show that she had warm relationships and obtained valuable work experience there.

Taylor had mixed with non-Jews at her high school in the Bronx, but none of the students there were African American or Asian, so her working and social life in Manhattan exposed her to much that was unfamiliar. In an entry dated December 31, 1921, when she was barely seventeen, Taylor described spending New Year's Eve with a boy named Joe and eight other friends in Greenwich Village and Chinatown. Recalling the surging, intemperate crowds in the Village, she wrote:

> We walked with crowds and crowds of merry-makers, hooting, shouting, laughing, skipping, many rolling with a drunken gait, using kazoos—in short making as much noise as they possibly could. Into the rat holes—through dark stairways, rickety and dirty, thru dark, narrow and filthy passages, to dimly lit, crowded rooms, reeking with smoke, filled with the sounds of shrill laughter and singing—and the prancing feet on a wooden floor beating time with their shoulders to so-called music with an effort. And the society folks sit along the sides, smoking their cigarettes with a tolerant air, and watching, watching . . . It left one sick at heart, cold and afraid—and thoroughly disgusted.

The content of the paragraph aside, once again Taylor's diary writing shows her incipient talent as an author. She does not merely record that she went to Greenwich Village with a date on New Year's Eve; rather, she describes her sensory impressions of the event. Halfway through the entry, she switches from a black to a blue pen, but at one point in the first half she crosses out a word with the blue pen, meaning that she reread and edited her writing.

Taylor left Greenwich Village repulsed and feeling "afraid—of everything." She was angry with Joe for not realizing how she felt and for being so absorbed in the goings-on. By the time they reached their next stop, Chinatown, Taylor was already revolted, angry, and afraid. Yet her emotional state does not adequately explain the vitriol with which she describes the people she saw in Chinatown: "China Town with its hideous population. Crowds—and crowds—and still the crowds of besotted fools. One Chinaman looked at me and I could feel a chill running down my back. I shivered."

Just under a year later, Taylor writes about her Chinese employers at the Nantoon Company in wholly positive terms, in language that communicates little bigotry save for her paternalistic tone when she describes them as "my chinamen." Throughout the rest of the description, she portrays the men as individuals and not as stereotypes. Dejected because the company was about to close due to business losses and debts, Taylor explains that she is "the last of the office staff left" and that she feels "horribly blue" about losing the job:

> For I have liked my work here so much—everybody was so pleasant and so congenial—hours were short—pay much—$25.00. I could not have asked for anything better. My chinamen here—the bosses, are perfectly wonderful—remarkably intelligent and exceptionally kind for employers. I have even gone out to lunch with them at the Pennsylvania with Mr. Lee—at the Astor with Mr. Ling. My—but we were the cynosure of all eyes! I don't blame people for staring. I would stare, too, were I in their positions with no understanding and no appreciation of the circumstances. But that is neither here nor there.

Taylor suggests that sensitivity comes from working with people, that the workplace is where one learns that ethnic difference is not "hideous" but "perfectly wonderful." Not much later, however, when Taylor works for Sutta and Fuchs, she slips into the stereotype of the inscrutable Orient, recalling the faces of her previous Asian employers as "implacable" and betraying no emotions no matter what happened.[13]

Taylor's academic and vocational education fills fewer pages in her diaries and letters than her sentimental education. The books she read and the skills she gained in management and organization both in and out of school laid the foundation for her independent life as a working woman of artistic sensibilities—yet she was still a teenager curious about herself and boys. With two married sisters, she asked herself if that was the next step—and what kind of young man would meet her expectations.

From the day she left high school in 1920 to the day she met her future husband, most likely in early August 1923, Taylor's diaries paint the picture of a sociable and introspective young woman uncertain about her relations with young men. The majority of the letters Taylor kept from the early 1920s came from men. Taylor's female companions were frequently neighbors or workplace pals, so it was easy to talk with them in person. When her female friends did write letters, it was usually while they were on vacation, whereas the letters from young men were written at all times and were filled with mundane events and social chat.[14]

Four men expressed deep interest in Taylor, sending her dozens of letters. Without copies of the letters she herself sent to them, it is impossible to know to what extent Taylor returned their interest. Throughout all her romantic entanglements, Taylor sought literate, ambitious men interested in the arts, eager to have a good time, and intrigued by her sexually without crossing an ever shifting boundary of personal autonomy. Her beaux insinuated that Taylor kept herself at a distance, both emotionally and physically, and only occasionally voiced the opposite complaint that she was uncomfortably persistent or clingy. Peeking through the gentle romantic filigree is a Taylor who was not head over heels in love with any of her boyfriends, and who tentatively tested their affections.

Dating meant discovery of self and the world as much as it meant a relationship with a boy. In the diary entry of October 18, 1920, just before her sixteenth birthday, she mused, "I'm just beginning to understand the expression 'cherchez la femme.'" She adds, "I used to feel angry because I was not a boy. But I don't feel so now." Referring to her friend Oscar Chafetz, she says that she looks forward to being a "*good* woman," one of those who "shape— no—bring him back to light and make him want to succeed." Almost in the next breath, she talks about wanting a recent date to "get rash." Having revised her initial impression that he was the "new skirt, new fancy" type, she acknowledges Chafetz's intelligence and expresses awe at how deep and frank their conversations are, even more than her conversations with her girl-friends, although he does want Taylor to praise him.

The entry encapsulates many of the themes in Taylor's relationships with men over the next several years. Conscious of her own intelligence, Taylor chafes at her restricted opportunities as a woman, all the while fascinated by her power as a woman over men. She wants physical intimacy, yet does not want to initiate it. She is skeptical of men's assumption of authority, yet she adopts a stance of feminine submission. She wants respect for her work and her ideas, but she dances around the cockiness of her boyfriends. And she wants a companion with whom she can talk as an equal. In that same entry, Taylor expresses ambivalence about entering womanhood: "I don't want that time to ever come, and yet I wish it were already here. Somehow, I feel as if after sixteen, there comes a change in a girl's life—shall I say a throwing off of all childish customs and beginning of the upward journey of a woman?"

Enter Milton Berger as a conductor on that journey. He was Taylor's first steady, long-term correspondent. When she knew him, he was working part-time in a law office while going to school. The first letter from him that she kept was written while Taylor was still in high school in the Bronx and is dated February 5, 1920. Milton's tone is argumentative as he challenges her claim that she works harder than anyone she knows, and nothing suggests that they are more than acquaintances. Nine months elapse before Taylor saves another note from her workaholic friend, and then she preserves each of his frequent letters in her letter box.

Although the number and frequency of his letters indicate that Berger had strong feelings for Taylor, their tone and content express persistent irritation. Berger was as self-conscious in his own way as Taylor was about the process of letter writing. He constantly brings up the topic of address: how they address letters to one another—whether they use the word *dear* or another word; how they sign their letters—with *your, yours,* or something else. He finds fault with how often they write to each other, the length of each letter, the paper and writing implements required. But the underlying topic is his frustration with Taylor. He takes her to task for not writing often enough or for not writing substantively, and his tone can be snide: "Well, I have no more to say except to congratulate you on the wonderful way you can write six typewritten pages and say nothing."[15]

Berger is disgruntled if Taylor types rather than pens her letters and gets huffy if she does not respond to his questions and baiting comments.[16] He can be scathing that she will not spend time with him or lacks warmth when she does. In a letter of April 29, 1921, he writes, "I am really sorry that you persist in refusing to lunch with me. At divers times I have something I feel like saying to someone and when I ask you I always receive the same cool, flat, deliberate, unfeeling, unemotional no." A year later, on April 26, 1922, he snarls the same refrain about her refusal to have lunch and her froideur. Despite his proprietary tone and references to shows and parties they attended together, Berger never refers to Taylor as his girlfriend throughout his many letters.

In contrast, Taylor sprinkles her diary with phrases that indicate Berger was her boyfriend. He first appears in a retrospective entry on December 31, 1921, which opens, "I never once have spoken of friend, Milton." Then Taylor adds a caret and squeezes in his last name: "Berger." She muses, "I don't know why. But now—now that that epistle is closed—why am I bringing him up?" She devotes the paragraph to praising this man whom she allowed to get away: "I know now that I have never enjoyed anyone's company as much—I know now when I no longer see him—I realize now what a perfect gentleman he was—how courteous, kind and—well—likable (that word expresses him). I realize now having gone out tonight with one who in the present day world is termed 'Fast.' " The shameless one was Joe, that young man who dragged her through the horrors of a debauched New Year's Eve.

Taylor's diary continues the comparison of the two young men. Joe is "ordinary" and the type "who takes a girl out—gives her a good time but expects one in return." Milton "is a clean—frank—wholesome young boy who will take you to concerts and other interesting places because he likes your company." She berates herself—not for the last time—for letting Milton go: "What a fool I was to end our wonderful friendship."[17]

But as she continues, Taylor implies that Milton was out for a good time after all. Their rupture had occurred the previous April 2, "on a night I will never forget," because of a dress and a kiss. In this lengthy retrospective New Year's entry, Taylor tells how she looked forward for many years to her first outing in an evening gown: "It was pink—just as a first gown should be. And Milton thought I was perfectly exquisite. But I—I almost hate it for it started all the trouble." Milton, overwhelmed by the vision of loveliness, asked for a goodnight kiss. Taylor's response was in keeping with her upbringing, if not necessarily with her own experience: "I refused of course and then because I was so hurt at his having treated me as one would any sort of girl I cried after he had left."

Taylor's behavior seems inconsistent. She is, after all, the same person who played kissing games with boys not so long before. Yet in the context of female adolescence in New York City at this time, Taylor's apparent inconsistency becomes less puzzling. Many of Taylor's peers in age and gender were negotiating the double messages society sent: have fun with your hard-earned money, but do not have too much fun lest you be seen as unchaste. Cultural debate in the press dissected how girls should behave and dress, and fretted over young women's loss of a moral center.

Melissa Klapper attributes much of this societal consternation to the rise of adolescence as a category:

> With the beginning of the twentieth century and the 1904 publi-
> cation of G. Stanley Hall's seminal book, *Adolescence: Its Psychol-
> ogy and Its Relation to Physiology, Anthropology, Sociology,
> Crime, Religion, and Education,* came a new understanding of
> adolescence as a time for individuals to grapple with emotional,
> intellectual, economic, and sexual independence in a modern
> world. As the destiny of women destabilized in that modern
> world, girls' adolescent years of preparation for womanhood be-
> came a critically important but perilous period for both defend-
> ers and attackers of traditional gender roles and opportunities.[18]

From the year of Taylor's birth, American society argued about adolescent girls. In her horror at the request for a kiss from a man she has been dating for six months, Taylor reflects the double standard foisted on young women.

Although Ella intervened—thus demonstrating that Taylor's relation-ships did not develop in a familial vacuum—and explained to Berger his of-fense, and although Berger apologized the following night, "things were never the same after that. We scarcely wrote to each other . . ." Here Taylor draws a rare connection between the letters in her big binders and her dia-ries. By the end of 1921, she had come to realize that she had blown the epi-sode out of proportion. "But at that time—it was what was behind his words that hurt—hurt—oh so much. He intimated that I had showed him that I *cared* when I *knew* that I had acted as frank and open with him in as purely friendly a way as was possible for a girl to like a boy." Berger made one failed effort to see her in the fall of 1921, but as of January 1, 1922, they had neither met nor corresponded again.

The diary resumes only on September 4, 1922. During the rest of the month, the frequent entries focus on Taylor's relationship with Nat Moses, whom she had socialized with during her summer vacation, along with two boys she did not know well, Paul Miller and Eddie Goldfarb. Taylor was

both puzzled and distressed by the difficulties boys and girls face in developing uncomplicated friendships: "Oh, dear, I wish—I wish I had some real
good boy friends . . . Eddie & Paul are not what I could call *real* friends."[19]
She continued to think about Berger: "If only Milton could realize how much
I long for his friendship—I feel confident that he would resume it. If only—
conventionality permitted a girl to be able to say to a fellow: 'I like you and
would like to go with you. Can't we be friends?' " Even in a society in which
women were taking a more active role in courtship, traditional mores shaped
her outlook about relations between the sexes. Answering her own question
about whether she could tell Berger she wants to be friends with him, she
writes:

> No—no—that could never be. That would mean the change
> of a woman's nature entirely. Woman was always meant to be
> reticent, thus giving cause for man's drawing out of her womanly
> nature. *She* is to be sought for and not to become the seeker. Why,
> all the joy of finding out the truth when Man's battle is won,
> would be lost were woman to take the initiative. 'Tis better things
> are as they are, even though conventionality is a trouble maker
> and a bore.

Taylor refrained from pursuing the romance with Berger because she felt that
she must behave according to convention.

Two months later, Milton unexpectedly entered her life again. Describing her surprise birthday party on October 30, which left her "dumb and
speechless" from astonishment, Taylor expressed pleasure with her gifts, listing the books she received and devoting space to the Halloween party deco-
rations and costumes.[20] She continued with a list of the guests, including
some boys she had not known before, ending with the biggest surprise of
all—"last but not least Milton. I can scarcely tell how queerly I felt. Here I had
been thinking of him continually, hoping and hoping that I would see him—
and now he was in front of me. We shook hands—hard, and merely looked at
each other. I gasped a surprised and happy—'Hello Mil-ton.' " Taylor deftly
conveys her flustered thrill at seeing Milton with the hyphen she puts between the syllables of his name, indicating the break in her voice. Taylor continues to recall the evening's festivities, the guests playing games such as

"dentist behind a sheet" and the "broom dance," singing around the piano, and dancing. In the midst of all of this activity, Taylor discovered that Berger was going to law school as well as working in a law office, and they arranged to meet again soon.

The following morning, Taylor received yet another surprise. Berger called her at the office to invite her to a theater party of the faculty of his prep school for a performance of *La Chauve Souris* on the roof of the Century Theatre.[21] On November 7, he wrote somewhat stiffly in more detail: "As I explained the members of the faculty are bringing their wives and sweethearts. The reason that the invitation to join them has been extended to me is due to the fact that I am president of the school. At all previous school functions I have escorted members of the school. They know I am bringing an outsider and are waiting expectantly to see her. Sincerely *Milton*." Taylor accepted with delight, thrilled that she was included among the sweethearts, and rushed to tell Ella about the swanky vaudeville show in her future.

Much ink is spilled over the buildup to Taylor's date with Berger and the date itself in the November 23, 1922, entry. Given that the date took place on a Friday evening, the entry, in addition to conveying Taylor's excitement, reveals that the family did not sit down for the type of Sabbath dinner that was so lovingly described as a weekly requirement in *All-of-a-Kind Family*. What the novel and its sequels did not depict was how the family gradually relinquished many of the practices required by religious tradition.[22] As Taylor inadvertently chronicled this shift in behavior in her diary, she noted no expression of consternation from any family members. On the contrary, her mother and sisters help her prepare for the Friday night date, suggesting that after two decades of assimilation, they were at ease with American customs and values.

Berger, described as tall and "with a big Jewish nose," is able to blur the gender barrier that so frustrated Taylor in her relations with boys. As they walk to the station, she muses on how "very, very frank" he is. She likes the way he "blurts out the truth in true boyish fashion," and how "he forgets I'm a girl and that he must be tactful else he might hurt me." Berger is her equal in candor, which puts them both at ease. But Taylor also wants to be seen as a woman. At some point during the evening, she takes note of a young woman Milton had previously dated. This young woman is dark-haired, dark-eyed, and, like Taylor, short, prompting her to think, "Milton must like them small."

During the trip home to Borough Park, Taylor and Milton patch over the quarrel that led to their breakup. Reflecting on the conversation, Taylor launches into a diatribe against herself and her sex.

> Why—why—why—I wonder did God make us so wicked and evil! From what I read and from what I'm told—I know that it's not only I who am that way. All women are alike. All women want to lead men on by means of their seductive power, a power which they want to test. Then when they have him in their power, at the highest pitch, they feel triumphant—at what? Foolish females to flatter themselves needlessly.

Essentially blaming herself for having worn a pretty pink gown without wanting to pay the price of a kiss, she adds that when women do arouse a man's interest, "*we* become angry when any liberties are taken. Bah!—Sometimes— though I have never admitted it to anyone—I *hate* and despise my sex. They are cruel—so cruel because they carry on their wickedness in an underhanded way, a smile on their faces—a smile which tends to become a laugh of gloating over the victim." Taylor declares she is worse than most other women in this regard, and pleads for understanding.

The two part ways concluding that theirs is a perfect friendship and that they want to see each other again, but Berger drops her. Taylor never mentions him again in her diary, and in 1923 saves only two short notes from him. Her reticence about his disappearance became characteristic of her introspective writing. Her pen fell silent about unrealized plans and failures, while feelings of hope and disappointment demanded lengthy exposition.

Feelings of fear also engaged her storytelling imagination. One November night in 1922, Taylor and her friend Fanny set out for a social hall where relatives of Fanny were sponsoring a dance. By traveling together, they followed social conventions meant to protect their generation's newly independent young women and their reputations.[23] In this case, defensive strategies failed. At the dance hall, Taylor and Fanny found the crowd "rough," the girls wearing too much makeup and dancing too provocatively and the boys pushing themselves on the girls. When they decided to leave, against their better judgment but having no other option at the late hour, they accepted some unsavory young men's company as their escorts back to Borough Park.

Taylor's companion accosted her, despite her telling him repeatedly that she did not welcome his attentions and that she and Fanny were not the kind of girls who allow boys to take liberties. He accused her of leading him on, an accusation she found so ironic and unfair that her eyes filled with tears. Upon getting off the train, he kept trying to put his arm around her, and about a block from her home he tried to kiss her. Struggling to get away, she stumbled. Running as fast as she could, she pulled Fanny away from her less obstreperous escort, and the two girls made it home without further mishap.

Missed cues and mixed messages between boys and girls are hardly novel, but women's increased mobility and opportunities for leisure pursuits gave them a specific cast at this time.[24] Unspoken, ambiguous rules guided the negotiations among men and women in the dance halls, where both genders anticipated the exchange of sensual favors—dancing cheek to cheek, stolen kisses, or more. On this occasion, Taylor landed herself in a perilous situation where a difference in expectations led to the young man's frustration and her anguished fear. Although the incident clearly shook her, she continued over the next few years to play with men's sexual desires.

Among those young men figures a girlfriend's brother, Julius Havelin, usually referred to as Julie. Their relationship reveals several important facets of Taylor's personality, goals, and interests at this time of her life, which include playing games with men, finding the right man, and writing. Taylor began to pursue Julie because of his aloof arrogance. She called it an experiment and explained that he intrigued her: "He was a Civil Engineer having completed that course at Cornell University in June, 1922 . . . he is clever, well-read, and a good conversationalist when you can get him to talk. But his indifference and manner of superiority irritate one. He ignores his family and slights his mother and father, by his close mouthedness." Despite these negative characteristics, the more Taylor hears about Julie, the more she wants to meet him.[25] She hides her interest, though, not wanting other girls to mock her, and finally engineers a meeting through his sister, a conversation she narrates in her diary as a dialogue. Characteristically, she employs metaphors of fiction in describing her actions: "I almost felt like a heroine in a cheap drama. I went to bed with crazy thoughts in my head."[26]

When Taylor tells her family of her interest in this superior fellow, Ella encourages the game playing: "You know what I would do in a case like this? I would make him fall in love with me and then I'd let him lay, spurn and taunt him. That would do 2 things—put a feather in my cap and cure him of his indifference." Taylor's response was one of amusement. "I laughed and told her that she was now dealing with *real* people and not book characters." But when she hears her own words coming from someone else's mouth, Taylor acknowledges the fiction she has constructed and tries to distance herself from it. She wants the relationship with Julie to be real, but at some level she knows she is making it up.

Once again, the fits and starts of a fraught relationship occupy Taylor's journal. Their shared enjoyment of literature and listening to records of violin solos on the Victrola pique Julie's interest. The game goes in Taylor's favor: "And glory of glories! I have won! I have not even made a conscious effort to win for I realized upon first meeting him that the best thing to do would be to forget that I am a girl and make him forget it too."[27] This comment reveals not only the game Taylor continues to play, but also the gender blurring she likes and that Julie likes about her. He admits, "It's seldom that one finds a girl like you who is a jolly good sport and clever."

As the romance develops, Taylor discovers that Julie and his friend Nat Moses have been playing a game with *her*. The two young men tell her they have been keeping a journal of *their* weekends. Taylor insists on reading it, and is surprised to discover that the two boys have been conducting an experiment to determine the truthfulness of their belief that "all women are the same," with Taylor the focus of the inquiry.[28] A week or so later, when Taylor doubts Julie's affections for her, she worries that she has been a "specimen" and that the two boys have examined her for sport, even as she realizes that she has done the same to them.

Julie's purpose in Taylor's diary is to provide a complex personality for character analysis, a task she undertakes at great length. Elsewhere in the diary, Taylor discusses how "analyzing" one another's character is all the rage among her friends. In entries from February 1923, Taylor talks about analyzing friends, attaches character analyses written by her friends about her, and includes an analysis that she wrote of her friend Anna. Thus, her examination of Julie is not unusual. Her detailed scrutiny of his character shows not only her fascination with him, but also her maturing literary muscles.

Unsurprisingly, Taylor was fascinated by what her friends discerned in her. Julie's sister thinks that she is a person "possessed of 2 conflicting characters," to which Nat responds:

> I can understand her perfectly . . . There is a good deal of that
> indomitable German spirit and will in her. If there be passion in
> her, it is so well-restrained, buried so deeply, that one cannot no-
> tice it. If she has any feelings—that spirit and will—does not per-
> mit her to even think about them. In addition, she has read an
> unusual amount. The authors have presented so many ideas to
> her mind, that she is bewildered—at a complete loss—and does
> not know what to believe. It is due to her reading that she seems
> modern in her ideas and actions. But that is not the real girl. At
> bottom she is an old-fashioned girl . . . She'll marry in a few years
> and settle down.

Those observations shake Taylor by their accuracy: "[I felt] as tho he had
stripped me naked and showed me myself in all my nakedness. I do not know
how he could have divined it—but he has shown me myself in the only true
light. I am grateful! I had wanted to know myself—yet—vaguely only, had I
been able to sense the feelings and spirits in me. But Nat has painted me truly
and it is good to be able to see myself."[29] Nat was neither the first nor the last
to feel the chill of Taylor's outward demeanor, but he may be the first to connect it overtly to the formative role of her German background.

Sexual dreams, even of the mildest kind, were also subjects of titillating
fascination. Taylor constructs play-like records of conversations she has with
Julie in which he dangles before her a dream he had of her kissing him—she
in dishabille, no less—to which she retorts with verve that it was just a
dream.[30] The young people flirt through discussions of Sigmund Freud's *Interpretation of Dreams*. Using the language of analysis, they thrust and feint,
test the depth of their feelings for each other, chafe at the loss of independence that a relationship entails, and question how sexual attraction can coexist with personal irritation. Julie twice initiates a conversation about an
erotic dream concerning Taylor; she shuts him down both times with a cutting remark. And so it continued, leaving Taylor "bewildered" as the relationship petered out in the spring of 1923.[31]

One characteristic that appears repeatedly in all Taylor's relationships
with men is her lack of responsiveness, which the friendlier ones consider an
old-fashioned propriety. Eddie Goldfarb described his momentary confusion when he walked Taylor home from a dance and she stopped before

reaching the door of her house. It took Goldfarb a moment to realize she was waiting for him to open the door. He mentally kicked himself for his lack of manners, but it struck him "as peculiar, cause one doesn't often, in these days of the saxophone and subway rushes, see such things out of the movies."[32] What Goldfarb thought of as etiquette from a bygone era, other young men interpreted as impassivity.

Taylor expressed both uncertainty and revulsion when Julie sought a more physical relationship, one that neither thought crossed a moral boundary yet still made Taylor uncomfortable. She claimed to feel no passion in response to Julie's caresses and wondered why she was confused, concluding that she was "but an inconsistent woman."[33] Taylor saw herself as inconsistent not because she allowed some boys limited sexual license while forbidding other boys to touch her; rather, she noted that even when she allowed amorous contact, which might suggest that she found it pleasurable, she did not respond to their touch.

Amid the obsessive prose about Julie, Taylor wrote about other people and events. As mentioned earlier, she regretted losing her job at the Nantoon Company in the fall of 1922. Her competence and ambition had been apparent to her employers. As the business began to fail, Taylor's duties increased due to the layoffs of other employees. Although her boss considered hiring a bookkeeper, Taylor asked to keep the books even though she lacked experience in that field and initially found herself "in a muddle." She pestered everyone for help, and soon her boss let her "have full control of the books." She felt overwhelmed at the end of the month but declared, "I shall not confess myself beaten." When the job ended, Taylor found another near the Garment District. She did secretarial work, including bookkeeping, for the furriers Sutta and Fuchs, located at 303 Seventh Avenue, across the street from the current site of the Fashion Institute of Technology. No matter the job, she exhibited a drive to learn, improve, and succeed that never weakened.

In addition to boyfriends and work, Taylor was absorbed with family matters. Ella had a son, Leonard, in October 1921, and Henny had a baby daughter, Harriet, in November 1922. Going farther afield, Taylor corresponded from at least March 1921 through April 1923 with her cousin Leo Brenner, who lived in Germany and was eight years older than she. The son of her father's brother Nathan, he worked in the family camera business in

Cologne.[34] Over several years, the cousins argued primarily about two subjects: womanhood and World War I.

Noting that Taylor had raised the topic of women ("a good idea of yours"), Leo seized the opportunity to excoriate women for pages on end. His words are so bitter that it is a wonder that Taylor kept up the correspondence. In a long letter of May 1921, Leo takes ten pages to tell "dear Syd" that women are inferior and "cruel," that their curiosity leads to men's doom, and so on in that vein. He claims that women will never be on an equal footing with men because they are incapable of it, although he marvels that his vehement cousin is only "sweet sixteen."

Apparently, Taylor was equally scathing in her defense of women, because Leo did not write again until November 26, 1922:

> My Dear, I won't conceal from you the last reason (better said the first one) of my silence. It was the sharp critique in your last letter who disarmed me. When I started the discussion about women, sure that the victory could not fail me, I hoped to have an easy play. Never had I expected such a strong and spirited opposition. But soon I was given understood that, I had made a vast mistake, not having foreseen the power of my opponent. Her maintenance seemed to be true and sharp, not to be denied. I felt something like embarrassment, shame, I did not know how to carry on the fight and instead of submit myself, to give in that, I feel conquered, now it would have been the most suitable way for a man, to be honest, I chose the other less honourable way: I mired myself in silence. It was an ugly mistake of mine, it was faint-hearted, unworthy of a man and therefore I beg your forgiveness. I give in, this time I am conquered. But I do not give up the fight forever.

Leo does not fully concede; rather, he retreats to take a better position.

In addition to showing that the American Brenners preserved ties to relatives in Germany, these letters reinforce the fact that Taylor was a feminist even at sixteen, long before she joined any organized political group. Feminism was not always an easy fit, as seen with her struggles in leadership positions at Morris and her dashed college plans, but she had a stubborn streak, as her forceful, articulate arguments reveal. Leo points out her relatively young age at the beginning of their heated exchange, and it was at an even younger age that Taylor changed her first name to one that was gender ambiguous. This young woman described by family and friends as quiet, obedient, conventional, or old-fashioned already wielded words to establish her identity and womanhood.

The other issue Leo raises, that of Taylor's feelings toward Germany, also indicates how fiercely articulate Taylor was. In their correspondence, she evidently expressed intense antipathy to Germany, reflecting the strong anti-German attitude that had persisted in the United States since World War I. On April 16, 1923, Leo complained that her last letter sounded like "a nationalist French newspaper" and claimed that her contemptuous hatred for his country was based on misinformation. The comment suggests a side of Taylor she does not show in her letters to her American friends—that she was passionately, polemically political.

Yet it was Taylor's companions at home who gave her an opportunity to engage in political activity. One of them, Paul Miller, invited her to a dance at the Hotel Astor to be held on May 16, 1923, saying the event was being organized by a club to which he and his friend Benjamin belonged.[35] That club turned out to be the Young People's Socialist League. Miller's letter provides the first mention of this "club" and of Benjamin Schlamm in any of Taylor's correspondence or in her diary. Taylor accepted the invitation, not realizing it would usher her headlong into the next phase of her life. For it was through Miller's club that she would meet not only her good friend Ben but also his first cousin Ralph, the man she would marry.

Political Awakening and Contentious Courtship

1923–1925

BEN SCHLAMM WROTE A LETTER to Taylor's friend Anna Kornweitz on May 15, 1923, about a hike at the Palisades planned for May 31. Serious in tone, Ben addresses Anna as "Dear Friend" and welcomes her to his "newly-born" chapter of the Young People's Socialist League, YPSL, the organizer of the hike. His informational letter about how the branch has been developing is typical of him in its methodical attention to procedure. It also urges Anna to invite her "friend and any other friend whom you might care to invite" on the hike. The friend in question was Taylor. Adding a reminder about YPSL's weekly meeting on Monday evenings, with explicit directions to the location in Brooklyn, Ben exhibited his distinctive mix of exuberance and officiousness. That Taylor kept this letter addressed to Anna and only vaguely referring to herself indicates the importance she gave both the YPSL organization and Ben.

Within two weeks, Ben was writing to Taylor directly, and with a more personal tone. By then Taylor had attended the YPSL meeting on Monday, May 21, another function on Thursday of that week, and the hike at the Palisades on Thursday, May 31. Her sudden interest in socialism was as social as it was political, and Ben evidently floundered in his valiant efforts to mix the two. In one letter, he enclosed a clipping from the *Daily News* about women's suspicions that men often handed them a line to mask self-interested intentions. Apparently, Taylor had questioned Ben's motives when he tried to recruit her for his club. Ben's indignant response accompanied the clipping:

"Do you consider my statement to have come from a desire to flatter you? Do you believe I was not sincere in what I said? That it was an attempt to please on my part? Should I have omitted the words I expressed? Was it pure propaganda in relation to your entering the club? Should I have worded that which I meant and felt? I repeat 'I consider you a valuable asset to our club.' I'll say it again. And again. And to Anna, too." Ben signed off curtly with "Ben Schlamm Young Peoples Socialist League Circle 9." Taylor's words had rubbed him the wrong way, and he was characteristically effusive in his defense.[1]

Despite this rough start, Ben and Taylor became fast friends. By midsummer, Taylor was fully ensconced in a group of YPSL members and attended their events so often that other activities were crowded out. She recorded the occasional date with nonmembers—the importunate Jack Schwartz bored her to tears—but such engagements became increasingly rare.[2]

Taylor mentions the organization in her diary for the first time only on July 17: "Since Anna and I have joined the YPSL I have had but little time left to devote to writing my thoughts. And I miss it because there is ever so much that I can write about. Our activities (committees, etc., etc.) have thrown us into contact with two boys who are the only two truly interesting boys in the club. Of these, Dan, our musician (a violinist) holds but little interest for me as compared to Ben."

Taylor then describes the slim, six-foot one-inch Ben's looks and personality in detail, trying to pin down every nuance of his physical appearance and his manner of walking. She devotes an entire paragraph to his voice. She goes on to describe his character, emphasizing his idealism, sentimentality, intelligence ("in his own way"), and kindness: "As for being truly wicked or ever telling a lie—one cannot couple them with Ben. Proof of his sterling quality is the fact that the club looks up to him in adoration and hangs on his every word when he speaks to them. There is not a one that does not like him." In this section of the entry, Taylor records snippets of conversations with Ben during which she expresses her worries for him as if she were writing a story, setting off dialogue with quotation marks.

As Taylor continues to write about Ben, sometimes typing up entries at the office, she relates significant conversations as stories, using suspense and commentary, interspersing her tales with character analyses and literary references, and playing with elevated diction. The July 23, 1923, entry opens with a preface that sets up a conversation as a sad drama. She begins, "Somehow the conversation with Ben last night has been ringing in my ears. I can think of naught else. The strong inclination to weep that was in me yesternight as he spoke, is still with me and it is with difficulty that I restrain myself." Our romantic heroine of exquisite sensibilities reflects on Ben: "Poor, poor human! How pitiable you are!" She explains he is pitiable because he feels and thinks so deeply, "with every fiber of [his] being," and seeks a reason for his thoughts, while others "merely live from day to day, caring not for the whys and wherefores, ignorant, blissfully so, thank God, of the depths of their own thoughts."

Rather than divulging what Ben said that was so affecting, Taylor employs more delaying tactics with a literary comparison. It is not unusual for Taylor to refer to books she has read in order to make a point, but here she does more than make a point: she builds suspense. "Now, only now, do I truly understand Sherwood Anderson for Ben is a Sherwood Anderson character—a human being frank enough to tell of his own thoughts and dreams. Besides that, there is in him the same earnesty (to coin a word), the same nervous tension, and above all the same desires that one would find in a Sherwood Anderson character." Taylor considered carefully the word she coined—*earnesty*—because she added the *y* at the end of the word with a pen. She also thought about the composition of this entry. Under the Sherwood Anderson comparison, she types a row of asterisks, to indicate separation of this three-paragraph preface from the story itself.

It takes Taylor another page before she discloses Ben's startling comment. After describing the particulars of their conversation, Ben's "thin hands gesticulating nervously—his pale, earnest face, his speech, halting at times, words stumbling over each other at other times," she gives over the narrative to Ben's voice in order to prolong the delay: "Syd, there is a desire in me which is so strong it permeates my very being—it is ever in my thoughts. Someday I am going to tell you about it." Taylor asks him why he cannot tell her now, since he already brought up the subject, to which he replies, "I realize I am not consistent. I know I should not have mentioned it if I did not want to finish my statement. At the same time—I want you to know—I want to tell you and I realize that if I did not care to have you know, I would never have brought up the subject. Besides, you would laugh at me." Taylor types out her reply as if typing a story: " 'Laugh at you, Ben—no—. Don't you believe me capable of understanding' I answered." She then buries Ben's confession in a long exposition of several paragraphs, drawing out the suspense until, finally, she gives in to the big reveal. Having Ben narrate in his own voice, she transcribes his persistent fantasy about suckling a woman's naked breast, including his detailed analysis of its meaning. She concludes with the literary frustration of attempting to record an affecting discussion: "I wish I could remember his conversation and put it down here word for word. Alas, I do not. I could never write as he spoke."

In the past, Taylor had written frankly about kissing games and more evasively about romantic kissing, and she addressed her feelings of longing and expectation, but she was never so straightforward and detailed about any sex act before recording this episode. Although Ben shrugs off the sexuality of his desire, it is clear that he imagines the suckling as part of a romantic encounter. He says he wants to be in the "guise of a helpless babe," but it is as a grown man and not a baby that he imagines himself suckling a woman's breast. And it is as a grown man that he titillates Taylor with his story. As her prologue showed, she was aghast at the strangeness of his confession and his "pitiable" self, but her passionate and surprised response was in part romantic.

Taylor leaves several pages in her diary blank, as if the entry of July 23 forced her to take a break, or in order to create distance between it and any others. The effect was also to build anticipation for the next entry, which proved to be far more important. On August 6, 1923, Taylor wrote, "The day we joined the YPSL's was a momentous one for us! Thru them we have acquainted with some of the dearest people." She then began a new paragraph: "Dan and Ben and Ben's cousin Ralph. Curious how some people will turn themselves round your hearts! These people have and how happy it has made Anna and myself." For the first time in writing, Taylor mentions Ralph Schneider.

This tall, serious, ambitious young man who became so dear to Taylor was born on April 7, 1904, to Fannie née Schlamm and Simon Schneider, immigrants from Latvia who had married in Manhattan on June 7, 1903.[3] He was the first of their three children, Milton following in 1907 and Lucille in 1914. On his birth certificate, Ralph's parents gave him the recognizably Jewish name Rubin and listed their address as 71 East 98th Street. Rubin or Reuven Schneider changed his name to Ralph Taylor soon after 1930, when he was in his late twenties, the new surname being a translation of *schneider*, the

Ralph Taylor in baby carriage

Yiddish word for tailor, and the entire family followed suit.[4] Little is known about his childhood, except for one notable incident. In a letter to a young friend in 1965, Taylor mentions that she and Ralph have become acquainted with relatives in Paris who originally hailed from Riga. She casually adds that when he was six, Ralph had accompanied his mother back to Riga and lived with her there for a year and a half.[5]

An eighth-grade report card issued by P.S. 25 from the term beginning February 1, 1918, reveals little about Ralph except that he was a straight-B student. While in elementary school, Ralph had already begun to work. At age twelve, he became an errand boy at the historic Caswell-Massey pharmacy, and by age sixteen he had been promoted to bottle washer.[6] Founded in 1752 in Newport, Rhode Island, as an apothecary shop called Dr. Hunter's

Dispensary, the business opened a branch in New York City in 1833, and its name was changed to Caswell-Massey in 1876. Before the Depression, it owned a warehouse and ten stores in the New York area.[7] Little did teenage Ralph know that he had embarked on a decades-long career that would make his fortune.

Ralph also worked for a family business, the American Cap Works, which was owned by his uncle and Ben's father, Louis Schlamm. That enterprise was located at 27 St. Marks Place, and in February 1920 a local trade paper announced that Ben had been made manager and that Ralph Schneider and Joseph Brenner would be salesmen.[8] Even though Joseph was a Brenner, there is no evidence of Taylor and Ralph meeting before 1923.

Ralph's need to work did not derail his schooling as it had Taylor's, and unlike her, he graduated from high school. In 1919, Ralph registered at Stuyvesant High School, located since 1907 at 345 East 15th Street in Manhattan. Known for the quality of its math and science curriculum, it began to restrict enrollment based on academic achievement the very year Ralph began his studies there. Little documentation remains from his high school years and it does not speak to his scholastic prowess. On April 12, 1920, the school newspaper, the *Spectator,* announced that Reuben Schneider had won the student government's cheer contest with the following composition: "Wolla Wolla Whee! / Wolla Wolla Wow! / Wolla Wolla Winkee! / Yow! Yow! Yow! / Yip! Yap! Yip! / Yip! Yap! Yow! / Stuyvesant High School / Wow! Wow! Wow!" The article goes on to say that first- and second-place cheers would be printed in the Songs and Cheers pamphlet.[9]

In the summer of 1921, Ralph enrolled in the College of Pharmacy of the City of New York, affiliated with Columbia University. He kept several receipts from the college, the first being for a $5 registration fee dated July 15, 1921. The second, bearing the date September 19, 1921, was made out to "Mr. R. Schneider" who "has paid one hundred ninety-five xx/100 dollars for 1st year." On September 19, 1923, a receipt records that "R. Schneider paid the Five dollar fee for Examinations," and on September 26 "Ruben Shneider" received his grades.

While a student in pharmacy school, Ralph became an active socialist through the YPSL. Signed by the secretary Morris Novik, Ralph's green membership card in Circle 6 of the Greater New York Branch of the organization shows that he was admitted on June 3, 1922, and attended meetings regularly. Ralph's enthusiasm carried over to at least one family member. His fifteen-year-old brother Milton composed a song in praise of internationalism with lyrics that read, "The coal barons and the steel trust shall go under for the people stands first / Yes! I know—Tomorrow that day will come for the working class and if the people only had their way / They'd pick a man like Eugene Debs I'll say."[10] Ralph eventually rose to join the leadership of the group. In April 1923, as a member of the Executive Committee, he was charged with organizing a circle in the Bronx, an apparently failed enterprise.

By the time Taylor and Ralph met at that fateful YPSL meeting in August, Ralph was the managing editor of the YPSL publication the *Vanguard,* the offices of which were located at 7 East 15th Street, the same address as the Rand School. His involvement in the production of this magazine foreshadowed his more substantial journalistic efforts a decade later, although that next venture concerned the arts rather than politics.

Having fun was an integral part of YPSL life.[11] The New York gang, including Ralph, Ben, Dan, Anna, and Taylor, with other friends mentioned occasionally, often traipsed off to the Palisades in the summer of 1923. Photographs of outings from this time show a lively bunch of young men and women. Taylor wears her hair short, as do the other women, and sports a curl over her forehead. She is easy to spot, since she is the shortest—like all but one of her sisters, she stood under five feet in height. This YPSL cell offered Taylor freedom. She did not initially associate the unconstrained relations between men and women with socialism, but on August 6 she did remark on the absence of constraint between the sexes: "I can safely say that never did we enjoy a day as much for in the company of these boys we act as freely as we would in the company of other girls, even to piling our hair on top of our heads (due to heat)."[12]

The group also appealed to Taylor because its members shared an interest in theater, which began at this point to assume great importance in her life. They improvised skits during their outings, and photographs capture their rollicking fun. The dramatists in the group were not put off when their friends seemed inattentive: "The actors cared not. We were so imbued with the spirit of the play that we completely forgot our audience and ourselves." Picking up on the word *forgot,* Taylor continues: "And to forget oneself is to forget all the hurts and bitterness. And there are hurts—like Julie which I would never admit before even to myself . . . When [the hurt] came—I was surprised. I was aware that the thought had been smouldering—but express-ing it only made me realize more poignantly how big a one it was." This con-nection between dramatics and self-discovery became the foundation of Taylor's later work in impromptu dramatics with children. Nurtured by her experiences in theater companies and with Jacob L. Moreno's drama therapy, discussed in the next chapter, Taylor later developed techniques of dramatic play for self-understanding and the resolution of emotional conflicts.

Playacting was not Taylor's only way of accepting the heartbreak Julie caused her. She ends the August 6 entry with "Ralph! If I could only tell him how truly much I thank him for the service he is rendering—a service that he is not aware of.—He is distracting my mind from its one path and directing my thoughts in his direction." While she perceives that Ralph causes her mind to shift from one man to another, she does not express any attraction to him or mention which aspects of his personality or appearance are appealing.

By the time Taylor returned from a brief vacation in the countryside with Anna, she seems to have resigned herself to the break with Julie. None-theless, when she heard the news that he was to be married in two months, she left the room "on the pretense of securing a coat." Summarizing her rela-tionship with Julie, her diary entry of August 29, 1923, muses about her ca-pacity to love: "Because I am young—because there is in me the capacity for love and because I was flattered by the attentions of an intellectual superior, I believe I cared." Echoing her remark about the "service" Ralph does for her, Taylor reflects on what Julie did for her: "Now that it has passed to being a mere incident in my life, I can more readily perceive the benefits derived from my association with Julie. He broadened my viewpoint, made me see things in a more understanding light, quickened my thinking power by his continu-ous reasonings, taught of the real enjoyment one can find in the contempla-tion of things, made me more keenly alive to my emotions and sensations." Taylor thinks the woman he is marrying—Marion—will succeed where she herself did not in bringing out "the goodness which I believe he has deeply buried in him."

One sentence in this rumination about Julie bears consideration for its implications for the future: "Even had I given vent to my illusory feelings of love by physical manifestations, I would still be glad that the incident had occurred." Taylor tells her thought book that she was never physical with Julie, and she apparently realized that she could have been and not have regretted her actions. Taylor's vacillation about physical intimacy persists even when she is not in a relationship. Hypotheticals about the past and uncertainty in the present came to shape her encounters with Ralph as well.

Taylor now completed the transition from Julie to Ralph. Back in New York, she recounts a dramatic story about the imperious Julie whose parents cut him off "merely" because his new wife was not Jewish: "The irony of it! Merely because Marion is gentile, his folks have refused to see him again. His pleadings on his bended knees (Julie! God! What an effort for him) to his mother to kiss him good-bye were futile. He left with a deep-rooted feeling of bitterness."[13] Exogamy was rare for Jews in 1923, and yet Taylor seems completely at ease with the idea.[14] Nonetheless, like many other young Jews of her generation, Taylor dated only Jews and was not looking to marry outside the Jewish community. Neither Taylor nor any of her siblings tested the senior Brenners' acceptance of intermarriage, although Charlotte came scandalously close to marrying a gentile. It was only in the next generation that members of the family married non-Jews, causing strain but not rupture.

Having related the story of Julie, Taylor draws her customary dashed line on the page. Her former boyfriend appears above the line, and Ralph after it. She starts the next section with "But so much else has occurred in the meantime. And it all came as a surprise." With this paragraph, she begins to refer to Ralph as a love interest. Despite gushing about him in her previous diary entry, Taylor sees him now as the pursuer: "I had been aware that Ralph liked me, but I was not sure just how much. I had wondered why he came to our club and committee meetings so often. But I had put it down to several reasons other than the real one. Somehow one hates to admit things to oneself."

One evening in early September, the YPSL meeting was held in her own apartment, with a Victrola and an evening stroll impressing themselves on Taylor's mind more than any substantive political discussion. Given that a typical evening might involve a debate between Ben Schlamm and Nick Lerner on, for example, "Resolved, American Socialist Party is dying because it has not lived up to the principles of Socialism," she can be excused for looking for livelier entertainment.[15] Characteristically, Taylor makes no mention of the meeting's agenda. In fact, unlike the young men in the group who corresponded frequently about socialist matters, she never once in her diary describes the political goals and activities of the club she loved so much that summer.

After listening to music, some members decided to get some fresh air, and Taylor ended up paired with Ralph.

> We had been walking in silence for blocks and blocks. I was busy with my own thoughts, and so his words spoken suddenly almost startled me.
>
> "Syd, isn't it queer our walking this way?"
>
> " 'Queer?' No!"
>
> R. "Doesn't the fact that we are walking mean more than anything we could possibly say?"
>
> S. "Yes. That is why I did not think it queer."
>
> More silence. Then—
>
> "Syd, do you think I'm a fool?"
>
> "No, Ralph."
>
> "Well, at least I am not deceived."
>
> "Am I to infer that I am being deceived because I do not consider you a fool?"
>
> More silence. Wonderingly, I asked
>
> "What is the trouble, Ralph? Tell me. Are you being a pathetic jackass a second time?"
>
> He nodded his head.
>
> He found it too difficult a matter to tell me that night. Besides, it was late, and Friday was a work day. He promised to explain when he saw me Friday night.
>
> When I said good-night and walked upstairs, he remained standing where I had left him. He looked so pathetic, I longed to turn back but it seemed best to wait for Friday.
>
> Needless to say that I could scarcely think of aught else. I kept thinking of the pathetic figure he made Thursday night.[16]

Drawing another dashed line on the page, Taylor continues with the next night, when a canceled lecture at the Rand School brought her closer to Ralph. The Rand School appears several times in Taylor's papers, and she addressed a letter to Ralph there in August. As for Ralph, in a letter dated October 17, 1923, "Comrade Schneider" received confirmation that he had been awarded one of four $250 Edward Berman Memorial Scholarships "for the full-time training course" at the school.[17]

On this evening in September, the scheduled lecturer failed to show up, and the young people seized the opportunity to pair off again.[18] Taylor and Ralph separated from their friends and had a heart-to-heart talk in a quiet spot in Central Park, which brought them ever closer. Reticent about much of the conversation, Taylor described its closing moments in a passage laden with infatuation:

> But it was this which made me like him most.
>
> [Ralph said,] "While you were away, I fought with myself, but it was useless. When your letter came, I read it several times. I could scarcely wait till Sunday when you would be back.
>
> ["]Now this may sound cruel and analytical, but when I saw you Sunday, you did not look well. Your face was sunburnt, there was skin on your nose peeling and you had some pimples on your chin, yet I wanted to put my arms around you and kiss you anyway."
>
> I had a desire to laugh because I realize the humor of it all. Would another boy have told a girl that? I doubt it. Yet I was glad that I had not looked well, that my face was sunburnt, that there was some skin peeling on my nose and that I had some pimples on my chin. For then it wasn't because of the external I that he cared. It was because it was *I* as I *am*.

As in her relationship with Julie, Taylor welcomed even unflattering attention if she felt it signified honesty.

This first time Taylor writes in her diary of Ralph's attraction to her, it is a negative attraction. Jo often related the story of her parents' first meeting. In her account, Ralph saw Taylor from the back, noticed her long, blonde hair, and assumed the woman's face would be as beautiful as her hair. But when Taylor turned around, "Eh," he said to himself, "she's not that great." Even with playful irony—a sense of "of course I find Syd beautiful now"—the story is still one of the backhanded compliments Ralph gave Taylor by telling her how attractive he did *not* find her.

By September 4, Taylor was already using the word *love* to describe her feelings for Ralph and his complicated feelings for her. She begins the entry of that date with "If I could not love Ralph for anything else, I could love him for the way he spoke to me last night." After writing that she remembers his words "distinctly," Taylor spends the next three paragraphs writing out what Ralph said:

> Syd, the world is moving on intellectually, and I want you and I to move on in the same fashion, with a broad and understanding view of things.
>
> After all, the mere words "I love you" do not mean anything. It is the understanding which 2 people have, that brings them close to each other. And I want to come close to you, as close as Anna is. If we are to develop the proper need for each other, we must go along the road of life side by side.
>
> Up until now you have seen only the best side in me. I have another side and I want you to know the other side too.
>
> You won't find me demonstrative. Somehow the more "spoon-ing" connected with a love affair that I see, the more shallow does that love seem. Love to me seems an intellectual union which finds its expression in physical manifestation.
>
> If I should ever ask you to kiss me, I want you to tell me just how you feel about the matter.

Serious, analytical, determined to be modern, and somewhat dry in tone—that is the Ralph who became Taylor's companion for over fifty years.

Ralph's assertion that Taylor should tell him how she feels about his kissing her when he *asks* to kiss her hints at how well he had studied her; it also suggests that he understood her ambivalence about whether her independence could coexist with social convention. Only a few days later, Taylor wrote in her diary, "Ralph, I fear, understands me far too well. He can read my very thoughts." Her response is to feel "very tender and kindly" toward Ralph: "To think it is I who inspires such sentiments within him. Why—why—why did he choose me? An unanswerable question."[19] Her conviction that Ralph is special and that his attention is a precious, inexplicable gift remained a constant in their relationship.

A subject that repeatedly comes up between Taylor and Ralph is sexuality. On September 19, Ralph wrote Taylor a letter with a self-described logical argument to demonstrate that human beings can know what others are thinking—he does not mention feeling—only through physical manifestations of inward thoughts. Some of those manifestations fall under the rubric of "Love and Passion," and Ralph objects that Taylor draws a false distinction between the two. Because she resists physical overtures from him, she indicates either that he is lying when he says he loves her—judging there is a disconnect between his actual feelings and their physical manifestation—or that he is indulging his animal urges, caring little which girl is the object of his attentions.

> Being a male, I have naturally been the aggressor, altho before I met you, I always felt that if by some overwhelming misfortune, I should ever "flop," I would have the one I loved propose to me, not only because I felt that I would want to be sure that she loved me (altho you don't half realize how important that is to the males generally), but because I would want no inhibition of "physical manifestations" on the part of my beloved—and that would be quite a good test.

Ralph proceeds to castigate himself for not adhering to his beliefs about female initiative. When Taylor did initiate intimacy, Ralph apparently took over, which caused Taylor's inhibitions to surface. He vows to let her lead the way from beginning to end going forward, however difficult that will be for him and however much it will cause Taylor to wonder about the intensity of his feelings for her. They have put themselves in a bind, but Ralph is convinced that his method is the only way Taylor will "*finally trust [him] wholeheartedly.*" Ever the man in control, he adds: "From now on, I do not want you to discuss our love with anyone. Even if this sounds like an order, Syd, I want you to obey."

Ralph never mentions social conventions as holding Taylor back and conveys instead that he thinks her resistance comes from anxiety about what "physical manifestations" could lead to, with his emphasized plea that she should trust him. Ralph subscribes to the notion that Taylor is averse to "physical manifestations" because of sexual politics. With those quotation marks, Ralph conveys that the phrase is Taylor's, but he also mocks it, suggesting that Taylor is overwrought. He does fear that he has been too intense, and his solution for this situation is to say that from now on, Taylor will lead the way in all lovemaking, not just starting it but finishing it.

Taylor wrote back the next night, September 20, a long, ruminative letter focused on emotions. From this point, Taylor starts to write to Ralph rather than write in her diary, although she would keep a diary for many more years. In terms of length and inward gazing, the letter resembles a diary entry, but at certain points she addresses Ralph directly. After writing that Ralph understands her so well that he even understands her half-formed thoughts, she addresses Ralph's proposed course of action: "You have confronted me with an unnatural talk. Ralph, you know 'tis the male's active, the female, passive. If I'm to take the lead *and hold it,* it will be a fight against all the instincts that are innate in a woman tho I have fought already and won." It is Taylor, not Ralph, who brings up the "natural" behavior of the sexes. In her adherence to classical stereotypes of male and female roles, Taylor shows herself to be more conservative than her boyfriend. Over the following weeks, Taylor and Ralph continue their discussion of what is normal male and female behavior, both in person and in writing. Taylor accuses Ralph of hurting her in his unnatural insistence that she be aggressive sexually, which to other "male beings would seem extremely unbecoming."[20] Pages of tormented conversations may make one wonder why they kept punishing each other, but Taylor and Ralph amused each other as well. Ralph drew humorous figures on his letters, and he wrote and illustrated a recurring comic strip styled on the melodrama *The Perils of Pauline.*

Ralph and Taylor's attempt to combine political action with romance annoyed some of the more doctrinaire members of the YPSL cell. While reading something titled "The Exposure of Socialism"—the "trickiest thing I have ever read"—Taylor was interrupted by a call from Nat, who shouted at her for missing a Circle 9 meeting. He accused her of choosing to spend her time with Ralph rather than with the YPSLs: "Give him my regards and kiss him for me, too, Good-bye!" he yelled as he slammed down the phone.[21] Taylor wonders "just how much he thinks he knows," indicating that she and Ralph tried to keep their romance private.[22]

Taylor's thoughts on what it means to be a man or a woman colored her experiences beyond her relationship with Ralph:

Came home in the side seat of a motorcycle tonight. Attired in a boy's red jersey buttoned high at the neck and a boy's cap stuck jauntily on one side of my head. I caused quite a sensation. It was glorious—racing along sometimes as fast as 30 miles per hour, the wind whistling past my ears—dodging now a car and now a truck. The young chap in the office who owns the car has promised to take me home more often since I so truly enjoyed it.[23]

In some respects, the image Taylor creates—that of a carefree young woman careening down the street, dressed as a boy—captures and updates the stereotype of the New Woman of the previous generation. Taylor does not ride a bicycle, but instead is in the sidecar of a motorcycle; she does not wear bloomers suggesting men's clothing, but rather a masculine jersey and cap.[24] Taylor relishes the notion that onlookers think she is a boy. The playacting, the freedom of being a gender other than her own, the sheer excitement of movement all combine to give her a thrill that she will soon seek to replicate through artistic expression.

This is not the only time Taylor expresses delight at being mistaken for a boy. To some extent, her enjoyment arises from women's social progress, but the sexual ambiguity also appeals to her, and her choice of a unisex name at age fourteen echoes through the motorcycle ride. Because Taylor continued to express pleasure whenever anyone mistook her for a boy, even several years after her marriage, more than gender is at play. Taylor is also a budding actress, and the role of Sydney is one that never ceases to fascinate her.

At this same time, Ralph and his cousin Ben corresponded about their ideas about women within the framework of their socialist ideals. Ben was in the midst of his own rocky relationship with a young woman who seemed too conventional for him, and Ralph clearly confessed to his cousin his difficulties with Taylor. In a letter of November 24, 1923, Ben suggests that Ralph and Taylor plan a camping trip together for the following summer, where they can iron out their differences by roughing it in the country away from their daily routines; in so suggesting, he blends practicality and theory in his typical fashion: "Would you both have the desire? Could parental objections be overcome? Will your jobs be the hindrance?" It suits Ben to think of Ralph and Taylor as participating in a social experiment by striking out for the woods, just as his own wanderlust was growing to the point that in the spring of 1924 he set off on a cross-country trip to work with the proletariat.

Ben sometimes switches from the voice of a radical philosopher to one that is endearing and friendly. As he draws the November 24 letter to a close, he writes, "Again from a very selfish motive, you can consider Syd as a treasure to be cherished and closely clung to. . . . [I]f you took all the vices and faults and weaknesses of Syd, their entire sum magnified ten thousand times could never conceal the value of certain characteristics. If one must be dogmatic, I call them golden." The conversation continues between the two young men, as Ben suggests a week later that Ralph would benefit from reading *The Elements of Psychology* by Edward L. Thorndike, drawing attention specifically to entries in the index on "sex differences in mental traits." He also recommends Havelock Ellis's *Man and Woman* and Helen Bradford Thompson's *The Mental Traits of Sex*. After more than one date with his girlfriend, Ben went to the Rand School library, where Ralph found him reading books about sex.[25]

Taylor's interest in sex paralleled that of the cousins. For example, she and her friend Martin North spoke on the subway about the cyclical nature of menstruation and its effect on the female sex drive, a topic unthinkable for public discussion a generation earlier.[26] The conversation itself infused their friendship with frankness, and it was chaste in the sense that they both professed interest in the female sex drive within the context of marriage. Martin admits he lacks experience and draws conclusions based on observation. His thinking about it at all is "in order to discuss with Leo (who is getting married Jan. 5) the particular care with which a husband must understand the subtle sex changes, desires and reactions of a woman. After all, the sex life during Marriage, should be the finest thing thru it all."

The conversation is remarkable not solely because the two young people discuss the menstrual cycle, but because they connect it to sexual desire. They do not link it to irritability, abstinence, or discomfort, but rather to pleasure and intercourse, even though they share the conventional and convenient wisdom of a woman's desire receding during the flow. Taylor agrees with Martin that "just prior to the menstrual period, sex feelings in a woman are at the highest point," but she does not clarify if she is speaking from personal experience or from what she has read on the subject. It is not clear whether she wanted Martin to think she was experienced or book-smart. In either case, she comes across as knowing. Still, Taylor seems a little startled by this exchange. She not only writes it out, but she also retypes it, which is unusual for her to do with diary entries, indicating how much it affected her.

Through Ralph's study of pharmacy, Taylor also found an opening to mention the intimate beautification procedures and products that she and her sisters use, as she walks the tightrope between candor and reticence.[27] The cod liver oil Ralph cajoles her to take for her health is hardly novel, being a fortifier from childhood, although his advice presages his lifelong conviction that he had the authority to determine how Taylor should look and how she should manage her health.

Among themselves, the Brenner sisters experimented with weight-loss pills, mudpacks, and depilatories. Skincare products appealed to first- and second-generation immigrants who wanted to conform to standards of beauty that preferred the light and fair to the dark and swarthy. Taylor refers to a type of depilatory called Zip, which a 1924 trade advertisement highlighted for use by "a dark-skinned woman, with the appearance of an eastern or southern European immigrant, [who] achieved social acceptance in America by ridding herself of superfluous hair."[28] Taylor says she will try it under her arms because Ella used it on the "down" on her upper lip, and "the result was marvelous."[29] For the fair Taylor, the depilatory serves a private aesthetic, while for Ella its purpose was to obliterate a public feature associated with Mediterranean minorities. How immigrant women looked was an obvious sign of their Americanization. Conforming to a particular ideal, even one shaped by a specific ethnic background, could be achieved through makeup and diet. Additionally, young working women knew they had to present themselves in an attractive way to please prospective employers and clients, as Taylor discussed in her diary several years later.[30]

From the end of 1923 through the beginning of 1924, Taylor's diary entries and letters continue to show the rocky nature of her relationship with Ralph, without stating their reasons for repeatedly breaking up and reconciling. Ella and Ben were intimately involved in the ups and downs of the relationship, tireless in offering advice and comfort.

On February 28, Taylor typed a long, rambling letter to Ralph while she was at work. In it she mentions having shared the "news" of their engagement. Explaining the reactions of various men in her office, Taylor notes that they all make complimentary remarks about Ralph, noting his size and good looks.

Taylor is "banging on her typewriter" while this parade of compliments passes by. She closes with "I am off to lie down where I shall lie flat on my back, arms crossed under my head and think about 6 feet of humanity. Your little Syd. P.S. I am repeating 3 little words in my head—Do you know them?"

This tiny woman who barely reached Ralph's shoulder was indeed becoming his "little Syd." The voice of the independent feminist appears to have been stilled. Apron around her waist, Taylor burns dinner one evening and patiently puts up with her mother's scolding and worry about her daughter's inability to care for a husband.[31] Taylor disapproves of a woman from Sutta and Fuchs who left her job to marry—not because the woman gave up her job, but because her approach to marriage was so selfish. When the woman came back to the office for a visit three months after her wedding, she had completely changed. Previously babyish, she had become a bored sophisticate. Explaining in detail what this woman's life is like—she has a maid, does not cook much, does not read—Taylor is convinced the woman married for material comfort and not love. She marvels at how few marriages are good ones with well-matched partners, and expresses happiness that she and Ralph are suited to each other. Upon Taylor's suggestion that the woman have a baby in order to be more content, her former colleague scoffs, declaring she is not interested and certainly does not want to ruin her figure. Taylor criticizes such selfishness, implying she would never put off childbearing for those frivolous reasons.

At this time, the Brenner sisters did not question the truism that married women do not work outside the home. Women in their class might work as seamstresses or as equal partners in a family business, but a job disassociated from traditional women's roles was improper after marriage. Charlotte describes how Ella quit her job a few months before her wedding date in order to find an apartment and set up house. When the postwar rise in rents made it impossible to find affordable lodging, Ella came up with a plan to continue working for a year while living at her parents' home with her new husband. That suggestion "released a torrent of reproach from both Mama and Tanta, for it was unthinkable in those days that a married woman should continue to work; even relatives and friends were astonished."[32] The older women determinedly tracked down a suitable apartment, thus avoiding a "scandal." All the sisters except Gertie did become working wives eventually, but in 1923 they expressed conformity to social convention.

Only a week after the ruined dinner, on March 14, things have fallen apart again. Ralph instructs Taylor not to call him, and within a few weeks she reluctantly agrees not to see him for a year, although for the next several months they remain in contact. The documents never state explicitly what caused the break, but they do make it clear that Taylor did not want it and pined for Ralph. She reverts to writing in her diary, explaining to the neglected thought book that she had not been writing in it during the romance because she had Ralph to talk to.[33] This new entry and the balance of the diary are now composed as letters to Ralph and no longer to the journal itself.

Taylor discussed her feelings with her mother, her friend Anna, and Ella, who loyally blamed Ralph. Other than to Ella, Taylor did not tell the whole story of the breakup. Taylor's decision not to tell Anna or her mother why Ralph did not want to speak with her for a year, for fear they would blame him, suggests that it was he who wanted the breakup. Taylor repeatedly construes herself as rejected and wronged, yet protective of her beloved: "I have told mother but not all. Somehow, I cannot bear the thought of having anybody misunderstand and condemn you [Ralph] and she would have hated you forever had she known the whole truth. [Mother] merely remarked that Time would prove whether this was for the best. She pleaded with me not to brood and sorrow since I was far too young to rail at Life. She knew something was wrong and she told me she had been waiting for me to come to her."[34]

It was unusual for Taylor to recount a conversation with her mother, and even more unusual for her mother, according to the diaries, to be sympathetic and forthcoming. Indeed, Ella, not Taylor, saw their mother crying because of Taylor, who received the indirect report: "Ella told me Mother had spoken to her. It seems she was crying, because she felt so sorry for me and because she believed that I thought she was glad it had happened. It hurt her—my thinking so—She had wanted to take me in her arms to comfort and sympathize with me but her old reserve kept her back."

Years later, Jo said that she thought there was tension between the two sets of parents, with the Schneiders disdaining the Brenners, and that may have contributed to the breakup. Already back in November 1923, Ben wrote to Ralph: "And if in Syd's family they are saying 'Hold on' and in our own 'Let go,' then allow me to be the rebel and traitor in our own ranks who says 'Hold on.' " Family lore kept alive the notion that no one was good enough for Fannie Schneider's son, but both sets of parents may have had reservations about the other.

Charlotte had a completely different take on the situation. She describes the relationship between Sarah and Ralph as "a quiet, gentle romance—no turbulent affair like Henny's, but rosy and warm . . . Ralph was tall and solemn—a rock the gentle Sarah leaned on."[35] For her own storytelling purposes, Charlotte telescopes time, and it is difficult to determine when events actually occurred. What is important to note, despite the uncertainties in chronology, is that she never indicates any tension between her sister and Ralph or mentions Ralph's long absence from New York precipitated by that tension. On the contrary, Taylor "had to make people happy," and she subordinates her desires to his.[36]

On Monday, April 21, Taylor begins her entry unusually, talking about the Jewish holiday of Passover. The plan had been for Ralph and Ben to be guests at the Brenner seder, a prospect that had filled Taylor with joy. Because they did not come, she wept at the table. To add insult to injury, another man tried to kiss her. Taking refuge in her bedroom, she resolved not to cry over Ralph again: "Tears will not bring you back. If I am to come back to you at all, I want to come back as a better, finer, and wiser Syd than I have been. Therefore from today starts my new life." She then writes that she will "plunge" into "new circles." She wants to meet different people, do different things, "read more and learn more." Determined not to think of Ralph, "I shall come to you only when I write these letters to you." She contradicts herself, however, at the entry's end: "I am anxious to see Ben if only to know how you received my message."

Taylor follows through with her plan of plunging into new circles, and within a week she is attending dance parties, club meetings, and movie outings with friends she had neglected, staying out as late as she can. Yet time and again, her attempt at carefree gaiety fails. She repeatedly says she is outwardly happy but inwardly sad. When she lies alone in bed, "all memories come flooding back—and I feel so lonely.—Then I call your name—speak to you . . . In the dark, you seem so close to me. I put my arms around the pillow and bury my head in it—And then I want you so—Ralph, Ralph."

While Taylor clearly experienced anxieties about her relationship with Ralph, which she tried to allay with an active social and working life, her shaping of that relationship on paper shows that writing was not only a means of catharsis, but also of artistic experimentation and of independence from Ralph. A set of three letters in June 1924 demonstrates how she was developing her critical voice as both reader and writer. On June 25, Taylor wrote a letter of appreciation to Boni & Liveright, the publishers of John Cournos's 1922 novel *Babel,* a modernist roman à clef that satirizes London's literary and political circles. Although Cournos has fallen into obscurity, he was well known in the 1920s and was spoken highly of by the likes of Marianne Moore, Ezra Pound, and F. Scott Fitzgerald.

In her letter, Taylor says that she often loans out her copy of *Babel* and hopes Cournos will write another book about the main character Gombarov, although she was less impressed by his 1924 novel *The New Candide.* In a letter dated June 26, John S. Clapp of Boni & Liveright replies that he forwarded her letter to Cournos. On June 28, Cournos sent Taylor a note from New Haven, Connecticut, expressing pleasure that she liked *Babel* and disappointment that she did not like *The New Candide,* which he considered his best book. He assures her that his next novel will resume Gombarov's story. Several aspects of this flurry of correspondence are striking. Taylor was only nineteen years old and not a high school graduate, yet her letter exhibits confidence in her literary opinions and in her right to be heard. Literature matters to her, as it does to Clapp, who forwards her letter to the author, and to Cournos, who takes Taylor's opinions seriously.

Taylor also demonstrated her independence in her choice of vacation that summer. She traveled to Camp Tamiment, a resort in the Pocono Mountains of Pennsylvania, in July 1924, the first of four times she vacationed there. The camp stood out both for its socialist ideology and its commitment to the arts.[37] Bertha Howell Mailly, executive secretary of the Rand School, conceived of the camp as a way to educate workers in a holiday setting while making money for the school, which was frequently short of funds. She succeeded in both aims. The school was expensive to run and was hit hard by a lawsuit that sought to shut it down during the anti-radical furor that followed World War I. Always looking for fundraising ideas, Mailly came up with the notion of creating a summer camp.[38] Run by the People's Educational Camp Society (PECS), Camp Tamiment opened on July 1, 1921, with thirty campers. By the last week in August, 175 campers filled the facility, with 285 booked for the Labor Day weekend. Members of PECS were required to belong to the Socialist Party. Pamphlets and brochures published in the 1920s indicate that socialist activities, frequently in the form of lectures, were a staple of camp life.

A vacation at Camp Tamiment was relatively inexpensive. In 1921, the cost was $24 for a week's stay in July, and $27 from August 1 through Labor Day weekend, with savings plans available throughout the year. For a young person, the fees could still be daunting. During Taylor's first stay, she received a teasing letter from Charlotte, who declared, "I won't go to Tamiment of course (I'd die before I spent all that money) but a plain 17-dollar camp."[39] It is worth noting that Taylor's first three stays at the camp took place in July, the less expensive month, and only in 1927 did she stay in August.

Tamiment catered to single young adults over the age of sixteen, most of whom were Jewish.[40] The Jewishness does not merit much attention from Taylor except in passing. During her stay in July 1925, she relates a conversation with a Rabbi Abe, who impresses her for being less superficial than other young men at the camp, but who also meets with her disapproval for showing an unwelcome interest in her. In the summer of 1926, she mentions a married, vegetarian Christian woman whose aloofness she attributes to being among so many Jews. Married campers were unusual. A family bungalow colony nearby was built in 1922 as part of Tamiment, but the camp remained primarily a single adult resort.

Unlike earlier resorts, which centered on a luxury hotel where parents could chaperone their children, Tamiment had rustic cabins constructed on nominally separated sides for men and women. The dining hall, social hall, and camp offices occupied the middle ground. The early cabins had a wooden floor, a roof, and about four-foot-high solid walls with canvas flaps above them to be rolled down during bad weather. They contained no furniture except cots, and had no closets, electricity, or running water.[41] During her first stay, Taylor was intrigued enough with her surroundings to elicit this complaint from Charlotte: "Next time tell us less about the place and more about how *you* like it. That's what we want to know, not the structure of your tent, materials used, etc. Will you make carpenters out of us? Thanks! If you're sure you'll like it very much, maybe I'll go there too instead of to a boarding house."[42]

At around seven in the morning, the wake-up bell rang, and soon after the campers gathered in the dining hall for breakfast: "Breakfast, like all meals, was ample, offering everything from pancakes to pickled herring. The rest of the morning was free for whatever one pleased—horseback riding, swimming, tennis, canoeing or relaxing."[43] Lectures and discussion groups were available in the afternoon, but attendance was not compulsory. Dinner was served around five or six o'clock, and then various types of entertainment filled the evening, ranging from sing-alongs and dances to elaborate theatrical revues. In the few letters and diary entries that mention Tamiment, Taylor refers to rowing, dancing, campfire activities, games such as peanut and potato races, and bunk and "necking" parties.

Taylor deliberately chose to vacation at a camp steeped in radical ideas concerning class, economics, politics, and literature. In the schedule section of the camp's daily newsletter *Breakfast Serials,* alongside events such as "canoe demonstration" and calisthenics, were announcements of lectures, such as "Dr. Goldenweiser will give the first of his five lectures on Theories of Social Progress" and "Scott Nearing will give the third lecture in his series on Economic Chaos and Reconstruction."[44] There is no record of which, if any, lectures Taylor attended. In a scrapbook she and Charlotte put together in the 1920s is a quotation from Eugene V. Debs, founder of the Socialist Party of America and perennial candidate for president on the Socialist platform, but otherwise it is difficult to find evidence of strongly held political beliefs.

Along with its recreational facilities, Tamiment shared another characteristic of the summer camps that proliferated along the East Coast in the 1920s—the chance to meet members of the opposite sex.[45] Mailly was aware of the need to compete with other camps by catering to independent young people who were conscious of their new sexual freedom. They no longer expected to have chaperones, and they had a different understanding of personal reputation than their parents.

Taylor's stays coincided with a period of intense experimentation with the social aspect of the camp, which reflected changes both in American camping in general and in Tamiment's clientele more specifically. As camps sprang up all over the Northeast, competition for customers intensified and the quality of entertainment became a major selling point. This was the time when the "Borscht Belt" entertainers began to thrive. At Tamiment, college graduates and white-collar workers with more tenuous ties to the socialist movement gradually replaced committed working-class sympathizers, and they sought a sophisticated cultural atmosphere.[46]

Initially some members of the PECS board worried about losing what they considered essential to the Tamiment experience, namely its high-minded intellectual and political atmosphere.[47] The first six years saw tension among board members, who grumbled at the frivolity of the entertainment while simultaneously wanting the recreational offerings to attract campers. They saw the need for professional social directors, yet wanted guests to be able to use their artistic talents.[48] Professionals gradually replaced amateurs and Tamiment's administration eventually supported the development of a resident theater, which gained a national reputation and fostered the careers of such stars as Danny Kaye, Neil Simon, and Woody Allen.

Taylor's diary and correspondence while at Camp Tamiment exemplify the trends described above, with a strong emphasis on men. She refers to no women by name and relates no anecdotes concerning them. Among complaints about missing Ralph, she boasts of being chosen "one of the most popular girls," and she clearly had fun. She bristles at any hint of proprietary behavior from men and even feigns tears in order to fend off unwanted kisses.[49] Taylor threw herself into camp life and embraced experiences that caused her to feel a range of emotions from amusement to indignation.

Taylor finally saw Ralph again in August. She sent him a note asking to see him after quarreling with Ella about the sincerity of his feelings for her. The night they met, they talked and walked for several hours, culminating in a dramatic conversation on Taylor's front steps. Taylor declared that she would like to see Ralph again "when the pain disappears," but Ralph responds firmly that he does not ever want to see her again. Both of them murmur vague, miserable statements about how the other does not understand what each "is going back to." Near the end of the 1924 diary, Taylor describes an upsetting letter Ralph sent her in which he confessed a dalliance with another woman, but this romance is evidently not the reason why he never wants to see Taylor again. The two of them never reveal what keeps them apart, although the evidence is strong that one reason was Ralph's feeling that he was more progressive about sex outside of marriage. Whatever the case, they are insistent that it is an insuperable obstacle.[50]

Ben meanwhile continued to serve as mediator and friend. A long letter to Taylor from Ben shows that he was trying to explain the root causes of their rupture to each of the distressed lovers. In his opinion, it was all about sex: "[Ralph's] harshness was a cloak to suppress his feelings. That night, Ralph was . . . a raging, restless, sex-hungry person—a mass of piercing painful pangs, deeply intensified by his aggressive, everprompting male sex makeup. He was hungry and he left you hungrier."[51] To his cousin he offered practical advice: "Yes, stick to your job & pass the Sept. exams & get the registered pharmaceutical license. I understand the feeling you are undergoing after the parting with Syd. Steel yourself."[52] Ever the advocate for physical exertion and the great outdoors as salves for emotional pain, Ben encourages Ralph to join the YMCA for its gym, swimming, and athletics, and to go on hikes. He repeatedly urges Ralph to join him and Nick Lerner on the cross-country adventure that they had begun in the late spring. Between August 12 and 28, Ben received word that Ralph had decided to take him up on his offer. He proceeded to give detailed instructions on how to join them in Chicago and what to pack.

By October 12, the young men were in St. Louis, Missouri. They proceeded through the Southwest and finally reached San Diego, California, by January 14, 1925. Along the way, the young men worked as agricultural laborers or found temporary jobs at hospitals and on construction sites. They traveled in their Tin Lizzie, known fondly as "covered-wagon Henry." Ralph's travels can be traced through several letters sent him by a May Garfinkel, who flirts with him over several months. Addresses and dates in her correspondence help trace his path.

Instigator of this proletarian adventure, Ben was swept up in the righteousness of rejecting materialism and the romance of standing shoulder to shoulder with working people. Conversations with young boys who had been raped on the road and encounters with coarse men did not dim his starry-eyed enthusiasm. The worst incidents could be dismissed as perversion, without shaking his commitment to fraternal solidarity: "There is a cooperation among us bums here. A rough give and take exchange. And most fellows here are good at heart beneath their skins. I'm happy in my struggling."[53]

Through it all, Ben remained a conscientious son: "Gee, I can laugh when I think of the 'all's well' letters I write the folks. They wrote me to come back middle of August. They don't know I won't go again into the shop . . . When I return, I'll tell the story to them from beginning to end, and then, oh boy, won't I have fun. There's no sense keeping the folks worried. Their minds are too shaped a certain way to be able to understand me."[54]

Ralph's relations with his family were also not ruptured by the trip. When he decided to return to New York and sent his clothes on ahead, his brother Milton described their father's amusement at the contents: "Papa wants to know if noses leak in California because the handkerchiefs seem to have been left untouched since Mama sent them to you."[55] His family sent him chocolate for his twenty-first birthday, and Ralph shipped a football and boxing gloves to Milton during the year. If Ralph omitted to correspond frequently enough with his family, it was due more to their expectations than to his negligence. "We have not heard from you for over a week and, naturally, Mama is in the incipient stages of anxiety," Milton wrote. "A little introspection on your part will soon disclose whether you observe your filial duty by your letter, besides being noted for its extreme brevity and lack of explanation."[56]

Once in San Diego, Ralph lodged at "The Hoover," an apartment house at 655 Sixth Street, where a furnished room cost 35 cents a day or $2 a week. He picked up work in a drugstore, but the three friends primarily occupied themselves with politics. Ralph, and presumably Ben and Nick as well, were members of the International Brotherhood Welfare Association, the national offices of which were in Cincinnati. The organization's object was "to unite the migratory workers, the disemployed, and the unorganized of both sexes for mutual betterment and development with the final object of abolishing poverty and introducing a classless society."[57] Under the direction of J. Eads How, "the Millionaire Hobo," who had tied up the income from his inherited fortune in a "people's fund," the members addressed each other as "Comrade" and sought to achieve "universal brotherhood."[58] How's mission was to improve the lot of the homeless and to change perceptions about hobos, so that society would view them as sturdy migratory workers and not shiftless tramps. Then based in Los Angeles, How sent several postcards and telegrams to Ralph about setting up committees and fundraising. He invited him to attend a class in public speaking at the "Hobo" Labor College at the Labor Temple, located at 538 Maple Avenue in Los Angeles, and mentioned classes being formed in social economics and industrial law.

Taylor meanwhile became increasingly reckless. Her family had noticed her carefree behavior for some time, and Ella saw her devil-may-care attitude as positive, especially compared with their mother's uptight ways.[59] Taylor's impulsiveness during this period of heartbreak, however, made some of her friends anxious. After a risky incident, one friend spoke up: "I believe that you are making the mistake of your life in taking those chances with men. You are very fortunate in that your companion had a 'spark of fineness,' as you say. Four chances out of five, there would have been a much more sorrowful Syd."[60] He goes on to relate a cautionary tale about a girl who said no:

Listen Syd, you haven't heard men speak of women as I have. Even some of the finest. There is one particular case I recall of some fellow taking a girl out, giving her a good time, and then taking her to a hotel. The girl knew what she was in for, but at the last moment, refused. She received a beating. I don't know how any man could do that; but when the fellow in this case, told his story to a group of men, he was applauded. They would all have done likewise, was the almost unanimous agreement. And there are times innumerable when this theme has been brought out in this very same manner.

I don't know the exact circumstances of your case, but from the little you write, you were in a pretty bad fix. Your pleadings or logic would not have availed you in most cases. All for a craving of excitement. You deserve a spanking.

Paul cannot refrain from inserting a sexist comment tinged with the violence he condemns, but his concern is genuine.

The serious side of Taylor and the one attracted to artistic expression did not completely disappear. At the Rand School, Taylor built on her solid foundation in reading to study how literature could express social views and attitudes, furthering her understanding of socialism on home ground. In addition to attending lectures at the school, she enrolled in at least one class—"Main Currents in Literature."[61]

As 1925 began, the twenty-year-old Syd Brenner had lived through a tempestuous few years. Like millions of other adolescents, she tested limits and matured. Unlike adolescents of the previous generation, she enjoyed and also suffered from more candid relations between the sexes. She benefited from an unprecedented situation where women were entering the white-collar workforce; as a daughter of immigrants, too, she was afforded a certain amount of leisure and spending money novel to the times. Coupled with a cosmopolitan mobility, Taylor embraced and struggled with unchaperoned independence. With all these possibilities, she actively looked for roles to play. She wanted to be worldly and an ingénue at the same time. That conflict led to repetitive, often harrowing experiences, but her adolescent role-playing paved the way for a lifetime of dramatic creativity.

SEVEN

Performance at Home and on Stage

1925–1935

TAYLOR CONTINUED TO EXERCISE a powerful pull on the distant Ralph. Much to Ben's surprise and disappointment, in May 1925 Ralph suddenly packed up and traveled by train back to New York, informing his cousin of his decision by telegram. While he initially thought that pride would keep Ralph from returning home and that he would travel solo around the country, learning the truth, Ben wrote: "I would consider it one of my greatest weaknesses to find myself so helpless and dependent upon one individual who was connected with my love desires that I surrender the opportunity of proving my mettle . . . You return with a loyalty to Syd that is due to your not having met a satisfactory mate on the road and also because you had a state of mind that restrained aggressiveness to other girls."[1] Ben remarks in passing that a letter from Taylor had reached him just as he heard of Ralph's departure. In it, "she asks me to tell you that she loves you and that nothing can ever change that." Ben was sure that Ralph conceded marriage to Taylor primarily for sex, but it was a bond that endured for over fifty years.

Ralph and Taylor obtained a marriage license and certificate from the State of New York in the Borough of Brooklyn on July 11, 1925. Our only source of information for the wedding and the dramatic events that ensued is Charlotte's memoir. Making no mention of Ralph's journey to the West Coast, the Charlotte of the memoir recalls receiving a phone call from Sarah while finishing up at work around 12:30 p.m. on a Saturday. She hides her astonishment at her sister's announcement that she and Ralph had just married at City Hall and invites Sarah to lunch at a local Italian restaurant so they

Ralph and Syd, 1934

can have a good talk. Ralph is not able to join them, since he had to go back to work and would not be free before six o'clock.

Charlotte offers two main reasons why Sarah and Ralph eschewed a formal wedding. First, she describes them as moving in "Bohemian" and "sophisticated" circles that disdained conventional marriage:

> Sarah and Ralph moved among friends who scorned such conventions as a formal wedding, complete with canopy, bridal gowns, brides maids, and all that "fuss." In fact at heart Sarah would have loved it, but timid little sweet Sarah tried to comply to all things with the man she loved. She was consoling herself by working on a trousseau—tablecloths, handkerchiefs, guest towels she embroidered, including monograms.[2]

Charlotte's conviction that Sarah was less committed to a rejection of traditional marriage and family than Ralph emerges in her description of her sister: "But Sarah didn't dare defy these 'Bohemians' like Ralph, who declared the war-torn society was no place to raise a child." As the conversation continues, the newlywed tries to explain her feelings:

> "You don't understand, Charlotte. Ralph says marriage is an artificial bond. Two people in love don't need a license. People not in love certainly *shouldn't* have one. Love should be honest and free." She recited her lesson well, adding, "It's too complicated. Anyway, as long as we both feel our union attests to our mutual feeling rather than a marriage certificate[,] it doesn't destroy the relationship to legalize it."[3]

Ralph's secular, bohemian views made the choice of the Sabbath for obtaining the license understandable from his point of view. He disdained organized religion and could get time off on a Saturday. But there were limits to the couple's rejection of convention. Even though Sarah reveals to her sister that she and Ralph had already rented a furnished room in the city before obtaining the license, they chose to acquire the sanction of marriage before living together.

The second reason Charlotte gives for the elopement is Sarah's concern about expenses. Sarah dismisses Charlotte's suggestion of a small, inexpensive family wedding, and Charlotte acknowledges that once a few relatives were invited, the event could well have snowballed into an extravagant celebration like Ella's.[4] Elsewhere, however, Charlotte describes a simple ceremony at the synagogue and a small reception at home for Henny and her husband "Paul" (Morris Fried), in part because the young couple had tried at least twice to elope.[5] It is not clear why such a modest celebration could not have been arranged for Sarah.

Continuing with the story, Charlotte recounts that when the two sisters arrived home after lunch, they beheld a distraught Mama. Having spoken with her son, Ralph's mother had telephoned the Brenners, but Cilly refused to believe the news until she heard it from her daughter. The main reason for Mama's distress was Papa's anger, but she also felt cheated out of the preparation for a wedding and was sensitive to community gossip. Once the news reached the parents, Papa did not move from his corner of the living room, where he sat "like a stone image." Sarah's attempts to mollify him fail, and he lashes out: "Hold your tongue, and don't talk to me. You're no daughter of mine. Without a Jewish ceremony, without a Rabbi to perform the religious ritual, this is not a marriage. This is the behavior of a 'Nafka' (prostitute). I have no daughter."[6] Papa remains in his chair for the rest of the afternoon, hand over his eyes, while Mama explains to Sarah and Charlotte their father's point of view and the three of them devise a compromise.

First Mama answers her daughters' question about the use of the word *nafka:* "It's a sin, to live with a man you haven't married." To Sarah's protestations that the couple are in fact married, her mother counters that they are not according to Jewish law. Ralph is requested to come to the Brenner home to discuss the wedding. He arrives at midnight and is met by the entire Brenner clan (except for the two little boys, who have gone to bed). The couple agree to arrange a "proper" Jewish wedding officiated by a rabbi, with the two sets of parents and two witnesses present. Sarah and Ralph consent not to live together until after that ceremony, and as a gesture of good faith, Ralph hands his father-in-law the key to the apartment they have rented.

Charlotte's reflections on this episode focus on the tensions raised by assimilation. She writes, "It was the inevitable clash of orthodox Jewish culture fighting the assimilative drift of first generation Americans. This dilemma had never been discussed at home, however." Her use of the word *drift* is significant, because this entire episode takes places on the Sabbath. Despite his complete identification with Jewish religious culture, Papa never mentioned that by working, traveling on the subway, and spending money on the Sabbath, his daughters transgressed Jewish law, and the sisters evidently did not expect that their father would pounce on Jewish wedding rituals. During their lunchtime conversation, the sisters focused on family expectations for a large wedding, not for a religious one. Charlotte ends the story with the handover of the key and mentions that a rabbi married Ralph and Sarah later.[7] What she does not mention is that the religious wedding occurred more than *two years* later. A rabbi issued their religious marriage certificate on September 3, 1927; however, the Taylors chose in later years to celebrate the 1925 date.[8]

Although Taylor continued to live with her parents until after the religious ceremony, some of her friends knew about the civil marriage.[9] In a letter to Taylor of July 22, 1925, one friend in New York indicated that her marital status was no secret: "It is with a little trepidation that I my pen in hand take—for it is unaccustomed I am to write to married ladies—but they say practice makes perfect."[10] Apparently the young man did not take the marriage seriously, because he flirted with Taylor near the end of his letter: "Don't let me forget to remind you that since you didn't send me a kiss in your letter—and since you won't write, you won't be able to do so—you'll have to deliver on your return." On June 17, 1926, however, Eddie Goldfarb asked when Taylor and Ralph planned to marry, so not all of the couple's friends realized that the two were legally wed.

Taylor seemed to treat her marriage lightly during the two years of limbo. Returning to Tamiment in the summer of 1925, she was surrounded by adoring men. She describes a "rather crude youngster" who strips down to his knickers, listing each item of clothing he removes, and relates how she climbed out the window because the door was barred, but they pulled her back in. She concludes, "Young boys are more or less exhibitionists, I notice. Presume this is a form of sexual excitement for them." Taylor did not strip, but again she put herself in situations of sexual play. In her own words, even a young rabbi "made love" to her.[11] Again at Tamiment in the summer of 1926, she resumed her flirting. She was pleased by compliments on her fetching white bathing suit and chatted about "necking parties" and being besieged with partners at dances.[12] While trying on the role of wife, she refused to relinquish the role of ingénue.

That Taylor enjoyed the role of wife surfaces in a letter to Ralph written in July 1925. It appears that Paul gave her a box of candy, and she writes in parentheses: "(Evidently [he] has not given up hope completely. Wonder would he still continue ministering to my comfort if he knew my true identity.)" Another letter to Ralph in that month describes how popular she is at camp. When she runs into the arms of her "big brother" Lester, he asks to see her left hand. She responds, "Nothing there, Lester—but he's home, waiting for me," and Lester says he knew it would all work out.

The lighthearted tone came and went. In a letter to Ralph from October 1925, Taylor indicated that her ambiguous situation took its toll. After "a night spent in crazy dreaming about linen showers," which lends credence to Charlotte's perception that her sister wanted a wedding with all the frills, Taylor poured out her frustrations about the angry resistance from both sets of parents to the marriage and to their children's lifestyle choices: "All this has its effect. One feels miserably depressed. You see, Ralph, I must needs turn to you for fresh courage and confidence. This letter—it is like saying,

Taylor in bathing costume on Brighton Beach, 1925

Ralph, give me your hand. Your Syd." Taylor felt caught in the middle, her loyalties torn between familial tradition and modern love.

Another reason Ralph and Taylor lived apart until the fall of 1927 was financial.[13] Near the end of her life, Taylor wrote to a young friend who was anxiously awaiting the results of her husband's professional exams: "It took me back so many years when Ralph had to take his pharmacy exams—first for Junior then for senior license. When he passed, it meant not only that he was ready to be a full-fledged pharmacist, but could also demand a bigger salary. Before that he had earned less than his wife."[14] Taylor's letter also reveals that when they were married, Ralph was not yet eligible for the senior pharmacist's exam because he had not completed his practical training in pharmacy. He was earning $20 a week, and two weeks after the marriage, he lost his job. Meanwhile, Taylor was earning $25 a week as a stenographer, "which wasn't too bad for a girl."[15] Each week, Taylor and Ralph took their combined income, sorting it "in little envelopes—so much for this—this much for that—and dreaming and planning for our future."

Jo surmised that her parents may have wanted to live apart and not be visibly married so that they could pursue their careers, which is supported by Taylor's continued identification of herself as unmarried on her tax returns. Societal and familial disapproval of married women in the workforce was a compelling reason to keep quiet, and Taylor kept the marriage from her employer until 1927 because she thought she would be fired.[16] Still living at home and not bearing any outward signs of her married status such as a wedding ring, Taylor may have preferred not to have any official tax documents that indicated she was no longer single land on Mr. Sutta's desk.

Finances do not explain all the tension in the early years, since the couple experienced the same problems that they always had, most notably their sexual incompatibility. As Taylor confided to the Ralph of her diary, "Confronted with the unhappy conclusion that the one is more sexual than the other—suppose that is the penalty of monogamy . . . Life with you is one heartache after another."[17] Nonetheless, Taylor declared she would rather have her heart broken ten times a day and then patched up by her beloved than "be wedded to one I love not—or who loves me not sufficiently to be sensitive to the pangs caused by love."

Despite the various obstacles, Taylor gradually settled into the role of wife. Her announcement at work that she was married was a significant step in that direction. She wrote to her employer in September 1927—after the religious ceremony:

Dear Mr. Sutta,

The prospect of an avalanche of questions and exclamations assumed such alarming proportions that I am frightened into not saying anything before I left.

It was so much easier to write a letter, go off on my second week's vacation and then have all that week's time in which to grow accustomed to the idea of my being married.

I had seriously considered keeping the fact a secret from the office, merely because I am somewhat skeptical about the attitude of Sutta and Fuchs towards married women employees, despite the frequent assurances (when I sounded for them) that it would not matter. However, I soon realized that it could not have been a secret for long, since outsiders know.

You see, it mustn't make any difference in my status at the office, for I have no intention of leaving, rather, it is my intention to remain self-supporting always.

I will be back at the office next week as

Syd Brenner

Although Taylor insisted on keeping her former job and name once her marriage was made public, she continued to wrestle with her role as a working wife. On November 10, 1927, she was moved to write to Dr. Beatrice M. Hinkle (1874–1953), a renowned feminist and psychoanalyst, asking for guidance about meaningful work for married women. In her response, Hinkle addressed Taylor's dissatisfaction with her job, which the young woman had described as neither mentally demanding nor particularly significant to her. Hinkle wrote, "I would say for a young woman like yourself that in order for you to gain a sense of the value of life and your own well being, it would be necessary for you to take up seriously some kind of work that would interest you and stimulate you, and train yourself definitely for it." Taylor took the advice seriously, or perhaps the advice suited her thinking, because soon after receiving the letter she intensified her involvement in the theater.

Hinkle made another, prescient, remark about the tension between career and motherhood: "Although you have been married two years you say nothing of children but speak of holding your position, therefore I presume you are not considering children. It is also true that children do not necessarily eliminate the discontent of the woman and can scarcely be used for this purpose." Charlotte wrote in her memoir that Ralph expressed reservations about bringing children into the post–World War I world, and here Hinkle addresses how motherhood effectively ends a woman's career. Taylor and Ralph did not have a child for another seven years as they both nurtured their artistic interests.

Not having children allowed the couple to devote a small part of their limited funds to travel, which for them meant short hitchhiking vacations. Carrying little more than a windbreaker, an umbrella, and a camera, they hitchhiked to Norfolk, Virginia, in September 1928, and then to Montreal over the Fourth of July vacation in 1929. Taylor reveled in being mistaken for a boy in her knickers (her "hiking togs") by policemen and potential rides,

Ralph in Montreal

and Ralph's obvious Jewishness got them a ride with a *landsman* and several restaurant recommendations, making them "grateful for Ralph's nose." They snapped photos of each other in fetching poses, collected menus and time-tables as souvenirs, and spent as little money as possible, sometimes having nothing more than a cup of coffee in the morning, sweeping up whatever crackers were in the diner, and finally splurging on a restaurant meal in the evening. Taylor typed up her notes, condescending to the toothless rubes who picked them up, expressing exasperation at running into yet another person like herself who worked for a furrier in Manhattan, seething with indignation at a white man in Norfolk who would not let the young couple ride in the back of the streetcar because it was for "coloreds" only, pitying the too numerous homeless men hassled by the police in public parks, remarking on

Ralph and Syd

the one female driver who picked them up, and chuckling at the assumption that she and her husband were going to Canada in order to escape Prohibition and enjoy a drink.

A telling line Taylor wrote after being overwhelmed by the solemn beauty of Notre Dame Cathedral in Montreal shows the direction of her thoughts: "It seemed to us that we were witnessing a play rather than viewing actuality." Taylor had been soliciting advice about alternative jobs as early as the spring of 1926. One friend wrote, "Remember some time ago—I think it was at that concert we went to, at Carnegie Hall—you expressed a desire to go in for something outside of the Business World—If you're still of the same mind—how about being a librarian—You, who are so fond of books, should be happy in a Bibliotequal (if I may coin such a word) atmosphere."[18] Libraries eventually played a significant role in her career, but at this time Taylor set her sights on the theater.

From 1927 through 1929, both Taylor and Ralph were involved with the Lenox Hill Players, an experimental theater troupe that evolved in part from the Provincetown Players.[19] In a biographical sketch that Taylor wrote in 1964, she recalled, "In my youth, I worked as a secretary in the daytime, but nights were devoted to The Lenox Hill Players, one of the important little theatre groups of the period pioneering in the production of many important plays." The earliest reference to the Lenox Hill Players in Taylor's personal papers is in a letter of November 10, 1927, from Jerome Seplow, the president of the group. Taylor had asked him about how the company was doing, and in his reply he chatted about plays the group was considering and directors asking for too much money. The fact that Seplow did not spell out all the details about plays and people indicates that Taylor was already immersed in his group.

In the Players' eleventh season, Taylor appeared in *The Fires of St. John,* a play from 1900 by German writer Hermann Sudermann. Depicting a love triangle and replete with Christian and pagan symbols, it opened on Monday evening, January 23, 1928. Later in the year, Taylor appeared as the ingénue Helen Atkins in Irving Stone's *The Dark Mirror,* which opened on Friday evening, November 9, 1928. According to the program, the work was "thoroughly an American play," and contemporary reviews suggest that the futuristic melodrama, replete with unemployment, suicide, prostitution, and poverty, was a social critique that accorded with Ralph and Taylor's ideals.

Along with acting on stage, Taylor worked behind the scenes in publicity, guided by Seplow, who gave her detailed instructions about contacting drama critics and editors at several newspapers. That job lasted at least until January 7, 1929. Taylor also served as acting secretary during at least nine executive council meetings in the late winter and spring of 1928, with the last record of her filling such a role occurring in June 1929.[20]

In his letters, Seplow flirted with Taylor. A handwritten note sent on the occasion of her birthday in 1928 reads: "Syd—Your birthday! There are *so many things* I *would* have liked to write you on this day—but—the fates have been unkind to us both and *allow* me only *one.* 'Best wishes for a happy birthday.' If everything could have been a little different—memories. Syd dear, I love you so much that I don't know *what's going to*————— *Jerry.*" He enclosed a pressed rose with the note on this and several other occasions. On November 22, 1928, Taylor wrote the following two-sentence dialogue in her diary, giving no indication of the circumstances or even whether it was completely imaginary: " 'What are you thinking about Jerry?'

Taylor in *The Dark Mirror* with the Lenox Hill Players

'Of the futility of loving a married woman who is in love with her husband.' "
Jo recalls that her mother spoke of Seplow and had a photograph of him in
the apartment, which from Jo's description was a publicity shot from *The
Dark Mirror*.

For his part, Ralph contributed his musical talents to the Lenox Hill
Players, playing the piano during rehearsals.[21] Charlotte adds that he "often
helped with the scenery, advised where to purchase materials they would
need, cautioned them on the threat of plagiarism when they sought to make
contact with a producer of a play they were practicing during a rehearsal."[22]
Whatever Taylor's initial reaction to Ralph's involvement in the Players, she
later expressed some resentment in her diaries.

Charlotte refers to the leader of the Lenox Hill Players as Louis Lazowitz, who can be identified as Lee Strasberg (1901–1982). In her telling, he was
an office worker by day and a generous, if stern and magisterial, theatrical
taskmaster by night: "Only Louis cared frightfully what the critics would say,
lacerated [the actors] with his professional criticism, sometimes made them
do a scene over and over just for the exercise, to punish them for not trying
hard enough."[23] In the 1928–29 season, Strasberg is listed on the group's letterhead as the "producing director." He staged F. Scott Fitzgerald's comedy
The Vegetable, which opened on April 19, 1929, and closed later that month
after 13 performances. "Syd Brenner" is listed in the chorus.

During this time, Taylor wrote at least two letters to Strasberg, and she
kept his friendly replies, which included regards to Ralph. She wrote him
asking for private and group classes for herself and other actors. Strasberg
started one reply (aside from some pleasantries) by jumping into the questions of what kinds of classes he would teach, class size, and the cost of lessons. Revealingly, he says he "was never interested in organizing a Lenox Hill
group but a theatre of a certain kind," responding to a question the Lenox
Hill Players had apparently asked him.[24] In the second letter, which he wrote
from the country, he states that he does not know how he will arrange his
schedule when he returns to the city, but that he could meet with some actors
after their Monday night dance class. Soon Strasberg would be known for the
Group Theater and eventually become famous for developing method acting
and the Actors Studio. Despite his claim to Taylor that "you know I don't like
to teach," he would be successful in teaching his method to several generations of celebrated American actors, including Marlon Brando and Al Pacino.

However exacting the director, Charlotte portrays the atmosphere in the experimental, creative world of the Village and off-Broadway as stimulating and sociable. She remembers "the young intellectuals" gathering in cafes where they discussed "politics, religion, literature, or music."[25] When the Lenox Hill Players "folded for lack of funds," Taylor became involved with the Impromptu Theater under the direction of Dr. Jacob L. Moreno (1889–1974), a Viennese-trained psychiatrist and an innovator in the field of psychodrama and group psychotherapy.[26] During the twenties, he was deeply involved with improvisational theater, and he immigrated to the United States in 1925 in order to develop his theories. Taylor jumped on board along with Ralph and Jerome Seplow. According to the journal of Moreno's organization, Ralph appeared on November 20, 1930, in *Morte d'Arthur,* an "Impromptu Play" presented at the Impromptu Theater in New York City. Six months later, on April 5, 1931, Ralph, Taylor, and Jerry were listed as members of the Impromptu Ensemble in a different, unnamed production.

The next phase in Taylor's creative career was spent with modern dance. As her correspondence with Strasberg showed, Taylor was interested in taking acting classes that included dance, movement, and fencing.[27] The Neighborhood Playhouse was a logical place to turn, and that was where the rising star Martha Graham (1894–1991) was teaching, as well as at her own studio in Midtown. Some of the most famous dancers in Graham's group, such as Anna Sokolow and Sophie Maslow, who performed with Taylor in the early thirties and went on to illustrious careers in modern dance, first began to work with Graham and Louis Horst at the Playhouse and were with her when she formed her group in 1929.

After briefly studying with Margarete Wallman (1904–1992), a disciple of German dancer and choreographer Mary Wigman (1886–1973), Taylor spent several years under Graham's tutelage. In her diary, Taylor never mentions her first meeting with Graham, but Charlotte explains how three Brenner sisters came to study with her. One evening, according to her memoir, Louis Lazowitz (Lee Strasberg) criticized the actresses for being "creaky" and ordered them to take a dance class.

They located a not-yet-famous Martha Graham, who was willing to concede the possibility that interpretive dancing might have a place in dramatic art. For a tiny fee, and the pleasure she derived

from teaching eager pupils, she taught them dancing on the roof-
top gymnasium of an apartment building in midtown. Here they
met and careened in leotards, or plain jersey tights, or pastel-
floating cheesecloth gauze. When they were finished with the lesson they deposited a quarter in a cigar box that paid the rent for
the gymnasium.[28]

Although not officially members of the Lenox Hill Players, Charlotte and
Henny were allowed to participate in the dance classes, where Henny
emerged as a natural talent.

Lazowitz/Strasberg remarked "that he seemed always to be bumping
into one Brenner or another, but their unitedness added stability to his
group."[29] Performing arts touched four of the five sisters. Ella had a gift for
singing and acting, and Henny for dancing. Taylor was an actress and dancer.
As for Charlotte, her ambition from the beginning was to be a writer. Because
she was expected to deliver her essays before large school audiences, she
wanted to develop her skills as a public speaker, and that drew her to Taylor's
theatrical world.

Taylor was typical of Graham's dancers in that she was a working
woman. From the office of Sutta and Fuchs, she moved to the firm of Baker,
Harden & Winans by the spring of 1932. She and her fellow dancers were exhausted by the classes and rehearsals held every evening, some of which lasted
until midnight, but Graham drew them back night after night. A formidable,
demanding woman with a vicious temper and a driving ambition, Graham
nonetheless inspired devotion. Group member Dorothy Bird recalls from the
summer of 1930: "If I were to tell you that she was an absolutely incandescent
teacher at the time, it would be only words. But it was a fact that she set the
students on fire; it was unbelievable."[30] It was Graham's ability to galvanize her
dancers and convince them of the need for total sacrifice that fashioned them
into a cohesive group that propagated her ideas.[31] Agnes de Mille recalled that
"there was always a level of fanaticism, even masochism, in the Graham dancers. They came to be known as the 'Graham Crackers,' and their fanaticism
held to such a degree that it kept the disciples from mentioning pain."[32]

The women Graham chose had other traits in common. They were
"older and often well educated. They came as mature, serious students of the
dance, interested in new ideas. And although they had to work for a living,

they had the time—they made the time—to read, to discuss among themselves, to go to museums, sometimes, if they were lucky, to go to concerts."[33]
Taylor fit that profile exactly, except that she attended *many* concerts, not to
mention numerous lectures and plays.

Graham's undeniable attraction for her dancers was frequently tested.
Several of the group's members recalled how the prima donna threw things
and slapped them when their inadequate work angered her.[34] Her demands
carried over into the women's private lives. Some of the members shared
cramped living accommodations and were expected to subordinate their private lives to Graham's artistic vision.[35] Dorothy Bird recalls her living arrangements in the early Thirties: "We lived about four in a room and there
was a little room off into which those who had a boyfriend or a husband went
about once a week for privacy. And anybody who worked brought hamburg-
ers or spaghetti."[36]

Although the evidence is scant, it appears that Taylor and Ralph rented
their own apartment rather than living with other dancers. Graham's erratic
rehearsal schedule would still have been maddening. Many of the dancers'
husbands thought Graham's unpredictability was intentional. She would say,
for example, that the women had the night off, and then demand a rehearsal.
Joseph Campbell, later known for his work on mythology, quipped, "We
never knew when Jean [Erdman, his wife] was going to be called. It was like
being a fireman. You know, the fire alarm rings and down you go."[37]

Looking back at that time, veterans of the Graham group repeatedly mentioned the relentless practice schedule, lack of income from dance performances, and shared poverty. The dancers' poverty was compounded by the
Great Depression, a situation Taylor found frightening: "This period of depression seemed scarcely to touch me and mine. I could feel sorrowful for so
many others but it was a sorrow outside of me. But I find it creeping in closer
and closer. It's like a deadly plague. We can only sit and watch with bated breath
wondering where next it will strike."[38] In fact, Taylor was never destitute, however tight the young couple's finances, and she acknowledged as much.

Ralph's connection to Graham's group was not only through his wife,
but also through his growing friendship with Louis Horst (1884–1964), Graham's pianist, mentor, and lover. A choreographer in his own right and a su-
perb teacher, the bearlike, charismatic Horst made at least one dancer feel she
got an advanced degree under his tutelage. Marie Marchowsky, a member of

the company from 1934 to 1940, recalled: "There were times when Martha was too tired to conduct rehearsals and Louis would take over. What a disciplinarian he was! He'd sit at the piano, smoking his cigar, and although his hooded eyes appeared to be closed, he didn't miss a thing. His caustic comments on our performance could be formidable. We called him Eagle Eye."[39] In addition to his other talents, Horst was a composer. Marchowsky remembered that Graham choreographed the dances without music, and Horst would see them and then compose the music for them.

All the drama in the studio was in service of a revolution. Considered to be Graham's first major dance in her unique, stark style, *Heretic* premiered on April 14, 1929, and featured the first appearance of her group. With its blunt portrayal of a solitary dancer (Graham) futilely trying to breach a wall of resistant figures, it mirrored Graham's perceptions of her relations with her dancers as well as with a disapproving public.[40] The three-part dance involved "straight lines, angular gestures, geometric formation," and the "group movements were machinelike and killing, those of the soloist (Martha) soft and sustaining."[41] *Heretic* was firmly ensconced in Graham's repertoire by the time Taylor performed in it. Playbills record Taylor's appearance in the dance on January 31 and April 8, 1932, and on March 25, 1933.

Another pioneering dance that explored the tension between a solitary figure and a monolithic group was the three-part *Primitive Mysteries*, which premiered on February 2, 1931. The score by Horst and the dance itself were so well received that the dancers had twenty-three curtain calls on opening night.[42] Native American rituals observed during her travels with Horst to the American Southwest inspired Graham. She was also influenced by Catholicism to create a dance involving sacrifice and an initiate among a group of acolytes.[43] Of course, Graham was the initiate and the center of attention, dressed in white, while the followers were dressed in navy-blue singlets.[44] The first mention in a playbill of Sydney Brenner performing *Primitive Mysteries* was from December 6, 1931, and she performed in it several more times over the next few years.

Taylor was serious about being in Graham's group, as indicated by a series of photographs taken on the beach during this period. On one of her days off, she was practicing dance moves on the sand, several of the positions being labeled on the photos as "stride," "movement 2," and "movement 3 in hipswing." Her bathing suit reveals muscular legs and a trim body. Taylor

Taylor at the beach in Martha Graham dancing
pose

reveled in her body and had no inhibitions about moving it in new ways in
public. When she held different poses, she demonstrated discipline and
composure, as well as strength and concentration.

Another sign of Taylor's seriousness was that she went on the road with
Graham, traveling to cities including Boston, Philadelphia, and Washington,
D.C. Although her scrapbook includes programs from those cities, most of
the performances were in New York, in part because of the expenses involved
in performing and touring.[45] It must be remembered that the educated audience for modern dance was quite small, that the dancers often performed for
other, equally impoverished dancers, and that the country was in the depths
of the Depression. All of those factors contributed to the relative infrequency
of performances compared to the many hours of rehearsal.

In addition to developing as an artist, Taylor benefited from dancing with Graham's group in that it allowed her to continue her involvement in leftist politics.[46] Graham developed dances that reflected the times and matched Taylor's socialist sensibilities. May O'Donnell, one of Taylor's contemporaries in the group, recalled: "In the early 1930s, the time of the Depression and social unrest, Martha created dances of social content that expressed the protest, anguish, frustration, and mood of the times—the angularity, the dynamic intensity, the beat of her body rhythms and movements, the search for the return to the primitive, were all part of this time. Martha could sense those things and in her dances she gave voice to those tensions and feelings that attracted an eager and responsive audience."[47] Graham herself is not seen as a political radical, but many of the women who populated her company in the early 1930s decidedly were, and many came from poor Russian Jewish immigrant families.[48] Women whose names appear alongside Taylor's in the programs for Graham's performances—Anna Sokolow, Sophie Maslow, Lilian Shapero, and Lily Mehlman—were Jewish radicals who went on to become prominent modernist dancers with leftist political goals. With Graham identified in the popular imagination as epitomizing modern American dance, Taylor and her fellow Jewish dancers tried to achieve through dance a drawing together of leftist principles and American identity.

Amid the turmoil of her creative life, Taylor confronted a personal crisis. In the spring of 1932, she resumed keeping a diary, presumably to think through a separation between herself and Ralph, one she called a "noble experiment." During this time, Ralph and Taylor did meet for meals and attend concerts together, but for at least the span of several weeks Ralph did not sleep at home. The first entries are not dated, but several toward the end are, beginning with April 29 and ending with May 10, 1932. As in the diaries Taylor kept when Ralph was hoboing, she composes entries as letters to him—in effect, one long letter she, again, did not send to her husband.

This diary confronts the couple's fundamental relationship, from new issues to old incompatibilities. One of the first words in the diary is *career:* "I have been wondering if perhaps the fault lies in my having made a career of everything but you. I have done so mainly because of you, but that may have nothing to do with it." Taylor believes that Ralph encouraged her to pursue her artistic vocation, but she has begun to question his sincerity. Although she admits that at the beginning of their marriage she might have found "creative expression" in raising children and being a housewife, by 1932 she no longer feels that way. The diary indicates that, like any young couple, Ralph and Taylor discussed domestic life and the possibility of raising children, but that over seven years Taylor's career had moved to the forefront.

The entry organizes many reasons for their marital discord. Those reasons include differing views on how much each of them should focus on outside interests—and by that, she means their artistic careers rather than the jobs they held to make money; the fact that her artistic career seemed on an upward trajectory while his remained static; her sense that she gives more to the relationship than he does; her awareness of change in herself over their seven years of the marriage, which she does not feel he acknowledges; her admission to being a hypercritical scold; his feeling that she does not praise him enough; his indifference to small romantic gestures that are important to her; and her resentment over painful episodes that occurred during their courtship.

Near the end of the diary appears a laundry-list form of argument, a style not reflective of her writing elsewhere. Rhetorically asking what marriage requires to succeed, Taylor identifies seven essential elements:

> Mutual respect and admiration I would put above all. Well, I
>   think there is that
> Physical harmony—not that
> Understanding—not quite enough
> Complete sincerity. I believe I can almost pass on that score. I am
>   not so sure of you.
> Freedom for outside interests. There was that.
> Financial backing—I don't mean a tremendous amount of money,
>   but enough to prevent narrowing of your means of living to a
>   bare existence. There was that.
> And last of all—a sense of responsibility towards each other. Just
>   so much responsibility as would exist between two good
>   friends. There is that—but it is irksome to you.

This is a marriage balance sheet that shows an organized pattern of mind. The frequent changes in verb tense throughout the list indicate that she was trying to encompass their marital history from beginning to end.

Although she considers a number of possibilities in compiling her list, the friction boils down to one thing: Taylor does not like sex with him. "But the more I think about it, the more convinced am I that our unsatisfactory physical relationship is at the basis of your and, consequently, my unhappiness." It will be recalled that Ben Schlamm had written to her about their sexual incompatibility when he and Ralph were hoboing across the country and that previous boyfriends had called her cold and repressed.

In her self-awareness, Taylor approached the problem of their sexual misery from a number of angles. She identified their working lives and incommensurately passionate natures as important causes. Both of them worked all day, and upon returning home Taylor felt there was a natural distance between them.

> You could bridge that gulf by your greater emotional nature, by a physical desire present whether I existed or not.
>
> Not so me—to have met your desire, I would have had to be an exceptionally passionate woman, whose emotions lay close to the surface—or I would have had to have felt myself wooed during the day—
>
> Ridiculously slight things, very unimportant and perhaps silly and childish to you, but necessary to me—
>
> A phone call to find out if I were all right—an occasional gift— a compliment on my personal appearance—to wait to do the thing you wished to, until I might join you—

Before they had sex, Taylor needed more courting.

Taylor frankly acknowledges that one common cause of marital strife is absent, and that is financial instability. Even though this diary was written during the Depression, and the couple knew what it was like to be fired, they were not living hand to mouth and apparently felt that losing a job would not be catastrophic, although Taylor's use of the past tense as well as the anxieties about money that lay in her future complicate that picture. Ralph did have a professional degree and work experience, and the pages of shorthand in the notebook she used for her diary indicate that Taylor was an experienced office worker confident of a steady income.

Taylor realized that not everyone was so fortunate, describing a visit to a woman who had missed a week's work due to illness, and consequently lost a week's salary. The emergency relief fund at her job was already depleted, she was a week behind in the rent, and she lacked a safety net. The visit prompted Taylor to recall Ralph once saying that emotions would fall by the wayside if basic needs such as food and shelter could not be met. She was aware how self-indulgent her focus on their relationship could appear: "It suddenly made me realize that my mental and spiritual troubles were unimportant, to be indulged in only when one's means of existence is secure." Taylor did not engage in a socialist critique of the system that led to her friend's plight, yet another example of her preference for human stories over political theory.

While sexual incompatibility loomed large as the primary reason for their unhappiness, Taylor and Ralph were also proprietary about their artistic pursuits, and Taylor resented Ralph's horning in on her acting and dancing. By this point, she had performed with the Lenox Hill Players, Moreno's Impromptu Theater, and Martha Graham's dance group, and she was confident in her abilities. Ralph had helped out with the Lenox Hill Players, performed with Moreno's Impromptu Theater, had at least taken classes with Graham, and was getting to know Graham's collaborator Louis Horst.[49] Nonetheless, his career in music—his true love—had stalled. Taylor suspected that he had doubts about his talent and the durability of his interest in musical performance. She saw him as envying her opportunities to attain emotional satisfaction through art, to perform in public, and to enjoy the stimulation of competition with a like-minded group of ambitious artists.

Taylor perceived that her interactions with Ralph failed to assuage his anxieties about his artistic talents. She thought that he wanted more effusive, vocal praise of his accomplishments and admitted that she was stingy with compliments. In a rare mention of her mother, Taylor mused in this long entry:

> My fault, that like my mother—I feel it wrong to give praise in person for fear of spoiling that person but think it all right to praise exorbitantly to others. A grave mistake in your case—since it was your realization of my great belief in you which was so necessary. My belief in you is there—always has been but I could not thrust it upon you. Such an expression of my firm belief in you would have to be the over-coming of an inhibition—the inhibition of showing my great affection for you openly.

This reticence in expressing admiration for the achievements of family members, which Taylor uncritically attributes to her mother's example, came to haunt her relationship with her own daughter as well.

Despite Taylor's implication that his artistic ambitions were stymied, Ralph actually played the piano for Graham long enough for her to remember his participation. Years later, Allen Wallace, the director of the Martha Graham Center of Contemporary Dance, wrote to thank Ralph for his significant contribution and also to tell him this story: "I spoke to Martha and she remembered you very well. She told me that you are a wonderful pianist and played for her for many years. She also told me an amusing story about a stray dog that she had found on the street that took a fancy to you and would lie under the piano while you played and not let anyone, including Martha, come near. Martha is a marvelous storyteller, acting out the characters and bringing a story to life with her delivery. I thought you might like to know the fondness she displayed in relaying these stories."[50]

As the Brenner sisters became more involved with Graham, Ralph's friendship with Louis Horst strengthened, and the two of them founded a monthly journal called *Dance Observer*. At the time, there was little professional dance criticism, particularly of modern dance. Few music and drama critics were sufficiently educated or interested in modern dance to be able to educate the public or evaluate authoritatively what they saw. According to Dorothy Madden (1912–2009), a pioneering dancer and choreographer who worked with Horst, inspiration for the magazine came from Ralph, who "rushed into Louis' apartment one day, outraged, infuriated by an article he waved in his hand." The offending article was an unfavorable review of Graham that music critic John Martin had published in the *New York Times*.

> "Why don't we try to fight against this sort of thinking?" Taylor raged, "Martha is more than a woman. She's a primeval force. We should counter this kind of criticism and promote the Modern Dance. Let's start our own magazine."
>
> Louis was interested. He replied, staccato, "Let's."[51]

Ralph contributed his skills for writing, editing, and graphics. At first, the two men put the journal together in their apartments, Ralph's being just one floor below Horst's: "When Louis's lawyer Louis Himber [Charlotte

Brenner's husband] visited in Ralph's flat he recalled bursts of music and pacing from above and mused later 'that's where the idea of the *Dance Observer* was born.' "[52] The editorial board of the first issue, which appeared in February 1934, included Horst, Ralph, conductor Lehman Engel, art administrator C. Adolph Glassgold, poet and critic Samuel Loveman, dance educator Martha Hill, and Winthrop Sargeant, who later became the music critic for the *New Yorker*.

Ralph and Horst stood at the doors of theaters where performances were held, selling copies at ten cents apiece (a year's subscription cost a dollar) until they built up a core of subscribers. Each issue was twelve pages long and featured sketches; by December, photographs appeared, which eventually exhibited remarkably high quality. The improvisatory nature of the magazine's founding is hinted at in the June/July issue, where the editors announce that they had decided to combine the summer issues, yet would honor their subscribers' expectations of receiving twelve issues by extending the subscriptions to fourteen months. Madden also recalls that Horst kept unsold copies under his mattress.

The editors set forth their goals in the first editorial, declaring that they would strive "by just encouragement, by the publication of authoritative studies on the dance, by uncompromising condemnation of the spurious and the pretentious and by serious endeavor to enlarge the intelligent audience for the dance, to permit the present and latent talent in the American dance its fullest scope for expression." The "authoritative studies" fell to Horst, who contributed historical surveys of classical dance forms, but he was not the only one. Naum Rosen wrote "The New Jewish Dance in America" for the June–July 1934 issue, which also had an article on the relationship between dance and music by composer Henry Cowell. Ralph, too, wrote analytic essays, chiefly describing the rise of modern dance in the United States. He focused on pioneers Isadora Duncan, Ted Shawn, and Ruth St. Denis. With its emphasis on American dancers and choreographers, the magazine attacked what it identified as a pervasive prejudice among audiences and critics toward European artistic endeavors, erroneously considered more sophisticated and technically superior to anything originating in the United States.

As for "uncompromising condemnation," it was a job that Ralph and his colleagues relished. While all the other contributors to the March 1934 issue had substantial credentials as choreographers, musicologists, and published critics, Ralph was described simply as "a young student of the dance." He proved to be an impassioned, often irascible, reviewer. He spared no one, not even Martha Graham. During the first three years, Ralph's numerous reviews indicate that he attended performances several times a week. His pet peeves included vapid posing and emoting, the absence of technical skill, and purely decorative exoticism.

A classic review by Ralph in the June–July 1934 issue reveals his acid pen, and records one of several instances when he left a performance early:

> What can the poor critic say when confronted with the problem of discussing the nostalgic sniffing of sprigs of lilac, the factual breast-feeding of a toy infant, billets-doux popping in and out of the bosom, or the harvesting of grain with a Hammacher & Schlemmer scythe, etc. etc., *ad nauseam?*
>
> Realizing that there are times when there is an unutterable futility to the puny process of adjectival description, this reviewer silently thanked an all-wise Providence for the feeblest efforts of our modern dancers, and waited hopefully for the intermission and deliverance.

Similar caustic remarks about other performances demonstrate that he thought modern dance as performed in New York often lacked structure and technical sophistication.

The editors were generally left leaning, so in addition to dance groups who have since been canonized by history, they paid attention to proletarian dance groups, such as the Workers' Dance League. Despite their socialist sympathies, the editorial staff's priority in the review process remained artistic excellence. As self-proclaimed nonpartisan observers, they criticized proletarian dance troupes for failing to achieve their own stated goals. In keeping with editorial policy, Ralph's focus on technical skill encompassed all dancers without favoritism, whether it was Martha Graham or the Workers' Dance League, and he found some of the latter's political subjects ridiculous.

Dance Observer remained in publication from 1934 until Louis Horst's death in January 1964. Ralph was on the masthead throughout that time, except during a break from January 1936 to October 1939. He and his brother Milton bought Caswell-Massey in 1936, which is probably why he reduced his involvement for several years. When his name reappeared on the mast-head, it was as manager and financial adviser rather than writer. He offered space in his new perfume factory on East 25th Street when the magazine needed more room for laying out, pasting up, and mailing, and he "also helped in getting the magazine to the printer, packaging and mailing and did baby sitting in steamy summers in New York when Louis had to teach else-where."[53]

Over the years, many famous people in the arts served on the *Dance Observer*'s editorial board, among them Joseph Campbell, Horton Foote, Lincoln Kirstein, and Marie Marchowsky. Writers for the magazine included John Cage and Woody Guthrie. Guthrie's March 1945 essay on the common man attending a modern dance performance took an "aw-shucks" approach, which showed that the magazine had a sense of humor about itself. Taylor also briefly worked on the magazine; using her maiden/stage name, "Syd Brenner" was listed as "executive secretary" from November 1934 through the summer of 1935.

With the exception of Madden, historians of modern dance and mem-oirists ignore Ralph's role in the founding and administration of the influen-tial arts publication, assigning all credit to Horst. In fact, Ralph's relationship with Horst was not limited to publishing. Eventually Ralph was the executor of Horst's will, suggesting a lifelong friendship. In a travel journal of 1963, Taylor described Horst as one of the only two people she ever knew who were "completely and utterly satisfied with life," the other being musician Walter Bergmann.

Known to show little interest in her dancers' personal lives, Graham did not pursue that same level of intimacy with the Taylors.[54] De Mille thought that Graham was so focused on her artistic vision that she knew she could not afford to concern herself with the details of her dancers' lives and that they all understood and accepted her attitude of indifference. Pregnancy, however, was not something Graham could ignore. In a small folded note from late 1934, Graham addresses a momentous change in Taylor's life.

Dear Syd—I am glad to hear you are better again—stay well—and have a beautiful baby—Personal greetings—and may the New Year bring you much happiness—in your baby and in your dancing— Love, Martha.

Although the note can be read as the casual brush-off of a woman who can no longer serve as a single-minded acolyte in the group, Graham left open the idea that Taylor would dance again, if not necessarily with her.

In a story that recalled Cilly's earlier attempts to end pregnancies, Henny told family members that Taylor tried to induce a miscarriage by falling down the stairs when she realized she was pregnant.[55] If true, the story shows that Taylor did not want to give up her career, and simply in the telling, it reinforced Jo's intuition that her mother did not really love her. In her letter to Mr. Sutta discussed above, Taylor had betrayed a sense of job insecurity when making her marriage public. Insecurity hardly describes her situation upon becoming pregnant, as even other working women such as Beatrice Hinkle assumed mothers did not work. Taylor's resistance to getting pregnant represents a decade of change in her thinking about work and motherhood. Ten years earlier, she had disparaged a newlywed co-worker who did not want to get pregnant for fear of ruining her figure. By 1934, keeping her own figure and personal freedom seemed essential to her artistic career. And yet when she could no longer deny the fact that she was, indeed, pregnant, she threw herself into the role of mother, progressive ideals and creative energies intact.

EIGHT

Progressive Motherhood

1935–1950

TAYLOR MAY HAVE FELT MIXED emotions about her pregnancy, but her niece Harriet Schaffer, Henny's daughter, remembered her happiness at the prospect of welcoming a baby. Physically, the pregnancy was difficult. Taylor suffered from jaundice and from an unrecorded but serious condition that caused her to permanently lose almost all the sight in one eye, a loss that prevented her from ever obtaining a driver's license. Later, when Jo's misbehavior angered her mother, Taylor would bring up the partial blindness that resulted from her pregnancy as further proof of the suffering her rebellious child caused.

When the birth was imminent, the perfectionist Taylor wanted to get her hair done before leaving for the hospital, until Henny managed to convince her sister that there was not enough time. On January 25, 1935, a girl was born to the Taylors. The printed birth announcement named her as Joanne and gave the family address as 87 West 169th Street. Although her mother always called her by her full name, the little girl came to be known as Joan to her grandmothers or just Jo.[1]

Clues to Jo's early days come from an album in which Taylor collected photos, notes on Jo's personality and health, and summaries of visits to pediatricians.[2] The photos show a contented, healthy baby and toddler, frequently in the arms of smiling parents. Jo's first words, tooth, and steps are meticulously recorded. Taylor expresses no sense of burden or impatience, even when remarking on the long nights spent walking the floor with a teething baby. From the photo album of Jo's early years, it is evident that Taylor and Ralph both doted on their daughter, taking note of and delighting in all stages of her development.

Taylor and Jo at four and a half
months on front stoop

Ralph and Jo

Taylor saw in Jo the interests she and Ralph shared:

At 9 months, Joanne starts to sing and dance in time to music. She is not very discriminating about the music—any sort of rhythmic sound is sufficient for her to commence performing. My using an egg-beater or chopping food in a chopping bowl will also act as her cue.

Her steps grow more intricate and varied as time advances.
*****
Ralph gives Joanne her piano lessons daily—it consists of her sitting at the piano and banging away to her heart's delight. We have decided that she is a modernist of the most advanced and atonal school. Schoenberg in comparison sounds like Clementi.

In addition to music and dance, Taylor also refers tongue-in-cheek to her earlier socialist leanings:

19 months . . . Joanne is a believer in one of the fundamental te-nets of communism, i.e. the joint ownership and use of property, the property in her case being toys. When she meets a strange child she always offers the first of her toys she can lay hands on and if that is not acceptable she tries the others, all this, of course, is a preliminary to her taking the other child's toys in exchange. Sometimes she gets into trouble because some of the other kids have a canny knowledge of values and will not yield an impressive toy for an insignificant one.

Making allowances for the dated clothes and the black and white of the photographs, much of the material in the album could be found in any baby book today, with one jarring exception: medicine. The Taylors' encounters with doctors show tension between medical instructions and parental prac-tice. Notes from doctors after regular checkups and visits for childhood ill-nesses reveal that Jo's pediatricians were in the mode of John B. Watson, a parenting authority who "criticized parents for their emotional excess and fail-ure to instill children with proper habits and discipline."[3] Jo's doctors repeat-edly labeled her as spoiled because she wanted attention, and they admonished

Taylor to ignore Jo's cries and refuse to give in to her. When Jo was two and a half weeks old, a doctor wrote: "Do not pick up, coddle and amuse."[4]

Demanding that not only Jo's grandparents but also Taylor herself limit contact with the baby, the doctors insisted on rigid schedules and tightly controlled behavior. One note instructs Taylor to feed the baby specific amounts of formula at four-hour intervals, with a last feeding between 10 and 12 P . M . : "If she does finish let her cry and wait until next feeding. May have water between feedings if crying and awake." Also regulated is the number of times the baby should be turned on her stomach and for how long. Furthermore, the mother is ordered to "stimulate to cry between 4pm–6pm by 'snapping her feet.' " The regimentation did not ease as Jo grew older: "After food give her 30 minutes to take it all. Then remove tray without comment. If she refused any one meal, give the same meal over."[5] It is difficult to know whether Taylor and Ralph actually indulged their daughter, who may or may not have been spoiled, or whether the doctors simply dished out the accepted parenting wisdom of the day regardless of individual circumstances.

One incident that Jo mentioned during interviews later in life was her hospital stay when she was about two years old. Taylor relates the episode at length in the album:

> Symptoms of diarrhea having reached an alarming stage and Joanne not eating a thing for days, we brought her to the doctor again. After examining her, he induced us to leave her at the Babies Hospital for observation. His belief was that the baby was 5% sick, and 95% spoilt but that did not seem to jibe with her physical symptoms as far as we were concerned. Leaving her was naturally quite a sorry mess. The baby yelled her head off and the parents shed a few tears too. We went to see her the next day but only Mother saw her. The nurse reported that she was eating and that the diarrhea had stopped. Since the child was heart-broken at Mother's leaving, it was decided not to see her the next day. We could not continue this Spartan denial for long and showed up the day following. We could tell from our visits that she must have done plenty of crying.
>
> During her confinement at the hospital (5 days—she learnt how to eat without assistance. Also on the advice of doctor, ar-

rangements were made for her to sleep in a room by herself. This latter caused plenty of trouble the first few days at home but perseverance brought excellent results.

When Joanne got home, she tried to make up for all the strict routine she had experienced at the hospital by trying to get all the attention she could from us. We had a miserable time all around for 2 days but finally parents won out and baby was a much better girl thereafter.

We later decided that the above mentioned attitude was probably due to the fact that she was afraid that we would leave her again.

Taylor the writer switched to the third person in recounting the period of enforced helplessness when both she and Ralph were kept away from their sick child, and the memory of her brother Ralph's death almost twenty years before surely passed through her mind.[6]

Taylor herself had been raised by a mother who valued discipline. Taylor's remarks about her mother in diaries and letters were infrequent but consistent, describing Cilly as aloof and stinting in the expression of love and praise. Taylor perceived that her upbringing had repercussions for her relations with Ralph, and she later acknowledged it carried over to her parenting approach. Except for reservations about Jo's hospital stay, Taylor expressed no impatience in the scrapbook with other instructions given by the doctors.

As a new mother, Taylor might have been heavily influenced by her doctors' punitive advice, but when Jo was old enough for school, Taylor and Ralph chose institutions with philosophies toward children that were diametrically opposed to those of their pediatricians. The couple's choices also reflected a shift in attitudes toward educational reforms in the New York school system, which had moved from John Dewey's (1859–1952) practical philosophy of improving society through education to one that "turned inwards and concentrated on freeing individual potential."[7] Describing the 1920s, educational historian Lawrence Cremin observed: "As the intellectual avant garde became fascinated with the arts in general and Freud in particular, social reformism was virtually eclipsed by the rhetoric of child-centered pedagogy."[8] The distinction between social responsibility and individual freedom was never unequivocal, and the rhetoric was one that the

Taylors responded to because it echoed what they had discussed so avidly as teenagers and continued to hear among their bohemian friends in Greenwich Village.

Jo attended nursery school at the Bank Street College of Education, known for its progressivism and child-centered philosophy.[9] The college was conceived by Lucy Sprague Mitchell (1878–1967), an adherent of Dewey's ideas on social reform who had been the first dean of women at the University of California at Berkeley. Mitchell, who saw building "a new kind of education as essential to the building of a better world, a more rational and humane society," became the driving force behind the Bureau of Educational Experiments, which observed how children learn, developed innovative curricula, and mentored student teachers.[10] Educators at what came to be known as the Bank Street School for Children emphasized children's creativity and curiosity, took them on field trips, and in other ways moved away from traditional rote learning confined to the classroom. Harriet Merrill Johnson, who had a background in nursing and had worked at the Henry Street Settlement, directed the nursery school, which opened in 1918.

In 1930, the Cooperative School for Teachers (CST), a teacher training school directed by Mitchell, was established in the same building as the nursery school. Its faculty included Johnson, Elisabeth Irwin (the director of what would be Jo's elementary school), and Polly Korchien. The last was a close friend of Mitchell and taught dancing at the CST. She had studied dance in Germany at a Mary Wigman school and circulated in the New York dance world, the students of Martha Graham and Isadora Duncan among her acquaintances.[11] Students worked with experienced teachers in a variety of schools from Monday to Thursday, and then took classes at Bank Street from Thursday night until Saturday afternoon. A weekly dance class was mandatory, and the curriculum also included music and drawing. The CST drew its students from graduates of elite private colleges, rather than from the working-class women found at most teacher training institutions, and it was some of those highly educated young women who worked in the nursery school. The goal of the school was to train progressive teachers who could spread new methods of learning.

Mitchell also saw the need to improve the quality of children's literature. A new philosophy of writing for children arose because of the rift between powerful New York City librarians and educational reformers. The

librarians, who wielded power because they were the gatekeepers to reviewing and purchasing books, wanted juvenile literature to be comforting and
fanciful, promoting fairy tales and classics such as the works of Lewis Carroll,
Mary Mapes Dodge, and Beatrix Potter. The educational reformers believed
that children's literature should reflect the actual lives of the readers, to be
"here and now." In 1921, Mitchell published the *Here and Now Storybook*,
which became a bestseller among children's books. It included stories to be
read aloud to two- and three-year-olds and ones that could be read by sec-
ond- and third-graders on their own.

In 1937, the Bank Street staff founded a Division of Publications for
writings about and for children. They also established the Bank Street Writers Laboratory, which encouraged writers to "produce books for children
that are consistent with the Bank Street understanding of how children develop."[12] Writers associated with the Lab included Maurice Sendak (*Where
the Wild Things Are*) and Margaret Wise Brown (*Goodnight Moon*). In keeping with the experimental approach of the school, Brown listened to the children in the school, viewing the toddlers through a one-way mirror and taking
notes, and wrote *Goodnight Moon* based on their chatter.

In 1930 the bureau had moved into the old Fleischmann's Yeast brewery
building at 69 Bank Street, where it remained until 1970, when it relocated to
the Upper West Side. The Taylors were living on 21st Street between Seventh
and Eighth Avenues when Jo started school. They were both products of the
traditional public school system, and Taylor had liked school, yet they chose
a progressive, private school at least a fifteen-minute walk away instead of P.S.
11 William T. Harris, the relatively new public school right down the street.
Given their social and professional contacts with liberal, creative people in the
Village, and their interest in psychodrama, it is not surprising that Bank Street
appealed to the Taylors, even though the financial cost taxed them.[13] With
psychologists who focused on the individual child and on creative play as a
method of learning, with staff members who included a dancer from the milieu of Wigman and Graham, and with sympathy for social-democratic values,
the Bank Street School represented an extension of their views.

In 1941, when Jo was six, Taylor made inquiries about getting pregnant
again.[14] She eventually turned to Dr. Alvin J. B. Tillman, a specialist on Park
Avenue, who presumably examined her or at least discussed her situation
with her. On March 11, he sent this letter:

Dear Mrs. Taylor: I have gone over your chart and case very carefully. While it might be possible for you to go through another
pregnancy, it would be taking a very definite chance. Just how
much of a chance, I can't say. You might get a recurrence of your
kidney trouble, as well as a flareup of your eye condition. I would
have no means available to determine whether or not you could
get by this future pregnancy, because I am uncertain as to what
your course would be. Having no way of predicting the outcome
of this pregnancy, I will still advise you against it.

Neither the blind eye nor warnings from doctors deterred Taylor from trying
to have another child in the 1940s, but she was unable to carry a pregnancy to
term. Ethel Brenner, Irving's wife, recalled going from her home on Perry
Avenue in the Bronx to visit her "very ill" sister-in-law in a hospital in
Manhattan after Taylor suffered a miscarriage sometime before 1945.

At this time the Taylors received help from Taylor's parents, her brother
Irving, Tanta Minnie, and Henny's daughter Harriet and her boyfriend Sheldon Schaffer, who married in 1942. For some period during her childhood, Jo
spent every Saturday with her maternal grandparents, where there were no
children to play with. In discussions as adult women, Jo and Harriet realized
that they had vastly different memories of Cilly. Jo perceived her as a "stern
German woman," who was "cold as ice." She recalled snitching a bag of chocolate chips from her dreaded grandmother's kitchen and getting slapped for
her naughtiness. In her grandmother's apartment, every doily had its place
and woe to the child who moved one. Harriet, on the other hand, saw Cilly as
loving and affectionate. They did homework together at the kitchen table
when her grandmother was taking classes to improve her English. Because Jo
was twelve years younger than Harriet, she knew an older, more austere
woman, while Harriet herself, only three years younger than her uncle Jerry,
knew a livelier person accustomed to having young children underfoot.

The Taylors seemed distant from other members of the Brenner family
during the 1940s owing to both occupation and geography. After buying Caswell-Massey in 1936, Ralph and his brother Milton threw themselves into
making it a success, Milton handling its retail division and Ralph taking
charge of the wholesale business. They capitalized on the company's reputation as purveyor of luxury products in The Barclay, the elegant hotel at 48th

Fannie and Simon Taylor with Jo

Cilly and Morris (Courtesy of Judy Magid)

Street and Lexington, as well as cultivating a mail-order clientele.[15] During
World War II, Caswell-Massey faced a labor shortage, and, utilizing her office
skills, Taylor worked for her husband.[16] Meanwhile, many of her relatives
were swept up into military service. Jerry Brenner, Murray Schiner, Sheldon
Schaffer, and Leonard Kornweitz (Ella's son) were all in the armed forces.
Even Irving went before the draft board in the spring of 1945, but was spared
enlistment by Germany's surrender. Because of his age, there was never any
question that Ralph would serve. The concerns of the Brenner soldiers and
their families were young wives and babies left behind, care packages, tight
finances, and survival, while the Taylors had a child with no cousins her age,
a business to run, and relative economic comfort.[17]

The Taylors also stood apart from the rest of the Brenner clan because
they lived and worked in Manhattan, while most of the family lived in the
Bronx. They did join family gatherings, but were not in and out of their relatives' houses to the same extent as the others. In writing to her husband Jerry
during the war, twenty-three-year old Norma Brenner indicated how seldom
she saw her sister-in-law by underlining Taylor's name on the rare occasions
she saw her at family gatherings and remarking on the number of months that
had passed since Taylor had appeared. In contrast, Harriet, Ella, Gertrude,
Ethel, and especially Cilly visited Norma regularly and spoke with her on the
telephone. The Taylors' contribution was often financial, especially helping
Cilly and Morris afford vacations at different resorts, and it is clear that
their economic and social status was recognized as higher than that of their
relatives.

Taylor's marginal position was exemplified by the one memorable care
package she sent Jerry, soon after the harrowing Battle of the Bulge. Having
endured weeks in a combat zone in Belgium, Jerry wrote to his wife about his
sister:

> I ought to scorch her behind. She sent me a box of Pinaud's stuff
> (Caswell-Massey) containing a bottle of *Lilac* lotion for *after
> bathing* (I haven't had a bath in over a *month!*) a box of Lilac tal-
> cum and a fancy jar of the same brand of shaving cream. What
> ever will I do with that stuff. I suppose she meant well. My moth-
> er's pkg was much better. It had tuna fish, cheese, jam, crackers,
> cookies and strudel in it. I ate everything at one sitting!

Family gathering, late 1940s; clockwise from left, Charlotte with baby Susan, Gertie with baby Judy, Murray Shiner, Joe Kornweitz, Lou Himber, Ella, Ralph, Syd, Tanta (in the rear), Cilly, a European cousin "Alfred," Jo, Morris Brenner

Norma commiserated, "Syd must be nuts to send you lilac, anything. A salami would have been better."[18]

Ralph's efforts to support the war effort with Caswell-Massey resources were more successful. At one point he received an order from the British commercial attaché in Manhattan for two hundred leeches "for immediate shipment by air to London . . . Mr. Taylor got in touch with the Hirudorium in Long Island City that breeds leeches and put them, neatly embedded in mud, on a fast ship for Britain."[19] A top-secret order to provide four thousand pounds of oil of birch tar came from the Chemicals Procurement Division in Washington. Ralph "found a neglected supply—just the right amount—in a warehouse at Third Avenue and 170th Street and saw it on its way one dark night, to Turkey." The orders were so top-secret that Ralph never knew the purpose of his clandestine shipments.[20] His business interests intersected with the interests of ordinary soldiers as well. He issued a warning to GIs overseas, especially those in the Mediterranean and North African theaters, who were buying bottles of perfume "concentrate" in the belief that they could return stateside and have the concoction made up into large quantities of Chanel No. 5 or Shalimar. Ralph cautioned that the bottled potions were nothing more than oil and vinegar.[21] Those episodes provided good publicity, but again the Taylors seem remote from the nitty-gritty of wartime life.

After Bank Street, the Taylors enrolled Jo in Greenwich Village's Little Red School House, known for its progressive politics as well as its experimental educational philosophy. Founded in 1921 by educator, psychologist, and reformer Elisabeth Irwin (1880–1942) in an annex to P.S. 61 at East 16th and Avenue B, "Little Red" developed an international reputation for a curriculum that integrated cutting-edge developments in social work and developmental psychology. Although established as an experiment in public education, based on the belief that modern methods of educating the whole child could be implemented on a mass scale, it faced constant attack from public school administrators. Parents also did not always trust that delaying reading until a developmentally appropriate stage or going on field trips would truly educate their children. Progressive reformers and "Villagers" who championed the school found themselves opposed by local residents who considered the focus on emotional development a threat to their children's mastery of traditional subjects. In 1932, the school lost the support of the public school administration, whereupon, sustained by loyal parents, it became a private progressive school, which it remains to this day.

When Jo enrolled in 1941, the school was located at 262 Sixth Avenue (at Bleecker Street). Jo took the subway every day to school. One of her parents walked her to the station, where she paid her nickel, rode the train for two stops, and then walked over to Bleecker Street. By sending Jo to private institutions, even only two subway stops away, the Taylors removed themselves from ongoing struggles in the public schools over funding, staffing, and the use of children's time. The choices they made for Jo's schooling kept the small family within the experimental, avant-garde world in which the parents had been living since the 1920s, from Camp Tamiment to the bohemian haunts of Greenwich Village.

Jo contends that her parents chose Bank Street and Little Red because "they were such progressives." Historian Julia Mickenberg's work on progressive education and progressive parenting analyzes the circumstances that would influence such a choice. Mickenberg links educational and parenting theories to socialism and progressive politics, tracing the evolution of parenting advice in the 1920s and 1930s, which, by the end of the latter decade, emphasized "permissivism," "freedom," and "progressivism," in contrast to the advice Taylor had received from Jo's doctors.[22] Taylor herself must have become aware of this shift, for the Little Red School House actively promoted progressive education, linking it to democracy, which it saw as inherently about equality, creativity, and individuality—much like the values of the YPSLs in the 1920s.

The emphasis on democracy took on added urgency in the 1930s because of the rise of fascism. As the decade came to a close, the Little Red School House published a handbook titled *Democracy,* with a foreword by Elisabeth Irwin. In the section about how democracy is taught to six-year-olds, Mabel Hawkins wrote:

> With the growth of fascism and the terrific attacks on our ideals and institutions and rights, I have felt very strongly that we teachers must lay the groundwork for democracy right here in our primary departments. . . . One does not use the word itself nor does one discuss the clash between fascism and democracy in the world today. But one builds up gradually a cooperative kind of living in the school—a living situation in which sharing is a major social practice.

She went on to explain how the children take turns with chores, help each other with their tasks, and are encouraged to observe and discuss the society they live in, including shabbily dressed, unemployed men and workers on picket lines.

Once World War II broke out, ideals had to be reinforced with practical decisions so that the students could safely continue their socially engaged education. A look at school bulletins from the 1940s gives some idea of how the war shaped Jo's education. Air raids demanded a response, so committees of teachers and parents developed an evacuation plan that would cost $50 a month (about $780 in 2017 dollars). The evacuation was not used, but discussions about air raids and civilian defense, the economic effects of rationing, the production of goods on a war basis and its effect on the consumer, censorship, and Fifth Columnists entered the curriculum.[23] A first-aid course offered by the school enrolled sixty-nine parents in 1942, and small parent committees were established to contact parents in case of emergency, because many of the mothers were at work during the day. With the school's emphasis on engagement with the world in which the students lived, even in the elementary school, as well as her own relatives' military service, Jo was exposed to information about World War II on multiple fronts.

In encouraging the children to ask questions about their environment, teachers and administrators at the Little Red School House opened themselves up to charges of spreading propaganda as early as the 1930s. To an outside observer, the charge of spreading leftist propaganda was not groundless. When asked what she remembers about Little Red, which she attended from 1941 to 1949, Jo says, "This was, at the time, truly 'little Red' as they had us making little dioramas of the Ukraine. We watched as many of our little friends, their parents and our teachers—wearing Henry Wallace campaign buttons—marched in the May Day parade."[24] Historian Arthur Liebman's analysis of the midcentury curriculum of the Little Red School House pointed out how the courses on socialism, labor history, and minorities predisposed the students to radical social change.[25]

In emphasizing respect for all, the administration consciously integrated Jewish and Christian cultures into its programs, even if it sometimes missed the mark. Taylor later told her friend Nettie Frishman that nonsectarian publications had taught her to spell Chanukah with an initial *H* instead of *Ch:* "I am always reminded of the principal at the liberal progressive school my daughter went to—the Little Red School House—at a combined Hannukah and Christmas celebration (before such things were the norm)—spoke to the audience about Chinooka—That is exactly the way he pronounced it. Understandably when you spell it Ch."[26] Furthermore, for all its leftist leanings, the Little Red School House promoted values that complemented Taylor's traditional, German-inflected upbringing. A pamphlet titled "Aims of the Experiment" from November 3, 1939, shows that the values of "organized thinking, industry, [and] order" were important to Little Red's ethos, beginning in kindergarten. Little Red promoted order as necessary to learning, as opposed to paying for individual freedom with classroom chaos.

While the curriculum in Jo's schools was progressive and her teachers committed to the well-being of the whole child, attending the Little Red

School House had some social drawbacks for Jo. Perhaps most notably, because the neighborhood children attended the local public school, they never became her friends. The Little Red School House drew its student body from as far away as Queens, so their tight-knit community was restricted to the school day.

A detailed note from one of Jo's teachers sent to Taylor on February 18, 1946, showed that at least one observer sensed tensions in the home. The teacher had several concerns about eleven-year-old Jo:

> Joanne is a capable child. She's a diligent worker, and she achieves good results, but her work does not contain much sparkle. She herself is rather apathetic a large part of the time. I feel that she is not free or happy the way a child should be. Somehow, and I have practically no knowledge concerning her background, she gives the impression of being a neglected child, and this is something I should like to discuss with Mrs. Taylor after this report is read. The other children's acceptance of her is very great.
>
> In the fine art classes, Joanne's work has developed in skill and maturity. Here, as in the classroom, she is discouraged very easily. On the playground, she is awkward and self conscious, and she needs to be encouraged to play. In school, generally, Joanne reflects a real need for warmth and praise. I hope Mrs. Taylor will call me soon so that we can discuss Joanne's needs and make certain everything possible is being done to meet these. I feel sure she has many potentialities which for some emotional reason, she is not able to develop.

The note was signed by Judith Ehre, who later became a well-known educator at New York University, but no further mention was made in Taylor's papers of a meeting or of other responses to the teacher's concerns.[27] Another teacher's report asked if Jo had been adopted.

The flexibility of the academic program and concern for the individual child in progressive institutions was tailor-made for Jo's emerging rebelliousness. The Taylors demonstrated sensitivity to her needs for independence in the summer as well by seeking out an alternative to the Cejwin Camps, which the Brenner sisters were associated with for decades. Jo attended Cejwin briefly, but she found it too Jewish and did not like being surrounded by relatives. Considering one of the benefits of summer camp to be freedom from familial oversight, she felt cheated at Cejwin. In response, the Taylors sent Jo to Buck's Rock Work Camp in New Milford, Connecticut.

Buck's Rock was founded in 1942 by Austrian therapist Dr. Ernst Bulova (1902–2001) and his wife Ilse, refugees from the Nazis who had studied under Maria Montessori. The program combined manual labor (during World War II, the children were employed at local farms to meet the shortage of manpower), a vibrant arts program, and education in the civic life of small rural towns. Alumna Erica Jong's daughter, Molly Jong-Fast, says she heard from her mother that Buck's Rock was "like a socialist summer camp, a big Jewish liberal Upper West Side camp, where they did chores and cooked the food themselves."[28] Jong also said, "It was the kind of camp for creative kids who were miserable in the kind of camps that made you do color war."[29] Regular activities were scheduled, but the campers could vary their program each day if they chose. Jo later attributed her choreographic success to her three years at the camp.[30]

It was at Buck's Rock that Jo met her first love, a thirteen-year-old girl who completely swept her off her feet. Hannah, a student at Hunter College High School, swaggered, smoked, and seduced. Jo says that Hannah became her girlfriend when she was twelve, and letters show that they were friends by 1948. Several mash notes Hannah wrote to Taylor in the winter and spring of 1949—the only evidence for the relationship between Jo and Hannah at this time—reveal that some sort of crisis developed, which prompted Taylor to interfere in the girls' relationship.

The first extant letter that Hannah wrote to her "Aunt Sid"—corrected in later letters to "Aunt Syd"—tries to clarify a misunderstanding.[31] Taylor had been annoyed to find a locked box in Jo's room. Hannah explained that she had arguments with her parents and she confided in Jo about them via letter, which Jo was discreet enough to store safely away. Jo recalled, however, that most of Hannah's missives were in fact love letters. From January 1 to March 21, Hannah wrote at least one hundred such letters to Jo. Taylor saw through the story, and her initial response was to guide the girls toward a platonic relationship, one Hannah called a more "normal" friendship. Jo's resistance to almost any suggestion from her mother complicated Taylor's efforts.

Ralph, Syd, and Jo at Buck's Rock

Throughout the letters, Hannah portrayed Taylor as a teacher and mentor. She expressed gratitude that Taylor used difficult words, knowing that Hannah would be forced to use a dictionary. Taylor gave her guidance on a birthday present for Jo, suggesting a Jewish star and a photograph of herself and implying that Hannah's original idea was too extravagant or inappropriate in some other way. Taylor also offered advice about how to improve Hannah's somewhat rocky relationship with her family, and Hannah gushed with gratitude and admiration for her friend's parents, addressed as Aunt Syd and Uncle Ralph. Those are the names by which the Taylors were called at Cejwin, and Taylor's tone with Hannah was indeed maternal with a dash of camp counselor and teacher.

Taylor struggled to preserve that tone, given that she was sitting on an emotional powder keg. Hannah was effusive, explosive, and titillating in her letters. On January 20, 1949, she made it clear that Taylor knew that she and Jo kissed. She repeatedly mentioned her "big chance" on the upcoming Saturday to prove to Taylor and to herself that she could keep her emotions in check. Even in a letter from April 25, after Taylor seems to have stated that Hannah blew her chance and that all communications must cease, Hannah pleaded with Taylor to write back to her. She resisted "the drastic steps" Taylor took and begged her not to break up the girls' friendship. Hannah mentioned kissing and holding hands and referred to Taylor's anger that Hannah went behind her back to meet with Jo. Whatever Taylor's orders, Hannah continued to write to Jo at least until August. In fact, the women remained friends for years, and Hannah played a significant role in the breakup of Jo's marriage in the early 1960s.

Taylor gave off mixed signals to the two young girls who fancied themselves in love. Although according to Jo, Taylor knew Hannah was "notoriously a lesbian," Jo thought her mother felt an obligation to help her. Jo maintains that Taylor encouraged the relationship, pushing the girls together and "suggesting we take naps together," but she tried to modify their behavior as well, as glimpsed in Hannah's letters. That the girls discussed gay desire with Taylor at all showed her to have been progressive and cosmopolitan as well as protective.

During Taylor's lifetime, middle-class understanding of and attitudes toward lesbianism passed through several phases. When Taylor was young, romantic attachments between women could be considered normal and even spiritually uplifting. Girls had crushes on each other and on female teachers, wrote passionate notes, and gave sentimental gifts. As adults, women might choose to live with other women, especially if they were committed to the independence of a professional life. The progressive educator Elisabeth Irwin, who played an essential role in both schools Jo attended as a child, had a relationship with a woman that lasted over thirty years. The two women raised several adopted children together, and were buried next to each other.[32] Although documentation is spotty, passionate emotional attachments between women often did not involve genital sexuality, something later generations had difficulty believing.[33] A recurring theme in Charlotte Brenner's memoir is her relationship with a young English teacher, which filled the girl with the exhilaration and confusion of love, but did not seem abnormal or perverse. Such a crush was not seen as inappropriate.

By the 1920s, sexual possibility between females was more openly addressed. When Taylor frequented Greenwich Village in the 1920s, it was a time of "lesbian chic" and the Village was one of the freest places in the United States for sexual experimentation.[34] According to historian Lillian Faderman, a community of lesbians formed in the Village, its social activities centered on a block of nightclubs near the Provincetown Players, where the theater group that was the precursor to the Lenox Hill Players performed. The Taylors' long involvement with the artistic community of Greenwich Village guarantees that they had first-hand experience of homosexuality.[35] When the relative license of the 1930s and '40s gave way to the strictures of the 1950s, the Village remained more hospitable than many other places to lesbians, especially if they exercised discretion.

Not all women who experimented sexually with other women claimed a lesbian identity. Many intellectuals of the time, bohemian or not, were greatly taken with Freudian theories of sexuality and floated the view that lesbianism was a phase that women needed to pass through, sexual repression being a more acute form of neurosis than engaging in love affairs with other women. Some lesbians internalized that idea, which they considered preferable to being viewed as mentally unbalanced, perverted, or sinful.[36] The implicit assumption remained, however, that lesbian relationships could never be as serious as companionate heterosexual relationships.[37]

Others found the experimentation a disturbing sign of illness or immorality, even political subversion, and it was that condemnation that eventually dominated discussion during the late 1940s and 1950s.[38] Childhood feelings formerly treated with sympathy were stigmatized as abnormal and in need of treatment as soon as they presented themselves. Being lesbian in the late 1940s was considered by many a sin, a crime, or a sickness, and any parent would be concerned about what a romantic relationship between girls signified. Attraction between young women could indicate deep friendship, but faith in psychology led parents to identify it as the poisonous manifestation of deep-seated problems of childhood. It is in this context that Taylor's involvement in Hannah and Jo's relationship should be seen. Circulating in the bohemian atmosphere of the Village was not necessarily correlated with acceptance of lesbianism for one's own child.

Hannah's letters reveal Taylor's anxiety about the potentially unwhole-some nature of the girls' friendship, but her approach seems cautiously flexible rather than condemnatory. As revealed by her actions, Taylor saw Jo's incipient lesbianism as both undesirable and malleable. It was during this period that popular understanding of homosexuality passed from limiting it to discrete sexual acts to considering it a definition of individual identity. By putting an end to acts of sexual intimacy, Taylor had every reason to think she might put an end to her daughter's unproductive development as a person. At that time, it was not common for women to be self-supporting, and lesbianism would preclude a financially secure, safe, heterosexual marriage. Furthermore, as a Jew in a society that countenanced anti-Semitism, Jo risked being doubly marginalized if she pursued homosexual relationships.

Taylor's concern for her daughter appears benign compared to the re-actions of other parents. Some women were disinherited, and one family set up a gravestone with their daughter's name on it and announced her death in the newspaper when she came out in the 1950s.[39] Others institutionalized their daughters in psychiatric hospitals, where electroshock therapy was con-sidered legitimate treatment for homosexuality.[40] It cannot be overempha-sized that middle-class girls and women were frequently constrained by discomfort with the open discussion of sexuality. Gertie's daughter, Judy Magid, says that theirs was the generation that "did not talk about things." Harriet Schaffer remembers that when she was about to marry, her mother, Henny, could not talk to her about sex: "She just told me I better not get pregnant. She couldn't talk about menstruation; she gave me a book. She couldn't talk about sex at all." If heterosexual relations were not spoken about, homosexual ones were buried even deeper.

It was not only social taboos that led to silence, but also the absence of a vocabulary for intimate relations among women, which increased the diffi-culty of distinguishing between socially acceptable crushes and deviant be-havior. Many women of Jo's generation who were questioned about their experiences did not know "lesbian" as an identity. Some said that they did not think of their feelings for other women as lesbian, but as "two people who love each other."[41] When same-sex affection became interpreted as a sign of mental illness that could lead to a woman's institutionalization, the tendency toward secrecy only intensified.

That lack of vocabulary and reticence toward speaking openly about sex may help explain why much of Taylor's involvement with Hannah and Jo was conducted by letter. Letters allowed writer and reader to avoid a face-to-face confrontation, to use euphemisms without being forced to expand upon them, and to have time to consider a volatile situation. In Taylor's case, an added aspect to the use of letters as a way to address her daughter's emerging sexuality is her history of viewing emotional turmoil through a literary lens. As we have seen, Taylor was conscious of herself as a writer who experimented with shaping a narrative when she wrote in her journals. Here, too, she was collecting material. Taylor kept the letters from Hannah to herself and Jo and put them in binders. Jo speculates that her mother considered writing a book about the girls' relationship.

Taylor's attempt to grapple with Jo's sexuality included giving her the classic lesbian novel *The Well of Loneliness*. Even though letters attest to Taylor's efforts to break up the relationship, Jo ventured that her mother gave her the book because she saw how Jo felt about another girl and wanted to help Jo understand who she was, using literature as the means. Published in England in 1928, the novel by Radclyffe Hall concerns an aristocratic woman, Stephen Gordon, who realizes from an early age that she is attracted to women. Her father "protects" her feminine mother from the knowledge, and when he dies, the mother comes to loathe her unnatural daughter, whose mannish behavior repels her. After a scandal erupts over Stephen's relations with a local woman, her mother orders her to leave the family home. Before departing, Stephen comes across a volume in her father's study about human sexuality by the psychiatrist Richard von Krafft-Ebing (1840–1902). She discovers that her condition is called "inversion" and realizes that her father had purchased this and other books in an effort to understand his unusual daughter, this "man trapped in a woman's body." Stephen becomes a famous author in London, but still experiences ostracism. She finds female camaraderie in an ambulance corps in France during World War I and settles in Paris, where her lifestyle causes no scandal. She spends many years in the capital, developing a sexual liaison with young, feminine Mary Llewellyn, whom she met during the war. Stephen ends up alone when she insists that her lover follow her heart and marry a young man who can provide her with children and respect.

Because of the subject matter, the book became the focus of an obscenity trial in England when it was first published, and was banned. By the 1940s, legal challenges to its publication in the United States were in the past. Jo said her mother gave her the book in 1949, and although she remembers it being banned at that time, it was not actually illegal to publish or own it.

Hall's novel comes up repeatedly in interviews with lesbians of the 1940s and '50s.[42] It was sympathetic to the main character, readable, and conversant with the language of psychiatry, which was the filter through which society viewed homosexuality. Faderman asserts that although it was published in the late 1920s, it "remained important into the '50s and '60s in providing an example of how to be a lesbian among the young who had no other guide."[43] Seventy years later, Jo said she "fell in love with Stephen Gordon and has been looking for Stephen all her life." Although the aristocratic world of wealth and upper-class British privilege portrayed in the book was far from that of Jewish girls in New York, the novel presented comfort through its fictional world. Young women faced with the complexity of their sexuality gravitated toward books that helped them tell their own stories, not academic tomes on abnormal psychology.

The Well of Loneliness was also one of the few sympathetic literary works about lesbians available in the 1940s. Much other literature about lesbianism consisted of either academic studies or pulp novels in which deviant women committed suicide, went mad, or saw the error of their ways and were saved by heterosexual marriage. The endings of those books often erased lesbians because they were written for a heterosexual readership. Furthermore, censorship rules encouraged publishers to condemn deviant behavior, which could not be rewarded with a happy ending. In contrast, even though Stephen Gordon ends up alone, her identity as a lesbian remains unshaken.[44]

The question can be asked whether Taylor gave her daughter the book as a deterrent or as a form of acceptance. The latter seems more likely, because Stephen is too sympathetic a character and the book too complex for it to be a warning. Had Taylor wanted to eradicate lesbianism from her home, she hardly would have given Jo such a book. Taylor and Jo were also not unique in having a struggle over sexuality be a flash point in the mother-daughter relationship, a tension not exclusive to girls attracted to girls.[45]

Jo's determined independence asserted itself in her artistic and educational choices as well. Like her parents, she was interested in music, studying the piano, and in modern dance, which she learned at the New Dance Group, where many of Martha Graham's dancers were active. The group had been founded in 1932 with the goal of promoting social change through dance and movement. The students included ordinary workers and professional dancers. For a dime, participants could participate in an hour-long dance class, an hour of improvisation based on a social theme, and an hour of discussion on social issues. They performed under the umbrella of the leftist Workers Dance League, whose performances Ralph had reviewed in the 1930s. Despite their shared interests, Jo showed her independence by playing popular music and taking tap-dancing lessons at the Jack Stanley School of Dance at Broadway and 51st Street. Her mother may not have chosen those forms of expression for her, but she thought it was better than nothing.[46]

Because of her artistic interests, Jo pushed to attend the High School for the Performing Arts (HSPA), located at 120 West 46th Street in the Times Square area. Established in 1947, it was a public specialized school created for students to concentrate on dance, theater, and music. Jo auditioned for the dance program, and retains to this day vivid memories of the creative fervor that pervaded the halls. Robert Joffrey and Sidney Lumet, "two starving teachers before they were famous," taught dance and drama in the early 1950s. Many of Jo's classmates also carved out distinguished careers in the arts.

At first, Taylor objected to Jo's choice of school. She wrote to her parents that Jo "chose this school on her own volition—I didn't want her to go there. I pleaded with her from the beginning to give it up because I wasn't impressed with their academic work. But she wouldn't listen—this is what she wanted."[47] At HSPA half the day was spent on the student's artistic specialty and half on academic subjects; to be sure, any program with a dual curriculum raises reasonable concerns that it favors some subjects at the expense of others.

In the spring of 1952, Jo put her parents in a quandary when she declared she wanted to change schools in order to get an academic diploma. This time it was her parents who insisted that her arts program provided all the academic subjects necessary for college entrance and that she should stick with what she started. Taylor wrote, "It would represent a giving up of something in the middle. I feel that for her character's sake, she should be forced to see it through. If she wants to give up dancing afterward, it'll be all right with both of us."[48] From a practical point of view, none of the district high schools in the neighborhood met the Taylors' standards, Jo was not eligible to enter a different specialized high school, and neither parent wanted to spend the money on a private school. They let the matter simmer over the summer, and Jo stayed at HSPA.

Choreography turned out to be Jo's strong point. She pursued choreography at Buck's Rock during the summers of 1950 though 1952, and at the high school she formed a dance company in September 1952, organizing a group of fifteen dancers, eight boys and seven girls, ages fourteen to seventeen.[49] Her choreography and the company's dancing won the school's choreography award, and the young artists performed around New York, including at the Henry Street Playhouse, and appeared on television. Like her parents, who had been active in the formation of arts organizations such as the Lenox Hill Players and *Dance Observer* magazine, Jo was eager to take charge and make things happen.

Also like her father, Jo wrote about dance. She published several pieces for *Dance Magazine* in the winter and spring of 1953 when the monthly periodical invited a group of dance students at HSPA to serve as guest editors of the "Young Dancers Section." Each student was responsible for a specific month, and in months when other students were the principal guest editors, Jo contributed pieces on the advantages of having parents interested in dance ("An Embarrassment of Riches"), on the tribulations of sitting in the cheap seats at dance recitals ("Heaven on the Side"), and on the stereotype that dancers are stupid and uneducated ("Dancers Dumb! Sez Who?"). In the March issue, Jo took charge of the entire section, which she filled with a long article of her own titled "The Experience of a Young Choreographer in Working with a Group."

Opening a window into her relations with her parents, Jo's articles suggest that Taylor and Ralph supported her, yet expected her to be independent. They also reveal a tension between her increasing maturity and a hunger for the radical experimentalism of youth and its unfettered independence. In "An Embarrassment of Riches," Jo admits that she wanted nothing to do with her parents' artistic milieu until it suddenly dawned on her that the presence of Louis Horst and Sophie Maslow in her home provided her with unmatched access to a world she found increasingly engaging. Adults were not expected to step in and solve her difficulties, and in general, they seldom intruded upon the world of dance and friendship depicted in the articles. That is not to say that family members stood on the sidelines. Bemoaning the difficulty of providing costumes without money or sewing skills, Jo acknowledged receiving help from her relatives.

Jo's company originally planned to rehearse in her family's apartment on 250 West 24th Street, but, her article continues, "After practically being evicted by the lady downstairs for dancing on her head (I live in an average New York apartment with a big studio mirror in the living room), I realized all too fully the necessity of rehearsal space." Discouraged by her inability to find an inexpensive studio in New York, she had a moment of inspiration and found room at the YMCA just down the street. She and her company were required only to pay $2 a year for membership, which included use of the gym and pool, and to perform periodically: "I now carry around a white card stating that *Miss* Jo Taylor is a member in good standing of the Young *Men's* Christian Association" (italics hers). Her writing reveals her pride in finding a creative solution to a potentially intractable problem.

The picture Jo draws in her articles of family harmony and shared love of dance is contradicted by her adult memories of her high school years, during which her relationship with her parents became increasingly contentious. Conflict broke out not only over Hannah, but also over how Jo dressed and wore her hair. Jo was a chubby child who became enamored of glamorous Hollywood movie stars. She shopped for high heels and luscious red lipstick, wore lots of jewelry, and hid in her room to dye her wild "mousy brown" hair jet black. All that stood in stark contrast to Taylor's classic style, which included long hair pulled back tightly in a bun and no makeup. Jo retains a vivid memory of her mother's indignation when she came home with a pair of precariously high-heeled shoes that she considered the height of fashion, and her mortification when Taylor dragged her back to the store and demanded that her daughter return the offending purchase, exclaiming that she could not believe the salesperson would sell such shoes "to a child!"

Taylor's correspondence with Cilly corroborates her daughter's memories about their tense relationship. Taylor worried that Jo did not apply herself enough: "Her philosophy is so different from mine—or even Ralph's. She is bent upon enjoying herself without understanding that the truest enjoyment comes from creative efforts—That without work, one can never be happy . . . In Jo's case, Ralph and I hope it is merely a manifestation of teenageness."[50] It was Cilly who reassured her daughter that Jo was a bright girl who would turn out just fine: "Please don't worry so much about Joanne. Just because everyone tells her what to do she becomes stubborn and does the other thing believe me she is a Taylor and let her take her time what she want to do you will see in the end she will do the right thing and you will be proud of her yet."[51]

Taylor did try to be supportive, and she expressed tremendous pride in her daughter's achievements to her literary acquaintances.[52] In the winter of 1953, describing the excitement of the teenage dance group's successes, Taylor wrote to her editor: "It's been good for Jo. She needed some triumph of her own—and it's certainly adding immeasurably to her self-confidence."[53] She mentioned to acquaintances that Jo's dance group had performed at the 92nd Street Y ("one of the cultural centers in New York City particularly where the arts are concerned") and won a $200 prize on television and that Jo appeared in a profile in *Seventeen* magazine.[54] Taylor's letters reveal awareness that having an award-winning mother and a financially successful father was not easy for a child, and she expressed regret for neglecting Jo after the publication of *All-of-a-Kind Family*.[55] Taylor's obligation to cope with an obstreperous teenager just when marvelous opportunities for her own creative development suddenly opened up would reasonably lead to tension on both sides, and drama was ingrained in the family's approach to problems.

Jo felt her mother wanted nothing to get in the way of her partnership with Ralph and that her father always took her mother's side. The strain finally drove Jo to leave home during her senior year of high school. She could not wait to get out of the house, and her rebellion suddenly became decisive over wanting to shave her legs. She bought a razor and shaving cream, the sight of which made her father erupt. He declared, "Nobody in this house shaves her legs!" So Jo picked up her razor and left.[56] In an interview, she claimed that her parents never came looking for her. They knew where she was and that she was safe, but they did not check out her situation for themselves. The Taylors' apparent detachment led to unresolved, persistent anger. They did keep themselves sufficiently informed to attend Jo's high school graduation, but she did not speak a word to them that day. No hint of this episode appears in Taylor correspondence.

Jo was not alone in her struggles with a Brenner mother. Every daughter interviewed remembered her mother—whether Henny, Taylor, Charlotte, or Gertie—as domineering. Harriet said, "Even when I was a kid she was the kind of mother who told me how to do it. If I had a toy she had to show me, tell me, push me . . . Let me tell you, all the Brenner girls were pushy. They were ALL like this." Susan confirmed that her mother could be controlling, saying Charlotte used to monitor what she ate all the time, and Judy made similar remarks about her mother, Gertie Schiner. Competition drove the family dynamic as much as generosity and companionship. Harriet said, "Among the sisters I always had the impression of very intense sibling rivalry. They were always cutting each other in indirect and direct ways." When mealtime discussions grew heated, Judy recalled, Charlotte's husband the attorney refereed: "Lou was like the monitor, telling people when they could speak. The sisters were always shouting and interrupting each other."

One way personal conflicts expressed themselves was through food. The family often gathered on Friday nights at the apartment building in the Bronx where the Schiners lived in the unit below Cilly and Morris. Henny would pick up several boxes of cake from the bakery on her way to dinner, even though she was repeatedly admonished not to. Charlotte's obsessions with diet and nutrition appeared at an early age, and she was convinced that, at five foot four, she towered over her sisters because of her healthy eating habits. Many of the cousins have memories of food being used to control or undermine other family members—Henny's insistence on cakes, Taylor's focus on low-fat, healthy meals, and Charlotte's implied anorexia being mentioned in numerous interviews. They remember their relatives as grossly fat or exceptionally thin, pushing food on them or withholding it. In response to a thank-you note from Jo for a gift of nuts, Cilly injected a warning: "Glad you like the nuts but you probably have to be careful with them as you have to watch your weigh [sic]."[57] Jo's development from chubby child to dieting model is a story she tells with relish, and her letters to her parents in the 1950s rarely lack some mention of dieting or weight loss.

Even amid the commotion of those Sabbath meals, coolness between various family members could last for years. When Jerry was discharged from the army in early 1946, he did not want to return to Morris Brenner & Sons, located at 55½ Columbia Street on the Lower East Side since the late 1930s. He had worked in the shop while in high school and hated the brutally demanding work, especially in the cold of winter, which left his hands filthy. Morris had a heart attack in the early 1940s, and the family hoped that he would close the store. When it looked as if Irving would be drafted, the end of the rag business seemed inevitable, but Irving remained a civilian, and Morris continued to commute to the Lower East Side via subway as long as his health permitted. Even if he only sat in a chair as Irving did the work, he clung to his identity as a working man.

Jerry was invited to work for Ralph, who was developing Caswell-Massey's mail order business. After two years, during which time Jerry took advantage of the GI Bill to take classes at the Columbia College of Pharmacy in perfumery and cosmetics, Ralph fired him. Jerry speculated that Milton worried that his growing influence would jeopardize his own sons' position as heirs to the business and pressed Ralph to push him out. According to Jerry, he and Ralph did not speak for years, even though they sat at the same Sabbath table, and Jerry held a grudge against his sister for not taking his side or even showing a modicum of sympathy. After Ralph fired him, Jerry found work in the trucking company of Henny's second husband, Harry Davis, where he stayed until Davis's death in 1963.

While choices of job and house can lead to distance among siblings under normal circumstances, spouses and cousins noted that Irving and Jerry were sidelined and never had as close a relationship to their sisters as the women had with one another. Irving's wife, Ethel, remembers the sisters being close, and although she was included in family activities, "sometimes you felt you couldn't get into the clan, you were an outsider." Charlotte and Lou were especially close to the Taylors, with similar interests in dance and psychodrama. Lou and Ralph also shared a personal connection to Louis Horst. Susan recollects accompanying her parents to the Taylors' apartment, where the intellectual adults talked about books and music.

Tanta helped temper the dominant role the Brenner sisters played in the family. At Morris and Cilly's golden wedding anniversary in 1949, Cilly made a speech in which she kvelled that she was such a lucky woman to have five daughters, just like the five fingers of her hand, omitting any mention of Irving or Jerry. Tanta Minnie called out, "Just remember you have two sons!"—a feisty interjection that became part of family lore. Jerry had fond memories of his aunt fixing enormous lunches of kreplach, pot roast, and chicken for him when he worked in the rag shop, insisting that she was a much better cook than his mother. Into the late 1930s, Tanta lived in a ramshackle walk-up on Sheriff Street around the corner from the store, with a wood-burning stove in the kitchen and the toilet down the hall. Eventually she moved to the East Bronx, but what everyone remembered was how much time she spent in their homes, caring for the children and taking charge of the housework. Taylor acknowledged her aunt's role in their lives by dedicating *Downtown* to her.

The Brenners' competitive nature turned to creative, as well as contentious, outlets. In all the interviews and documents, artistic expression emerges as one of the family's most revered values. Everyone painted or sewed or sang or wrote. Morris made elaborate dollhouses for his granddaughters and gardened. The family treasured his papercut, as we have seen, and heated disputes arose over who should get it when he died. Publishing articles in newspapers, the more prestigious the better, mattered a great deal to Charlotte from an early age, and she basked in her father's pride when her essays appeared in Jewish publications.[58] As an editor for the YMCA, in 1942 she wrote *Famous in Their Twenties*, a collection for young adults of inspirational biographical sketches about contemporary figures such as Norman Bel Geddes, Paul Robeson, and Margaret Bourke-White.[59] To research the book, Charlotte traveled to the home or office of almost every celebrity she profiled, where she met with them personally or with a close relative. In her letters to Jerry in the mid-1940s, Norma noted that Charlotte had articles published by *Parents Magazine* and *Woman's Home Companion*, for the astounding sums of $50 and $250.[60] Obtaining recognition of and payment for artistic efforts spurred on the Brenners and increased their value within the family circle.

During these years, the Taylors remained close to Ralph's family. Simon and Fannie lived in the Bronx and worked at the Caswell-Massey store in The Barclay hotel. The older generation still enjoyed reasonable health and were not yet the source of anxiety and strain that they eventually became. Ralph's sister Lucille had married Rabbi Abraham Ruderman and went wherever he found a pulpit, yet visits to the city were frequent enough that Taylor grew quite fond of her nephew and niece David and Naomi.[61]

Taylor continued to take dance classes while working at home and at Caswell-Massey, yet a completely different chapter in her artistic life was about to begin. When Jo was about seven, Taylor began writing down the bedtime stories she told her daughter about her own childhood. As Jo was bringing home from school the fruits of her progressive education in the form of school projects and newsletters for her parents, Taylor was putting on paper the words that would define her as a writer and bring Jewish children's literature into the mainstream of American society. But before Taylor became a published author, she honed her skills of writing for children at an important Jewish institution—Cejwin Camps in Port Jervis, New York.

Camp Cejwin

1942–1960

BEGINNING IN 1942, TAYLOR JOINED ELLA as an employee of Camp Cejwin, in Port Jervis, New York, ninety minutes from Manhattan by train. Cejwin was founded in 1921 under the auspices of the Central Jewish Institute (CJI), and by the early 1940s it was a flourishing institution in constant expansion. Through Ella's connection to the CJI in Manhattan in the early 1930s, all of the Brenner sisters eventually worked in some capacity for the camp, several for decades, and some of their children later worked as counselors.[1] Until the mid-1970s, Taylor served as the drama and dance director of the Hadas camp for younger girls (ages seven to eleven), writing new plays and pageants each year, in addition to choreographing dances and directing performances. Her summers at Cejwin combined many strands of her life: attachment to her sisters, involvement in progressive education, interest in molding a Jewish American life, and experimentation with artistic expression. Because she went to Cejwin for so long and had similar experiences summer after summer, this chapter occasionally jumps ahead chronologically, before returning to 1950 and Taylor's transformation into an award-winning author.

Complementing the role of public schools in the Americanization of immigrants, Jewish summer camps shared a primary goal of nonsectarian American camps, which was to raise healthy, independent citizens. In the years after World War II, as many as one in six camper-age children attended camp each summer, so the impact on American childhood was significant.[2] For Jews, summer camps also became places to promote knowledge of and pride in Jewish culture and to reshape tradition for their modern American children. The historian Jonathan Krasner has shown that the rise of Jewish "cultural camp-ing" was guided by an innovative group of educators, the so-called Benderly Boys, whose mentor and teacher was Samson Benderly (1876–1944), who in turn was greatly influenced by John Dewey. Albert P. Schoolman (1894–1980), the founder of the CJI and of Camp Cejwin—and later, Ella's husband—was one of Benderly's disciples. The camp Schoolman created exemplified some of the ideas of Dewey and other progressives that were familiar to Taylor from the Bank Street School and the Little Red School House.

As mentioned, the massive immigration the Brenners took part in led to overcrowded cities, with their attendant poverty, disease, and crime. Social reformers and philanthropists eyed vacation camps in the country as yet an-other mechanism for social progress, allowing poor urban children to escape to the fresh air, thereby both benefiting public health and reducing delin-quency. Often motivated by epidemics of influenza and polio, Jewish philan-thropists and organizations subsidized that goal of safeguarding children's health. Trends discussed earlier about progressive education surfaced in these summer camps, including an emphasis on direct experience, on the development of the whole child, and on democratic relations among teachers and students.

By the 1930s, Jewish camps were a mass phenomenon for all socioeco-nomic groups. Just as it became hard to define a mainstream "American" camp, as the initial antimodern institutions that romanticized the great out-doors and frontier life expanded to include a vast range of ideological camps catering to different socioeconomic or politically inclined groups, Jewish camps also came in different flavors. Some were private commercial estab-lishments, while others were associated with Jewish organizations. They each coped with the effects of modernization and assimilation on Jewish identity and encouraged campers to marry among themselves. Yiddishists and Hebraists, Labor Zionists and cultural nationalists, Communists and so-cialists, Reform, Conservative, and Orthodox—the full range of Jewish life in America found expression in summer camps.

Camps of all varieties became laboratories for progressive ideas after World War I. As progressive Jewish educators perceived an opportunity to apply their theories in a novel environment, they, too, began to hire social workers and innovative teachers as camp staff. Samson Benderly's disciples believed that observing children in order to understand their psychology, quantifying those observations, developing a modern pedagogy using scientific methods, and engaging students in the experience of education would produce a system of Jewish teaching equally at home in an urban classroom or a camp nature center. Schoolman saw summer as a "difficult school problem," because educators had to promote fun outside an academic setting while continuing to teach their young charges. He set out to solve that problem by perfecting the Jewish summer camp.[3]

Historian Jenna Weissman Joselit identifies two primary goals of Jewish progressives: assimilation and "ethnic persistence."[4] The purpose of outdoor activities was to produce healthy American children, thus demonstrating that Jews could be like everyone else. Camping also allowed progressives to gather Jewish children together away from distractions and to give them a Jewish education in an enjoyable way, without their awareness that they were being educated. The goal was to make them active participants in Jewish life, hopefully for the rest of their lives. Camp activities were to be imbued with Jewish values and culture in order to ensure the survival of the Jewish people then buffeted by modernism and anti-Semitism.

The combined strands of identity were so integral to the CJI, Cejwin's founding institution, that the phrase "Judaism and Americanism" was carved above the doorway of its Manhattan building. The CJI was created in 1917 in order to provide quality Jewish education to the New York community. As traditional immigrant communities assimilated and their children grew up with widely varying standards of education and practice, community leaders realized that they needed to build new kinds of institutions in order to strengthen Jewish life in America. Some envisioned the synagogue as the future of organized Jewish life, while others, like Albert Schoolman, looked to the school. Under Schoolman, the CJI served as a model school and community center.[5] Gathering recreational and educational facilities in one building in order to serve families, regardless of background or affiliation, was a revolutionary idea, which led to tension with more conservative Orthodox synagogues in New York, but it eventually became a model for American Jewish life.

That tension was attenuated in the setting of a summer camp, which by definition existed to provide both recreation and education. The origins of the CJI Camp (a name changed to Cejwin Camps in 1933) lie in a two-week vacation provided to some twenty girls and their teachers in 1919, little more than a summer school in the country. Schoolman quickly realized that he could use summer vacation to apply his vision of modern Jewish education, and the CJI Camp was founded in 1921 as a Zionist, pluralistic camp. At first, the camp continued to serve a working-class population by providing free or heavily subsidized vacations in modest rustic surroundings, along with an intensive Talmud Torah education and an emphasis on Jewish living. Schoolman held that "the program of activity should be directed to strengthen the curriculum of the Talmud Torah and to broaden it, especially along lines of experience in *the art of Jewish living.*"[6]

In part, Schoolman developed his ideal camp to correct what he considered the faults of other institutions. He disparaged Jewish camps of the early 1920s for their lack of strict standards of kashruth (Jewish dietary laws) and their focus on Sunday rather than the Sabbath as the day of leisure and spiritual renewal. Yet he, too, made decisions about religious observance that reflected the fluidity of Jewish practice in the interwar period. He sought to avoid denominational divisiveness and believed that bringing children together from a variety of backgrounds encouraged independent thinking and social cohesion. Although boys and girls attended separate camps, bat mitzvahs were celebrated at Cejwin long before such ceremonies became mainstream, prayers were abbreviated depending on the ages and backgrounds of the campers, and the traditional Talmud Torah education gave way to more purely cultural activities, such as plays and arts and crafts with Jewish themes.[7] Schoolman's vision underwent modification as his clientele and the camps' financial situation placed new demands upon him. Nonetheless, he persisted in trying to build an orderly environment in which Jewishness was normal and pervasive, with none of the contradictions of the outside world.

Even with its foundation in Jewish culture, in many ways Cejwin differed little from non-Jewish camps. Memories of hot dog roasts and singing around the campfire belonged to any camper in America. In terms of staff organization, routine, and recreational program, the expectations for a summer camp were the same across the board. It was Cejwin's creation of its own standards and rituals that made it unique to the thousands who worked and played there over several generations and contributed to its success. By 1946 the camp served one thousand primarily middle-class children and hired a staff of four hundred. In 1958, Schoolman proudly declared that some twenty-five thousand families representing three successive generations had passed through Cejwin. His pride in that accomplishment reflects the importance of denominational inclusiveness and generational continuity in the Jewish camp movement.

Parallel to the growth in clientele, the physical plant expanded. Weathering the Depression was difficult, but by the late 1940s and into the 1950s, Cejwin was financially stable and pursued an ambitious building campaign. A map of the site shows bungalows, dining halls, infirmaries, social halls, playing fields, a canteen, an auditorium, and a central flagpole next to the main office—all surrounded by forests and situated on either side of a lake where children are swimming and canoeing. Those facilities were to be found in most camps, whether or not they were Jewish. All that sets the map apart is the Hebrew nomenclature for various locations.

Upon arrival, the children settled into rustic bunkhouses that lacked running water and were open on the sides, with canvas flaps to be rolled down in bad weather. Boys and girls arrived together, but once at camp, they led largely separate lives, eating in separate dining halls, performing separately in plays and dances, pursuing separate interests. The sections for boys and girls were a mile apart. The children did pray together on the Sabbath, dressed all in white, on boys' and girls' benches divided by an aisle. Such gender separation was hardly unusual at the time, and Schoolman dismissed the issue in his essay on Jewish summer camps:

> A completely co-educational approach in camping would not be helpful to the objectives of a Jewish cultural camp. The co-ed question, in itself, is an exacting problem, begging careful and extensive exploration and experimentation. To introduce this problem in the type of camp under discussion would only confuse and distract. However, limited elements of co-ed activity among the campers along social and cultural lines can be incorporated in the program.[8]

After a wake-up call at 6:30, daily prayers followed the morning lineup. Religious services varied in content and length with the age of the campers, from a brief flag-raising ceremony for the younger children to slightly longer prayer services for the older ones. Mealtimes were also occasions to establish rituals specific to the camp, from set-up and cleanup chores to seating arrangements to special foods. Schoolman made kashruth nonnegotiable, regardless of what children ate at home. A brief grace was said before and after each daily meal, with longer prayers included on the Sabbath.

The Sabbath featured prominently in recollections of blissful summers at many camps. Taylor's description of the Sabbath, written to a young fan of her books in 1953, includes details that were mentioned by campers and counselors alike over the years:

> We make much of our Jewish ceremonials—like a specially won-
> derful meal on Friday evening. Our little girls become Sabbath
> angels (some of them) and they march into the dining room sing-
> ing a lovely Sabbath eve song holding lighted candles in their
> hands. All that afternoon our little girls are busy polishing their
> white shoes—all heads are scrubbed and beautifully combed and
> by evening everyone, dressed in white, and shiny clean, goes to
> the mess hall (dining room) for the service and the meal. The ta-
> bles are spread with white cloths and a small candle burns on
> each. Our head counsellor makes the kidisch [sic] since we have
> no boys on our side of camp . . .
>   We do lots of things that are purely American also but it is nice
> to know that we can live so happily as Americans and still main-
> tain our own customs and beliefs and ways of doing things.[9]

The satisfaction derived from ritual persisted, even as it was modified by social and political changes in the American Jewish community, such as acceptance of women's leadership roles and embrace of the State of Israel. Encouraging Zionism was part of Cejwin's mission from the beginning. Through naming of camp locations, performing plays with Zionist themes, adopting the Maccabiah games, and encouraging the children to donate to Israel, the camp administrators integrated commitment to Zionism in the daily life of the campers. Pairing Cejwin with children's villages in Israel, they taught their campers that Israeli children were in need and that American Jewish children had an obligation to help, thus combining progressive ideas of individual responsibility for the community with Jewish loyalty.

On Friday nights before services, each bunk donated to the charity Keren Ami (Fund for My People). Established around 1925 in Chicago by teachers led by Benderly's student Alexander Dushkin and his colleagues at the Board of

Jewish Education, it soon spread to other cities in the Midwest and on the East
Coast, including the CJI. According to Krasner, "The object of Keren Ami was
to utilize the weekly collection of *tzedakah* [charity], which was common in
many schools, as an occasion to train students 'for intelligent participation in
Jewish community life.' "[10] In conjunction with collecting donations, students
prepared presentations about different charitable organizations to which the
funds could be allocated, and then, several times a year, the entire student body
decided which causes should receive their donations. That basic structure was
modified at camps like Cejwin, where cabins "took turns on successive Fridays
performing skits about various organizations, and an elaborate ritual was created for the public collection of the Keren Ami boxes shortly before the Sabbath."[11] By combining theater and tzedakah, modern methods and ancient
values, Cejwin developed yet another tool to educate, socialize, and entertain.

The camp experimented with reinforcing its lessons during the winter
with follow-up programs.[12] Administrators tried to establish home study
groups in Manhattan two or three times a week. They also organized winter
reunions, which were purely social affairs. The program for such a reunion
held on December 26, 1949, at Textile High School on West 18th Street was
designed to provide a distillation of Cejwin goals. The events included singing "The Star-Spangled Banner," opening remarks by Schoolman, movies,
refreshments, and songs led by Ella and Taylor, among others. Two of the
songs were secular love songs, and the rest were on Jewish themes. Taylor
regularly mentioned the reunions in her letters to family and friends, focusing
on gossip she picked up about her fellow counselors—their marriages, births,
and deaths, and their disputes with the administration about salaries and job
descriptions. Because much of the staff lived in the New York area, informal
gatherings were held as well for purely social purposes.[13]

Just as Cejwin administrators reached out to the world beyond Cejwin,
the world intruded on its idyllic setting in ways that sometimes painfully reinforced its sense of community. During World War II, the names of staff
members in the armed forces were displayed on a mural in the canteen, and
stars were put next to the names of those who were killed. In subsequent
years, the mural served as a reminder of the camp's patriotic sacrifices for the
war effort and for America.[14]

Surveys of former campers uniformly show that the Brenner sisters
were remembered with fondness and respect. The women, always impecca-

bly dressed with ironed blouses, shorts, and skirts, were in constant motion. As head counselor, Ella went to Cejwin in May to supervise maintenance and grounds crews and to make sure the facility was ready for another season. After she was widowed, Henny often joined her in the months before camp officially opened, while Taylor spent a weekend at camp at the end of June to set up her quarters, returned to the city, and then traveled back to camp with the busloads of youngsters.[15]

The Brenner sisters were deeply involved in the day-to-day running of the camp, but it was in the arts that they shone, especially Ella and Taylor. Creativity in the service of an integrated American Jewish life shaped Cejwin's physical plant and its scheduled activities. In 1935, artist and arts educator Temima Gezari, a product of Benderly's schools in New York, painted *Harvest Mural,* which dominated the Syn-Aud, as the multipurpose building used as synagogue and auditorium was called. Cejwin had an annual Dance Fete, "where interpretive dances on a Jewish theme were performed to Jewish music."[16] In one such dance, older girls swirled in formation, their costumes conjuring up Hasidic garb with traditional prayer shawls draped over their shoulders.[17] Modern American girls were thus able to explore their connection to their immigrant parents and grandparents in an experiential way.

Taylor's background in writing and dance and Ella's in music qualified them to develop a challenging performing arts program. The sisters' progressive artistic ambitions stand in a direct line with those of the Neighborhood Playhouse in the Henry Street Settlement House, and of drama programs in Jewish institutions of the Lower East Side, which had played such an important role in their childhood and in Taylor's development as a dancer.[18] Throughout the *All-of-a-Kind* series, the sisters, and especially Ella, are shown as thoroughly engaged in all aspects of play production. The plays are performed at the settlement house, in Hebrew schools, and in the streets. Describing her dramatic endeavors as a child, Taylor told her editor in 1953 that, although the settlement house "served as a non-sectarian refuge for East Siders, still children of orthodox parents like mine, mostly used the Hebrew School for a kind of settlement house. That's why the Purim Play was given through the Dramatic Club in the Hebrew School."[19] Between their involvement as children in the settlement house and in Jewish institutions, the Brenner sisters had models for including the performing arts in children's educational activities. Their emphasis on the arts in childhood development went beyond nostalgia to become a professional preoccupation.

Several other factors made employment at Cejwin attractive to the Brenner sisters. As seen above, it was a family tradition to go to the seaside for recreation and to escape the city's heat and diseases. From a day on Coney Island in the first book to a summer in Rockaway Beach in *More,* the fictional Brenner family took pleasure in the cool breezes and amusements of vacation spots, just as the actual Brenner family did throughout the decades. Ralph and Taylor also had positive memories of weekend outings with youth groups and of summers at Camp Tamiment, and their friends had written them during that period about their own getaways to farms and holiday camps, most located within a few hours of New York City.

Furthermore, with men off to war in 1942, summer camps employed women at much higher rates than before and in more responsible positions.[20] Those women developed professional confidence and friendships that lasted for decades.

Last, Taylor and her siblings had young children to occupy during the summer and working at the camp helped with expenses. Schoolman prided himself on Cejwin's affordability, claiming that the camp fee was about two-thirds that of a commercial camp.[21] In 1946, the fees were between $250 and $300; by 1958, the cost had risen to $445, and in 1960 to $500. Thus, it made financial and familial sense to work at Cejwin.

Of two primary features of summer camping—outdoor living and separation from family as a way to build character—the latter was not a Brenner custom. Charlotte was the only sister who did not work at Cejwin consistently over the years, but even she showed up on visiting day to see her sisters. A worker once quipped that no one over five feet tall was allowed to work in Hadas, because of Ella, Taylor, Gertrude, and their friends Sarah Lang and Gertrude Holz, who were all short.[22] In 1957, Taylor told a fan that four of the five sisters worked at camp that summer: "My mother claims we ought to call it an All-of-a-Kind camp. But that wouldn't be exactly correct because you see Henny does not work there. Henny, as usual must be a little bit different from the rest of us."[23]

Campers and counselors knew "Aunt Ella" in different capacities, and she excelled in all of them.[24] At various points during her long career with Cejwin she was head counselor of Hadas, supervisor of laundry and transportation, and chief administrator of logistics. As music director, she composed music for plays and other performances and sewed costumes. Campers remembered her beautiful voice in song and story, and her vivacious charm. She might seem busy and distracted, but this woman not much taller than her campers was gentle and funny, and noticed small details such as "shoes unshined! Hair needing to be brushed!"[25] Ella always had time for "her girls" and remembered their names even after they had graduated to the older camps.

Ella's impact on Cejwin's administrators and counselors was equally great. Her talents and warmth made a lasting impression, and it is a rare letter to Taylor from her friends at camp that does not ask that the writer be remembered to Ella. One of Ella's contributions to camp life was how she made her little cabin into a homey gathering place for the adults. "No one is like Ella you know," Taylor wrote. "Even when exhausted, she allowed people to invade her privacy and stay on and on and on, too kind to tell them to go."[26] Taylor often mentioned how closely she and her sister worked preparing for camp and making its dramatic productions a success. Writing about a camp song Taylor had mentioned to her, Jo asked, "Isn't that song . . . one that Ella has used previously—I really seem to hear it ringing a bell somewhere—as you pranced around the living room while she hammered it out . . . are you two like Rodgers and Hammerstein—with your album of classics?"[27]

Henny did eventually become an employee of the camp, driven by financial need when she was widowed in 1963.[28] As dining room supervisor, she directed her formidable energy to running the kitchen, and she also ran the laundry, a demanding job that required coordinating the truckloads of soiled clothing and linens that were regularly sent for washing in New York. Charlotte worked for several summers as head counselor of Yonim, the youngest group of campers (ages four to six), before it was discontinued, and planned programming for staff, as well as providing informal counseling. She apparently exhibited the same perfectionism as her sisters, but was more relaxed. Susan Baker credits her mother's study of educational psychology for her success with the youngest children, as well as her tremendous experience taking care of her siblings. Gertie interacted less with the campers on a daily basis because of her secretarial positions. She cut back her involvement after she married, although when her daughter Judy became a camper in the 1950s she again spent more time at Cejwin. Irving's wife Ethel worked year-round

in the camp's Manhattan office for twenty-five years, supervising the paperwork generated by registration and the employment of a large staff.

How well their children adapted to camp life did not necessarily determine the length of their mothers' careers at Cejwin. Taylor continued to work
there even after it was clear it was not a good fit for Jo. Ethel's children never
adjusted to any camp life at all, so she continued to work in the Manhattan
office while her boys attended summer school. She made sure, however, that
her eldest son got a job as an errand boy in the office the summer after his
high school graduation because she worried about how he would spend his
time without a legitimate occupation. Her concern shows that the potential
for trouble caused by unemployed city children was considered as much of a
problem in the 1950s as it was when camping first began. Ethel did not always
feel safe working alone in the 23rd Street office, so she also brought in her
sister's teenage sons to work with her and run errands. Taylor relatives also
attended Cejwin, including Naomi Ruderman, Taylor and Ralph's niece
through Ralph's sister, who attended the camp beginning in the late 1950s.

Husbands came up on the weekends, and the Brenner group developed Saturday customs for their days off, such as going to Flo-Jean's, a favorite restaurant off-site. Campers remembered how anxious Taylor was for
Ralph's arrival on Friday afternoons. Except for those few weeks in summer
when he attended various adult music camps in New England, he would
show up in time for a shower before the Shabbat ceremonies, and Taylor
paced fretfully when he was late. Not only did "Uncle Ralph" visit his wife,
but he also entertained the children, and in the 1970s was writing original
music for some of Taylor's plays. His performances on the recorder were
regular summer events.[29]

In addition to their energy and warmth, the sisters were remembered
for their intense sibling rivalry. Their loud arguments at the dinner table took
on a different form in the camp setting. Henny thought her work in the
kitchen less prestigious than Ella's supervisorial work. Camper Susan Addelston recalled that "decades later than the actual event Syd, Ella, Henny
were still discussing/blaming each other—or maybe one of the sisters who
wasn't there! For borrowing a dress, staining it and then returning it to the
closet. I think Syd told that story in one of her books—it DID happen, and
they still hadn't gotten past it."[30] Addelston was right: Henny's effort to dis-
guise a tea stain she got on one of Ella's dresses, which she had borrowed

Sisters at Cejwin; from left, Ella, Gertie, Syd, Henny

without permission, creates the drama in "Tea Party," the second chapter in *Uptown*. In the narrative, Taylor is able to resolve all the tensions: Henny successfully dyes the dress beige, which renders the stain imperceptible; Mama intuits the truth and makes Henny confess to Ella that she took the dress and lied about it; and Henny cheerfully accepts the punishment Mama imposes, which is to dye a pair of curtains for the parlor and do all the family's laundry that week. Henny makes no protest, and is in fact relieved that everything is out in the open. As she begins to scrub, "it was as if her wrongdoings were being washed away too" (34). The real-life Brenners found the past more of a burden than their fictional counterparts.

Like Ella, Taylor wore several hats, serving as assistant head counselor in Hadas and as theater and dance director. As counselor, she paid attention to all details of the girls' lives: "She'd train us to walk in properly and as 'ladies' on Friday nights if we got picked as Sabbath angels in the dining room.

Manners! Deportment! Her girls were going to be perfect in all ways—always! She'd line us up, straighten our posture, count us off with just the right number of steps prior to walking in correctly to the sounds of Sabbath Queen sung a cappella of course."[31] In numerous replies to fans of her books, she described her activities at Cejwin in response to questions about what she did besides write or about how she knew what children liked.[32]

From the beginning, Taylor was at Cejwin to develop its theater program. The earliest plays with her name on them date to 1942, where she is listed as providing lyrics and dance choreography. Some of the early plays were improvisational and emphasized group participation, a type of production that remained meaningful to Taylor for the rest of her life.[33] By 1947, she was drama director, a position she held until 1975. In the spring of 1951, when she was trying to coordinate publicity appearances for *All-of-a-Kind Family* with her job at Cejwin, she told her editor that she had an eight-week contract beginning the first of July and, although she was entitled to several vacation days during the summer, she needed to make sure her substitute was not overwhelmed: "The camp season is so short, it is necessary to work at top speed to prepare programs. As I am entirely responsible for the activities of dance and dramatics in my division (125 children), such preparation will necessarily have to be suspended during my absence." She had spoken to the director of the camp about leaving for a few days in July to attend the American Library Association Conference in Chicago, and Schoolman "agreed to extend this privilege to me, pending the approval of my head counselor. My head counselor is my sister Ella, so of course it'll be all right. But it won't be easy for her."[34]

Taylor and Ella worked together on theatrical productions. Taylor is usually listed in programs as responsible for original scripts, lyrics, choreography, and direction. In addition to providing original material, Taylor supervised a staff of counselors who wrote, composed, and directed. As mentioned above, Ella wrote original music and was choral leader in different productions, as well as creating costumes. Taylor's duties included organizing dances for Cejwin's celebrations, which reflected the hours of planning and preparation she put into them. Taylor amassed packets of choreographic notes, each summer adding new pieces such as "Oriental Dance in Pharaoh's Court."

Taylor thrived in the environment of hard work, lively and demanding children, and creative freedom.[35] Even after she became a popular author,

Cejwin dominated her calendar. Each January she negotiated her contract with the current director. What became her annual four- to six-week vacation in Europe was scheduled for the spring so that she could be back in New York to write, choreograph, and polish that summer's productions. Her editor knew she might decline invitations to speak throughout the summer because of her obligations to Cejwin, and that camp determined her writing schedule.[36] During the winter months, her professionalism drove her to take weekly yoga classes, Hebrew lessons, and dance classes with teachers such as Dvora Lapson (1907–1996), a pioneer in Hebraic dance. She considered her studies preparation for her work in the summer, so much that she deducted the fees as business expenses on her taxes.[37] Never one to tolerate an idle moment, she went so far as to seek out Israeli dance classes during her book tour/vacation in California in 1964.

Taylor's scripts show the importance of theater in progressive Jewish education. They embody some of the values considered necessary to impart to new generations of Jewish children, who were moving farther and farther away from the traditions and experiences of their parents and grandparents. The use of drama in Jewish educational institutions dates back to at least the 1890s when the Bloch Publishing Company sold playlets to be used in religious schools, and by the 1940s, their usefulness for revivifying tradition in a rapidly changing culture was assured.[38] In 1946, Schoolman stated that in a Jewish camp such as Cejwin, "the dramatic plays deal with episodes of Jewish history or of Jewish values rather than with American Indian life or with 'Minstrel' shows."[39] Taylor recorded Schoolman as repeatedly declaring: "I don't care how good a play is[,] if it has no Jewish content, I'm not interested."[40] General themes could be dealt with in regular public school—the summer should be for Judaism.

Taylor later wrote that it was in a Jewish summer camp that she "learned how important it was not to belabor the points of Judaism but rather to come upon them gently in rich and colorful expression."[41] Such ideas had been percolating in her mind for many years. In 1930 she had written in her diary:

> I am no longer religious in the sense that is commonly considered
> so. That is, I observe none of the rituals in relation to my religion.
> And yet, I think back with a good deal of inner glow to my child-
> hood days when the observance of the ancient and time-worn

customs played so important a part in my life and I feel glad that my parents enabled me to have such memories.

What, I often wonder, can we offer our children in its place? How can we imbue them with the festive spirit of a religious holiday, the strange mystery surrounding the performance of an old rite, and the accompanying awareness of so many years before their time? True, such expression of religion is infantile and recognized as such by adult minds. But in the minds and hearts of little children, it is filled with a rare and treasurable beauty.

Could close and active association with the arts of music, dance and theatre fill religion's place?[42]

Taylor's seriousness about the connection between the arts and religious experience colored her summers at Cejwin and how she approached her young charges. Because Hebrew schools and Sunday schools already spent so much time on holidays and holiday pageants, Taylor felt she had a tremendous opportunity and responsibility to expand the children's understanding of the spirit and culture of Judaism through methods and topics of her own choosing.[43]

The question became where to find suitable material, and Taylor's solution was to write her own plays, at least three each summer. It was a point of pride with her to come up with new material every year, and even when she adapted the plots of other works, she reshaped them significantly for her campers.[44] Taylor always kept in mind that she was writing plays for children. Most of the scripts note how long they should last, with 25–30 minutes being the usual length. Taylor was sensitive to the challenges of memorization and included rhyming speeches in some of her plays to make it easier for the young thespians to master their lines. Her scripts also include detailed notes on choreography, because Taylor was not the only adult supervising the theatrical productions. The stories sensibly featured children as the heroes and combined pathos with playfulness.

Taken as a whole, Taylor's plays form an eclectic set, partly because of her wide interests and partly because of the sheer volume of writing that was required over the decades. The subjects of the plays fall into the following categories: non-Jewish legends that embodied Jewish values; biblical stories and Jewish legends; Jewish observance; Jews in America; and modern Israel. In the 1950s, Taylor's love of classical music inspired her to write two plays about Haydn and Grieg, and she made a foray into Greek legend with "Perseus and Andromeda," but such topics were the exception. Since the plays were written mainly for the girls' camp, it is not surprising that they include numerous stories about princesses.[45]

Whatever the subject, didacticism invariably prevails. The lessons to be learned are not to judge hastily, to be honest, not to do to others what you do not want them to do to you, to persist in the face of difficulty, and so on. It is in that preachiness that the camp's educational agenda becomes evident. Taylor was praised for the finesse with which she taught important lessons in the *All-of-a-Kind* series, but those were novels to be savored at leisure through independent reading in the tranquil rooms of a library or in the privacy of the home. In Cejwin's communal setting, clear, simple lessons had to be imparted to large groups of children in a limited period of time and in a way that kept them constantly engaged.

The non-Jewish legends co-opt fantasy elements in order to teach a lesson. In "The Three Gifts," a king learns that it is in helping others and being constructive that one will be happy. The play opens with the king overcome by an inexplicable melancholia. His court tries to lift his spirits with entertainment, feasting, and good company, to no avail. A wise old man brings him a gift of magical eyeglasses that open his eyes to what is going on in his kingdom— the building of a house of worship, scholars struggling to study and teach, and poor people who work hard yet cannot feed and clothe their children. The king realizes he was blind to the needs of his kingdom because he was "wrapped in self," and he vows to take action. He orders the construction of hospitals, museums, beautiful parks, and a fine town hall. Of course there must be schools, so that "in my land, there shall be not even one ignorant man!" As for the poor, "Just a minute. I have not finished. There are too many poor in my country. I must go see them. They must be well housed, well fed. For those who can work, we must find jobs and see that they are well paid. I swear to God I will not rest until there is no more poverty in my land!" The YPSLs may have been deeply buried in Taylor's past, but her idealism about a country where everyone works, is paid a fair wage, and benefits from public services was thus imparted to another generation. The story of royalty is milked not for romance or adventure, but rather for a work ethic with a socialist twist. The king learns that worthy work is undertaken not for the sake of productivity or keeping busy, but rather for the collective good and the eradication of poverty.

Literal dramatizations of Bible stories are rare. Among biblical figures, Elijah the Prophet and King Solomon are featured, and it is their legendary rather than biblical personas that held dramatic interest for Taylor. One play retells the tale of how King Solomon learns humility from the bees and comes to realize that only God is omniscient; another has him granting the wish of loyal hoopoes for golden crowns, which they quickly realize make them a target for hunters, so they ask for a crown of feathers instead—a Jewish "Just So" story. The possibilities for dramatic action in the story of Daniel in the lion's den are obvious, but Taylor's choices were not always so understandable. One of her plays uses fairy-tale motifs to tell the story of Athalia's defeat when the child Joash claims the throne, basing it loosely on the account in 2 Kings 8–11. Although a biblical story centered on a child makes sense on a superficial level, Athalia's is a gruesome tale filled with betrayal, filicide, and massacre, and it comes as no surprise that the director of the camp expressed reservations about Taylor's choice of subject.[46]

Dramatic elements explain the appeal of Rabbi Yochanan ben Zakkai's escape from Jerusalem in a funeral bier when the Romans besieged the city, and a tale about Maimonides and Saladin has both suspense and humor, but Taylor used rabbinical stories to hint at more complex realities. "Jingle-Jangle" relates the story of a rabbi who uncovers corruption among a kingdom's tax collectors. At first glance, the play teaches a straightforward message— liars will get caught, the guilty will be punished, and the innocent will be rewarded—encapsulated in the overtly didactic closing song. What makes the play more complex is that it sets up an economic conundrum. The king needs more money to benefit everyone, but the people cannot give him more money in taxes, so he is unable to act on his subjects' behalf. Taylor eliminates the conundrum by attributing the cause of the problem to cheating tax collectors rather than by questioning the inherent inequity of the economic system. She also takes an oblique approach to a canard about Jews that would have been familiar to her actors and audience. One of the tax collectors advises against trusting a rabbi: "You know you can't trust the word of a Jew." The rabbi of course proves himself trustworthy, thus reassuring the children that the prejudices of the non-Jewish world do not reflect reality.

In plays on American themes, Taylor intertwined American history and Jewish culture. She has a Jewish girl be a "brave little soldier" during the American Revolution, using the ploy of Rabbi Yochanan ben Zakkai to smuggle herself past British lines. "Three American Heroes" presents vignettes from the lives of Asser Levy (1656), Francis Salvador (1776), and Judah Touro (1838). By situating the protagonists in three successive centuries and having them interact with heroic Jewish children, Taylor encouraged the children of Cejwin to play a part in the tradition of American Jewish patriotism in their own historic era of the twentieth century.

The cultural medley can be dizzying. For example, "The Peddler" is a short, largely plotless play about a pioneer family living in semi-isolation in 1880 somewhere on the Great Plains. When Aaron, a Jewish peddler, arrives, the family examines his wares and invites him to join them for supper and stay the night. He joins them at a barn dance the following night, and everyone dances a quadrille followed by an Israeli folk dance. The atmosphere is that of an imagined Jewish Little House on the Prairie. The peddler's role is to bring Jewish identity to the pioneers, which is shown by his teaching them an Israeli folk dance. He forms the link between nature (the plains) and civilization (the sale of goods, including a skillet, calico, and pins), and between American identity (pioneers) and Jewish identity. The sheet music used is a song called "The Peddler," a Russian song translated by Jacob Robbins and published in 1921. Russian words in the Cyrillic alphabet are included. Taylor's choice of a song for a play about American pioneers that included the line "O the steppes lie far and wide!" conjures up syncretic images of homesteading Russian immigrants not quite sure of where they are—a linguistic collision most children would have ignored.

Some of the plays about American Jewish children take place entirely in the present, and their purpose is to encourage players and spectators to embrace their role as active custodians of Jewish tradition. In "Spirit of the Sabbath," for example, two angels visit a sleeping girl in a dream, followed by a personified Kiddush cup, challah, and finally the Sabbath Queen herself. The mother and father wake their daughter, who then recounts her dream. The parents remember Sabbaths from their childhoods and agree to celebrate it once again. In addition to accommodating fantasy and creative costumes, this play promotes Cejwin's mission of guiding its campers to assume responsibility for their culture. The adults are forgetful or negligent, but love of their children makes them accede to a reversal of roles as they accept the tutelage of the younger generation.[47]

Taylor's plays addressed the attenuation of Jewish tradition through assimilation and also through the devastation of the Holocaust. Given her audience, it is not surprising that she sought a positive message in that bleak horror, softening the suffering of European children with Zionist hope. Presented on Sunday, July 28, 1968, "The Sad Melody" is set in Israel in 1947 during Purim. It focuses on Naomi, an unhappy eight-year-old European orphan, who is eventually found by her uncle and reunited with relatives. In a reversal of fortunes appropriate to the holiday, she once again has a family. In the course of the action, a girl sings a Purim song in Yiddish, and it is that song that leads the Israeli family to recognize their European relative. The old world of Europe and the new one of Israel are bridged by art and tradition. The language of the old world is the catalyst for a child's freedom and security in the new. The play is emotional and affective, tapping as it does into both fairy tale (the family reunion) and the Holocaust.

The fictional children in Taylor's plays about contemporary Jewish life shoulder the burden of adult problems of Jewish identity and history imposed on them by Taylor and her fellow educators. The real children who acted out those literary parts seemed untroubled by the worries of their elders, however. In the *Hadas Bulletin* of the summer of 1968, the girls wrote about "The Sad Melody" without any mention of Taylor. The concerns of the girls were the mistakes they made or their pride in getting the lead part. One, Cyrisse Sarway, wrote: "I was a dancer in the play. I was so nervous I made a big mistake. Well, it turned out that nobody noticed till I said, 'Omigosh' and put my hand over my mouth. Well it turned out GREAT!"

Taylor did not shy away from the tensions that tempered the hope embodied in the State of Israel. One play focuses on a Moroccan Jewish boy on a kibbutz who is ostracized by members of Eastern European ancestry until he proves that he is as good as everyone else. Set in Israel in 1948, "On the Border" involves conflicts between Arabs and Israelis. A little girl named Rochael saves the day, but it is only with the help of an Arab woman that Rochael and her father escape danger. The cast of characters in "Shalom Good Neighbor" includes Jewish settlers and Arabs. On the cover of the script dated August 8–9, 1951, are pictures of Arab and Jewish boys shaking hands, as well as a quotation that reads, "Israel is ever ready to achieve a lasting peace with the Arab nations," which is identified as spoken by David Ben-Gurion on June 1, 1951. In the play, the Arabs abandon their initial hatred for the Jews when they see how decent the Jews are and how they have improved the land. At its climax, the Jews save the Arab children from sickness. However clumsy the plots sound in summary, they guided Cejwin campers to work through difficult problems by means of drama.

Campers remembered Taylor as a demanding director, the two most frequent adjectives used to describe her being *talented* and *perfectionist.*[48] She was "demanding but patient—always expected one's best—no excuses!" Some campers hinted at Taylor's playing favorites, but that must be balanced with the warm memories of campers who worked on plays with her. Taylor clearly expected her young performers to follow directions and to excel. Those children who rose to the challenge thought highly of her, crediting her with giving them self-confidence and leadership skills. Barbara Lieberman recalled that it was "just fun for me to be with her as a kid." Another, Wendy Pflaster, wrote in the bulletin, "Aunt Syd is our dramatics teacher. When she tells us to do things, it's so much fun. When she tells us to pretend to be Elves, we do it."

Even a passing encounter with Taylor could make a lasting impact. In a letter, a Cejwin parent (identified only as AIE) expressed gratitude for all Taylor did for his children. She had made his awkward daughter graceful and helped another daughter overcome her stutter, and instilled pride in both at being Maccabees. Taylor had also danced with the father at a camp event and explained to him what "expressive dancing" meant. He felt "wealthier" for having been exposed to "such unselfish giving of one's self." The key elements that Schoolman and his cohort of progressive Jewish educators sought to inculcate in the new generation were all there: self-confidence, a sense of individual worth, creativity with a purpose, participation in community that joined parents, teachers, and children, and pride in Jewish identity.

Some campers wrote years later to express their fondness and admiration for their former counselor. Karen Love, a theater major in college, sent a letter to Taylor on September 3, 1977, having heard she was in the hospital. After explaining the circumstances for her writing, she continued:

> I just wanted you to know how much you meant to me my first two years at Cejwin. I went there for 5 years . . . I remember writing home to my mother and telling her how much I loved the dramatics classes. It was always my favorite. My second year Hadas bunks 18–22 were in our play, *In Gods Hands.* I was Mutke. My first big part. When I tried out I sang "America the beautiful."

You said I had a sweet voice. And I remember when you fitted me
for my costume. Oh and I had to wear a little red wig which was
in a page boy style. I will never forget those days. I will never
forget you. My first two years at Cejwin were my best because you
gave me something to love and look forward to.

Love attributed much of her enthusiasm for the theater and her decision to
major in drama in college to those formative years at Cejwin.

The younger staff members liked Taylor, although she was somewhat
removed from their social circle. Attending to the staff's needs was Ella's responsibility, and she figured more vividly in their memories, being from the
outset more outgoing than her younger sister. The word *aloof* comes up in
descriptions of Taylor, qualified by "if you didn't know her well." One of the
staff members who did get to know Taylor well was Janet Schwartzman,
known at camp as Ginger. She and Taylor developed a working relationship
beginning in 1955, Ginger eventually serving as Taylor's assistant. From
those first intense months of working together, the two women developed a
warm friendship of deep mutual affection. As Ginger navigated college, boyfriends, family, career aspirations, marriage, and children, Taylor was always
there to read her letters and write long, thoughtful replies. At first she saw her
devoted acolyte as yet another emotional, needy teenager, but she gradually
came to recognize in the young woman her own traits of relentless hard work,
love of the arts, and commitment to family and Judaism.

Jo had a more jaundiced view of Cejwin. Even though her parents allowed her to attend a different camp, Jo could not escape the dominant role
that Cejwin played in her family. In 1955, married and struggling to establish
her independence, Jo snapped at her mother's praise for a dancer at Cejwin
who had been one of Jo's classmates at the High School for the Performing
Arts. The young woman had made a career for herself as a modern dancer in
Israel, but Jo would have none of it: "I can conceive of her improving with a
great deal of work, but it sure would take quite an effort because she was so
lousy. The foremost dancer in Israel???? this I can't see . . . You must remember that in Cejwin one loses all perspective completely. What's good in Cejwin would be mediocre elsewhere and you know that as well as I do."[49]
Taylor did not press the point, for she did not return to Cejwin year after year
because it was exceptional—rather, she returned because it was familiar and

preserved the closeness of the Brenner sisters, for whom it was a stage on which to exhibit their talents, whether in the theater, the kitchen, or the office.

Taylor's time at Cejwin also witnessed her emergence as an important writer for children. Early in the 1950s, when asked by a parent about her occupation, Taylor replied that she "writes children's books." A camper who started in 1956 was excited to meet the author of a book she had read and thought she was a "he." The girl was surprised to find that was not the case. Taylor's evolving identity as a children's book author, with all its ambiguities, was a subject for speculation not only for Cejwin campers, but also for the Brenner and Taylor families, and for Taylor herself.

Award-Winning Author

1950–1960

THE SUMMER OF 1950 PROCEEDED like the summers before it, with Taylor busy at Cejwin and Ralph working at Caswell-Massey during the week and spending weekends with his wife at camp. Yet on one fateful day Ralph set in motion a series of events that affected the entire family and soon touched the lives of millions of children. Without informing his wife, he submitted one of her manuscripts for an award he had seen announced in the newspaper— an award that the book won.[1] Thus began Taylor's career as the author of the *All-of-a-Kind* series. Taylor went on to win awards, accolades, and most important, an audience. Thanks to Ralph's impetuous act, she learned to be a professional writer, a public speaker, a businesswoman, and a spokeswoman for the Jewish American experience. Although her husband continued to support her creative endeavors, Taylor's success exacerbated tensions with her daughter, and it changed the dynamic among the Brenner sisters.

Over the years, Taylor explained in a number of speeches and letters how she came to write the first book, adding or subtracting different details while keeping certain themes constant. She told fans that her daughter was often lonely at bedtime, so Taylor spun stories about her own childhood with four sisters and eventually a baby brother on the Lower East Side.[2] She wanted both to soothe her daughter with tales of a large family and to preserve and share the values of a vanished lifestyle in the neighborhood where she grew up. She felt compelled to write down the stories and read them to Jo and her friends; then she put the manuscript in a box where she kept her play scripts and other miscellanea. She did not specify how long the manuscript languished there, but intimated that it was several years.

At the end of the summer of 1950, according to the speeches, Taylor asked her husband to dig out a script she wanted to use at camp. He saw the family stories among her papers and, having recently noticed an announcement for a prize for children's literature, had his secretary type them up and mail them to the sponsor of the prize, the Chicago publishing house of Wilcox & Follett, without telling his wife what he had done. When the letter dated November 21 arrived announcing that Follett planned to publish her stories as a book, Taylor was "flabbergasted" and Ralph's activities on her behalf were revealed. She sat for a while rocking in the rocking chair in Jo's room, which her daughter had long outgrown, then grabbed her coat and went to see a movie. Taylor was even more astonished to learn that she had won the second annual Charles W. Follett Award in children's literature. She had no idea what the prize entailed and had to ask the publisher as late as February 1951 to learn that she had won $3,000 (approximately $30,000 in 2017 dollars) and a gold medal, as well as the publishing contract.[3]

In Taylor's telling, she then called her mother long distance because her parents were wintering in Florida.

> When I got her on the phone, my first words were—modestly— "Mama you're going to live forever." And Mama replied, "Yes I know—everyone tells me how well I look." When I explained what I really meant, she was so excited, she spluttered. A few days later I got a letter from her written at 4 o'clock in the morning. She hadn't been able to sleep. Well neither had her daughter. But her letter ended with the characteristic question—"Did you say $300.00 or $3,000.00?"[4]

Cilly was, indeed, tremendously proud of her daughter. In subsequent years, she encouraged her daughter to write a sequel, and wondered about adapting the book for the movies.[5] Morris was also pleased by Taylor's success. In a touching note that responded to several questions she asked about Jewish practice, he revealed his fondness for his daughter: "I hope that it will give you so much Plasure in your Life ... I will allwais be glad to give you any information you will ask me if I will only know. it is only to bad that I am not so Educatet in Jewish as I should be, but I will do the best to ansfer your kwasktions."[6] After the book was published and met immediate success,

Taylor started a career of visits to schools and library groups and began to receive thousands of fan letters, which she conscientiously answered and filed away.

Those bare outlines of the book's publication were modified as Taylor gave more speeches and interviews, depending upon the audience and Taylor's growing confidence. As she retold the sequence of events, Taylor was inconsistent in attributing agency to her storytelling. Sometimes it was Jo who demanded stories, and other times it was Taylor who felt the need to share the experiences of the Brenner family with her child and was then gratified that Jo and her friends found them interesting. Sometimes, she explained, it was a compulsion to describe the vanishing world of the Lower East Side that drove Taylor to write, as visits to the neighborhood with Jo failed to capture the excitement and promise of immigrant life in America. Occasionally Taylor depicted the process of writing as casual, almost accidental, and dependent on her husband to move her stories from the box to the marketplace. That became the prevailing myth.

Taylor complicated the myth by saying at one point that she had herself submitted a completed manuscript for publication in the 1940s. In that telling, she said she typed the stories at a table next to the kitchen when her daughter was asleep and her husband worked late. After the manuscript was rejected, she stored it in the box, which she sometimes described as having been made by Jo as a project at the Little Red School House. Laurie, Jerry Brenner's daughter, remembered hearing the account of the rejection—a version that, however, went against the myth and was not as useful for publicity.

By 1958, Taylor spoke openly about another reason for her writing. She insisted in a letter to a fan that Jo's consciousness of her Jewish identity was a factor: "In those days (my daughter is now close to 24) you could not get any books about Jewish children in our public libraries. And even those published by Jewish concerns were far from attractive or appealing to youngsters."[7] In a speech Taylor developed for Jewish audiences, she polished that account:

> [Jo] said to me one day "Mother why is it that every time when I read a book, it's about Gentile children. Why isn't there a book about Jewish children?" And then I remembered that that was exactly the way I used to feel when I was a little girl. I had no an-

swer for her. It wasn't a sufficient explanation to say "Well Jo, we're members of a minority group." After all, the Eskimos are a minority group and certainly plenty of books have been written about them. So I said to myself somebody ought to do it. Thereupon came another thought: Why not I?[8]

In several letters, Taylor claimed that the impetus to write about Jewish children dated to her own childhood rather than to her daughter's: "I remember when I was a little girl and read books from the library (which was the only way we got them in my day) they were always about Gentile children and never about Jewish ones. So when I grew up and had a daughter of my own, I determined I'd write a book for her about Jewish children. And this way she has been sharing the stories I told her with lots and lots of other children."[9]

The children's book editor at Follett, Esther K. Meeks, originally resisted Taylor's public declaration of the role Jewish identity played in the creation of the book. It would be facile to describe her reservations as anti-Semitic. The fruitful and challenging relationship that developed between the two women over the next two decades—one the consummate professional and the other a professional in the making—was too complicated for such a characterization. Born Esther Kelly on December 4, 1909, in Joliet, Illinois, Taylor's first editor spent her entire publishing and writing career, until her retirement in the early 1970s, with Follett Publishing, part of a family-owned firm established in 1873 in Wheaton, Illinois, and headquartered in Chicago since 1876. Meeks authored several beginning readers and science books for children but was most influential as an editor in the 1950s and '60s. She was one of several Follett employees who encouraged ethnic diversity in American children's literature and sought out books for children from other countries.[10]

Meeks's first letter to Taylor is dated November 21, 1950.[11] The salutation was "Dear Sydney Brenner" and Meeks frankly admitted that she knew little about this author whom Follett wanted to publish: "I would like to know something about you. Actually I don't know if Sydney is a man or a woman, though I feel quite sure a man couldn't write this story."[12] After informing Taylor that Follett would like to publish her book, she proceeded to introduce elements that dominated the two women's relationship for the next two decades. Although the women proceeded from "Dear Mrs. Meeks" and

"Dear Mrs. Taylor" to "Dear Esther" and "Dear Sydney" over the spring and summer of 1951, and although they met each other with their spouses on social occasions and exchanged bits of family news, they never seemed to develop a close friendship. Beginning with the first *All-of-a-Kind* book, Meeks exerted her authority to demand editorial changes, treated Taylor as a rank amateur, paid close attention to every word and punctuation mark in the text, and displayed ambivalence toward its Jewish content.

Meeks made it clear from the outset that the manuscript needed extensive revision. She wanted the first chapter dropped and its descriptions of the Lower East Side and the family incorporated more naturally into the story, so that the first chapter would jump right into the action of Sarah's loss of her library book. Taylor disagreed. To her, the Lower East Side represented freedom, respect for learning, and appreciation for the myriad opportunities available in America even amid the hardships of immigrant life. Because she adamantly insisted on filling the first chapter with a sketch of the tumultuous, optimistic neighborhood before launching into her story, Taylor clashed with Meeks, who had equally strong opinions about good writing, as well as concerns about marketability.

In their correspondence, Meeks positioned herself as the professional and Taylor as the amateur, competent in the kitchen perhaps but ignorant about the book business. In her first letter, Meeks pushed Taylor to revise quickly in order to get the manuscript to press. When, later, Taylor disagreed with some of her revisions, Meeks implied that the novice was not experienced enough to know how to shape the manuscript properly and in a timely manner. The changes Taylor made in response to her suggestions made the story "bumpy . . . the parts that have been added remind me of lumps of flour belatedly added to gravy. They just don't mix with the rest." Condescension continues to pervade this letter as Meeks urges Taylor to drop the introductory chapter: "There isn't room in a book for something just because it is dear to the author. If this something is admissible in a story, though not exactly what I prefer, I am happy to do it the author's way. But if I know that it hurts the book, then I have to persuade the author to see it my way. In the case of this introduction, six readers, including four judges in the Follett Award Competition, have stated independently that the story should begin on page six."[13] The two women went back and forth on the introduction, and it is clear from Meeks's letter on March 29, 1951, that she simply decided to drop it: "Cutting this manuscript and tying up the loose ends was a terrific job. I hope you like the way I did it." In April, Taylor sent back galley corrections and requests for the restoration of parts Meeks had cut, but the published book shows that by and large those requests were ignored.[14]

Meeks had little patience for Taylor's self-portrayal as the hapless housewife whose typewriter perched on the kitchen table. Taylor's chatty letters to her in the first year of their relationship often run to at least three single-spaced pages, full of details about her progress with editing, her husband, her feelings about winning the award, and later, her delight at the attention being paid to her because of her book's success.[15] Meeks's letters, in contrast, include little personal information and focus on editorial changes and deadlines. At the end of December 1950, Taylor blamed domestic chores for her delay in revising the manuscript and positioned Ralph as essential in making her a responsible author: "My poor household suffered by my lack of attention. I tried to make some order out of chaos on Sunday but made my long-suffering husband follow me around with the manuscript. Said he 'I want you to know not every housewife has a reader follow her while she works.' " Taylor's attempt at humor flopped. In her reply, Meeks dealt primarily with revisions. Although she mentioned that the book promised to be one of Follett's great successes for 1951, at the end she brusquely remarked, "I sympathize with your family, but that is the fate of a writing woman's family. Later on they may share in the jollier aspects of being an author's family."[16]

Lest Meeks be seen as an arbitrary editorial tyrant, her instincts and her close attention to every detail in the unseasoned author's manuscript proved sound. Some of the chapters most beloved by readers took shape under her guidance. It was she who pushed the transformation of a young woman friend of Sarah's who lived in an apartment upstairs into Kathy the Library Lady, minimized the librarian's involvement in the daily life of the family, and encouraged Taylor to develop the plot of the separated lovers, Kathy and Charlie, who find each other in the family sukkah. Meeks helped provide a narrative arc for Taylor's collection of self-contained stories.

Where Meeks's instincts proved less acute concerned Judaism. The editor was never completely comfortable with the Jewish aspects of the stories. That discomfort resulted from her own, admittedly limited, exposure to a more Americanized Judaism than that of Taylor's immigrant childhood, and from her concerns as a businesswoman. Meeks disliked the portrayal of the Purim play, for example, thinking it must have been more of a stately pageant that included all the biblical characters, rather than the humorous, lively show of song and dance portrayed by Taylor. Taylor enlisted Dwight Follett himself after she met him in early January 1951 to allow her to stick with her version of how Purim plays were performed on the Lower East Side in 1912. Similarly, Meeks protested that Simchas Torah, a notoriously raucous service, surely must have been characterized by more solemnity and dignity.[17] She occasionally mentioned that she had checked with a local rabbi or an editor with "an orthodox Jewish background" about certain details and felt, based on their answers, that Taylor could alter the tone of particular passages.[18] In her opinion, too many unfamiliar details about religion would turn readers off. This was to be a book about a family, not about Jews.

In addition to making the Jewish holidays conform to how she thought Judaism *ought* to be practiced, Meeks wanted the Jewish community of the Lower East Side to be more American in other ways. She did not try to minimize Judaism so much as to Americanize it, and establishing the right balance of Judaism and Americanism preoccupied her in the process of revision. She urged Taylor to change the text so that the charming and happy family would not appear isolated because she considered one of the strengths of the story to be how easy it was for American children to identify with its fictional family: "An added value, of course, is in the fact that though this family is Jewish, the daily life is such that this could be any family . . . [but] this family seems to live in a world of its own—the Lower East Side, not America." Meeks questioned whether that insularity really existed and asked whether the family indeed celebrated no holidays except Orthodox Jewish ones: "If they did celebrate the Fourth of July, for example, it would certainly make them seem more like Americans (also) to celebrate with a picnic."[19]

Over the next few months, Meeks pushed Taylor to include a Fourth of July celebration, which she did. Early drafts included lengthy passages about the history of Independence Day, which were gradually excised, until, under Meeks's tutelage, a lively chapter of firecrackers, fire engines, and romance emerged. Judaism and Americanism are in harmony when Charlie, the gentile romantic hero, sits down to a steaming platter of kugel—"potato pudding," as Taylor has him call it for the benefit of non-Jewish readers—prepared especially for him by Mama, before setting off magical fireworks for his Jewish friends and their neighbors. Without being overly didactic, Taylor has her family participate in a holiday that celebrates freedom "all over the country," because it is precisely for freedom that Mama and Papa immigrated to the United States (*AKF* 133, 138).

Hovering over the entire correspondence between Taylor and Meeks was the indictment in August 1950 of Communist Jews Julius and Ethel Rosenberg for espionage and treason, and their trial, which was set for March 1951. In this time of the Red Scare and Senator Joseph McCarthy's anti-Communist crusade, when Meeks, in her early requests for revisions, adamantly declared, "I do think it important, too, particularly today, that this family show some signs of being American as well as Jewish," she did not have to spell out what she meant by "particularly today" in order to get across the careful handling that Taylor's book required.[20] A significant proportion of citizens brought before the House Un-American Activities Committee were Jews, a fact that escaped no one's notice.

After details of holiday celebrations were ironed out, Meeks put her mind to publicity. She admitted to Taylor, "For a number of reasons this book is not easy to write about." What she meant was, the Jewishness posed a problem: "Though I am very glad the story has this feature it is not the sort of thing I would use in publicity at the outset particularly."[21] Taylor was instructed to say in her public appearances that she decided to tell her daughter stories about the old days, wrote them down "as a logical next step," put the stories in a box, remained oblivious to her husband's efforts toward publication, and greeted her unexpected win with gratification.

Based on the correspondence and the scripts of Taylor's speeches, Taylor did as she was told, even though not all of that explanation originated from her. While acknowledging that Taylor's reasons for writing included more than solace for an only child and nostalgia for a vanished neighborhood, Meeks encouraged her neophyte author to downplay Judaism. She knew perfectly well that the stories were written because of the lack of Jewish children in children's literature: "The item you wrote me about Jo wondering why there were no stories about Jewish children will be very good for talks and perhaps for later publicity."[22] She insisted that Taylor emphasize that Jo, like other children, wanted stories about her mother as a child, and as an only child, she loved stories about her mother's sisters. It was not unless Taylor spoke to Jewish audiences that she made a point of deploring the lack of stories for children that featured accessible Jewish characters.

Taylor and Meeks may not have realized at the time how pioneering *All-of-a-Kind Family* would prove to be, but Taylor was conscious early on of her desire to bring diversity to children's literature. "I wanted also to show the world that children were children first and Jewish afterward—something perhaps Gentiles did not appreciate. Also I hope to be able to make this Gentile world of ours see and understand the warmth and beauty and graciousness inherent in Jewish living. To have succeeded—I must assume I have since so much of my mail comes from Gentile children—has made me very proud and happy."[23] Most of Taylor's fan mail did, in fact, come from non-Jews. Jewish readers might mention how a grandmother confirmed Taylor's description of the Lower East Side or that a book in the series had been a Chanukah present, but for the most part the popularity of the series did not depend on religious or ethnic affiliation.

Over time, Taylor became more vocal about the constraints she had been under when the book was first published. In a speech she wrote after the publication of *Downtown* in 1972, she said:

> Especially in the light of present day's overwhelming concern with minority groups, it may be difficult for many to comprehend what courage it took for Follett & Co. to publish my first book many years [ago]. Though they believed in its value, they were still concerned that given prior knowledge of its contents, the Christian world might shun it. In the beginning, all mention of the word Jewish was avoided in their blurbs and in their advertising. I was cautioned to say "the newcomer" or "the immigrant" when referring to the Jewish inhabitants of the lower East Side.

That caution carried over into many reviews of the book—in newspapers from the *San Jose Mercury Herald* in California to the *Rutland Herald* in Vermont. Not one review reveals an anti-Semitic bias, but many of them omitted mentioning that the delightful All-of-a-Kind family was Jewish. What the reviews picked up on was how effortlessly the book balanced the tension between the universal—all children can relate to the stories in the book—and the specific—the particular customs, food, and language of immigrant Americans. The book and its successors describe Jewish customs, but every reader can relate to the siblings, and even an only child can relate to the loving parent-child relationships. Taylor was specific to just the right degree.

Some idea of just how unusual it was to publish stories about Jews for the general public emerges in letters exchanged about a short story that Josette Frank of the Child Study Association asked Taylor to write after *All-of-a-Kind Family* appeared.[24] The subject was to be a Jewish holiday, and Taylor used material about Sukkos that had been deleted from her novel in part for reasons of space.[25] Meeks asked that Taylor send her the rough draft because Meeks "might be able to make useful suggestions." Her main suggestion was to rectify the lack of dignity in the religious festival: "Even on a joyful occasion like this, I should think there would be some impression of the solemn as well as the festive spirit. For example, Christmas is one of the most joyful among Christian celebrations, yet always there is a very solemn and awe-inspiring atmosphere along with it—at least in the religious festival."[26] Taylor replied that she had tried to increase the sense of solemnity in the synagogue itself, but assured her that as soon as services were over, it really was a rambunctious holiday.[27]

As reported by Taylor, Frank's response to the story was similar to that of Meeks:

> The story I did . . . created quite a todo. Miss Frank was both fascinated but somewhat frightened by it. She wanted the dancing in the synagogue scene to be toned down. I was reluctant because it was a true description of an actual ceremony. She submitted it to her book committee. Result—half were for it because it was so unusual—half against it for the same reason. On it went to the . . . publishers of the anthology. Miss Frank reported the editor was terrified. I could understand their reasoning. Since the anthology was to cover a wide general range of holidays, they felt they wanted something which would not give too extraordinary a picture of Jewish life.[28]

In the end, Frank liked the story enough to ask for more. Taylor continued to write about Jewish holidays for Frank and in 1963 wrote an easy reader for the Child Study Association. The remarkable aspect of the exchange is how Taylor internalized the views of outsiders and accepted without protest that her religious practices were strange. The reaction of the Child Study Association editors actually lent Meeks more credibility in her efforts to have Taylor normalize Judaism for a mainstream audience.

The question becomes why Follett anticipated that publication of *All-of-a-Kind Family* would be profitable and why they chose to bet on an unknown author to introduce Jews into children's literature. Some insight can be gained from looking at the other book published in 1951 by a mainstream publisher that featured a Jewish family—one that did *not* receive rave reviews or lead to sequels and has been virtually forgotten. That book was *Carol's Side of the Street* by Lorraine Beim, published by Harcourt, Brace. In contrast to Taylor, Beim was an established children's author whose previous work dealt with subjects such as racism, divorce, and polio, thus putting her in the forefront of authors of "problem" stories. *Kirkus Reviews* said *Carol's Side of the Street* introduced "another adult-nurtured contribution to childhood (and adult) unhappiness—the tragedy of anti-Semitism."[29] As the story unfolds, an ordinary sixth-grade girl, recently relocated to a new neighborhood in a suburb of Boston, must learn how to get along with a girl living across the street who spouts hateful remarks about Jews. Other narrative strands show how Carol's entire family addresses the challenges of living as Jews in a Christian world, deciding whether going carol singing at Christmas is a "pleasant custom" or a betrayal of Jewish heritage, and balancing the late hour of the Passover seder with the need to attend school the following day, homework in hand. They explore the boundary between conformity and ethnic identity in their middle-class suburb.[30]

Because of its contemporary setting and its author's interests, *Carol's Side of the Street* drew a sharp distinction between the inclusive ideals of American society and its complicated reality and hinted at a Jewish embrace of American material culture that could tip into caricature.[31] It could not fall back on nostalgia to soften social conflict, because it took place in the present. The very title of the book encapsulates division, and the lectures given by Carol's parents about the ignorance that underlies anti-Semitism indicate to the children that the scourge will remain endemic in society, so Jews need to learn to live with it (97). Plot developments emphasizing friendship, togetherness, and cooperation fail to erase that underlying pessimism.

Overt didacticism frequently interrupts the story. For example, the thesis of the book is voiced by Carol's father, speaking to his mother-in-law at a

Chanukah party during which several adults have tried to explain to their children the difference between Christmas and Chanukah: "Maybe if we all understood each other's customs and rituals a little better it would be a better world" (49). Later on, he adds that although Jews have their own religious holidays, "we do celebrate the Fourth of July, and Thanksgiving, and all the national holidays because we are first of all Americans. We have freedom of worship and our freedom gives us the right to be Jews, American Jews" (55). A staunch advocate of "show, don't tell," Meeks eliminated such preaching from Taylor's writing, and her rigor produced a better book.

It was not only that Beim was killed in a car accident the summer before her book was released that led to its obscurity. Aside from containing glaring factual errors about Jewish holidays, it lacked Taylor's ease of storytelling and charm. It was geared to a slightly older audience than the *All-of-a-Kind* series, yet failed to grapple in a sophisticated manner with the serious problems it raised. As mentioned in chapter 3, Meeks rejected the *Downtown* manuscript in part because it dealt with troubling subjects she did not consider appealing to young readers. *Carol's Side of the Street* may be seen as a precursor to books like Judy Blume's *Are You There God? It's Me, Margaret,* but Meeks's instincts told her that consumers of children's literature—librarians, teachers, parents, as well as children—preferred straightforward optimism in 1951.

The adjectives that appeared most frequently in book reviews published all over the country and in the hundreds of fan letters received by Taylor, primarily from girls ages eight to twelve, were *funny, heartwarming,* and *wholesome.* Critics praised the book for its portrayal of a hardworking, poor, yet indefatigably cheerful family full of love and support for one another, guided by patient, caring parents who teach their children time-tested values. The critical approbation reveals as much about expectations for children's literature in 1951 as it does about the books themselves. Like Laura Ingalls Wilder and Maud Hart Lovelace, who also wrote about girls in turn-of-the-century America, Taylor sidestepped confrontation. The immigrant neighborhoods of the All-of-a-Kind family constitute a secure world despite poverty and disease. The girls in the family do not question or push against their parents, who are seen as wise counselors.

Like Beim, but in a more reassuring way, Taylor explored how Jews fit into American society, and both authors asked how Jewish children in

America should grow into their roles as American Jews. Their books defined American Jewish children as respectful of adults and authority, friendly, responsible, religious without intolerance or parochialism, and moderately materialistic. Where they differed was in their confidence about society's response to Jewish faith in American values. In their premise that there is something "American" that absorbs all other identities, they are evidence that ethnic separatism simply was not a value in children's literature in 1950.[32] That explains in part why Fourth of July celebrations appeared so frequently in children's literature. In *All-of-a-Kind Family,* Taylor's description of the festivities on the Lower East Side in the early 1900s laid out a historical foundation for Jewish participation in American culture; in *Carol's Side of the Street,* American children from a variety of ethnic and religious backgrounds celebrate their American identity together on Independence Day.

As Taylor suggested, it was impossible to find books about Jewish children at bookstores or public libraries before *All-of-a-Kind Family.* When she became known as "one Jewish writer who has managed to invade the Gentile book market for her principal source of income," she excoriated Jewish publishing houses for failing to provide good, appealing literature for the avid readers Jewish children were known to be, offering them instead cheaply produced, unattractive, morally heavy-handed, and parochial publications.[33] According to Taylor, Jewish educators were largely to blame because they were so mired in finer points of dogma that they lost sight of every child's love of a good story.

Most of what appeared before 1950 did, in fact, consist of biblical and ritual stories, published by small Jewish presses, with the avowedly pedagogic purpose of explaining Jewish scripture, holidays, and life cycle events. In 1947, Fanny Goldstein (1895–1961), librarian with the Boston Public Library since 1913 and founder of Jewish Book Week, published an article in the *Jewish Book Annual* of the Jewish Book Council titled "The Jewish Child in Bookland," which discussed Jewish books for children and included a nine-page inventory of what was available.[34] Her Jewish-themed reading list, dominated by Bible and holiday stories, shows how few books of fiction with leading Jewish characters existed. Through the 1950s, Goldstein contributed an addendum of three to five pages to the *Annual,* and in 1961 she published a slim thirty-six-page pamphlet, "The Jewish Child in Bookland: A Selected Bibliography of Juveniles for the Jewish Child's Own Bookshelf."

She included a few works of historical fiction in which Jews play peripheral roles, but stories about ordinary Jewish children living ordinary lives are absent until the *All-of-a-Kind* books appear. In contrast, Linda R. Silver's *Best Jewish Books for Children and Teens: A JPS Guide,* published in 2010, fills 375 pages. The *All-of-a-Kind* series was crucial in initiating that extraordinary change. It appeared at just the right moment, when the market for children's literature was growing and editors realized that telling inclusive American stories promised increased sales.

Non-Jewish librarians also responded to the change initiated by *All-of-a-Kind Family.* Lionized by the American Library Association for her positive portrayal of librarians, Taylor was thrilled to meet and be praised by Anne Carroll Moore, superintendent of children's work at the New York Public Library from 1906 to 1941 and grande dame of children's literature even after her retirement. Moore initiated a brief correspondence with Taylor in October 1951, congratulating her on winning the Follett Award and promising to attend the upcoming luncheon in Taylor's honor. The two women met at the banquet for the presentation of the award held at the Hotel Pierre on October 15. Their meeting led Frances Clarke Sayers (1897–1989), Moore's protégée and successor at the New York Public Library, to invite Taylor, Ralph, and Jo to the St. Nicholas Eve party on December 5, 1951, a celebration held annually in Moore's honor at the library's Central Children's Room.[35]

Moore sensed in Taylor a potential ally in the rapidly changing field of juvenile fiction. In a letter of October 4, 1951, she lauded Taylor's contribution to children's literature "in an era when racial and religious themes have been too often thrown off balance by the failure to trust the family or the individual character sufficiently to capture the reader's imagination." She thought Taylor succeeded in avoiding dull, heavy-handed preachiness about race and religion. Taylor's engaging story of a Jewish family, with unique, appealing characters and imaginative adventures, was, in Moore's view, more effective than stories that assumed it was absolutely necessary to articulate tension as inherent in racial or religious identification.

In a later letter, Moore identified a book she considered "thrown off balance": *Ladycake Farm* by Mabel Leigh Hunt. The novel tells the story of the African American Freed family of five as they move from a small town to their own farm in an entirely white community. During their first spring and

Luncheon for the Charles W. Follett Award: Taylor with Frances Clarke Sayers, D. W. Follett, Anne Carroll Moore, Patricia Cummins (executive secretary, Children's Book Council), October 15, 1951

Taylor between Morris and Cilly Brenner, with D. W. Follett at award ceremony

Taylor with D. W. Follett and Esther Meeks at award ceremony

summer, the Freeds encounter both neighborly kindness and crude prejudice in their new home. The characters verge on stereotypes, and incidents are contrived so that the community must confront its racism. Moore expressed reservations about the book and asked for Taylor's opinion. Taylor respectfully pushed back, even though she agreed the family was unbelievably and relentlessly cheerful:

> I came to it with a slightly prejudiced mind because I had heard your comments about it. Nevertheless when I finished the book, I had the feeling that Miss Hunt had done rather well with the racial problem. Though it plays an important part in the story, her treatment was rather delicate. Mr. Taylor and I have a colored girl who works for both of us and when I consider how carefully we must tread not to hurt her oversensitiveness, I feel Miss Hunt minimized rather than bore down too heavily.[36]

Setting aside for the moment the undisguised racial prejudice, the interesting point is that an influential woman in the world of books consulted Taylor on "minority" children's literature.

In seeking Taylor's opinion, Moore implicitly placed Jews and African Americans in the same category, and indicated her disapproval of religious and racial "problem" stories.[37] *Ladycake Farm* resembled *Carol's Side of the Street* in that the families in both books treated prejudice as something unlikely to disappear, surmountable only in individual instances through strength of character and dignified courtesy. Moore preferred America as portrayed by Taylor. In that idealistic world, society rewarded hard work and time-honored values without reservation, and the innocence of childhood remained unsullied by social, if not natural, ills. Disease and accidents might claim their victims, but kindly doctors and settlement nurses did their utmost to cure and shelter, and librarians and teachers offered an education that would lead to a better world. In Moore's view, the purpose of literature was to delight the imagination. Juvenile literature should convey the enchantment of childhood and the magic of language rather than the stark realities of flawed human nature.

Taylor certainly thought she was living an enchanted life in 1951 and 1952. Beginning with the banquet on October 15, for which she received a corsage from Benn Hall, the publicity agents, sent via Western Union, and an invitation for her parents, Taylor began a round of appearances up and down the East Coast on radio shows and in schools and libraries, interviews with newspapers, and luncheons and cocktail parties with the likes of Anne Carroll Moore, Fanny Goldstein, and Iphigene Ochs Sulzberger.[38] *Child Life* magazine chose *All-of-a-Kind Family* as one of the ten best children's books of 1951. The accolades made her giddy: "I'm in a constant state of excitement. Every day brings something new and more wonderful. If it keeps up, I'll be standing on my head."[39] From the beginning, just as she had kept scrapbooks to record her trips with Ralph and Jo's early years, Taylor kept a scrapbook in which she methodically pasted newspaper clippings sent by a service to which she subscribed, photos, radio scripts, publicity flyers, invitations to book fairs and luncheons, and drawings from schoolchildren.

Aside from the hitchhiking jaunts to Norfolk, Virginia, and to Quebec with Ralph soon after they married and a few out-of-town performances with Graham, Taylor had rarely traveled. Follett now provided her with all-expenses-paid trips by airplane to cities as far afield as Chicago, Detroit, and

Fayetteville, Arkansas, and by train to most major cities along the East Coast. Taylor also visited dozens of schools and libraries in the New York area, modifying her talks to make her book seem personal to each audience. When speaking to librarians, for example, Taylor had a speech that used childhood memories not in her book to romanticize and revere them as custodians of learning and magic. Meeks coached Taylor in public speaking, urging her not to try to be someone she was not—namely, a dramatic orator—but rather to rely on her own particular appeal and to appear spontaneous even when she had a speech manuscript in hand: "So you just keep on doing what you are doing, and you need not feel like a little mouse."[40] Meeks misinterpreted Taylor's self-deprecation, given Taylor's experience on stage as actor and dancer and as coach to children of various talents and attention spans. Taylor mentioned in more than one speech that she was a "ham," joking that her audience was obliged to listen to her, unlike her husband.

Although Taylor polished set speeches for her various audiences—librarians, book fair attendees, teachers—improvisatory dramatics with children was her true love. As early as November 1951, she transformed school auditoriums and children's reading rooms in libraries into stages where she interacted with students—with no props and an endless fund of story ideas. On a visit to the Teaneck Public Library on November 30, she made a small speech, read a little from her book, "and got a big kick out of hearing the children laugh in certain places. I could not tell, though, whether they were laughing in response to the reading or to the subject matter itself." She conducted a question-and-answer session and then "noticed a kind of restlessness in the audience." Spotting two of her Cejwin campers among the onlookers:

> I couldn't resist the experiment I next made. I invented a new technique for use in story hours at the libraries. At least Miss McDonald said afterward that she would try to employ that technique herself. Using my own 2 little campers to start things off, I did impromptu dramatics with the children—just like the kind of work I do at camp. My plots were all related closely to the neighborhood and the library itself . . . The children were a bit stiff at first but I acted right along with them and soon there were more wanting to perform than I could possibly use. It was a good afternoon—I don't know who had a better time, the children, or me.[41]

Taylor doing creative dramatics with children at Seward Park Library

Taylor with schoolgirls in Chicago

Photographs from similar sessions show rapt audiences of laughing children focused on the diminutive Taylor who has a big grin on her face or a finger raised in mock scolding as she participates with the lucky students chosen to act with her.

Taylor's camp work dovetailed with her literary work through creative dramatics in a way that pleased both children and adults. A loyal participant in the *New York Times* "Reading Is Fun" program, in which authors visited schools in the New York metropolitan area, Taylor heard from the director of the program, Dorothy McFadden, about a principal's appreciation: "She said you were wonderful and the children just loved you. She particularly liked 'the expressive reading of a chapter from her latest book.' "[42] Taylor's participation in the program was also good publicity, for McFadden informed Taylor that a review of *More* would soon appear in the Sunday *Times*.

Meeks had been right that Taylor would be free to discuss the Jewish features of her book once she accepted speaking engagements. On several occasions, Taylor inquired in advance if the audience of school children or library patrons was likely to be Jewish so that she could include relevant anecdotes in her talk.[43] She was invited to speak at synagogues, addressing the parents of their religious schools.[44] In 1957, she was asked to speak at a conference in November sponsored by the Jewish Book Council and the Theodor Herzl Institute on "Jewish Writing and Jewish Writers in America."[45] There she spoke about literature for younger readers and seized the occasion to scold the Jewish publishing business for doing so little to promote quality literature for Jewish children.

Taylor felt she could speak with some authority, because she saw her impact on Jewish children in the hundreds of fan letters she received. Children of all backgrounds wrote to her as school assignments or because they were curious about the life of a writer. It was only the Jewish readers, however, who could tell her how much the books meant to a parent or a grandparent or how happy it made them to recognize their customs and foods in the stories. Upon receiving one of Taylor's kind replies, a fan in Milwaukee wrote back: "That very night we had our first Seder. I was so thrilled with your letter that I decided to share it with the family. After the religious portion of the Seder was completed, I read your letter at the table, got your book and read your chapter on Passover. This led us into the wee hours as we started to reminisce and discuss our funny childhood experiences."[46] Taylor felt compelled to answer every fan letter, and it was responses like the one quoted that made her compulsion more than a reflexive response to her "darn Germanic conscience."[47] She saw in just how many unexpected ways she could touch the lives not only of Jewish children, but of Jewish families more generally, through words.

Taylor's literary achievement earned her more than speaking engagements in the Jewish community, for she also won several awards from Jewish organizations. For example, in 1952 the Jewish Book Council of America awarded her the $250 Isaac Siegel Memorial Award for best Jewish juvenile literature in English, which was presented at a ceremony at the 92nd Street Y and written up in the Jewish press, both English and Yiddish. In the Golden Pen Playwriting Contest of 1956, sponsored by the Jewish Theater for Children, Taylor's play *In God's Hands* won honorable mention for being among the best plays written in English on a Jewish theme.[48]

Taylor delighted in the feeling of accomplishment and the attention she received in the months after the publication of *All-of-a-Kind Family,* so it is unsurprising that she continued to write.[49] To her dismay, it was not so easy to get more of her writing published. As *More* was going to press in 1954, Taylor drafted a speech, which she gave on numerous occasions, titled "Adventures of a Prize Winner."[50] It was a lighthearted, slightly rueful look at what happened after the success of her first book. Taylor opened with a brief summary of how she came to write *All-of-a-Kind Family* and win the Follett Award. She once again attributed agency to Ralph: "Now my husband, still carrying the ball rushed out and brought me the latest book on how to write for children. He seemed determined to keep me working." Unable to feign interest in the manual—because she was, after all, a celebrated author— Taylor pounded out a new story on her portable typewriter. She was under obligation to her editor in Chicago, who, she was sure, "must be simply drooling with impatience." After several months, she sent off a manuscript she was convinced was superior to her first book in style and construction. Months passed during which her correspondence with Meeks concerned Taylor's numerous speaking engagements, without one word said about the new "masterpiece." Finally, Meeks came to New York, and over lunch, the editor broke the news to her overconfident author: " 'Put it away for now,' she said gently and then added, not very diplomatically, 'it might ruin your career.' " Into the famous box went the manuscript.

Taylor then tried to write about teenagers from an adult perspective, convinced she knew a lot about them since Jo and her friends were always around her apartment.[51] She submitted the manuscript to three women's magazines, and it was rejected three times. Taylor concluded, "Maybe my husband was right after all. He always maintained the reason I had been so successful with my children's book was because I was so childish myself." That manuscript, too, ended up in the box. Taylor thought her mistake had been to write about teenagers from an adult point of view, so she composed five chapters of a book about teenagers from their point of view. Again over lunch in New York, Meeks told Taylor that books for teenagers do not sell as well as those for younger readers, and those chapters ended up in the box as well. Taking a cue from all the fan letters she was receiving for her first book, Taylor wrote a sequel to *All-of-a-Kind Family*, which did not impress Meeks. Taylor claimed that at this point she was ready to throw in the towel and content herself with cooking, dancing, and perhaps a hobby like weaving.[52]

Meeks did not give up on Taylor: " 'You know,' she said earnestly, 'a professional writer never stops working' . . . 'But I'm not a professional writer,' I wailed. 'But you will be,' she replied with such assurance, my mouth snapped shut. For once I was speechless.' " As was her practice, Taylor wrote during the winter before she started preparing material for Cejwin, and she developed a superstition about not discussing her project before it was ready. On January 21, 1954, she assured Meeks: "Though you have not heard from me, I have been working. But I don't want to talk about it yet. I have been working against odds." The acceptance letter for that manuscript—the book set in 1915 that became known as *More All-of-a-Kind Family*—arrived less than a week after submission, accompanied by glowing comments, a contract—and no revisions. Indeed, the entire publication process went quickly, and Taylor had a copy in hand by November 6.

Part of the reason it went so quickly was Meeks's decision not to consult Taylor on certain matters. After receiving a copy of the book, Taylor admitted to the illustrator Mary Stevens, "Esther kept your work a secret from me all the while you were occupied."[53] Meeks had wanted Taylor to check the illustrations for the first book, primarily for accuracy of Jewish garb and of the appearance of the sisters, but she had learned over time that Taylor was as much a stickler for detail as she was, and time was of the essence.

When *More* came out, accolades poured in yet again. Fanny Goldstein gushed: "I was quite thrilled with the delicate format of the book and the jacket. I have not as yet been able to read the book because the minute it arrived, I took it straight to an exhibit on the Tercentenary at the Copley Square Library, and there it is in the main lobby in a case."[54] Taylor's name spoke for itself, and Goldstein assured her she was welcome to come speak at the Boston Public Library any time.

Elated to have a second book out and conscious of the need to give it good publicity, in the "Adventures of a Prize Winner" speech Taylor downplayed just how tortuous the process of arriving at a second publication had been. She referred to the "agony of creation," but the overall tone of the speech was that of a self-mocking homebody. Taylor mentioned that she preserved discarded typed pages in a large shopping bag, even though they outnumbered the ones she kept: "This shopping bag is a device I arrived at through lamental [*sic*] experiences. Once I used to tear up the pages I thought I didn't want anymore, and feed them into the hungry mouth of the incinerator only to discover when it was too late, that I'd burnt up sections of my manuscript as well." Throughout, Taylor played the role of the hapless housewife with hidden talents. When asked by children if she had ever experienced failure, Taylor turned her experience into a lesson in perseverance and character-building, echoing her mother's admonitions from years past: "Yes I have had failures only I don't call them that. You learn from everything you do and though something you've written is not thought worthy of publication by some editor, it does not mean that it hasn't some merit or that it has not served to improve your writing."[55]

That was a gentle way of alluding to what was often a tough fight between editor and author. For example, Taylor increasingly refused to water down her past to suit Meeks's blueprint for a successful children's novel. Before Meeks rejected *Downtown*, she tried to polish it to her satisfaction. Among her editorial comments was the suggestion that Taylor make the social worker more a figure of fun. Taylor bristled: "The social worker of her day was a dedicated person who came from a much higher strata in the social scale and had deliberately chosen a life of self-denial and sacrifice to help correct some of the social and economic evils existing in the crowded portions of the city . . . They were highly respected by the community and were actually, to a large degree, Lady Bountifuls."[56] The truth of Taylor's past was not to be sacrificed to the whims of the market.

An even more horrific suggestion Meeks offered was for the All-of-a-Kind family to adopt gentile Guido, the Italian boy. While retaining a polite, almost regretful tone, Taylor went on the offensive:

> It would be highly unlikely that the Italian community would not take care of its own. And still less likely for a Jewish family to play foster parents to a person of another faith. Lack of charity would not be the issue here. Having the family work together with the parish priest would be unthinkable at that period as the various religious communities had no contact with one another whatsoever. If we emphasize Guido's religion at all and put him into a Jewish home, and then have him take an active part or even explain to him the various ceremonials, it will appear to the reader, I am afraid, that the child is being proselytized. This would not only create a bad taste all around but also would be against Jewish custom which forbids proselytizing.[57]

It was one thing to create understanding and promote harmony in the American ethnic and religious landscape. But for a non-Jew to distort the past, with its unique religious and cultural features, and to expose Jews to yet more unjustified attacks was something Taylor rejected categorically.

Meeks did appreciate that Taylor produced reliably popular stories about her lovable fictional family, which had readers, especially girls, asking for more almost as soon as a new book in the series appeared. Meeks pushed for another book as early as January 1955, only two months after *More* hit the bookstores: "I have been thinking about what you should write next. Maybe you have already started something . . . the logical thing seemed to me to write about what happened in the new neighborhood. The adjustment to a different environment must contain some very interesting situations."[58] And indeed, Taylor presented Meeks with the manuscript for *Uptown* by the spring of 1956. She was, however, less than enthusiastic during the editing of the book: "You wished for something that would be characteristic of the neighborhood. Unfortunately there wasn't anything that was very characteristic. Actually the outstanding quality of the Bronx at that particular period, was that it suffered for the most part from the drab uniformity of the areas along the subway circuit."[59] Follett's 1956 list was already closed when Meeks received the first draft, so Meeks hoped to publish the book in 1957—it did need some refining, after all. The name was settled by January 1957, but the novel did not appear until May 1958, in part because of illustrator Mary Stevens's other commitments.[60]

An omen of things to come was the rejection of subsequent manuscripts. In January 1959, Taylor sent Meeks a fantasy about a personified recorder.[61] In that letter she mentioned another submission as well, *Goodbye Is Hello,* a novel about dancers and choreographers, which shows she had not given up on her plans to publish something for teenagers. Meeks turned down both manuscripts in March. She herself did not care for the personification of musical instruments and she did not think that there was a market for the story. As for the book aimed at girls aspiring to be dancers, "I think its appeal would be limited, and in general I don't believe the story has any real importance. As always I could help you to make it a better story, but no amount of work could make this story good enough to be worthy of your reputation."[62] That motif—that a book by Taylor would receive unfavorable comment and disappoint readers—came to haunt the frustrated author.

With her popularity still intact in the 1950s, however, Taylor's writing became more assured and more complex, and she saw her books as conveying significant messages. Her goals changed from simply retelling stories to pursuing her own complicated ideas about Jewish Americans, including their socialist activism. Although Taylor was not involved in leftist politics in the 1950s and is not grouped with writers such as Crockett Johnson or Carl Sandburg, who were known leftists whose personal politics have been traced in their works for children, she still moved in the leftist circles prevalent in the fields of theater, dance, and education.[63] As she interpreted the past through the filtering lens of her left-wing sensibilities, she retrofitted her progressive values to memories of her presocialist youth. In a 1952 radio interview, Taylor extolled the values learned from living in a large family, and by extension a larger social community: "In a large family we got the best possible preparation for living in an adult world. We learned to cooperate—to divide the work to get it done . . . No member of a large family can expect his needs to be considered over those of others . . . [Understanding in families] will broaden out to an understanding of all peoples of the world—without regard for their race, color or religion."[64] That classic progressive message comes straight from the YPSLs by way of the Bank Street School and Little Red. Taylor's focus was domestic rather than economic, but it was political all the same.

Just as Taylor reshaped her past through progressive ideals of gender equality and female independence, as seen in the discussion of Henny's election at school, and promoted ideals of enlightened parental authority and social responsibility, so her portrayal of work and workers in the 1910s reflected her progressive vision. In the first book of the series, the issue is secondary, except that the reader knows that everyone in the family works hard and that Papa welcomes and assists workers of the lower class, specifically the peddlers who sell their goods to him. Taylor introduces the peddlers who frequent Papa's shop by name, giving each a nationality and a personality, and shows that Papa's children are comfortable with the multilingual group (*AKF* 35).

In *More,* Taylor subtly integrates her politics into her portrayal of the past. In the chapter "Queen of the May," she relates how a celebration of spring that the family organizes—with maypole, neighborhood children in fairy-book costumes, and an Uncle Sam outfit for little brother Charlie—turns into a party with Papa's peddlers in his cellar junk shop when rainstorms make an outdoor parade impossible. By converting an ancient British holiday into a day off and a time of celebration for workers—May Day as labor rather than mythical holiday—Taylor chose the Americanization of socialist principles over the Anglicization of Jewish characters. With the participation of a little Uncle Sam, support for workers and celebration of a labor holiday become acts of patriotism.

In real life, the Taylors faced a business crisis in 1955 that marked a turning point in their approach to the working classes. This softening of socialist principles is representative of many second-generation Jewish immigrants; in Taylor's case, there was a catalytic story. Until 1955, the Taylors were able to live as if they were socialists, their political leanings not in conflict, in their minds, with the way they lived. Taylor had never been particularly ideological, but she was sympathetic to the working poor, the homeless harassed by policemen in public parks, and children doing odd jobs to earn a penny. She knew from experience that getting fired or business reversals could not always be avoided and were not necessarily anyone's fault. And those sympathies endured—as long as they did not threaten her husband's business.

While Taylor had been enjoying her fame as an author and struggling to come up with new material, Ralph and Milton had been making a success of Caswell-Massey. In February 1952, the store received a glowing write-up in the *New York Times,* complete with photos of antique apothecary equipment, the storefront, and pages of an old formula book.[65] The article noted that "a cologne water made up of orange, lemon, neroli, oil of rosemary and berga-mot (among other ingredients) delighted Dolley Madison, George Washington, Captain Kidd, the Marquis de Lafayette, Jenny Lind, and is still a favorite with Caswell-Massey patrons." Ralph is described as "tall and grave" and deeply informed about the store's history, showing the reporter prescriptions with the names of Diamond Jim Brady, Edwin Booth, and Sarah Bernhardt, among others. Herbert Hoover, William Saroyan, and assorted Vanderbilts and Astors are mentioned as current patrons. According to the reporter, Ralph and Milton "feel a heavy responsibility for maintaining the dignity the shop has always fostered. They never show astonishment, no matter what requests or prescriptions come through." And some of those requests were for leeches, bear grease, turtle oil, and two-hundred-year-old beauty remedies.

In March 1952, the store celebrated its bicentennial, with champagne and highballs pouring from the soda fountain and the Taylor brothers slicing a birthday cake topped with a model of an apothecary's mortar and pestle. Between four and five hundred guests who had accepted formal invitations passed through the store's doors, including Anita Loos, Mrs. Lou Gehrig, and top academics in pharmacy.[66] Less than two months later at a luncheon at the Waldorf-Astoria, the apothecary shop was one of 231 businesses honored for being in operation in the city of New York for a hundred years or more.[67]

From Taylor's point of view, her hardworking husband deserved his success.

> Ralph is very busy—even to working on Saturdays. Which I suppose I ought to be grateful for because it means that his wholesale business is finally catching on. He has put forth a great deal of effort in that direction, it being his hope that someday they [Milton and Ralph] will both be able to retire from the retail industry which takes too much of a toll of their health and energy.

> You cannot possibly work the hours necessary for a retail estab-
> lishment and if you stay away from the store, you always have to
> feel uneasy because it is in the hands of strangers.[68]

Another advantage of the wholesale business was that Ralph did not have to
manage staff. He had one secretary and a boy who worked part-time, just as
Ralph had many years before. Both brothers had the support of their parents
as well. Simon Taylor was described in his obituary as "secretary and senior
member" of the firm when he died of heart disease on November 6, 1953, on
a subway platform while on his way to work.[69] His widow became a constant
presence in the store, working the cash register and engaging customers with
her lively conversation.

In 1955, the elegant emporium came under threat. Taylor first mentioned trouble at the store in a letter to Meeks in April: "What am I doing?
Helping my husband fight a strike situation in our lovely shop. I am thus being afforded the opportunity to gain a liberal education in labor politics.
Life's become a game of cops and robbers and the battle waxes so hot and
furious, there's no time, nor energy, nor thought for anything else."[70] Taylor
did actually continue speaking at schools in the *New York Times* program,
reliably filling in for other authors who backed out at the last minute. But
much of her time was spent at the shop, and she noted that she typed her letters with the store typewriter, not being able to get home to use her own. That
spring, friends included good wishes for the end of the strike in their notes to
Taylor and hoped she and Ralph had regained their peace of mind.

But the strike dragged on and the Taylors grew increasingly hostile to
the union. Taylor said she could not get away "till the situation here at the
store resolves itself—for that matter I don't know if it actually will since we
have no intention of working with this particular local—before I shall be able
to resume a normal social existence."[71] Milton's wife Zelda complained, "The
strike situation is so damn depressing that I don't like to even think about it,
although that is really impossible. However, Milton says he doesn't care
about the strikers if he can get good help."[72] Jo put in her two cents during the
summer, glad to hear "that at least a partial condemnation of some of the
Union organizers has been achieved finally."[73]

Beginning in October, Meeks regularly inquired whether the strike
situation was improving.[74] A few months later, Cilly in Florida expressed

surprise that her daughter still could not get away from New York because of the strike, for she thought it was settled.[75] Taylor responded with information about a court case, to which Cilly replied, "If only the Union would stop the picketing so you and Ralph could go on that long plan vacation."[76] In July, Jo still fretted over her parents' labor troubles.[77]

In her correspondence, Taylor did not say what exactly was going on. It appears that the labor dispute began in March 1955, when Ralph and Milton fired a soda fountain washer after his supervisor complained he was too slow. The fired worker appealed to Local 1199 of the Retail Drug Employees Union, claiming he had been fired for being a union member. Caswell-Massey's soda men all went out at the union's call and the union set up a picket line that lasted a grueling twenty months. A police detail protected customers during business hours (Taylor's "cops and robbers"), while picketers reportedly chanted that going into the store was "un-American." Truck drivers who made deliveries to the store were beaten or threatened near their homes. Caswell-Massey's three phone lines were constantly jammed, and once a union sympathizer lobbed a stink bomb into the store from the door leading into the lobby of The Barclay.

The dispute was part of a comprehensive push by Local 1199 to expand its membership among drugstores in the metropolitan area. It turned out Caswell-Massey was one of seven pharmacies targeted by a phone-jamming strategy, which ultimately led to felony accusations against several union organizers. The maximum sentence for the charges was two years on each count, but on December 7, 1956, those convicted received suspended sentences.[78]

Another case that wandered through the courts from 1956 to 1959 caused the Taylor brothers yet more headaches and was what Cilly had referred to as "the case." With all its fancy accoutrements and perfumed soaps, Caswell-Massey was still a working pharmacy that filled prescriptions. Health inspectors delivered summonses to Milton and Ralph on the charge of violating the New York City Sanitary Code on the sale of barbiturates. The pharmacists "refilled sleeping pill prescriptions at least five times between July and December without proper authorization. The purchases were made by health inspectors."[79] The Taylors claimed to have phoned the relevant doctor's office when clients came in for a refill that was not marked on the written prescription. The health inspectors disputed their claim; Milton and Ralph were fined, but appealed. The State Court of Appeals finally reversed the lower court decision in July 1959, with one dissent, asserting that the law as written was vague concerning refills authorized by telephone.[80]

Through all the troubles, Taylor seized every opportunity to advertise her husband's business. In her travels to book fairs and conferences, she invariably sent cologne or some other toiletry item to her hostess, promoting it as a Caswell-Massey product. For many years, Caswell-Massey soaps and colognes were her standard Chanukah gift to her friends the Frishmans in Los Angeles. If fans asked about her husband, Taylor always mentioned that he was the president of Caswell-Massey, "the oldest chemists and perfumers in America."[81]

Taylor also participated in the glamorous men's fashion show that Caswell-Massey initiated in 1958 and sponsored for many years thereafter, an event that attracted fashion houses from Rome, London, and Paris, as well as American firms.[82] The awards for excellence in menswear design were presented at a gala dinner dance and fashion show at venues such as the Four Seasons restaurant and the Plaza Hotel, and the show expanded to other cities in the United States and Canada. Among the judges were Richard Avedon, George Balanchine, and Serge Obolensky, the Russian aristocrat and war hero who was then vice-chairman of the board of Hilton Hotels.[83]

Taylor wrote to friends and family with lengthy descriptions of her custom-made gowns, all the while avowing that it really was not her type of activity. To Sarah Lang, a friend from Cejwin, she admitted: "I'm all prepared in a gold long sheath slit on the side. It doesn't look like me—it doesn't even feel like me though I had it made to my measurements. Sarah, I was never meant for this kind of life."[84] Still humble when writing to the teenage Ginger, Taylor at least expressed pleasure: "I wore my sumptuous new dress—it was very lovely—people liked it but there were so many other magnificent clothes one more beautiful dress did not matter."[85] The difference in tone accords with Taylor's different relationship with each woman: Sarah was Taylor's peer at Cejwin and it is clear from their correspondence that she had to watch her finances, while Ginger was an admiring teenager, interested in fashion and the fashionable world. As Ginger and Taylor developed an increasingly adult relationship, Taylor's tone modulated:

Damn it, I can't appear in last year's gown much as I love it and much as I hate going through the trouble and time-consuming effort of getting a new one. I suppose others might welcome the opportunity for dressing up but I don't. It seems so absurd to me—I am not a society woman or one who makes a point of night-clubbing where such clothes can be displayed—so my closet will soon be bulging with evening attire. I wish someone I knew were my size so that I could lend them out.[86]

Taylor considered herself not a "society woman" but a businesswoman. When she knew which shows Ralph planned to attend ("of course I plan to go with him"), she contacted Meeks about the best choices for her own publicity: "Which . . . would be more advantageous for publicizing Follett & Co. and specifically my books? I haven't been to either [Dallas or Miami Beach] so I'll leave it up to you to decide for me . . . I will then let you know exact dates so your publicity department can get busy."[87]

It took time for Taylor to reach that level of confidence, and in the meantime, she and Ralph faced new challenges as parents. Whatever Jo remembers about her stormy senior year, the rift with her parents, while painful, did not constitute a complete severance of relations, which might have derailed Jo's academic success, nor did it prevent the Taylors from financing their daughter's education. Already in 1952, Taylor entertained hopes that Jo would go to college, preferably out of town: "If she doesn't get a college education, there'll be no future of any kind for her."[88] Jo's parents did indeed support her decision to enroll at Sarah Lawrence, an expensive, elite women's college.

In several ways, Sarah Lawrence fit the pattern of educational choices the Taylors had been making since Jo was born. Located in Yonkers, some fifteen miles north of Manhattan, it offered highly individualized, personal curricula. Founded in 1926, it was the "first liberal arts college in the United States to incorporate a rigorous approach to the arts with the principles of progressive education, focusing on the primacy of teaching and the concentration of curricular efforts on individual needs."[89] Educational reformer Harold Taylor, hired as president in 1945 at the age of thirty, was friends with John Dewey and employed Dewey's method at the college.

Working toward her liberal arts degree, Jo continued to choreograph modern dance pieces. The school newspaper enthusiastically reported on her dance group's television features to be shown across the country. Jo was as intrigued as her mother by interactive performances, for questions were to be asked of the television audiences and incorporated into the shows. The cast was to create its own commercials, and "although Jo isn't dancing, she ironically confesses that she must lose 35 pounds in order to qualify for one line in a commercial."[90] When she graduated in 1957, Jo was still working with her dance group from the High School for the Performing Arts.

In the college, Jo worked on *Dido and Aeneas* in 1954 with Bessie Schonberg (1906–1997), the director of theater and dance at Sarah Lawrence from 1938 to 1975 and one of the foremost dance educators of the twentieth century. Again, Jo's world and that of her parents overlapped. Just as Joseph Campbell taught at Sarah Lawrence and was on the editorial board of *Dance Observer* in the 1940s, so Schonberg, a German immigrant, collaborated with Martha Graham in the early 1930s. She performed in *Heretic* and *Primitive Mysteries*, before giving up dancing when she injured her knee in 1931. Like Graham, who envisioned certain colleges as venues to develop modern dance, and who was on the faculty at Sarah Lawrence between 1935 and 1938, Schonberg realized the possibilities of heading one of the first dance departments in American higher education. Jo also had an article titled "The Psychology of Creative Expression" published in *Dance Observer* in December 1955.

Despite her continued involvement with the dance world, Jo realized that what she really liked was not dance so much as working with people, so she started studying social work. In at least one project, she was able to combine her interest in choreography with social work. Taking a class called "The Artist in Modern Society," she undertook to research the place of choreography in the dance world. She wrote letters to choreographers, drafted questionnaires, made telephone calls, and conducted personal interviews: "The cooperation was really remarkable, and I heard from almost all of the people that I contacted, including Balanchine, Agnes de Mille, Jerome Robbins, and Doris Luhrs, the business director of the Ballet Russe, and a Sarah Lawrence alumna."[91] Reaching outside choreography, Jo sought field experience in more traditional branches of social work, volunteering at the Youth Consultation Service in nearby White Plains. As Jo shifted her academic focus, Sarah Lawrence continued to be a nurturing institution; the school's ethos emphasized political activism and volunteerism, which fit Jo's drive to improve society.

The atmosphere of freedom that prevailed at Sarah Lawrence allowed Jo to explore more than intellectual interests, and she soon presented her parents with an unwelcome fait accompli. As Taylor wrote to Esther Meeks in 1954, "Life with Jo is always dangerous but never dull!"[92] She was referring to Jo's choreographic accomplishments on television and at Sarah Lawrence, of which she was proud, and gave no indication that she suspected the bombshell her daughter was about to drop. In December of her sophomore year, Jo eloped with blue-eyed and blond Steve Marshall, a non-Jewish soldier without a college education, who lived with his elderly Russian father in Greenwich Village.[93] News of the couple's marriage was not made public until September 1955, and it stunned friends and family. Sarah Lang's early-October response was typical:

> Now I may be doing the wrong thing to write to you before I hear from you personally regarding Jo Anne's marriage. I don't know whether you know that I received an announcement from Jo Anne and Steven Marshall announcing their marriage last December. Naturally, I was quite shocked and surprised, but I do hope everything will turn out for the very best for Jo Anne and that she will have a full measure of happiness and contentment in life and that you'll have lots of joy together with her.
>
> None of us know what our children will do—we try to guide them and advise them according to our more mature judgment and all we can do is hope and pray that when they marry, they will better their own lives and bring joy to their families, too.[94]

Although little was preserved on paper about the elopement, it is not difficult to imagine the rash of phone calls and emergency family meetings.

The letters Jo sent in the summer of 1955 are chatty, happy, and completely at ease with both her parents and her exciting life as a soldier's wife at a military camp in Augusta, Georgia. She talks about books and movies, funny incidents with her husband's colleagues, her summer job, dieting and health concerns, and above all her deep love for Marshall, whom she praises as intelligent, serious, mechanically gifted, shy, considerate, and hardworking. Once the marriage was made public, the Taylors' friends rallied around and were soon sending regards to Jo and Steve in every note to Taylor.

Jo's marriage presented three problems. First, her family feared that she would leave college. That was underestimating Jo's intelligence and ambition, and those worries were quickly allayed. Jo and Steve lived apart during the academic year while Jo finished her studies and Steve worked, and she wrote often to her parents about teachers and class projects. When Jo graduated in 1957, Taylor wrote proudly, "My daughter graduated from college. She has won a fellowship to the New York School for Social Work (an offshoot of Columbia) where she goes for her Master's degree."[95]

The second problem was Steve's lack of the social, economic, and educational background the Taylors expected in their daughter's husband. Cilly bluntly criticized Jo's carelessness: "Her Letters are so lovely and intelligent that one is surprised of her infatuation to such inferior boys when she can choose the finest and best of them Oh well lets hope she will wake up some day."[96] In Cilly's mind, Jo was old enough to make her own choices, and if the marriage turned out badly, she could always walk away from it. What Cilly did not want was for Ralph and Taylor to torture themselves over their daughter's decision, or to nag Jo about her foolishness, which served no purpose.

In Jo's recollections, her parents initially did not like Steve. Yet since Steve himself felt the lack of a college degree, they refrained from holding it against him and encouraged his efforts to get an education. Over time, they came to appreciate his good qualities and to hope that his steady personality would anchor their restless daughter. Certainly Jo's letters to her parents over the next few years were those of a curious mind, completely engaged by new experiences and fascinated by this man who shared her life. Before long, Ralph was sending advice and medication for Steve's ulcer, and vitamin pills for Jo, while Jo informed her parents of Steve's promotions and salary increases. The Marshalls tried to get along on their own earnings, and their thriftiness must have reminded Ralph and Taylor of their own days as newlyweds when they rationed their salaries and hitchhiked to make their limited budget cover a weekend getaway. Steve stayed in the Taylors' apartment when, benefiting from the GI Bill, he traveled to New York to take entrance exams for the engineering program at Pratt. Jo and Steve rented an apartment near the Taylors when they later settled in New York. In 1958, Taylor dedicated *Uptown* "to Jo and Steve," a relationship she freely explained to fans who asked.

The third difficulty was that Steve was not Jewish. Cilly and Morris were in Florida when they received the news, and Cilly voiced objections to the intermarriage as coming from her husband. She herself made it sound as if having yet another family member to knit and cook for could not have pleased her more. According to Cilly, when cousins Rafael and Nelly Brenner visited with the young couple in the Washington, D.C., area, they reported, "Aside from Religion [Steve] seems to be a very nice and intelligent Boy and they actet very happy."[97] Cilly was indefatigable in reassuring her daughter about the headstrong Jo:

> We had expected this only not so soon and as everything turned out alright there is nothing to worry . . . Well it seems you taking your Son in law more to your hart from what you write he must be very fine and considerate I only hope he dosent humble himself to much towards Joan I am sure once they have their own home she will make it a happy one for him and as they are so much in love it should be a happy marriage. Every member of the family who invited him wrote us what a wonderful impression he made on them . . . am only glad Pop has soffent and is willing we shall invite them at your house as soon as we come home.[98]

In Cilly's telling, Morris was the one who was upset and embarrassed. Wintering every year in Florida, the senior Brenners had become quite close to Charlotte's in-laws, who spent the season near them and whom Cilly formally referred to as Mr. and Mrs. Himber. In early December 1955, several months after the public announcement of Jo's marriage, Cilly wrote to Taylor: "Mrs. Himber still dosent know that Joan is married or perhaps she does know and don't want to talk about it."[99] In January, Cilly clarifies: "Even Pop is more reconcildet toward it and even tell me to tell Mrs. Himber."[100]

Once again, the story is not so simple, and it is unlikely that the disapproval came only from Morris. Susan Baker, Charlotte's daughter, recalls that when she married a gentile, the difference between her two Orthodox grandmothers was remarkable. Her paternal grandmother—Mrs. Himber—accepted Susan's husband, feeding him matzo ball soup to make him feel welcome. Her maternal grandmother—Cilly—saw the intermarriage as a great tragedy, it being the third in the immediate Brenner family.[101]

Taylor and Ralph were not in a position to object as strenuously on religious grounds—cultural perhaps, but not in terms of ritual observance. Taylor acknowledged that she and her siblings had moved away from the practices of their ancestors: "As we grew older and had families of our own, we lived more like atheists than Jews. In my own home I observed none of the customs I'd enjoyed so much in my childhood—principally I suppose because my husband was so irreligious. I know it came as a shock to me when I first met him to find that he thought nothing of writing a letter to me on Yom Kippur eve. But I loved him so dearly, whatever he wanted or did I was happy to do also." Taylor at least had memories to draw upon when the pull of the past grew stronger as she aged; as for Jo, "all religion of any faith seems absurd to her."[102]

The disruption introduced by Jo's marriage seemed to be resolved within a year or so. Marshall may not have been the Taylors' choice as a husband for their daughter, and they worried about the impetuosity of youth, but the newlyweds appeared to be sincerely in love, worked hard in their respective fields, settled in Manhattan near the Taylors, and showed every indication of fulfilling the family's hopes for a happy, secure future.[103] Not only was that dream to be shattered, but in 1955 the first of many illnesses to devastate the family began to appear in Taylor's correspondence. Joe Kornweitz, Ella's husband, showed signs of a disease that was eventually diagnosed as muscular dystrophy, and afterward Taylor's beloved sister was repeatedly referred to as "poor Ella." Cilly and Morris continued to vacation every winter in Florida, but their health was failing. The Taylors knew financial success without ever feeling completely secure, and Caswell-Massey grew into a business from which Ralph could not retire.

By 1959, the gleeful award winner of 1951 admitted that she did not love writing, but she did love the perks of being a writer: "Sometimes I wish I could throw the typewriter out of the window—at other times I could kiss it for the happiness it has brought me. The rewards for writing are marvelous—meeting friendly, warm-hearted people all over in far off places—meeting them personally or by letter—gaining some faint shred of immortality (for a time at least)—The economic return is one I need not concern myself with since my husband fortunately is well able to take care of that end."[104] Taylor's outlook became more severe as family, work, and health were hit with one blow after another in the 1960s, yet she continued to lecture and to write, giving no hint of that turmoil to anyone outside her immediate circle of friends and family. Her speeches and replies to fans were public statements, geared to sell books, a goal she ceaselessly pursued. Eliding the many difficulties that she experienced, her lectures and books continued to shape her tumultuous life into something appealing.

Personal Loss and Artistic Anxiety

1960–1970

FIVE DEATHS AND A DIVORCE hammered Taylor between 1960 and 1965. Beginning with the death of her father on August 15, 1960, followed by that of Cilly a few years later, the losses piled up. All of the siblings in the All-of-a-Kind family reeled from the loss of Mama and Papa. The deaths of Ella's and Henny's husbands in short succession further drew the sisters together as they looked out for one another's financial and emotional welfare. The death of a friend and colleague from Cejwin, Gertrude Holz, marked a change in Taylor's relation to the camp, while the collapse of Jo's marriage increased her parents' anxiety that they might never have grandchildren. Throughout the personal turmoil, Taylor continued to write, but the results of her efforts disappointed her, as did much else in her life.

Morris suffered from the ordinary aches and pains of age throughout the 1950s. Cilly reported regularly from Florida on his eczema, asking Ralph to send down Caswell-Massey salves to relieve her husband's discomfort and informing the Taylors of improvements in his condition. Her infrequent remarks about Morris were interspersed with news of Cilly's own health, especially the faintness that made walking difficult, and her busy life of bingo, knitting, fundraising for Jewish women's organizations, and socializing. Cilly included the occasional line about Morris ironing while she writes letters and doing the shopping when she cannot walk, or his imminent return from shul (synagogue), where he met his friends year after year, or his strictness about changing the dishes and kashering for Passover. When Cilly complained that she could not ask her husband for money without having an argument, it was the gentle bickering of a long-married couple that rustled through the stationery, rather than any ferocious antagonism.[1] The Brenners had a good laugh over Ralph's amusing suggestion that Morris was womanizing down in Florida: "As for Pop chasing the young women on the beach there are none only old one like me so he has to stick with me."[2]

When Morris died, Taylor was at Cejwin. Seeming to take it in stride, she went to New York for the funeral, but soon returned to her job at camp. Ralph's letter to Taylor on August 20 was full of news about his move from one music camp to another and his continuing success: "I just looked at the bulletin board and see I am assigned to a Sammartini quintette, with me the solo recorder. David [Dushkin] must think I'm good."[3] In a quick note on August 22, Jo mentioned that she and Steve saw the movie *Psycho*, reported on her weight, and asked for travel advice for the Labor Day weekend. Although she assured her mother that she had been in touch with Grandma, her note lacks any urgency or sorrow.

Cilly's amusing remark about her immortality when she learned of Taylor's Follett Award was an indication how the family came to interpret their fictional counterparts in the *All-of-a-Kind* books, as seen also in the condolence note from Taylor's sister-in-law Lucille: "There is the consolation that your father lived a long, full and worthy life. His immortality is assured not only in the memory of his dear ones, but through the important role he plays in your books. A person need never die provided he leaves behind a legacy of memories that are an inspiration and a blessing."[4] Taylor had originally wanted to crystallize a vanished world of the Lower East Side through tales of her childhood—but inadvertently she had created timeless images of her relatives, cherished not just by a commercial audience but also by future generations of the Brenner family.

Cilly was in failing health when she lost her husband, and she faded noticeably afterward.[5] During most of the year, she lived in the same building in the Bronx as Gertrude, who assumed much of her care. Gertrude's personal attentions won her little recognition, Taylor claiming that "harum scarum" Henny, who even as a married woman had given her mother such problems, was "the one most devoted to my mother—the most considerate and kindest."[6] Cilly stopped going to Florida, where she had too often seen her neighbors taken to the hospital only to die within days, with no family to comfort them in their last hours.[7] During the summers when Ella, Taylor, and Gertrude were at Cejwin and Charlotte worked, Henny kept an eye on their mother.[8] For several weeks, Cilly went to resort hotels in the New York area where her sons could visit more easily—their job situations were tenuous at this time—and she continued to enjoy the company of Mrs. Himber.[9] Cilly insisted that she did not want support from the families who were less well off, but all her children contributed financially to her care, with the Taylors and Himbers chipping in the most.[10]

After an almost fatal heart attack, Cilly ended up in a small private hospital in the Bronx, where Taylor traveled daily by train and taxi.[11] Henny thought their mother's days were numbered already in February 1963, and insisted it would be a kindness to let her return from the nursing facility to her own apartment. Like many families coping with aging parents, the sisters felt pulled in different directions. Henny and Cilly's unrealistic expectation that Cilly could return to her apartment was too much for Taylor to take. Although she praised Henny to outsiders, self-pitying Taylor wrote a three-page, single-spaced letter, punctuated with one exclamation mark after another, informing her sister of just how misinformed and misguided she was.[12] When Henny had been hospitalized for exploratory surgery that winter, Gertrude had come down with the flu and yet another of many attacks of erysipelas, so Taylor had to visit Cilly every day bringing food, because "in her willfulness" Cilly refused to eat hospital food. Taylor told Henny how completely unrealistic it was to impose on Gertrude for the care of their mother, who would never trust a housekeeper from outside the family to manage her food, run her errands to the library and post office, and oversee the use of medical equipment, such as an oxygen tank.[13]

Taylor further complained about the time and expense she had devoted to finding a facility for Cilly after she left the hospital. She spelled out that she had paid the lion's share of their parents' support over the years, so it was time to use up their mother's funds before making further contributions. The litany of woes continued with Taylor's nosebleeds, Ralph's bout with the flu, and Cilly's relapse. Taylor felt that unnamed siblings dismissed her work from home as just "playing around," and therefore thought she should be the one to take care of their mother, similarly expecting that Ralph and Taylor should provide all of Cilly's medications—a "list of 6 different expensive drugs on it right now." Taylor disdained Irving's and Jerry's "crocodile tears" not backed up by practical action, and resented that Jerry and Norma thought the $120 a year they contributed to Cilly's care entitled them to dictate the conditions of that care.

For all Henny worried about how much weight she had lost after her surgery, Taylor could top it: "The shilly-shallying back and forth—the constant talk, talk, talk about what to do is over! I for one can't take anymore. I went down to 101 pounds without an operation—Am only now slowly returning to some semblance of health—Despite the fact that there are 7 in the family, right now and for the past 5 weeks, the brunt of this has fallen on Gertie, Charlotte and me—and mostly me!" Nor, Taylor commented, was Cilly so sick she could not write letters to friends and family complaining about how badly she was being treated, how Gertrude and her daughter Judy fought constantly and considered her a burden, how she was parked in a facility with mean nurses. Her ingratitude, even if attributable to senility and pain, was more than Taylor could handle. Taylor continued her rant to Henny: "I am so sick of the phone conversations—I have just told Ralph that he should answer all phones from now on. We have had to give up all social life—all plans for any vacations or trips—everything! My God, we have to live too!"

Only two months later, in April 1963, Henny's husband, Harry Davis, died suddenly of a heart attack. Taylor wrote to Nettie Frishman:

> One sister who always kept her eye on Mother each summer in our absence (Henny) has just lost her husband this week—heart attack also but he was only 63—tall—6 foot 3, an athlete all his life—and beautiful. One never expected it would happen to him. Now she is completely prostrate—she herself only just got over a serious operation which left her weak to begin with. We cannot tell Mother about the loss—we're afraid it would be too much of a shock.[14]

Aside from expressing shock at the unexpectedness of Harry's death, the Brenner sisters did not mourn him, because he was a womanizer and had acted inappropriately with their daughters. Their primary concern was for their mother and Henny. By April, Cilly had been moved from the hospital to a nursing home, where the sisters visited daily to appease the harassed nurses and indulge their mother's whims.[15] Charlotte softened the blow about Harry's death by saying he had taken a turn for the worse. The next day Gertrude and Henny delivered the news, armed with a sedative for Cilly. Charlotte wrote to Taylor and Ralph, who were in Europe, "Of course for the rest of the afternoon it was Henny who was consoling Mom for Mom's misfortune . . . We're all telling her how important it is for Henny at a time like this to know she at least has a mother she can turn to."[16]

Rallying around the first sister to be widowed, the Brenner women worried that Henny was not eating properly, that her spendthrift ways—the "terrible spending impulses" she fully admitted to—would impoverish her, and that she would be overcome by loneliness, despite the fact that her marriage had been troubled and she was close to her daughter Harriet, then living in Birmingham. Henny had been in Alabama all winter to recuperate from her operation, and the sisters feared she would return there, where she had no friends or family aside from Harriet. Lou Himber gave her legal advice, and Ella found her a position supervising maintenance at Cejwin starting June 9, finagling that position into a job in the kitchens for the rest of the summer.[17] Henny, who had been working with her brother Jerry in her husband's trucking business, considered undertaking a small business venture with a friend.[18] The family did not trust her business acumen, however, and Ralph soon stepped in to employ her as a bookkeeper at Caswell-Massey during the rest of the year.[19]

Although her letters revealed a pervasive loneliness, Henny continued to travel, involve herself in family matters, and work, so the family's focus remained on Cilly. Cilly resented being hovered over by people with whom she felt she had nothing in common. Charlotte reported Cilly as saying, " 'Ich kan nicht mich unterhallen mit a Schvartza' [I can't keep up a conversation with a black woman] and she's right. They are no companions for her."[20] The sisters worried about how their mother would cope when most of them went off to Cejwin, with Charlotte working long hours at her job in the Wall Street area, a significant commute from the Bronx. Ever the brisk advocate of self-reliance, Charlotte concluded it did Cilly good to be left to her own devices so that she would be forced to socialize with the other residents of the nursing facility.[21]

During the last months of her mother's life, Taylor was torn between filial responsibility and a desire for personal freedom. She debated whether to take her annual trip to Europe in the spring of 1963. "Thus though I feel guilty about it," Taylor admitted to Meeks, "I am nevertheless running away for a while to renew my spirits. Anyway, Ralph has to go for business, so it would have meant staying home alone."[22] Her letter to Nettie was more expansive, but again there is a cavalier steeliness. After noting that she and Ralph would not stay in Spain as long as she wanted because he had business in Paris and Switzerland, and they also wanted to visit their "great love," England, Taylor revealed that they planned to be away for almost five weeks: "I had to cut it short—In fact until two days ago I wasn't even sure if I would go this year. We've had so much trouble—Mother's had a heart attack—she's 82—was on the terminal list—still is as a matter of fact, but it was touch and go for days and weeks. Right now she is in a very fine nursing home—terribly expensive but as nice as one can expect—because she needs constant nursing care. She's not happy—wants to come home." In Europe, Taylor could not escape her worries about her mother. Expressing disquiet with the modernization of the Mt. Royal Hotel, where the Taylors had stayed during previous visits to London, Taylor used her feelings of unease, of returning to a "changed home," to empathize with Cilly: "If we have this disturbed feeling, isn't it understandable how Mother—at 82 feels?"[23]

Cilly committed suicide on September 10. Charlotte copied and kept the following message with the heading "Note left by Mother upon her death":

> My Dear Children
> Please forgive me what I intend to do. I am to sick and old to run a household. I can not be a burden to you children. I reach a ripe old age and it's time to end it. You made my life very happy and rich and the pills I brought from the home which I saved by keeping one a week since June. So don't blame anyone. You all are very good and kind. It's time for me to go.
>
> Mother

Taylor had seen her mother yearn for death: "She longed for it desperately—used to say over and over again 'I have lived too long.' But then my mother was close to 83—and very ill—dying by inches over a period of years. Also despite her 7 children, terribly lonely for the person she had shared her lifetime with was gone—her husband."[24] Cilly's daughters voiced the opinion over the years that it was depression that killed their mother, although they did not discuss her suicide outside the family.

However matter-of-fact Taylor's tone during the spring, her mother's death hit her hard. Cilly's little admonitions that Taylor should stay in bed longer and not run herself ragged with entertaining and lecturing, to eat a little more, to take a vacation; her pride in Taylor's achievements, the promises to knit an afghan for her, the reassurances that Jo would turn out just fine—all of that maternal solicitude came to an end. Five months after Cilly's death, Taylor wrote to Sarah Lang, "I cannot tell you how many times I think of my mother and feel so alone. Her character now seems so remarkable, so far above that of her children, and particularly when I compare the little she asked for compared to my mother-in-law, then I truly see we had no business being annoyed or irritated at any time. But that's the way life is—you realize only too late."[25] Aside from the dig at Fannie Taylor, who had not yet been canonized in family lore as the remarkably tough, independent old lady she turned out to be, Taylor's grief is palpable.

Her mother's last years burdened Taylor for a long time. When Meeks's mother-in-law died in 1965, Taylor sent her condolences with an admission: "I know how bereft you must feel because I know how I continue to feel the absence of my own parents. It's odd about the emotional tieup with parents—even though in their last years you may have been entirely responsible for their welfare, you still feel the child—abandoned by parents when they are gone . . . You were spared much agony watching slow spiritual and physical deterioration. My mother suffered her infirmities with great mental anguish—and so did we all suffer with her."[26] In light of those remarks, Taylor's decision to take a five-week trip to Europe the spring before her mother's death seems less selfish than self-protective. The emotional toll was simply too much for her without a break.

The loss of the elder Brenners continued to reverberate through their daughters' lives, especially around Yom Kippur, the Jewish Day of Atonement. Taylor lamented to her own daughter in 1965, "Always before, at this time of the year, my family would gather around my mother and father because holidays are a time for family closeness. I remember Papa saying "I will pray for you." Who prays for me now? We feel so desolate, my sisters and I—we try to keep together to assuage some of the loneliness."[27] Ella echoed those sentiments three years later when she was in Alabama for the holidays:

> I particularly miss Papa and Mama on Rosh Hashanah and Yom Kippur. This year especially—altho the services were dignified— and the singing lovely I felt alone and lost and an exile! . . . I wanted to be back on Willett and Delancy over the *carriage*

and horse stable—with Papa and Mama—the smell of snuff—and
(ammonia drops) in my nostrils. I was the only one who fasted—
I missed Papa's coming home with a cheerful grin and saying *Gut
gefast heint!* And enjoying Mama's coffee cake and coffee.[28]

Morris's religious sincerity lingered with the sisters: "My father was a man of
deep faith in God, always used to say—and heaven knows he had to say it
often enough—'For every child born, God will provide.' And he thoroughly
believed it."[29] As for Cilly, she was recognized as the standard of good manners, fastidious housekeeping, and constant activity against which all the sisters measured themselves.

The last of the four deaths in the family was that of Ella's husband Joe,
who passed away on August 20, 1964, after a long struggle with muscular
dystrophy. His illness was first mentioned by Cilly in February 1956: "How is
Joe does those treatment help him and has he still got the Store?"[30] Those
twin anxieties—health and income—appeared over and over in subsequent
letters. By April 1957, Joe had indeed given up his store, and dithering about
Ella's finances peppered the family correspondence year after year.[31] Friends
from Cejwin, such as Sarah Lang, were equally concerned.[32]

Joe's deepening depression and declining physical state increased his
anxieties about being sent away from his home, yet everyone noticed that his
care had become too much for Ella. "I do not see how much longer Ella can
go on taking care of him at home," wrote Taylor to Sarah Lang. "He has to be
moved about by someone else's strength and certainly no woman has that—
he helps himself very little—makes no attempt to rehabilitate the few remaining muscles—he never did want to go to the M.D. center . . . Ella seems
greatly distraught by it all. I fear she can't take it much longer."[33] A few months
later, Taylor was brutal in her helpless anger: "Ella still has her Joe problem—
and it is a problem. He's confined to a wheelchair all day now—goes for treatment to the M.D. foundation but it's silly. Mostly his condition now is one of
deep depression. Well who wouldn't be depressed in his state."[34] Ella did get
help with housework, and Joe had some good days, but Taylor remained ob-
durate: "It is just that she is a prisoner having to stay with Joe so much."[35]
When Ella received a pay raise from Cejwin, Taylor grumbled that the administration simply dumped more work on her to go with the extra money
instead of easing her life with Joe.

In the first few months after Joe's death, Ella betrayed a sense of guilt, but Taylor would have none of it:

> She's depressed and a little lost—had to go through all of Joe's belongings at home—and rearrange her household and it made her weep—she feels she wasn't very nice to him and we have to keep reminding her that there were plenty of times when he wasn't at all nice to her—that no one could have put up with more. She counters with the information that he had the excuse of being ill—it affected his mentality she feels but that she had no excuse. NO EXCUSE! God I sometimes wonder if I would have stayed with Joe in similar circumstances.[36]

Ella's sadness after caring for her invalid husband for so long is not surprising, nor is a devoted sister's vehement loyalty, but the writer in Taylor transforms their feelings into narrative speculation, becoming a story that she might have told.

After Joe died, Ella turned her impressive energies to a dizzying array of activities. She joined a choral group, took painting classes, exercised at the YMCA, sewed her own clothes, and became active in a synagogue where she attended classes in Judaism.[37] Everyone held her up as a model to Henny about how widows should get on with their lives. But underneath was loneliness, that mournful word punctuating the sisters' correspondence. Ella went down to Florida with Henny, but spent time simply waiting in the lobby of the Marseilles Hotel for mail to arrive: "Nothing helped to dispel the 'aloneness.' It took me years to adjust and accept Joe's condition—and I did finally make a way of life for myself that in the main gave me some satisfaction but—I doubt whether I'll ever adjust to the awful feeling of being a widow—I can't even bring myself to *say* the word—it's like a stigma and I hate being the victim."[38]

The fifth death appears slightly out of chronological order here because it was not a family member, and serves as a gateway to a discussion of Taylor's literary career during these trying years. One of Taylor's dearest friends from Cejwin, Gertrude Holz, died from cancer on March 31, 1964.[39] Holz supervised arts and crafts for the younger girls at Cejwin, and the two women became as close as sisters.[40] Taylor and Holz worked together at camp for ten years, and they often spoke on the phone during the rest of the year, so the written record is sparse, but their mutual affection colors every mention of Holz, "the little sparrow," in Taylor's correspondence. They checked up on each other's minor ailments, sympathized about the difficulties of caring for aging parents, and fretted over their daughters, both married while in college and exhibiting a drive for independence that felt like ingratitude.[41]

Already in the fall of 1962, the women knew Holz's health was precarious and faced the prospect that her waning strength would prevent a return to Cejwin the following summer.[42] Taylor was determined to have her back for Holz's own good: "Personally I think it would be the best thing in the world for her. She needs to be absorbed in work."[43] Taylor's protectiveness included deceiving her friend about just how serious everyone knew her condition to be. As late as February 1964, Holz, refusing to accept her imminent death, told friends she was suffering from arthritis. "Oh the deviousness of love!" Taylor exclaimed to Ginger. "But what can one do? The necessity for lying in Gertrude's case is desperate. She cannot face the end at all—never will be able to."[44] Upon hearing the news of Holz's death, Taylor broke down in the only display of raw emotion that Ginger ever saw from her. When the headstone was to be placed on Holz's grave a year later, Taylor was reluctant to attend the ceremony, knowing it would open up old wounds of sadness, "because that last winter I saw her almost every week—lying to her all the time about her condition."[45]

The two women were not just chatting about inconsequential matters in a desperate attempt to avoid talking about Holz's spreading cancer. True to form, Taylor put Holz to work. In the evenings at Cejwin, when the adults gathered in Ella's cabin, Taylor had been enchanted by her friend's stories about her childhood in Hungary: "It was a life that was so utterly different from anything that we had ever known or could even imagine. It was like going back a century ago in our own country."[46] When the sick woman lay exhausted in her hospital bed that winter of 1963, Taylor suggested Holz dictate stories from her past as a distraction: "In the weeks that followed I would gently prod her with innumerable questions. She told me as much as she could remember. But sometimes when she could not recall things perfectly, she would call up her mother or her sister and ask them questions. Thus she would talk and I would listen and make notes. I'd go home and write up what we had talked about and then bring the sections back to her. I could see that it pleased her. In the re-living of her little girl days, she was able to forget her pain and illness."[47] After Holz's discharge from the hospital, Taylor continued to visit, listen, and write until the end.

Taylor completed the final chapters of the book based on Holz's memories, *A Papa Like Everyone Else,* after Holz's death, signed a contract in September 1965, and saw the book published in the fall of 1966. It represented Taylor's effort to achieve immortality for her friend. In a speech at a book fair, Taylor said that the character Gisella was based on Holz, that being the Hungarian equivalent of the name Gertrude: "For all of us who knew and loved her, she has not gone . . . In this book I have tried to capture for my readers, some of Gertrude's sweetness and her great love of beauty. If when you read the book, you feel some measure of the true loveliness of the real Gisella, then for you too Gertrude will always live."[48]

Another distressing event further darkened Taylor's days in the early 1960s: Jo's divorce from Steve Marshall. After graduating from Sarah Lawrence and pursuing a master's degree at Columbia, Jo became a social worker. Steve finished college in the spring of 1960 and went for graduate studies at Syracuse, which took the couple away from New York City for the academic year 1960–61.[49] As of the summer of 1960, Jo was writing her parents the usual chatty letters about her cultural activities, diets, Steve's work, and her own summer job with the Youth Consultation Service of the Diocese of New York. She displayed an imaginative curiosity in the cases she was assigned and was determined to have her research published in the *Social Work Journal.*[50]

Jo was just as buoyant when her parents went to Europe the following spring, joking about Taylor's double-entendre in her description of Ralph's musical activities in Holland: "Holland sounds Dutchy—only your famous sentence about Ralph—'playing [recorder] with a divorced woman on Saturday night' gets a big laugh from all who hear it. It's a lucky thing we knew what you were talking about."[51] Jo's use of the first person plural in this letter clearly refers to her and Steve, who are attending plays and taking the Brenner and Taylor grandmothers out to restaurants. Jo also describes experiencing a national air raid drill.[52] One paragraph must have raised an eyebrow, though, and that described the visit Jo and her secretary took to Planned Parenthood to get "that Enovid stuff," which is supposed to be "100% effective as long as you remember to take one from the fifth day of the month on and don't miss a day." Enovid was the trade name of the first hormonal birth control pill; the product was cleared by the FDA for sale in May 1960 and went on the market on June 23. Jo was ambivalent about using the new drug, in part because she was scared to try it, having "visions of growing a mustache or beard or something," and even with all the medical precautions, thought it was "a little weird."

Taylor's concerns about birth control followed a completely different track. She wrote to Nettie Frishman, who was worried about her daughter's single status: "My own child married at 19—put her husband through school (or rather Papa and Mama lent a hand)—and here she is married 7 years with no offspring. So actually she's no further advanced than yours. So I'm depressed about that. I would so love a grandchild. Thus you can see that with a child it's always something—till the day you die."[53] Several of Taylor's siblings became grandparents in these years, but in addition to sibling rivalry and seeking an outlet for affection, Taylor wanted grandchildren because she saw them as a bulwark against loneliness, both her own and that of her daughter.

When the Marshalls returned to New York, they frequently dined with the Taylors. Taylor wrote to her young assistant Ginger, "My daughter and her husband seem to eat in my house about half the week . . . and I had forgotten how much a young man can eat!"[54] Jo accompanied her parents to the Caswell-Massey Fashion Show, "looking very beautiful."[55] But Taylor drops hints in her correspondence that all was not well. Writing from Cejwin about Gertrude Holz's troubled marriage, Taylor warned: "Ginger whatever you do, don't get married until you find someone you know you can be close to all your life. For at best a person is alone—married to one she loves deeply, she is at least alone together with someone. But to be always and forever alone . . . is dreadful. I am so dependent upon Ralph for my very existence, I can hardly imagine a life like hers [Gertrude's]."[56] In the letter, Taylor urged her protégée to resist social pressure to marry, just as she shook her head over young people's rush to get married in her letter to Nettie. Taylor recalled that when she was eighteen years old, society *expected* young women to date and take their time before marrying. Since the three older Brenner sisters married barely out of their teens, Taylor clearly had something other than her own past in mind. In fact, Jo's marriage was in trouble, and its dissolution was the source of much drama and heartache in the years to come.

By the spring of 1963, Steve and Jo were no longer always living together. On May 8, 1963, Steve wrote to Ralph and Taylor that he had seen

Jo twice since the Taylors left for Europe: "The letter you wrote, Syd, has had little effect on Jo's outlook on life, she still clings to her negativism and insists that 'no one cares for her.' Many of the details of our meetings will have to wait until your return."[57] Steve was still involved in the life of the family, promising to visit "Grand Ma Brenner" and hoping his in-laws enjoyed their trip. When the Taylors returned, Jo ignored mail from her parents. Ralph showed no sympathy, especially after Jo refused to come to the phone when Taylor called, leaving her mother to feel "humiliated" and the telephone operator "embarrassed." Ralph stated categorically, "If she wishes to have anything to do with us, she knows where we are." But Taylor assured her daughter that her outlook as a Brenner was different from that of the Taylors: "In our family we are never mad and glad at people even though we are deeply wounded by them or have just cause for severing relationships. If you remember when you were a child, everytime Dad did not speak to you, it was I who brought you two around. In Ralph's family I have known his mother not to speak to a brother or a sister or an aunt or uncle or cousin for years at a time. Besides I'm a Mother."[58] In that same letter, though, she regretfully agrees that Ralph is right, and says it is up to Jo to contact them, their door never being closed to her.

During the summer of 1963, Steve stayed in the Taylors' apartment while they were at camp and Jo was on vacation. In a letter to Ralph of August 4, he sounded breezily cheerful: "Jo's back [from vacation] and looks extremely well! She's coming to some valid conclusions concerning her present position—there's hope!" Two days later he was a little more explicit in a letter to Taylor:

> Jo returned from her vacation last week looking extremely well; she has a rich dark tan and has lost some weight. I told her to see Ralph and let him observe her new found complexion. Jo states she has been doing some serious thinking about her present problems and feels the need for some constructive changes . . . Where there's a will there's a way . . . trite but true. At this point I have no idea what the future holds in store for Jo or myself . . . I only hope we both can find some sort of happiness . . . together or apart . . .
>
> Love, Steve[59]

A friend from Lenox Hill Player days, Rae Rosenblum, ran into Jo at a restaurant and confirmed her blooming appearance, while hinting at some knowledge of the situation: "She certainly looks most glamorous and the least likely to be mistaken for a social worker. I hope she is happy and so are you."[60]

The written record remains spotty because, as Taylor pointed out, so much needed clarification that visits in person were required, the telephone, let alone letters, proving inadequate for the serious discussions they needed to have. One would not, in any case, realize from the letters alone that Hannah, Jo's crush from Buck's Rock, had once again become an important part of her life and that the two of them had spent several vacations together on the island of St. Thomas.

Cilly Brenner having just died in September, the family drew together and made a concerted effort to meet regularly, but the gatherings were torture for Taylor and Ralph, who sat silently while the Brenner siblings celebrated milestones in their children's lives. Just three days after Yom Kippur, a holiday embedded in Taylor's consciousness since childhood as a time of familial forgiveness and reconciliation, Taylor's grief at the loss of her parents and her guilt at not having treated them as well as she thought she should have merged with her guilt over having made mistakes with Jo. That welter of feeling expressed itself as frustration with her daughter, as seen in a letter to Steve: "Since my daughter pays no attention to the tenets of our religion, this [the opportunity for reconciliation on Yom Kippur] would make no impression on her."[61]

In a manner that became increasingly pronounced for the rest of her life, Taylor addressed emotional turmoil by focusing on finances. In that sorrowful Yom Kippur letter, she explained to her son-in-law the distribution of Cilly's estate. Two-thirds of Cilly's assets were to be distributed between Ella and Gertrude—Ella because she needed it more than the others and Gertrude because she took care of Cilly for so many years. The remaining third was divided among the other siblings. Taylor had debated whether to donate her inheritance to a charity in her mother's name or divide it among her nieces. Almost casually, she added:

And then I thought—why not give it to Jo? The supreme sacrifice my mother made in order not to be a burden to her children—she would consider well worth while if through it she could help her grandchild, because despite all of Jo's indifference and lack of attention, my mother was very fond of her—very proud of her— This would mean no hardship at all on my part—and I could have the sum deposited to your name or hers—and she wouldn't even have to see me about it. Could you tell her this for me.

Taylor closed this tormented letter with the reassurance that Steve was not alone, and that she and Ralph would not forsake him: "Were I Jo, I could not help but love you—could not help but appreciate the qualities which one finds so rarely in humanity today. Please keep in touch with us—Not only because you are the link between our child and ourselves—but for your own sake."

The deterioration of the marriage dragged on. Reversing her earlier promise to keep the door open to Jo, in January 1964 Taylor brusquely wrote to Paul J. Woolf, a professional photographer and clinical social worker: "Nothing has changed in our relationship with our daughter except that perhaps we have shut the door even tighter than before."[62] After a year of arguing and contention, Jo entered therapy; Steve continued to work in his government job, and characteristically, Taylor kept silent to friends such as Sarah Lang about her daughter's marital troubles.

Matters came to a head while Taylor was at camp in 1964. Hannah reappeared in the correspondence when she and Jo came up to Cejwin for what turned out to be an emotionally wrenching weekend. In four pages of closely typed text, Hannah engaged in what she saw as her mission to help Jo establish a warm relationship with her parents and urged Taylor to be "aggressive in your desire for her company," but the relationship between the two young women was an obstacle in itself, Hannah recognizing that it was a source of "hurt and embarrassment" to the Taylors.[63]

In her long letter, Hannah acknowledged that the Taylors wanted no more personal meetings with her.[64] From what she wrote, it is clear that the relationship between parents and child had disintegrated. As Hannah tried to be both psychologist and mediator, the gist of Jo's complaints about her parents emerged: "The constant criticism, over the years (though the motivation was constructive) has put her in such a state that her value of herself is practically non-existent." Jo interpreted admonitions from her parents as denial of her self-worth, even though Taylor was copying the demanding parenting methods she knew from her own youth. Rather than inspiring Jo to strive for greater self-improvement, Germanic criticism shattered her. Jo felt she had her face rubbed in her lack of accomplishment, even as her parents felt she squandered and failed to appreciate the sacrifices they had made for her.

Hannah was supremely confident in her own role as accurate observer and mediator: "Her doctor has suggested that she should discontinue any contact with her parents because it upsets her so. I can't see that. I keep encouraging her to see you people, to speak to you, hoping that through such contact she will learn to understand that she is loved and wanted and needed. I guess I have erred in such thinking." It was Hannah who informed Taylor that Steve asked Jo to get a divorce as soon as possible, and she thereby presented herself as Steve's mouthpiece. She quotes him as saying "he never really loved [Jo] as a wife but rather as a sister, that he certainly wouldn't give her any means of support because she's big and strong and can work, etc." Her own goals in speaking for Steve are never made explicit, but although the magnetic bond between the two women remained strong, Steve and Jo stayed in contact even after they separated, and their emotional bond as family for each other was never broken.

The attitude of the Taylors, on the other hand, came across as "We told you so" about Steve and about marrying so young, which further wore away the parent-child relationship. Their blatant desire for grandchildren also backfired, according to Hannah: "She's terrified of the true responsibility of being a wife and mother . . . Chastising her and having the wisdom of hindsight will not help her make a better decision the next time." After Jo took Hannah's advice to call Ralph, matters worsened: "I didn't expect him to tell her that since she didn't cook and have babies (and they both agreed on this before marrying) that she couldn't expect to keep any man. There are many women who marry and have careers in preference to motherhood and the domestic life." When Jo told Ralph about the divorce, he apparently "told her not to come to him with her problems, that she should learn to be independent." From Hannah's point of view, times of crisis were precisely when children should expect parental support and it should not have surprised the Taylors that Jo decided never to call or see them again.

Yet Hannah's agenda remained inconsistent. Just after stating Jo was too insecure to marry, Hannah reported that her friend wanted to try dating seriously: "She doesn't want to go off and involve herself with some musician or artist, etc., who is confused himself. She wants to give the average adjusted kind of fellow a chance." Jo felt her time-consuming, difficult work limited her social life, but when she mentioned to Ralph that she thought of going to resort hotels such as Grossingers or the Concord, "her father told her that those places have no intellectual atmosphere and so she felt that his comments were more of disapproval than anything else. So, once again she feels rejected and alone."

Hannah's passionate sense of responsibility for Jo hinted at a relationship that disturbed the Taylors, but she hoped for some understanding from Taylor: "You could not have tolerated my presence at camp if you really didn't care for her, this I know. I know that her father didn't come to the dance festival [at Cejwin] because he knew I would be there. She was terribly disappointed. She had gotten all dressed up, her hair done, little make-up, etc., and even made reservations for dinner at a restaurant up there. I guess he didn't come because he felt his presence would indicate an acceptance. We all know that is not so." Hannah's agitated rhetoric is laced with the lexicon of psychology, yet the sincerity of her affection for Jo shines through. It is only because of Jo's subsequent relationships with women and her own memories of her sexual identity at the time that the Taylors' distress over Jo's lesbianism can be extracted from Hannah's indirect hints.

Some attempt at reconciliation was attempted in September 1965—again during the emotional period of Rosh Hashanah and Yom Kippur. In an overwrought letter to Jo, Taylor berated her daughter for once again storming out of the apartment, leaving Steve with Ralph and Taylor. Taylor insisted that her lack of demonstrativeness should not be equated with lack of love, that all she wanted was to provide Jo with peace and security without making her feel imprisoned by parental expectations. She repeated her lecture about the meaning of the Day of Atonement and begged Jo's forgiveness for any wrong she may have inflicted. Jo's joy and sorrow, success and failure, were experienced by her parents as if they were their own: "It is always so with parents—particularly Jewish parents."[65]

Pulsing through the letter is fear of loneliness. Having lost their parents, Taylor and her sisters responded by drawing closer together. "But who consoles you in your loneliness?" Taylor wondered. "And all we can do is stand by helpless and tongue-tied, and full of pain." Fannie Taylor's efforts to reach out to her granddaughter had also been rebuffed. Taylor's doggedness about the importance of family eventually led to a resumption of relations, however laced with resentment and disappointment. By 1968, Taylor indirectly made it clear that she was at least on speaking terms with Jo. Nettie Frishman's daughter was contemplating adoption, and she reassured her friend about the process, quoting "my daughter who worked for many years with the Louise Wise [Adoption] Agency."[66] Jo's postcards from her travels carried neutral messages, but at least she sent them. Extrapolating from the many letters Taylor exchanged with her sisters over the years, in which they often sniped at each other, it is evident that in Taylor's mind, any relationship was better than silence, and criticism remained an expression of love. Jo was unable to convince her mother that any other way was possible and came to understand that it was up to her to forge an adult relationship with her parents on her own terms and with full knowledge that they were unlikely to change.

Taylor, too, had her methods of coping with emotional distress, focusing on finances to create a sense of order. Although she had been thrilled to accept speaking engagements in the early days of her success, practically pinching herself to prove it was true that so many people wanted to hear from her, in the 1960s she began to ask for more compensation than simply reimbursement for travel expenses. She initially charged $25 for an appearance in the New York area, occasionally waiving it out of concern for limited library and school budgets. By 1968, her fee rose to $50, and by 1972 to $75. Earnings became a measure of self-worth.

With the increasing success of Caswell-Massey and the steady revenues from Taylor's writing career, Taylor and Ralph organized their savings in a manner typical of those who had lived through the Depression, suggesting that they had not been as carefree in those days as the journals implied. In the 1960s, they opened more than a dozen savings accounts with different financial institutions, starting with deposits of some $2,000 each. When combined deposits and interest payments reached $10,000 several years later, they closed all the accounts within a few months and invested them elsewhere. People of their generation who had seen banks fail during the Depression kept a close eye on the maximum the Federal Deposit Insurance Corporation would reimburse depositors in case of bank closures. In the early 1960s, when the Taylors were engaged in these transactions, the limit was $10,000.[67]

Taylor's other method of coping was work. During the 1960s, she published four books: *Mr. Barney's Beard* (1961), *Now That You Are Eight* (1963), *A Papa Like Everyone Else* (1966), and *The Dog Who Came to Dinner* (1966). *Papa* carried emotional weight for Taylor, but the others were experiments in juvenile literature that were not particularly memorable and gave her little satisfaction. Aimed at a younger audience than the *All-of-a-Kind* books, *Mr. Barney's Beard* told the story of a little bird that makes a nest in a man's beard. Taylor signed the contract in May 1960, and the book came out the following spring.[68] The *Chicago Tribune* called it a "delightful nonsense yarn," pointing out it owed much to an Edward Lear limerick, yet as a book for beginning readers it drew little media attention.[69] Its winning the Boys Club of America Junior Award showed up in a few of Taylor's biographical sketches, but she never made much of it.

Taylor's writing became becalmed in easy readers, and writing them bored and aggravated her. The Association Press/YMCA in conjunction with the Child Study Association (under Josette Frank) commissioned her to write one of their *Now That You Are* books. Taylor's contribution was *Now That You Are Eight,* which she completed by June 1962, although the series was not launched until the following spring.[70] The series was to include up to twelve small books for different ages to be sold in card stores and bookshops as a substitute for birthday cards. Each book would tell the child what to expect in the coming year, in terms of school, family, friends, and so on. Taylor became exasperated by the whole enterprise:

> It was a real ordeal—a committee voted on the material—and of course each member of the committee had to put his two cents in. Also I was given a huge list of items to try to cover—(all within 68 pages of writing)—and I had to sneak in as many as I could. I had many arguments—much discussions—and re-writing—and finally I put my foot down when what they were asking for was becoming ridiculous. So many times older people, particularly in the psycho fields—I mean the child study organizations—etc. are so filled with what is right and correct, they spoil your writing.[71]

The revisions the editors wanted, she went on, were "stupid, inane things— the kind of things adults think about." Then the editors sent out a questionnaire to children with a copy of the manuscript, a procedure Taylor found utterly stupid, because in her opinion, children answer the way they are expected to or are automatically negative. The questionnaires she kept show that adults filled them out for the children, and the answers were as stilted and insubstantial as Taylor expected. Taylor finally refused to make any more changes. She told the editors that they had no clue how to write for children and that their demands made her book increasingly dull from a child's point of view. To her surprise, they accepted her refusal to revise further; to her disappointment, they delayed the release of the book for a year. Taylor ended her tirade with what turned out to be premature appreciation for Follett: "All the things I thought about Follett I now take back completely—Heaven help me from having to deal with child psychologists—child studists—etc."[72]

Taylor kept few reviews of *Now That You Are Eight*. The assessment of the *Bulletin of the Children's Book Center* was lukewarm: "Realistic anecdotes, but Mrs. Taylor's usual easy writing style is hampered by the contrivance necessitated by the purpose of the series."[73] Taylor kept an eye on sales, but this was clearly an experiment never to be repeated.

That same spring of 1963, Taylor sent Meeks a sequel to *Mr. Barney's Beard,* which was rejected within four days: "I wished and wished and wished that your new little story about Mr. Barney would be something we could use. But alas, none of us can see a book in it."[74] More crushing than that rejection was Meeks's evident fatigue with the All-of-a-Kind family. Along with the *Mr. Barney* sequel, Taylor had sent chapters from what eventually became *Ella of All-of-a-Kind Family,* in addition to other material that was never published. In this same March letter, Meeks threw out a few half-hearted ideas for improvements and suggested Taylor try to sell some of the chapters to magazines as short stories, but she had no intention of pursuing it: "The book as a whole is not publishable."

Taylor had discussed with Nettie already in 1961 her plans for a book about her sister Ella and reported even then that forcing her character to choose between marriage and career met resistance from her editor. Nettie supported her friend: "I've been thinking of what you mentioned . . . and your idea about Ella's choice between career and marriage. Somehow, I think that in the late '20s and early '30s, and especially in a Jewish family, the choice would always be that of marriage. A career was not a choice—just a necessity. And then, too, young marriage is such a popular theme with the teen-agers!

Besides—you have the rest of your wonderful family to supplement Ella!"[75] Meeks disagreed. It was not that she thought the choice was contrived, but rather that Taylor's depiction of life on the stage was so dreary, it did not offer a plausible alternative to marriage. Meeks also questioned whether immigrant parents wanted artistic careers for their daughters, and indicated that Taylor had told her about Cilly and Morris's opposition to such a future for Ella.[76]

Meeks's fundamental concern was sales. By this time the *All-of-a-Kind Family* was a brand, and Meeks did not want it cheapened. Repeating her views from 1959, Meeks stated that readers who loved the original book "will expect any other books about the family to be as good or almost. The second book was not as good, but was still a good book. *Uptown* is readable, but not as good as the second book. The new story is not as good as *Uptown*."[77] Taylor's many fans asked for more about the family—perhaps Charlie's bar mitzvah or another baby—but Meeks was convinced that tastes were changing.

What sold books in the 1950s had become outdated in the 1960s. Meeks moved with the times, embracing "problem" books and turning away from romanticized portrayals of children's lives. She encouraged Taylor to do the same: "You are living an interesting life and encountering new people and situations all the time. Why don't you write a book about today? The remembrance of things past is charming and appealing, but there is a need for stories that children today can identify with. Not sweet little stories, but strong realistic ones. I don't mean there shouldn't be fun in them, but there should be problems and heartaches too. They should be about life, which is made up of all these things."[78] *Carol's Side of the Street* might have met a different reception in the 1960s, and Judy Blume was poised to become a bestselling author for young adults, with her candid look at real-life problems. Because rapid social changes were making Taylor increasingly anxious, she was not eager to move in the direction Meeks was suggesting. This was a woman who wrote to a friend, "Sometimes I am glad (aren't you?) that I lived in a quieter, more secure, more 4 square kind of world when I was growing up—we knew what was right and what was wrong and there was no doubt about it."[79]

Taylor continued to sell stories to magazines—*Highlights for Children, American Junior Red Cross News, World Over*—by her account all commissioned by the publications and not solicited by her, and it continued to thrill her to see her work in print.[80] Even here, though, she was subject to editorial challenges. A story about the High Holidays, "Josh Balances the Books," gave rise to doubts from the managing editor at *Highlights,* Caroline Myers: "We wondered how some children would react to the idea of God writing down everything a child does."[81] Myers consulted Rabbi Jerome Folkman, a member of the magazine's advisory board, who suggested modifications in his reply, which Myers enclosed, asking Taylor to alter the first page of her story in response to his remarks. The rabbi wanted it to be made clear that Taylor was drawing on a legend from Talmud, a poetry that should not be treated as fact, and conceded that "the ethics are a little mechanical and might be offensive to some." The requests from *Highlights* for stories came less frequently than before, which Taylor attributed to the magazine having a rabbi on its staff, and Taylor claimed to be relieved: "It was getting hard finding new gimmicks to surround the occasion so as to make it palatable for the reader."[82]

Taylor tried to sell a collected volume of her short stories, primarily holiday stories that had appeared in *Highlights,* to publishers other than Follett. Thomas Crowell rejected it in January 1962, and Abelard-Schuman turned down "Mr. Taylor's" *Danny Loves a Holiday* in February 1963, as did Jonathan David. Dutton, the publisher that did finally issue it, did not publish the book until 1980, two years after Taylor's death.[83] Over several years, Taylor shopped around her book *Ricky the Recorder,* which Meeks had rejected in 1959, and again failed to find a buyer.[84] A self-confessed recorder player, Jean Karl at Atheneum did not like Taylor's anthropomorphic approach any more than Meeks had: "Your manuscript . . . is done in a style that is not suitable for a children's book. Factual things for children should be given as fact, and need not be dressed up with personified objects." Elizabeth Riley at Thomas Crowell responded similarly. She regretted having to turn down such a respected author, but "children today will not accept nonfiction material in story form. They like their information given to them directly." She expressed a willingness to discuss a nonfiction book about the recorder and other wind instruments. The editors framed their objections to *Ricky the Recorder* as reflecting children's aversion to anthropomorphism, but of course what they were really saying was that they did not find Taylor's fanciful approach pedagogically or commercially sound: it was not the kind of book editors, teachers, and librarians now wanted to put in children's hands. Meeks tried to interest Taylor in writing a children's biography of Revolutionary War financier Haym Solomon, but Taylor did not bite.[85]

Follett ended up modernizing Taylor despite herself, while keeping her in the genre of beginning-to-read books. In a note dated March 22, 1963, Meeks thanked the Taylors for their hospitality while she was in New York, which included a dinner at the Four Seasons, where she had never eaten before. She acknowledged that her editorial staff liked *The Dog Who Came to Dinner*, although they found the ending "a bit flat." Taylor responded five days later with a new ending for the story about a homeless dog that interrupts a dinner to which the Lane family had invited their neighbors the Browns. On June 3, between her return from England and her departure for Cejwin, Taylor asked Meeks what she thought of the second ending, never having received a reply, and repeated the request on September 10. The following May, she persisted: "By the way is that dog of mine ever going to get his dinner? He's been hanging around your office for a mighty long time."[86]

Out of the blue, on September 10, 1965, Meeks wrote: "Surprise! Here are the contracts for *The Dog Who Came to Dinner*. Perhaps it isn't a surprise, though, because I think you probably have the check for the advance already." The real surprise came in the next paragraph: "I've been thinking about making this an integrated book. This would not affect the text, but there would be some Negro people in the pictures. There is a need for this kind of book for young children." No doubt, Meeks had noticed the success of Ezra Jack Keats's *The Snowy Day* in 1962, paid attention to changing expectations of juvenile literature, and drawn her own conclusions. Nothing in the text or her correspondence suggested that Taylor ever intended to address race relations in the book. Taylor responded: "I think your idea of having some of the cast Negro is good. So go ahead."[87] Given the restrictions of easy readers as a genre, with their limited vocabulary and length, the book was not reviewed as widely as a novel would have been, but it was well received. Not all the reviews mentioned integration. The *Chicago Tribune* gave "neighborliness in an integrated community" as the theme, and the *Bulletin of the Children's Book Center* said it "treats with pleasant nonchalance the fact that the Browns are white and that the new neighbors, the Lanes, are Negro," but the *Sacramento Bee* simply mentioned that it was "fun" and had a new-word list at the back.[88]

Outside the world of publishing, Taylor was ambivalent about the civil rights movement. It was not because she had lost faith in American ideals of equality and freedom, but because she felt those claiming their rights were going about it the wrong way—namely, they were not coping with poverty and prejudice the way she remembered her immigrant neighbors had. Violence repelled and frightened her and became associated in her mind with the civil rights movement. The fact that Hasidic Jews in Brooklyn felt they had to form vigilante groups to defend themselves shocked her: "One of their school teachers was murdered by a negro one night—On the following gangs of drunken colored teen-agers held up the motorman on a subway train—broke up the cars—beat up some of the passengers—What's going to happen this summer when the kids are all loose? . . . it is no doubt that all this vigorous campaigning for civil rights on the parts of the negro population have loosed all the accumulated hatred of years. I'm glad I shall at least be out of it for a couple of months."[89] Taylor's books were a return to a seemingly more secure age, and Cejwin, too, existed far removed from the tumultuous times and increasingly dangerous spaces of New York City and the country at large. When her book tours took her to public schools and libraries in low-income neighborhoods, her letters reflect the condescension of a Lady Bountiful gratified to bring joy into the otherwise bleak lives of less fortunate people. Change came too fast for Taylor and lines blurred too quickly, which made her anxious.

As seen above, *A Papa Like Everyone Else* also came out in 1966. As a novel from the author of the *All-of-a-Kind* series, it received more attention than *The Dog Who Came to Dinner*, but no reviewer was particularly enthusiastic. *Kirkus Reviews* called it a "slight story": "Only in a few instances . . . is the tremendous potential in the situation realized; generally it is a catalogue of customs and celebrations in which the bread gets baked but nothing much happens to anyone. Good butter and eggs, not enough yeast."[90] Reviewers who were fond of the *All-of-a-Kind* books described the new work as a "warm-hearted little charmer," but many criticized the episodic plot structure and weak characterization. The fidelity of this "quiet little book" to a time and place and its portrayal of a tight-knit family constituted its appeal, but reviewers did not rave about it as they had about *All-of-a-Kind Family* fifteen years earlier.

Along with chafing at the difficulty of getting work published, Taylor felt Follett was failing her in terms of publicity. When she visited schools and libraries across the country, she noted each instance when she was told that copies of her books had not been made available or were sold out at book fairs because insufficient numbers had been shipped. Scolding letters to Follett followed, demanding immediate action.

In the same way that writing gave Taylor less joy than before, so Cejwin ceased to be as magical. Gertrude Holz's death was not the cause of Taylor's growing disenchantment with Cejwin, but after the loss of her friend Taylor grew increasingly frustrated with the camp. In the late 1950s, when becoming a full-time author and lecturer had seemed a tantalizing possibility, she had dropped hints that she might not always be at Cejwin.[91] The camp itself did not account for her evasiveness at the height of her literary career; rather, Taylor was intrigued by the prospect of pursuing other occupations. Beginning in the 1960s, however, changes at Cejwin became the stated reason for her discontent. Holz's death marked the end of an era, which Taylor bathed in nostalgia in the years to come, as colleagues chose not to return, uncomprehending administrators replaced those with whom she had grown comfortable, and a new generation of campers exhibited behavior that baffled and repelled her. With the departure of friends, those "wonderful happy useful times" were no more.

Sarah Lang was the first of Taylor's close friends to stop working at the camp, explaining that her job during the rest of the year and her devoted care of her aging mother made it too difficult to get away.[92] Taylor confessed to Ginger, "I can't stand this breaking up—it's as if a tight circle were having links chopped off. With Sarah I have spent 21 years—Ella too is utterly abject . . . But anyway, for the old-timers these changes are hard to accept—You get into a rut—you expect things will continue as they always have."[93] With the loss of Gertrude Holz, the situation only worsened. "Oh Sarah, it is so hard to get older and have to know that this is over—never to come again."[94]

When Ella changed positions at the camp in 1964, she moved to another part of the facility, and Taylor feared that the cozy evenings of gossip and stories in her homey cabin—the "koffee klatches"—would end. That became another source of lament:

> My oldest sister has a way of gathering people around her . . .
> it was she who had made her little house cozy—with curtains
> at her windows and covers on her bed-couches—We gathered—
> everyone—every evening—drinking coffee and munching on

matzah or cookies—and gossiped, gossiped, gossiped about our children, our work—or tried to solve problems, or just plain laughed. Laughter I think resounded in her house more than anything. It is this we will miss—Sure she'll be there—but not close to us. She will be heading the maintenance staff—What will we discuss with her—how a porter got drunk and did not show up to clean the bathrooms?[95]

Despite Taylor's anxieties, Ella continued to draw family and friends to her new cabin, and they still savored their Saturdays off, when they lunched at Flo-Jean's, "the loveliest little restaurant made out of an old toll bridge" and relaxed together for the rest of the day.[96]

Amid the changes, Taylor remained a dynamo. The camp itself grew in enrollment and physical size, and her responsibilities grew commensurately. "The camp is so huge," she wrote Nettie in 1965, "it's as big as many a town in our country—1200 children—about 600 staff—spread over a large area though and separated into 6 different camps, each functioning separately."[97] Taylor was in charge of daily classes in dance and dramatics and supervised up to 220 children in plays, sometimes directing six plays in two months; she also supervised a Fourth of July pageant, the commemoration of Tisha b'Av (the fast day in midsummer that commemorates the destruction of the Temple in Jerusalem, among other tragedies in Jewish history), and the final closing-night program.[98] Her days and nights were filled with one task after another:

> It is not only that I have definitely scheduled 3 or 4 periods a day which means 3 or 4 hours—but in between the scheduled times there are rehearsals—the typing of scripts—and parts which I always do myself—the collecting of costumes either from the costumer down below eked out with those we have collected over the years right in our own division of camp—fitting, repairing, ironing them—making out programs like the one enclosed—worrying about props—writing reports of my activities for camp—and generally pitching in whenever it rains or there is some free time when the youngsters have nothing special to do ... At night I am too exhausted to even sleep—also my head

buzzes with the little items—how to direct a scene—what next step in the dance I am choreographing—etc. But to give it up would make me miserable. Actually I am completely fulfilled in this work—more so than in my writing.[99]

Years later, Ginger reminisced: "I'll never forget how frustrated I'd get when I'd rush back to set up benches or get costumes out or something else, only to find you had already done it! You set a speedy pace that was hard to beat. I found the only way to exist was to join you or be one step behind."[100] Taylor even described herself as "a nut with too much sense of responsibility."[101]

Taylor never failed to take her increased responsibilities seriously, preparing with the diligence she had displayed for decades: "My winter life has ever been geared to a kind of preparation for summer—the dance classes I take—the Hebrew lessons—the reading and research for material for story telling, for the writing of plays, etc. One needs that kind of motivation."[102] The flip side of that acknowledgment was that without the motivation of camp, a huge hole would open up in Taylor's life.

Taylor's sense of duty did not allow her to flag, but she became increasingly critical of the perceived shortcomings of her colleagues. Some change was natural; Taylor acknowledged that she and her peers were getting older and that young counselors would move away or have other job opportunities—that was to be expected, if regretted. Other complaints stemmed from the incompetence or insensitivity of other people. She did not like the current executive director, Dr. Abraham Gannes (1911–2003; at Cejwin 1956–67), because she disapproved of some of his personnel choices and resented his interference in her writing.[103] She thought he harangued the children, showed no understanding or appreciation for her work, made ridiculous suggestions about the kinds of plays she should write, and played favorites with the staff.[104]

Parallel to her attention to book sales and royalty payments, Taylor became more conscious of salary as an indicator of respect: "I find it repugnant discussing and haggling over salary—I never once in all the years I worked there even mentioned the subject—I was underpaid terribly for year after year—and then when at last some measure of equality was aimed at, the increases were granted to me without any comment or discussion on my part."[105] In that same letter from 1965, Taylor vented her anger at discovering that less experienced staff members with fewer responsibilities were paid more than she: "I don't need the money—but money seems to be their only way of showing their recognition and judgment of your work there."

Ginger did not return for the first time in 1968. Taylor acknowledged the decision was sensible, given the lack of social life available to her friend, but it meant the loss of someone who understood how she worked and who really liked her. Ginger's replacements were no substitute for the devoted, hardworking young woman Taylor had seen mature under her tutelage. Taylor complained that other counselors were lazy shirkers. She might have adapted to new assistants, but more was at play than a change in personalities: Taylor was out of sync with the younger generation. The little girls she supervised still retained the innocence of youth, but the older ones seemed a different breed. At summer's end in 1968, the staff found a pile of beer cans and whiskey bottles in the sitting room of some of the counselors: "Horrified—(where was their advisor in all this we wondered)—the director of the camp called a meeting and asked for an explanation. Do you know what the reply was—'What are you getting so worked up about? You ought to be glad we're not smoking pot.' "[106]

The question everyone asked was why Taylor stayed. Gertie, the youngest Brenner sister, made the break in 1969. Her daughter, Judy Magid, was expecting a baby in June, and Gertie gave that as her reason not to return, but Taylor knew her sister no longer found the work interesting or the country air beneficial to her health, struggle as she did with asthma.[107] Henny needed a paid occupation, but that did not apply to Taylor. Loyalty to Ella was Taylor's primary reason for returning summer after summer during the 1960s. Ella needed the paycheck, and furthermore, she was romantically involved with Albert Schoolman; Taylor was not about to leave her sister without her support for an entire summer. The women had collaborated for so long and knew each other so well that the prospect seemed impossible. As early as 1956, Sarah Lang said, "I'm assuming that you'll be back—you just couldn't let Ella down."[108] In 1970 Taylor wrote, "I hate the thought of going back—and yet if Ella and Henny return, I shall have to."[109]

Admittedly, Taylor still derived satisfaction from the job: "It's work that I love above everything else."[110] It kept her young, "particularly since I remain with the same age group all the time. One gets the illusion of never growing any older."[111] It also kept her busy, for Cejwin had become a way of life that would leave an unnerving void were she to stay away. And while Taylor liked being acclaimed as an author, writing did not give her as much pleasure as interacting directly with children:

> When I consider staying home with nothing definite, I am frightened. You know how much I have always loved the work I do. It gives me a sense of completion and gratification that no other kind of work can give me—certainly not the writing because that is a solitary vocation whereas in camp I work with living people— with children. To watch them open up and expand and grow under creativity, is a joy which I would hate to forego.[112]

Taylor loved the immediate response from the children, so different than sitting "utterly alone, locked up with one's characters." It was thrilling to see children respond to the books she published, but nothing compared with guiding children directly.

Selling her books was integral to the thrill Taylor felt in being known as an author at Cejwin. From her correspondence with the marketing department at Follett and her sales receipts, it is clear that she saw Cejwin as a market waiting to be tapped. She ordered books to sell every summer, insisted on her special rate as an author, and complained when shipments were delayed. Some afternoons she sat under the shade of a big tree where signs in Ralph's beautiful script advertised the sale of autographed books. Just as every visit to a book fair or letter to a fan was an opportunity to promote both her books and Caswell-Massey products, so were all those Hadas campers—precisely the age group most enamored of the *All-of-a-Kind* books—potential buyers of her stories and the teenage counselors potential customers for Caswell-Massey toiletries.[113]

Sales also were part of the annual trips to Europe. Way back in 1929, on the ferry to Provincetown during the Taylors' Canadian hitchhiking jaunt, Taylor wrote, "We were able to image ourselves travelling to Europe for were we not on the Atlantic Ocean and no land in sight?"[114] Thirty years later, they finally made that journey, and except for 1964 when they went to California on Caswell-Massey business, they returned to Europe each spring until 1977. The Taylors started out in England, each year adding destinations: Italy, Spain, Switzerland, France, the Scandinavian countries, Greece, Turkey, Yugoslavia, Belgium, Portugal, Scotland, Ireland, Germany, and Israel. While Ralph and Taylor took their first trans-Atlantic journey to fulfill a life-long dream and finally enjoy the economic success they had worked so hard to achieve, business was not shunted aside for the sake of untroubled leisure. Ralph scoured flea markets and visited bottle factories to find unique items to sell back in New York. On the trip to Spain in 1963, he crowed over finding fifty-five old-fashioned apothecary jars that he would be able to sell at 1,000 percent profit, thereby covering the costs of the entire vacation and then some.

The Taylors shaped their itinerary to meet business needs.[115] While Ralph's meetings with suppliers and search for new products provided the original impetus for combining business with pleasure, Taylor quickly saw opportunities to gain an international readership for the *All-of-a-Kind* series. She initiated negotiations with Blackie & Co. of England in 1959, before turning the matter over to Follett.[116] In the course of the next year, arrangements were made for distribution and royalty payments. Taylor felt she scored a coup when the book came out in the fall of 1961 with illustrations by a young refugee from the Hungarian revolution of 1956, Victor Ambrus, who went on to have a distinguished career in England.

Even before the book appeared, Taylor convinced Blackie that the appearances she made in the United States improved sales, and she pushed them to arrange visits to libraries and schools, where she read from her books and engaged the children in creative dramatics. From 1959 until 1975, sporadic visits with English schoolchildren were a high point of Taylor's trips. She mentioned to all her American correspondents how much more restrained the English children were, but how she always won them over, children being children the world over. With every visit, she checked bookstores to make sure her books were stocked, and nagged Blackie to take action if supplies were low or nonexistent. She failed to interest a publisher in France, where Hachette turned her down in 1962, or in Israel, but it was not for lack of trying.[117]

Both Ralph and Taylor always felt some anxiety before their departure—Ralph about leaving Caswell-Massey and Taylor about her writing and preparations for Cejwin. Because Murray Schiner (sister Gertrude's husband) worked as a manager for Ralph, the Taylors had more confidence that Caswell-Massey's laboratory was in trustworthy hands while they were away than if they left the business in the hands of strangers.[118] And Taylor's fussing over her work seemed reflexive, for no one ever accused her of being unprepared at Cejwin or slow in responding to her publishers. Flying itself was worrisome, so the Taylors developed a ritual of holding hands and smiling at each other as the plane took off, thinking, "This is how we shall go if it should turn out to be our final journey." Safely in the air, they let go of each other's hands and Ralph quipped, "Well—not this time."[119]

In each country they visited, the Taylors took bus tours. Many of Taylor's travel journals read as summaries of whatever tidbits of historical information their guides rattled off, her personal judgments coming across as superficial and focused on her personal comfort. Harsh in her assessments of hygiene, central heating, and courtesy, Taylor was noticeably uncritical about politics. This former socialist noted that Franco was liked in Spain and that thanks to him Jews were free to practice their religion as long as they gave no outward sign of their beliefs. Some time later, a visit to Raymond Duncan, dancer Isadora's eccentric brother in Paris, led Taylor to question her perceptions on this front, but without any sense of urgency. Duncan's daughter had also visited Spain, where she was overwhelmed by the poverty, fear, and constant surveillance. Her own observations having been so different, Taylor wrote in her journal, "Did the government tour show us only what we wanted to see? After all, we did wander around by ourselves. I never felt watched. True, I never discussed the political situation so perhaps we could not really know." She ended, "How could we both be right—or so wrong?"

When the Taylors wandered off on their own, it was often to spend time in Jewish neighborhoods. Taylor noted the size of the Jewish population and the availability of kosher food in stores and restaurants, and she made an effort to attend services on Friday or Saturday. She mentioned when other Jews were on the tour, and when there were none she wondered if her failure to feel comfortable with some of their traveling companions came from being the only Jews in the group. Yet when an outspoken woman Taylor liked used the expression "to jew down" about the Taylors' successful forays to the flea markets, Taylor merely remarked that the woman caught herself, but was not embarrassed, and the incident proved no obstacle to their companionship.

Bus tours allowed the Taylors to cover a lot of ground without having to make arrangements for lodging and meals, to avoid driving, and to absorb information without preparing for the trips in advance. The couple balanced

those weeklong excursions with stays in major cities, where their itinerary
was an extension of their lives in New York, as they enjoyed cultural and cu-
linary exploration, business activities, and family visits. For Ralph, the trips
came to include music camps similar to those he attended in New England
each summer.[120] In 1963, Ralph pursued his acquaintance with Walter Bergmann (1902–1988), a refugee from Germany who became a pioneer in the
revival of recorder playing in England, which gave Taylor an opportunity to
hear more about the harrowing escapes of Jews from Hitler's Germany.[121]
The Taylors often sought out amateur musical soirees, which Taylor loved
for the chance to get away from conventional tourist activities and interact
with people in their homes.

They went to art exhibits and attended dance and theatrical performances, comparing ticket prices with those in New York. Taylor kept a record of favorite restaurants, noting that Ralph liked gazpacho in Spain, which
Taylor likened to borscht. She tried snails for the first time, bemoaned the
absence of green vegetables in restaurant meals, and thought herself quite
daring for breaking her teetotaling ways at a sherry tasting in Spain, although
she was not tempted by Scotland's whiskies. In Paris, Ralph insisted on finding Isadora Duncan's burial place, which led them to Raymond Duncan,
mentioned above, with whom Ralph had performed in Moreno's theatrical
group so many years before.

As much as Taylor hungered to shed her role as tourist, her interactions
with Schneider relatives in Paris challenged her Jewish and American chau-
vinism. Ralph had a paternal aunt in Riga, Brocha Jankelowitsch, who was
murdered in the Shoah in 1941, along with most of the Jankelowitsch/Sch-
neider families. Her daughter Bluma had been sent away in the 1920s because
she risked arrest in Riga for her Communist activities. She had married Adol-
phe-Abraham ("Adek") Landau, born in Warsaw to a family of distinguished
rabbinical heritage, who had also left his home because of his involvement
in Communist organizations. The two settled in Paris, where they had two
daughters and started a movie production business. When World War II
broke out, Adek served briefly in the French army, before joining Bluma, who
had fled with their daughters to the "Free Zone" of Vichy France. Adek refused to register as a Jew or don the yellow star when anti-Semitic regulations
were instituted. Among other activities, he helped ferry Jewish refugees to
safety across the Pyrenees when the family was in hiding in the Perpignan

region, where their third daughter was born. At war's end, the family returned to Paris. By 1962, the Landaus had achieved financial stability with the commercialization of the widescreen camera technique they helped develop.[122]

The Landaus welcomed the Taylors warmly in 1962 and 1963. They drove them to see the sights of Paris, wined and dined them, and invited them for a long weekend at the couple's summer home in the Norman seaside village of Villerville.[123] Although Taylor spoke fondly of the Landaus in letters to Nettie, her journal tells a more nuanced story. The Paris relatives rubbed her the wrong way for two main reasons. First, they displayed what Taylor considered the unjustified and rude French contempt for all things American—food, fashions, and friendliness. According to Taylor, they had no interest in meeting their American neighbors in the upscale suburb of St. Cloud, despised the British, and disparaged Ralph's gift of a bottle of bourbon as an undrinkable beverage that tasted medicinal. Second, their Parisian sophistication came at the expense of their Jewish identity. Taylor decided Bluma drank wine with her meals and ate snails in order to consciously turn away from Judaism. When the subject of their youngest daughter's non-Jewish husband came up, Adek defended him "with a hand of defiant pride," while in her journal Taylor mused about the untrained, uneducated young man, "Where's the bargain? . . . What's so marvelous about this goy?" Taylor was gratified to see Adek, "the self-hating Jew who professes no Judaism," blissfully devour chopped liver and other traditional Jewish delicacies at a kosher restaurant.

Bluma was both familiar and not. Taylor found the French woman's housemaids shockingly young, but she recognized herself in this cousin by marriage when she saw the energetic Bluma stripping sheets from the beds and doing laundry for her married daughters: "I thought of myself. When a person is too swift in execution, too efficient—then everyone else is easily discouraged from pitching in—It is so much easier to sit back and let Mother do it. Thus we spoil our children." And Taylor envied the Landaus their grandchildren. During their emotional parting in 1963, Bluma brought up the murder of so many of her relatives, and the Taylors comforted her with mention of her children and grandchildren. Taylor plaintively asked her journal, "Who will carry on for Ralph and me?"

Aside from short asides about choosing a particular destination for Ralph's business, Taylor rarely justified why they traveled where they did. The search for luxury merchandise suitable for Caswell-Massey, the ease of being in a country where they spoke the language, and the welcoming early music community always made England a pleasant destination. In contrast, Taylor emphatically disliked the French. No matter how nice individual Frenchmen were, she was not drawn to them for "there is something in the French character which rubs Americans the wrong way." She thought the French were contemptuous of others and suspicious, especially about money matters, watching every penny and charging for every little thing—a peculiar grievance for Taylor, who enumerated each episode when she felt cheated in France. She also noted the influx of immigrants from Africa, which did not bode well, in her opinion, for social harmony. After two visits, she did not need to return, relatives or no.[124]

Two other countries also resonated personally, standing out as more than casual holiday choices—namely, Germany and Israel. As we have seen, Taylor felt she had absorbed her mother's German culture, particularly her work ethic and domestic fastidiousness. She did not hesitate to identify certain of her own behaviors as Germanic, because in her mind German and Jewish cultures were inextricably intertwined in the person of her mother: "I am still my mother's daughter (and my mother was a German hausfrau with all that entails in thoroughness)."[125] While recognizing that aspect of her background, Taylor was matter-of-fact about what the Germans had done to her European relatives (she does not use the term *Nazi* in her correspondence or journals). When Rafael Brenner—the older brother of Leo, Taylor's Cologne correspondent in the years after World War I—fled Nazi persecution for the United States, the two branches of the family quickly reestablished ties. The Nazis had appropriated the family business in Cologne; Italian fascists had persecuted the family in Rome and Milan, where they tried to reestablish the business; and Rafael and Leo's mother, so dear to Cilly, was killed in the Shoah. Having sheltered their savings in Switzerland, Rafael and his wife Nelly eventually fled to the United States, where they opened a successful camera business in Washington, D.C. They pampered the elder Brenners in Florida, sent Morris birthday cards with $10 checks, hosted Ella and Joe for Passover seders, and were hospitable to Jo and Steve Marshall. Leo reappeared briefly in Taylor's papers as well when Cilly wrote that Morris had received "a very nice Letter from Leo of Israel in which he praised your two books very highly. He urged us to come for a visit to Israel but how will be ever able to do this but you and Ralph ought to now."[126]

In 1965, the Taylors considered a trip to Riga with the Landaus. Bluma had lost all her family there in 1941 and felt an obligation to return at least once. Adek, fearing the effects of the emotional turmoil on his wife, wondered whether the companionship of the Taylors would make it easier for her to bear. For her part, Taylor thought that having traveling companions who spoke the language would be useful. In the end, however, the plan fell through.[127]

Taylor's knowledge of Nazi atrocities thus came not just from research she did for Cejwin or general hearsay. She had immediate, personal connections. Her feelings were so strong on the subject that it was not until 1973 that she and Ralph visited Germany.

Taylor's ambivalence toward Israel was of a different kind. She had nothing but praise for the country and enjoyed her visits, but she could not see herself settling there. She and Ralph went to Israel for the first time in the spring of 1960, on their second trip abroad. Taylor prepared by studying Hebrew diligently.[128] Once there, she had "the warm, wonderful feeling of being at home—people there are the most hospitable one has ever met—you exchange a few words and are invited home to eat—the taxi cab drivers turn down a tip."[129] Friends from New York introduced them to interesting people, and Ralph made a "recorder trek" throughout their visit.

When the Taylors considered returning to Israel two years later, Nettie encouraged Taylor to think of writing for children about the modern country. Not many books on the subject were available, and, according to Nettie, those that were had contrived and confused plots.[130] The Taylors decided against going, but Taylor did not specify the reason. She reiterated that she loved the feeling of being home "as soon as you step on the El Al plane and hear the Hebrew words spoken and look about at the smiling faces of the passengers."[131] Three years later in a letter to Sarah Lang, she again stated her attachment to Israel: "You'd so love Israel—it is one place in the world where you'd feel immediately at home. I can very well understand Berel's [Sarah's son] wish to return after having spent a year there. I think about it often and long to go back myself. So does Ella."[132] But loving Israel and living there were two different matters. Taylor told Nettie she could not write about modern Israel for children without spending a significant length of time in the country, and she was not willing to be apart from Ralph for so long: "I lean on him heavily for guidance and inspiration and love. I would hate to be without him for extended periods of time—and at present he is not yet free to stay away from business too long."[133] Her classes, camp, visits to schools and libraries—all those made a full life, and Taylor refused to sacrifice them for a single-minded focus on writing.

The Taylors did return to Israel in 1968: a "marvelous trip—full of contrasting and exciting experiences particularly being in Israel for the much argued-over Independence day parade in the old city of Jerusalem. I sat on the stands and watched the passingby of equipment left by the fleeing Arabs during the six day war."[134] Nephew David Ruderman was studying in Jerusalem that year, and he sent his uncles in New York tapes in lieu of letters about his experiences. The family in New York gathered around to listen to and discuss his reports. After one such session, Taylor confessed in a letter to her nephew that her feelings about settling permanently in Israel matched his. Whereas their first visit in 1960 convinced the Taylors that they would retire in Israel, being so "enchanted with all we saw and felt," their views had changed. There were not enough hospitable, intelligent individuals to compensate for the rude, arrogant, and contemptuous masses. Taylor acknowledged extenuating circumstances, but her bruised feelings lingered. The heat was too intense, the food too monotonous, the hordes of bugs relentless, the plumbing inadequate.

> Even as I list the faults, I realize I sound like the typical American tourist but then how can one help it? Born and reared in a land like ours where creature comforts are so lavish, one does become inured to them. My childhood had a sufficiency of the lacks of good living in the way of food—housing—hall toilets, no hot water nor heat—but I was a child—I knew no different. No one around me in the ghetto had it any better. But when one grows older, creature comforts become increasingly important. Perhaps were I young—and idealistic, I might think differently. But I am not even sure of that now. I have met too many young idealists who left Israel to remain permanently here.[135]

Israel represented an idea of home, a destination for immigrants in search of a better life, but Taylor's actual experiences in the young country proved to her that she was the successful child of immigrants rather than an immigrant herself.

With all the personal losses and disappointments in the first half of the 1960s, darkness seeped into Taylor's letters and worrying about expenses became her default mode of containing emotional turmoil. An entire file box in the Kerlan Collection at the University of Minnesota is filled with her correspondence of complaint, beginning around 1959. Some of the complaints seem reasonable, although the tone can be shrewish. As mentioned above, Taylor became more insistent about her salary at Cejwin and outspoken about inconsistencies in the pay scale. That might be seen as the healthy assertiveness of a woman swept up in the feminist tide, joining the growing number of women entering the workforce and seeking pay parity. Taylor also scolded Follett for not forwarding in a timely manner fan letters that had been sent to the Chicago office and for neglecting to include the envelopes, often the only source for the return address. Again, this could be seen as fastidious professionalism and devotion to children: "What do you suppose a child thinks when she writes a note, taking the time and trouble to do so and straining in the effort—only to receive no reply for so long a period? Highly disappointed in the writer I am sure."[136] When Taylor complained that a theater sent her tickets she could not use because of her "commercial blindness" and was slow to send replacements, her reason for lodging a complaint sounds reasonable.[137] Her vision was, indeed, impaired such that she used a magnifying glass to read and always had to sit up close at theatrical rehearsals and performances at Cejwin.

But Taylor complained to Macy's about a standing food chopper, a broiler and rotisserie unit, a meat grinder, a Teflon pan. Products did not match advertisements, clerks were rude, stores were dilatory in addressing her complaints. The correspondence about the broiler unit persisted over twelve letters. The Royal typewriter Taylor received from her husband as a birthday present became a character in a lengthy, melodramatic letter of disappointment. Taylor complained to furniture stores about shoddy merchandise and then about their "highly insulting" replies. She complained to radio announcers that they were plugging inferior products. Phone bills, newspaper bills, the price of detergent in the grocery store, the inadequate labeling of oranges—all provoked her epistolary ire. Airlines lost her bags, gave her pitiful snacks rather than the first-class dinner she paid for (and she had specifically "made do" with a sandwich in the expectation of receiving a meal):

Now who needs your snacks? Dainty sandwiches with the crusts cut off (the best part of the bread) a slimy piece of pie with the lemon meringue all squashed—and for women concerned with calories what a mess! Also why go first class? I don't drink—I am very small less than 5 feet and weighing just about 100 pounds— economy would be just as comfortable for a short trip—what do you offer in first class for the difference?[138]

Taylor goes on to say that her baggage was mishandled, the suitcase being wet and scuffed upon delivery. PanAm received a two-page, single-spaced letter filled with complaints not only about their service, but also about the fact that they did not serve American food. Besides the absurdity of having the flight crew speak with English accents, the menu was French! Other national airlines served national food, so why should an American carrier not show just as much pride in American cuisine? Taylor even proposed a detailed menu of American wines, fresh vegetables, and apple pie.[139] Disappointment, sarcasm, and frustration were perfected in her history of complaint. The only businessman she treated with unfailing courtesy was Mr. Vlasik, her tailor in London. Taylor had been taught to do everything to the best of her ability, and she was bitterly disappointed when she did not get that same perfectionism from salesclerks and manufacturers.

A bright spot in this difficult decade was Taylor's friendship with Nettie Peltzman Frishman (1913–2005). This devoted children's librarian, born in Chicago to Russian immigrant parents, was raised by her aunt in Los Angeles when her mother died in the flu epidemic following World War I, and earned a bachelor's degree at UCLA and a degree in Library Science from USC.[140] She worked for the Los Angeles Public Library for thirty-three years, served on numerous library boards, and was a judge on the Newbery/Caldecott Committee. Her first husband died in 1940 when she was twenty-seven, leaving her with two young children, and she did not remarry until 1960, when she wed businessman Harold Frishman, who, she informed Taylor, "does not object to my working."[141]

In December 1956, Nettie Peltzman wrote to Taylor care of Follett. As children's librarian at a branch library in Los Angeles, she explained that she had been given *All-of-a-Kind Family* to review back in 1951 by Rosemary Livsey, head of the Department of Work with Children at the Los Angeles

Public Library. The book was sent to her because she was Jewish and "could possibly evaluate it more critically than most of the other children's librarians." She loved the book, "not only because it is the *only* book in our collection with a warm and human and loving Jewish family background—but because—first and foremost—it is a wonderful story." As she visited libraries in the Los Angeles area, Nettie witnessed the book's appeal to children, whether they be "Jewish, Japanese, Negro, Mexican, Protestant or Catholic." After lavishing more praise and informing Taylor that as a book on the "first purchase list," *All-of-a-Kind Family* is "well represented in every library in the city of Los Angeles," Nettie used her observations as a librarian to encourage Taylor to write some "good Channukah stories: because this particular holiday has taken on added meaning these last few years. In a big city like Los Angeles, with such a large Jewish population, branches throughout the city cry for a 'good Channukah story.' With your feeling and warmth, I can't think of anyone more qualified to write that story than you."[142] In response, Taylor mailed Nettie a copy of *Highlights for Children* that contained her Chanukah story.

Nettie's energetic enthusiasm blossomed into affectionate friendship. Four and a half years later, Nettie wrote again, telling Taylor she was excited to take her first trip to New York, "and part of my excitement and anticipation is the fact that you live (I think) somewhere in that area." After a litany of praise, Nettie closed with an invitation: "I would be delighted and most honored if you would be my luncheon guest when I come to New York . . . It would be the highlight of my trip if I could have the opportunity to see—and speak with you."[143] The rapport was immediate. Taylor chided Nettie for not finding the time to visit Taylor at home after she had gone to the trouble of inviting some friends over and baking a cake, but that was after an enjoyable luncheon: "You made me feel as if we had known each other for a long, long time. I hope that some day I shall be able to get to see you in California or that you will come again to New York."[144] In appreciation, Taylor sent Nettie her newest book. Nettie's reason for not showing up was unassailable: "I almost cried when I read your letter. We had so planned to spend that evening with you . . . but came back to find an unexpected visitor." Nettie's elderly father-in-law from her first marriage had come to their motel from Newark expressly to hear about his grandchildren, whom he had never seen.[145] Devoted to family herself, Taylor found Nettie's explanation yet another reason to be fond of her new friend.

A month later, "Mrs. Taylor" and "Nettie Frishman" became "Syd" and "Nettie," and not a year went by without chatty, newsy letters. Nettie's optimism, candor, and passion for books invigorated Taylor, who was more open with her about her thoughts and feelings than with any other correspondent. Both women loved dance, books, children, travel, and their husbands. In part because they saw each other so seldom and did not speak on the telephone, long-distance charges being prohibitive, Taylor described in more detail what was happening in her life than in her letters to family members or Cejwin friends, whom she saw and spoke with frequently. Perhaps also because of the distance, Taylor was able speak frankly without sounding constrained or condescending, as she sometimes did with her New York circle.

The openness between the women came primarily from Nettie's warm heart and unflagging admiration. Alluding to the miracle of Chanukah that was celebrated the week she wrote, Nettie exclaimed, "I'm always so delighted to find a letter from you. To me—this is a modern miracle—that someone I have admired so much and so long has suddenly become my friend! I'd like to keep it that way!"[146] Nettie sent Taylor jams from Knott's Berry Farm (and Taylor was exasperated that Ralph's sweet tooth compelled him to open every single jar for just a taste), while Taylor sent colognes and toilet waters from Caswell-Massey. Nettie was a one-woman public relations agency. At a meeting of the California Library Association, she told her "fellow children-librarians of my meeting with you—and I now shine in your reflected glory—every one of us know—and love your books; and hearing about you is like receiving news from home."[147]

No wonder Taylor was charmed, appreciating Nettie's "happy capacity for making me feel bigger than I really am."[148] While Taylor herself was militant about responding quickly to letters, she could hardly be annoyed by Nettie's reasons for a late reply: "It's been a too long time since I've answered your letter. I keep it here with me at my desk in the library—smile at it often—and keep up a running conversation with you—but unless you're clairvoyant—I doubt that you 'get the message.' "[149] The usually reserved Taylor ended her long letters with admissions such as, "I find I could go on and on—There is so much more I'd like to talk about but I'd better send this off now."[150] When Taylor and Ralph traveled down the California coast in May 1964, visiting the Frishmans was a high point.

As the years passed, the friends saw each other periodically at conferences, but their primary method of communication remained correspondence—spotty, depending upon their busy schedules, but guaranteed to resume during the High Holidays and around Chanukah. Nettie raved about Maurice Sendak ("an amazing young man") and reported delightedly on a conference where Dorothy Parker spoke, shot off flares about politics and railed at Christian Science, and shared with Taylor her efforts to integrate Jewish practice both into her second family ("without tradition and background") and into society at large. Taylor described the party atmosphere in her home during the blackout of November 1965, talked about her woes with publishers and Cejwin, and chatted about plays and concerts she had attended.[151] The two women discussed retirement, both their own and that of their husbands, regaled each other with descriptions of travels, and bemoaned the chaos that seemed to overtake the United States in the 1960s. Together the women worried about their children's marital status and about their prospects for grandchildren. Nettie managed to be forthcoming without prying, and Taylor responded to the extent she felt comfortable.

Taylor's other great friendship during these difficult years was with her husband. Just as Ralph encouraged his wife's writing, so she had nothing but praise for her husband's musical endeavors and respect for his ceaseless toil at Caswell-Massey. Aside from working, Ralph played the recorder in coffeehouses, attended summer music camps, and sang in a choir.[152] He made his peace with not pursuing a professional music career, especially when he saw recital halls half empty for world-class performances.[153] When loneliness threatened to overwhelm Taylor, Ralph held the darkness at bay as her protective equal: "My mother and father are gone—my mother-in-law even with all her annoyances was a measure of life and vitality and part of our Sundays—my sisters and brothers scattered—busy—All Ralph and I can do is cling to each other."[154] Taylor ran the household for her husband, arranged his meals—the main meal always eaten in the middle of the day, either prepared by her or eaten at a restaurant such as Stouffer's, where they had their favorite waitresses—and turned to him for business advice. When the couple left their cares behind on their travels, their Parisian relatives fondly called them "the two love-birds from New York."[155] As many who knew the Brenner sisters noticed, the women were ferocious in argument when they were together, but in their homes, they deferred to their husbands. Taylor was no exception: "Mostly I think of myself as a housewife with a wonderful husband to take care of."[156]

Last Years and Legacy

1970–1978

AFTER A DECADE OF PROFESSIONAL disappointments and personal sorrows, Taylor might have thought she had reached a safe harbor by 1970. She was a beloved author, camp counselor, wife, sister, and friend. Professional responsibilities and domestic duties occupied her days. Each year followed a steady rhythm of personal appearances, classes, summer camp, family gatherings, and multifaceted cultural activities and travels with Ralph. Taylor's books continued to sell well, and her fans exhibited the same curiosity about and devotion to her All-of-a-Kind family as they had twenty years before. And yet, her world still failed to meet her expectations. Publishers made decisions she did not understand or with which she disagreed, unrest and high costs in New York City drove her family away, Ralph seemed trapped by his business—and her body betrayed her. Until her death in February 1978, this tiny, elegant woman who was always in motion, who sought to express words through movement, faced one physical setback after another.

As early as the 1950s, Taylor had tried to get her Cejwin plays published, and the project simmered throughout the 1960s. In 1962, Nettie Frishman suggested various publishers who might be interested in them, part of an ongoing conversation.[1] In the spring of 1968, Meeks considered publishing some of the plays in book form, which sent her author into a flurry of activity through the fall, as she polished scripts and found music to go with them. Taylor's vision was to publish a book of short, easy plays for classroom use, and another book of her longer scripts for all-school productions. Taylor also approached CBS, which had announced a projected *Children's Playhouse*, based on the success of its adult *CBS Playhouse*, and contacted NBC about the production of a play on television. Neither project went beyond the planning stage.

By March 1969, Taylor had heard nothing from Meeks, and huffily stated, "I do think I have been more than patient."[2] Meeks dropped the axe by return mail. She claimed that cuts in federal funding had depressed the entire children's publishing industry and that the editorial staff at Follett, in the process of being downsized, did not see Taylor's plays as a viable commercial venture.[3] Because Follett had not published plays, and the plays themselves required more directorial skills than the average teacher possessed, Meeks decided to return the manuscript. In the same letter, she rejected Taylor's retelling of a legend about King Solomon and asked Taylor to reconsider Meeks's suggestion of a sequel to *A Papa Like Everyone Else* or another installment of the *All-of-a-Kind* series. In September 1969, Taylor admitted to Nettie that a project Follett had asked her to work on the previous year (an educational primer) had fizzled to nothing, and a book of plays she had modified for the general reading public, including only one or two of Jewish content, had also petered out.[4] She couched her disappointment as effort wasted, and professed a disinclination to peddle her wares, since she had no compelling financial need and lacked confidence as a saleswoman. Despite those claims of indifference, she did try to sell her scripts that fall to play publisher Samuel French, which turned them down for lack of a sufficient market, and she made repeated attempts during the 1970s to find a publisher.[5] When Meeks once asked Ralph what he planned to do upon retirement, he said he would publish all of his wife's rejected manuscripts— and he did, in fact, try to keep the play project alive even as Taylor was dying.[6]

In February 1971, Taylor and Ralph viewed the precipitous retirement of Esther Meeks as an opportunity to resubmit the manuscript of *Downtown* to Follett, this time to editor Bertha Jenkinson.[7] Bertha and Taylor had discussed the book over the phone in the summer of 1970, and Taylor now apologized that unexpected surgery had delayed her submission, admitting that she had only now "returned to her normal self."[8] In her publicity speeches and in a letter to Nettie almost two years later, Taylor told a slightly different story. She reiterated then that it was Ralph who mentioned the book to Jenkinson when the three of them had lunch in New York, and the editor asked Taylor to send it along: "I was reluctant to do anything about it but Ralph kept after me."[9] Jenkinson must not have known much about the book, since

Taylor had to explain that it fit chronologically between *All-of-a-Kind Family* and *Uptown*.[10] In a letter of April 14, Jenkinson expressed enthusiasm for the manuscript, while warning Taylor that there would need to be cuts and revisions. In order for bound books to hit the shelves in the spring of 1972, Taylor would have to finish the revisions before she left for Cejwin, and Jenkinson needed to find an artist who could produce illustrations as close as possible to those of Mary Stevens, who had died since the publication of *Uptown*. Because of budget constraints, illustrations would be fewer.

Jenkinson kept her eye on marketing as much as Meeks had. She was delighted that *Downtown* fit between two earlier books, for that would stimulate sales for the entire series. *All-of-a-Kind Family* was still selling well, *More* moderately, and *Uptown* the most sluggishly of all. The audience for the series consisted of eight- to ten-year-olds, and Jenkinson wanted Taylor to keep that in mind in terms of length and lexicon. She asked for cuts of about sixty pages and suggested chapters that could be removed in their entirety. She had every expectation that Taylor would comply, because Taylor signed a contract for the new book in May 1971.

By dropping episodes about Papa's junk shop and a Purim play, which she felt unnecessarily repeated material from earlier books, Jenkinson hoped Taylor could expand on the settlement house. She felt such an expansion would be educational and would provide a mechanism to overcome Taylor's weakness for producing episodic chapters lacking in overall narrative structure. Some of the changes Jenkinson suggested were simple. For example, Kathy and Charlie's reappearance was implausible and could easily be removed. Jenkinson repeated Meeks's implicit warnings that Taylor had lost touch with how tastes had changed since 1951: "There are certain stereotypes that one could get away with twenty years ago—like 'Polack' and the incorrect reproduction of Italian speech, etc., which we will be condemned for with even greater vigor today—and rightfully so."[11]

Taylor acceded to most of the suggestions, holding the excised chapters in reserve for future books and agreeing to remove Kathy and Charlie. Again, in her letter to Nettie in November 1972, she changed her story of how the book came to be published, crediting herself and not Jenkinson with the realization that many revisions needed to be made and claiming the revised manuscript had little in common with the version Meeks had seen in the 1950s. Having trimmed the manuscript to 125 pages, Taylor felt she had the right to refuse ideas that distorted the past. As in earlier revisions, she was open to improving her writing, but never at the expense of what she considered the truth of history or human character. Jenkinson did not want visiting nurse Miss Carey to be a widow who had lost a child, although, unlike Meeks, she did not object to the death of Guido's mother. It was not that death was inappropriate in a children's book, but Jenkinson thought that Taylor piled on the melodrama in a way that beggared belief. Taylor refused this change. She needed Miss Carey to have suffered acute personal tragedy in order to render credible the woman's choice of career as a settlement nurse and her decision to "step out of character" in involving herself so intimately with Guido's future. Taylor also claimed authority in determining what was or was not characteristic of settlement houses in 1913.

Jenkinson was less brusque than Meeks, and satisfactory compromises were more easily reached. Taylor's version to Nettie was that "I have become bolder over the years and have begun to ask for certain things." That assessment ignores the fact that Taylor had always asked for "certain things," and whether or not she got them depended more on market assessments than on her stubbornness. By November, Taylor was going over final galleys, which, Jenkinson explained, would look different to Taylor because Follett had switched to computer typesetting to bring down costs. Jenkinson was pleased with the illustrations of Beth and Joe Krush, but Taylor had to ask to see them in order to check for errors. She liked them enough to later request a signed illustration to frame. Nonetheless, it is noteworthy that the editors at Follett did not automatically seek Taylor's stamp of approval for the illustrations and had to be prodded into letting her see the artwork in advance.

Jenkinson's ambitious timeline stalled, for in March 1972 Taylor complained that she did not know what was happening with her new book. She did know that it had not yet been bound, because she asked for the copyright to be in her name and for the dedication page to honor Tanta.[12] The reason for the delay was Jenkinson's retirement from Follett—a fact of which Taylor had remained ignorant. To the editor who replaced Jenkinson Taylor admitted, "I feel very sad. It's heartbreaking to have one's close contacts change. But I suppose that is the penalty for growing older—changes of any kind come harder."[13] Taylor later glossed over how little she knew at the time, when she explained to Nettie that Jenkinson had resigned over unhappiness with changes at Follett.[14]

Her new contact at the publishing house was Sandra Greifenstein, a former assistant to Meeks known to Taylor since the early 1960s and subsequently head of the Children's Book Department at Follett from 1970 to 1972. Taylor repeated her requests about the copyright and the dedication. Not receiving an immediate response, she prodded Greifenstein for an answer, mentioning that she was soon off to Europe and that her numerous connections at libraries in England would want to know the status of the new book.[15] Greifenstein replied that it was the fault of the Krushes, who had been promising to deliver illustrations since December. The current plan was to have a completed book by June for fall release.[16] Even before the official launch, Taylor would have copies in hand to sell at Cejwin.

Follett had high expectations for *Downtown* and planned to promote it aggressively. They wanted Taylor to attend the annual American Library Association conference held during the last week of June in Chicago: "We know many, many librarians would be thrilled to renew their acquaintance with you or to meet the author of the renowned ALL-OF-A-KIND series."[17] Greifenstein piled on the flattery, calling Taylor one of Follett's "important authors" and inviting her to be Follett's guest of honor at a cocktail party. She did not point out that a major impetus for Taylor's participation in publicity was that no new *All-of-a-Kind* book had appeared since 1957, even though Dell had contracted to reprint the series in paperback in 1965 and it was still selling in the tens of thousands of copies each year.[18] Greifenstein was ever gracious, sending Taylor a color proof of the jacket unasked. Such courtesy did not go unnoticed, for Taylor remarked to Nettie that "she was very good in her job and extremely nice to me."[19] In October, Taylor was selling *Downtown* at her appearances at Hebrew schools and hoped it would do half as well as *All-of-a-Kind Family,* then in its seventeenth printing.

Downtown received a good notice in *Kirkus Reviews,* but Jean Fritz in the *New York Times* panned it.[20] Taylor was "terribly upset" by the negative review and, in a letter to Ginger, sounded bewildered and hurt:

> The new books for children contain what grownups consider is reality—a drunken father or mother—a mother who abandons her children—divorce in the family—unwed mothers—homosexuality— and you name it. Even the new Newbery Award is being given to a

book about an Eskimo girl of 15 who is given in marriage to an older man. On the wedding night she runs away because she does not want to consummate the marriage and lives with wolves or something. I haven't read the book just the report on it. But this is what they are choosing and exposing to children to today. Then they wonder why children are growing up so awful![21]

Even though enthusiastic fan letters poured in and the Child Study Association put Taylor on their reading list, that one unfavorable review in the *Times* stung. Ralph was so angry that he wrote a sarcastic letter to Fritz and had an employee sign it so he would not "appear prejudicial as a husband."[22] Also remaining silent about their connection to the author, Charlotte, Gertrude, and Ginger wrote in Taylor's defense as well.

Yet one more blow was Greifenstein's decision to move to San Diego with her husband, where she did freelance work for Follett and joined the staff of a new magazine for children, *Cricket*.[23] She solicited short stories and plays from Taylor for the fledgling publication and volunteered to work on any book manuscripts Taylor might have. But the manuscripts sent were neither sophisticated nor "singular" enough to meet *Cricket*'s aspirations to be a publication of high literary quality, so Greifenstein rejected some and sent others back to Follett for additional review.[24] At Follett, Taylor was handed over to Marci Carafoli, her last editor at the company.[25] Within months, her latest attempt at a picture book, *Jingle-Jangle,* was rejected, and Taylor took her complaints to Greifenstein. Ever the diplomat, Greifenstein intimated that once again Taylor was out of touch with current tastes and commercial realities: "Today adult reviewers, librarians, and many other buyers are predisposed to books of social value, sometimes to the exclusion of books with other values it seems. So the marketplace must be considered."[26] The marketplace apparently did not want Taylor's attempt at another *Mr. Barney* book either, and Taylor resisted Carafoli's attempt to interest her in writing a nonfiction book about dance.[27] In numerous letters, Taylor expressed consternation at the rapid changes in personnel at Follett: "I can't begin to tell you how I feel. Cut adrift—Relationship between an editor and author gets to be rather close. Now who will be the next one?"[28]

The one relationship Taylor could count on was with her husband. Ralph's role in Taylor's career as a writer continued. More than a cheerleader and defender, he was her first reader and editor. While his wife was at Cejwin, Ralph sent *In God's Hands* in answer to an ad placed in the *Saturday Review* by the Jewish Community Center of Cleveland. He also pursued contacts with illustrators with the thought that they could provide illustrations for Taylor's future work. When Taylor became too sick to meet with Follett editors, Ralph discussed editorial and financial matters as her proxy. He looked for an agent to represent his wife's work, choosing Meredith Bernstein of the Henry Morrison agency to help with the publication of the last *All-of-a-Kind* book, *Ella of All-of-a-Kind Family*.

Both Taylors grew disenchanted with, even distrustful of, her publishers. Ever since Dell began publishing paperback editions of her series in the 1960s, Taylor found her royalty statements difficult to decipher and seldom clear about the sales of each book. No matter how many demands for clarification and letters of complaint she sent, her mind was never at rest about the financial aspects of her writing career. At a book fair in Atlantic City in October 1973, Taylor was dismayed to see that Follett was selling *Now That You Are Eight* under its own auspices, when she had been told that the Association Press edition was out of print. Follett still had failed to reply to her queries by the end of January 1974.[29] Eventually Taylor and Ralph learned that even though the copyright was hers, Follett had bought the unbound copies of a later edition, made new copies, and sold them without notice or royalty to her.[30] Follett might mollify Taylor temporarily, but they used a form letter to inform her that *Mr. Barney's Beard* was going out of print in 1974.[31] Whatever personal touch there might have been was a thing of the past.

Taylor became increasingly elegiac when she considered her career as a writer. Fatigued at the thought of dividing her time between housework and writing, she wrote, "Part of me says 'how much of what has been published will endure anyway? Just think of the millions of written words gone down the drain.' The other part of me says 'well who will honor me after I am gone for the clean house I kept?' "[32] Yet the fires of ambition still burned. Taylor responded to the Kerlan Collection's request for her manuscripts of *All-of-a-Kind Family* and *Mr. Barney's Beard* and pushed (unsuccessfully) to get *All-of-a-Kind Family* published in Israel in 1974. And whatever Taylor thought about writing, she never flagged in her prompt, friendly replies to her fans and her insistence on proper accounting from her publishers.

Just as she refused to give up on her writing, so Taylor could not give up on Cejwin, even if she did think too many of the campers were "rotten spoiled brats."[33] Her dear Ella was still running registration during the year and supervising the maintenance staff in the summer, and Taylor was not willing to abandon her sister, no matter how much she disparaged the director, Rabbi Jerome "Jerry" Abrams (1926–2017; at Cejwin 1967–78), and the young, irresponsible staff.

Taylor's relationship with Ella, however, faced a new challenge. Ella's involvement with Albert Schoolman became public when his wife Bertha died in January 1974 after a long illness. On one hand, the change constrained how the Brenner sisters were able to speak about Cejwin matters, for now Ella openly had a foot in two camps. When the affair was not spoken about, the fiction could be maintained that Ella was a Cejwin employee like everyone else. Once Ella took on a more public role in Schoolman's life, she had divided loyalties, especially when her family complained about hiring choices and salaries.[34] But Taylor noticed that with Schoolman around, Ella's "whole personality seems to change. She had been looking so weary and worn—but she seemed so much more youthful—was so nicely dressed—her hair so well groomed . . . It's good—it should happen to Henny—make a new woman out of her."[35] Although Ella and Schoolman, now eighty, traveled together and had a full life in New York, Taylor and her sisters worried that Ella would once again be stuck caring for a sick man, even as they did not want to deny her a fleeting chance at happiness.[36]

Besieged by change, Taylor foresaw the closing of the camp. Registration slowly declined, the number of age divisions falling to two from a high of seven, as Jewish parents made other choices for their children's summer activities. In 1974, Taylor wondered whether Cejwin might receive a windfall from the energy crisis, for parents might choose camp for their children instead of vacation travel. As the camp experimented with ways to remain relevant, Taylor worked with boys for the first time in 1974, and the combined number of boys and girls (235) made for an exhausting, if rewarding, summer.[37] Taylor was not reconciled to the change even a year later, however, and not because of the added work. Remarking that both parents and children liked the switch to a co-ed camp, she grumbled, "Parents are so anxious to throw the sexes together—and I can't for the life of me say why they have to be rushed into things so much."[38] All Taylor saw was sexual license and yet further proof that the world had altered: "Life was so much nicer when we were young—even if we were at the other extreme of knowing too little perhaps. But we had rosy dreams and ideals—and we saw great beauty in love—the sexual aspect was something we hardly thought of excepting in connection with love. But if you could see what goes on in Aviv-Aviva!"[39] Young people were out of control, and Taylor's anxieties about aging into irrelevance fogged her memory of her own youthful escapades.

When Taylor was made responsible for older children, she bemoaned the lack of time to produce the requisite number of plays and dances. She acknowledged that she lacked the energy to teach the older campers Israeli and modern dancing: "I no longer wish to expend that much energy on the terrible hoppy-jumpy-swift numbers that teenagers like to do. I like them too but in moderation."[40] Nonetheless, she did not allow herself to be eased out of the dance program in 1975 without a struggle. Already sick, she took her lighter load as an opportunity to increase her involvement in the drama program.[41] Her sisters assumed camp was out for Taylor in 1976, but ill as she was, she showed up for a reduced schedule and was remembered by campers as a kind and devoted theater director. She even went to camp in the summer of 1977, seldom leaving her cabin, yet faithful to the end.

The love for theater that Taylor shared with campers in the magical, child-centered world of Cejwin continued to be part of her appearances in libraries and schools. Her belief in the value of improvisatory dramatics remained strong, and she extended her programs to include adults when she could.[42] Everywhere she went, Taylor remained attuned to the performative quality of human expression. On her trip to Italy in 1970, her eye was drawn to the drama of Italian speech: "Watching them talk is like watching a stage performance. Even without knowledge of the words you can understand them—and you reply with gestures. We get along just fine."[43] With so many years of training young people to find just the right movement to express a poem or a feeling, Taylor responded warmly to this Italian sidewalk theater.

The European trips continued to mix the new and the unfamiliar. Taylor and Ralph had considered and then rejected a trip to Austria and Germany in the 1960s, but by the fall of 1972 they decided to go. Taylor's dance teacher Katya Delakova, who fled Vienna in 1939, had discouraged Taylor from making the earlier trip.[44] Several years later, Delakova herself taught a

Taylor in Europe

dance class in Germany, "which proves that one has to forget—especially where business is concerned. When you consider that even Israel has resumed relations with Germany, why should we continue to hate them. After all the new generation wasn't even born at the time."[45] Still, Taylor hesitated. Although Ralph would enjoy playing recorder with the many fellow enthusiasts there, she mused, "I wonder if I won't be feeling upset and angry all of the time." By March 1973, however, it was settled. As Taylor asked Nettie, "how long must one go on hating[?]" The Taylors purposely left their itinerary open. Aside from starting in Mainz, home of Schott & Co. music publishers, they had no fixed plans: "We have felt that if we find ourselves unhappy in Germany and unable therefore to properly enjoy the trip, we will go back to England."[46]

The following year, the Taylors returned to Israel for the last time as a couple. They did not make a special trip for the wedding of their niece Naomi Ruderman (daughter of Ralph's sister, Lucille, and her husband, Rabbi Abraham Ruderman), choosing instead to visit the newlyweds during their regularly scheduled travel period. Taylor reported little about her feelings for the country, except to say in connection with Rabbi Abraham and Lucille's plans to immigrate to Israel upon the rabbi's retirement, "not for me . . . I want to retire right here in America and feel free to go around elsewhere when the mood strikes."[47] No one could accuse the Taylors of the fear Taylor claimed kept her sister Gertie from Israel, even when Naomi Ruderman wrote of acquaintances being killed in the Yom Kippur War the previous fall. Nonetheless, although Taylor and Ralph visited willingly and bought State of Israel bonds, they identified as Jewish Americans first and foremost.

Taylor remained attached to her Ruderman niece and nephew, sending gifts when their children were born, composing and receiving newsy letters and tapes, and praising them for their Zionism and commitment to Judaism in her letters to friends. She was close enough to David that his wife, Phyllis, felt comfortable writing letters about their life in Israel, Phyllis being one of the few family members to write about politics in any depth.[48] Phyllis enthusiastically offered all sorts of suggestions for hotels and tours before the Taylors' two-week visit to Israel in the spring of 1974, and delightedly shared the news that David's first job as a professor would be at the University of Maryland.[49] Naomi bubbled over with excitement about her wedding, her studies in Jerusalem and job as a social worker, and her fiancé's work with street gangs in development towns. When Rabbi Abraham and Lucille finally made aliyah in 1977 to fulfill a lifelong dream and live near their daughter and grandchildren, Taylor saw in the Ruderman family a happiness denied her.

Over the years, Taylor pondered why the Rudermans, of all her nieces and nephews, seemed so anchored, so uninterested in rebelling for rebellion's sake. She looked at how her siblings had raised their children in loving homes, with beautiful relationships until everything went wrong and they experienced nothing but tough times.

It's not the parents—it's the attitude of their whole generation. They infect one another. I have only one niece and one nephew who are so absolutely wonderful, I find myself thinking over and over—how is it they turned out so well? Their father is a rabbi—their home was always run with great spiritual feeling about their religion—The children were directed towards Young Judea at an early and impressionable age and through these organizations met some wonderful idealistic Israelis who indoctrinated them. So is religious training the answer? I'm not sure—I know a friend of my rabbi's son, whose father was also a rabbi who repudiated the religion altogether and will have none of it now. Who knows?[50]

It cannot have escaped Taylor's notice that many of her nieces and nephews had passed through Cejwin, yet even that Jewish organization had not inoculated them against the infection of their generation.

Taylor realized that what she was best able to accomplish was to present a view of the Jewish past to American children and their families. Contemplating how writers could address the Jewish minority in the present, Taylor concluded that Jews did not live so differently from other groups in America, and that the abundance of books about Jewish holidays reflected the fact that such celebrations had become the sole distinguishing feature of Jewish life.[51] She perceived no distinction between sisterhoods and men's clubs affiliated with suburban synagogues and their equivalent organizations in churches. With access to such social amenities as country clubs and exclusive private schools, Jews were no different from their gentile neighbors. Taylor was convinced that even Milton Taylor's two sons, who had attended an Orthodox day school and insisted on strict observance of regulations such as kashruth, would lose their religious determination once "out in the regular world of America." Intermarriage was becoming the norm, and "as for antisemitism, one doesn't meet it openly here in New York."[52]

While Taylor described American Judaism as disappearing into the larger culture, she did not see that as reason to give up on Jewish education: "A child who is brought up with a faith knows where he belongs. Also the beauty and color tradition can give to one's life is so important in later years . . . those who have immersed themselves in Judaism remain much finer in character than those who drift away. I think particularly of my niece and nephew David and Naomi Ruderman who find they cannot relate to the young folk in our county because of their moral standards and shallow view of life."[53]

The Taylors' own experiences with youthful rebellion finally seemed over by 1970. No longer estranged from her daughter, Taylor conveyed the normalcy of their relationship in complaining to Henny that Jo had neglected her health for too long, and it was high time she paid attention to Taylor's dietary and medical advice.[54] The Taylors fussed over Jo's unexplained heart flutter and made an appointment for her with a specialist, which she kept. By now, Jo recognized that her parents' smothering interest in her welfare was a sign of love, however irritating. In turn, she organized a surprise fiftieth wedding anniversary party for her parents in June 1975. Although the word *lesbian* does not appear in Taylor's correspondence, in 1976 Charlotte asked Taylor to give her love to both Jo and Virginia, Jo's female partner for several intervening years, in the casual way family members used to do with Jo and Steve.[55]

It had long been clear that Jo was not going to take over Caswell-Massey, the future of which remained in doubt. Ralph and Taylor murmured about retirement for years. Despite Taylor's repeated assurance to friends and family considering retirement that busy people would always find a gratifying outlet for their energies, she failed to convince her husband—or herself. At first their excuse was that business was finally booming and they needed to guide the company. Then it was that they needed to wait for at least one of Milton's two sons to complete his education and training in the business in order to take over. Then it was that the sons lacked genuine interest, and it was impossible to find a buyer for the company.[56] In 1968, Taylor had assured David Ruderman that Ralph would "retire out of business and into a purely cultural life."[57] According to her, Ralph hoped to fulfill a lifelong dream of studying music composition at Julliard. Two years later, Taylor told Nettie, "I only know that I wish he would get out."[58] Apparently Ralph did not want to retire from Caswell-Massey any more than Taylor wanted to leave Cejwin or stop appearing at schools and libraries. Even though Taylor repeatedly described Ralph's inability to extricate himself from the company as outside his control and "depressing," he continued to throw himself into his business.

Since Ralph could manage a packed schedule of lessons, performances, and music camps, in both the United States and Europe, while steering a multi-million-dollar company, he had little incentive to retire. In 1970 he made deliveries in person when the company contracted for a delivery job proved unsatisfactory.[59] He devised his own advertising campaigns, appeared on radio and television, and put in twelve-hour days during the Christmas rush, working even on Saturdays. In 1977, he came out with new products called "Modern Dance" and "Hot Stuff," and expanded the business through franchises.[60] The Taylors' trips to Europe continued to include business meetings, so Taylor could sympathize with her sister-in-law Zelda, whose first vacation with Milton in over a year included looking for items suitable for the Caswell-Massey catalogue.[61] The store occupied not only the Taylor brothers, but also their mother, who still worked there several hours a day well into her nineties.

It baffled Taylor's sisters why Ralph did not retire. Writing from Florida, Charlotte mused: "We talked of the cruelty of fate that keeps you and Ralph from enjoying this kind of winter. It seems a kind of trap Ralph is caught in, and I wonder whether he doesn't feel like bursting thru at whatever financial loss."[62] Taylor participated in this dramatization of her situation, seeing the ambivalence of Milton's sons as indicative of that deterioration in the young she had long deplored at Cejwin:

> The young of today are so different from us. One is now in the business but I feel it is only for the money—he would not take courses suitable for the business like pharmacy but physics. There being no chance of getting jobs in that field today he came into the business. I see some small growing interest but he will have to get back into some kind of studying to run it properly. As for his brother, he's quit college after 2 years even though he was on the dean's list—and is at the moment roaming around Europe. We did get him to take a course in Grasse with some connection of our company in the making and distilling of perfumes—but when he was through with the 6 weeks course, instead of coming home, he's traipsing around abroad. What's happening to our young? Why is it they're so little interested in what the future needs will be? They seem to live only for the present.[63]

The voice of the immigrant daughter is strong. Taylor shakes her head over the lack of seriousness and drive, the wasted educational opportunities, the lack of concern for the future—not only of her nephews, but also of American youth as a whole. She and her generation struggled to achieve financial security and professional success without the benefit of all that was given to the younger generation, and they were dismayed to witness how little stock their children put in their parents' values and aspirations.

With his interest in the theater and performance, it is no surprise that Ralph excelled at another skill of second-generation immigrants—inhabiting a self-made identity. When, in 1976, the city of New York honored companies that had been in business for more than two hundred years, the article in the *New York Times* opened with warnings about the departure of some of those enterprises for less costly, safer locales. Flight was not in Caswell-Massey's future, however. Ralph was quoted as saying his company would never quit the city:

> We've been aristocrats for more than 200 years and New York is the only place left where our kind of people come . . . We have resisted the commercial and we are an oasis of quiet contentment. We try to help New York by remaining the way we are. And that takes effort . . . We just had a burglary this morning and my brother said that if they come back, we should give them a catalogue . . . It is part of the adventure of living in New York and we don't mind. To be burglarized is unusual and nostalgic, just like our products.[64]

Those who knew Ralph would have detected the dry humor of this Jewish immigrant from Latvia, born Reuven Schneider. Ralph played the role of debonair aristocrat with aplomb, yet not without self-aware puckishness.

The Taylors had combined the different strands of their lives into such a well-balanced structure that removing any one piece threatened to upset the whole. They certainly were not tempted to join Brenner relatives in Florida, for their business and intellectual lives centered on New York; six weeks in Europe provided a sufficient break for them, along with Taylor's summers in the country. That is not to say that they were not critical of New York. When changes were made in rent control laws in 1971, Taylor got busy at her typewriter to complain to the City Rent Commission, the State Rent Administration, Governor Nelson Rockefeller, and even President Richard Nixon.[65] Ever the storyteller, she spun a dramatic tale for the politicians about how her elderly, widowed sister had been mugged in the Bronx yet, because of changes in rent control laws, could not afford to give up her apartment to look for a safer neighborhood. Her letters crackled with fiery tirades about the degradation of life in New York, the filth and noise, the ever-rising costs, and the condescension of public leaders.

Taylor used personal stories as a springboard to a passionate defense of the middle-class people of New York—"law-abiding, hardworking people who ask for the minimal of service from their government"—who were exploited by greedy landlords and indifferent public officials. It had been a long time since Taylor identified as a socialist, but her passionate advocacy of the working man had endured and became more articulate: "Why is it that in our country today only those who militantly scream loudest—make unjustified demands, can get their voices heard over T.V.—radio—and can have their words and faces spread across the news media—and violently demand—and abuse and lo and behold the demands are met. Must we who are long-suffering and silent, begin to organize and scream equally loudly before governmental officials will pay any attention?"[66] Six years later, Taylor went on the attack again, writing to Senator Daniel Patrick Moynihan to excoriate him for reversing his opinion on rent control.[67]

Politics remained singularly individual and familial for Taylor. Her antagonism toward communism and the Soviet Union, for example, emerged from her personal blend of American patriotism and Jewish identity. On their trip to Italy in 1970, Taylor heard from a rabbi in Naples that he noticed more anti-Semitism than during World War II, which he attributed to the Communists— "naturally they follow the line laid down by Russia."[68] As a Jew, Taylor enjoyed her role as citizen of the world. In a kosher restaurant in Florence, where she and Ralph met Jews from Iran, Mexico, England, and New York, Taylor noted: "The proprietor could speak Hebrew and Italian and English but no Jewish. Some of his customers (like the Mexicans) could speak only Yiddish or Spanish, so Ralph and I were the interpreters." The Taylors alone straddled the New and Old Worlds and brought them together.

Physically, however, Taylor and her family began to fall apart. Illness continued to plague the Brenner siblings throughout the 1970s. In 1970,

Ella's granddaughter was diagnosed with the disease that led to her early death.[69] Lenny was diagnosed with muscular dystrophy, and he too faced years of disability. Henny always had one complaint or another, at one point in the 1970s eliciting Taylor's diagnosis that she suffered from Ménière's disease.[70] Gertrude continued to seek treatment for her asthma and erysipelas, although Charlotte wondered archly about the convenient timing of her attacks. When they were not inquiring about or reporting on illness within the family, the sisters informed each other about sickness and death in the Cejwin community. Those reports, however, were far outnumbered by enthusiastic descriptions of their social and cultural lives in retirement communities, at home in New York, or on their travels: Ella's painting classes, which brought her into rivalry with Charlotte; Lou's golf, Henny's ceramics, and Gertie's trips to Mexico.

Taylor had suffered from various health problems throughout her life—the blind eye, nosebleeds, pulled muscles from dancing, occasional scrapes, and bouts with the flu—none of which were life threatening. She lived a healthy life, kept a strict diet, and had every reason to think that she was doing everything right. When she had her first serious operation—a hysterectomy in the fall of 1970—she was open about the procedure and betrayed no great concern. She had gone into the hospital for the removal of a fibroid tumor and ended up having the more radical operation.[71] In a detailed letter to Nettie, Taylor expressed only annoyance that she had to have the operation at all, which she blamed on doctors over-eager to prescribe hormone therapy as a way to slow the aging process in women.[72] Because she took their advice, she said, and was "one of the first guinea pigs to use estrogen," she ended up quite sick and under the surgeon's knife. In fact, it was Ralph who repeatedly urged her to pursue the latest anti-aging treatments, and she deferred to him as a matter of course. In keeping with past behavior, Taylor seized on financial matters in an attempt to assert control: "It's unbelievable the situation medically today. Tiny rooms which were once private rooms are doubled up into semi-private for which I paid $100.00 a day!"[73] Taylor's recovery was slow, at least to this impatient woman eager to return to dance and yoga classes.

By December 1973, Taylor had received a diagnosis of cancer and undergone a mastectomy. It abruptly became clear to her why she had been so tired at Cejwin the previous two summers. In her letters to Charlotte after the operation, she primarily voiced her irritation about how long it was taking to exercise without pain, and she groused at her doctors for not being clearer about what she should have expected. She also complained about the high cost of false silicone breasts. Katya Delakova had also had a mastectomy, after which she developed a dance program that included Tai Chi for women recovering from the operation. Working one-on-one with Delakova offered physical and psychological solace to the perpetually active, energetic Taylor, and the competitive performer in her shone through: "[Katya] says that of all the ones she's worked with, I'm in the best condition of all with a great deal of movability . . . she thinks by summer I'll be more than ready to work in camp."[74] Taylor was back fulfilling her speaking engagements by early February and entertained no doubts that she and Ralph would visit Israel that spring.

Charlotte sighed, "It's so sad that you should be struck so unfairly, considering how correctly you've lived."[75] At first, faith in the medical profession and Taylor's resilience buoyed the family's spirits. Various members continued spending their winters in the South or vacationing in Mexico, gathering for meals in New York, and spoiling grandchildren. Taylor and Ralph took all the expected measures, including seeking opinions from a number of doctors in New York. Taylor sought additional care from the Cleveland Clinic, staying with friends she had met at a book fair in 1967. While in Ohio, she appeared at schools for her creative dramatics even though surgeries and chemotherapy dotted her calendar.

Anyone given a frightening diagnosis can sympathize with Taylor's frustrated bewilderment when confronted with medical institutions. Because she was an articulate storyteller, her illness, too, became a drama in which she distanced herself from the action and assigned reassuring roles to the main characters in her life. To Dr. Caldwell Esselstyne she wrote: "A person confronted with the realization that he has cancer is very vulnerable. Thus he is ready to catch at straws—to rush into treatment immediately—to do something—anything—that might possibly help. That is precisely the way I felt when I was at the Clinic. But this is not true of Mr. Taylor. His customary sober judgment comes to the fore. He will not permit me to act precipitously without due consideration and the weighing of all possibilities."[76] As she came to realize, however, cancer did not lend itself to the therapeutic treatment of improvisatory dramatics, and her many complaints sounded increasingly plaintive.

True to form, Taylor's siblings rallied around their sister. In newsy letters, they wished her well during her treatments and were heartened when
she told them she was gaining weight or getting out to restaurants and plays.
Taylor continued to write chatty letters, but she was reticent about her condition. When Charlotte thanked her for a long and informative letter, she exclaimed, "You don't tell how you're *feeling*, but if the illness hasn't progressed,
isn't this the miracle you're hoping for?"[77] By December 1976, Taylor
confessed to her sister that her situation was dire: "The cancer in the initial
primary area seems to be looking better but there is proliferation elsewhere—
whether it is the body throwing it off or what I cannot say." Her wig may have
been beautiful, but she was crushingly tired. When her housekeeper caught a
cold and stayed away to protect her employer's compromised immune system, Taylor dragged herself through the motions of taking care of the apartment and preparing Ralph's meals. Even so, the training of her youth
prevailed, and she ruefully acknowledged to Charlotte that when her regular
cleaning woman came, "I have to prepare her lunch too—you know the way
we are—like Mama—it has to be a decent meal."[78]

   In 1977, the family still seemed to expect that Taylor would recover.
Charlotte's husband Lou wrote approvingly to Ralph, "We think her attitude
toward her illness and life are admirable. We *do* grow old, feeble, ill and weak,
but it's all a part of living. No sense crabbing or complaining. Just make the
best of what you have. Syd's letters are just like her—newsy and sparkling."[79]
The ongoing squabbling among her siblings signaled normalcy. If Henny's
feelings were hurt when Taylor turned down her offers of help and asked for
Ella's companionship instead, or Charlotte asked Taylor to intercede with
Cejwin on Henny's behalf to get her a job in the summer of 1976 when she felt
Ella was not doing enough, it meant that Taylor was still in the thick of things,
still part of her All-of-a-Kind family.

   The sisters were complicit in Taylor's attempts to keep the news of her
illness from anyone outside her immediate circle. Some of the reticence was
for professional reasons. Responding to a proposal in 1976 to develop a television program based on the *All-of-a-Kind* series, Taylor apologized for her
delay with the understatement, "In the last weeks of children's camp where I
am head of dance and dramatics, I became ill and am not yet recovered."[80]
She wanted to keep working at Cejwin, and even when that became impossible, Henny reported about a colleague at camp, "She doesn't as far as I

know, know anything about your illness except that you do not feel well enough to tackle the job."[81]

With Ella as her role model, Taylor refused to let up.[82] In 1976 she submitted the manuscript for *Ella of All-of-a-Kind Family* to Marci Carafoli at Follett and fought for her vision of how to tell her sister's story. Although there are chapters about the other children, the novel focuses on Ella's opportunity to pursue a career on the stage after a talent scout notices her. Tensions arise when her longtime boyfriend, Jules, returns from Europe, where he fought in World War I, and asks her to marry him. Framing the choice between career and marriage as an either/or decision offended feminist sensibilities in the mid-1970s, but Taylor argued that such was the choice facing a young woman in 1918. Were the story to "conform to the current popular trend giving emphasis to the 'feminist viewpoint,' " it would be false to history: "All of a Kind Family, if anything, is not a modern story. Nor is it even a commentary on the period involved. On the contrary, I have deliberately avoided second guessing, i.e. passing judgment on that era from today's viewpoint. The series adheres as accurately as possible to the mores of the times. It is as much as I could make it an authentic historical portrait of how it was in those days. Any hint of special pleading would amount to a subversion of my intent, rob the characters and situations of their validity and moreover, would be faking history."[83] Echoing Meeks from some fourteen years earlier, Taylor thought Carafoli's views on the character of Ella contradictory. If the character were to pursue her performing career longer and spend more time on the disappointing vaudeville tour, her decision to marry Jules would seem like no dilemma at all. On the contrary, it would come across as an antifeminist escape into marriage rather than an affirmative decision.

Taylor also fought Carafoli about Henny's reason for running for office in the chapter "Election in the Balance." In Taylor's telling, Henny and her girlfriends saw election to office as a wonderful opportunity to meet boys. When Carafoli objected, finding such a reason an unsuitable educational message for girls in 1977, Taylor insisted that it would have been a privilege of office: "Considering the constraints of the times this privilege was definitely exceptional." Taylor sent documentation about the separation of boys and girls in gym classes in 1919 to prove her points about how things actually were. Her books were to be true memorials to a vanished time and place.

Within months, Taylor signed a contract for *Ella,* but it was suddenly with Ann Durell at E. P. Dutton.[84] Carafoli, too, had left Follett—in her case, for the Robert Bentley Company in Cambridge, Massachusetts, when her husband took a new position in Boston. For the first time, Taylor began working with an agent. Ralph and the agent, Meredith Bernstein, eased Taylor's transition to a different publishing house. For the first time too, Ralph was openly involved in the editing. Because of Taylor's illness, it was he and not Taylor who met with editors, and he conveyed their decisions and suggestions to his wife. Taylor continued to make revisions under Durell's guidance. With Ralph's encouragement, Bernstein and Durell adopted the deferential, respectful, and supportive tone most likely to obtain Taylor's compliance. Durell was especially pleased with the ending Taylor devised in June, which offered the fictional Ella a chance to continue working under Professor Calvano with Jules's support: "Terrific! You made the ending even more effective than I could have imagined. You put your finger right on what I missed—the new scene with Professor Calvano suggesting that Ella can have a more compatible career opportunity singing with his group is perfect, as is the new ending with Jules. There was just one thing that seemed not to fit just right in the latter, and I'm enclosing the last two pages with a few suggested changes."[85]

The battles were far from over. Durell informed Taylor that there would be no illustrations. She wanted the book to look more "grown-up" for the older readers who would be attracted by Ella's more grown-up story. Durell was also struggling to keep costs down and feared that the search for a suitable artist would delay publication until at least the fall of 1978. Taylor was horrified, calling the decision "tragic."[86] She argued vehemently for the inclusion of illustrations, citing illustrated editions of *Little Women* as evidence that even older readers liked pictures. She drew on Ralph's connections to come up with names of artists, wrote personally to Enrico Arno in the hopes that he might illustrate her book, and eventually prevailed over Durell's objections.[87] However sick Taylor felt in the fall of 1977, she did not let up with detailed instructions to Durell about the type, spacing, wording, and coloring of the jacket cover, as well as the accuracy of the images. When Durell sent her the jacket cover, Taylor replied with compliments before criticizing the type, and concluded bluntly: "The blurb is pedestrian."[88] Having received copies of the illustrations, she proposed modifications to the piano stool, clothing design, and the apparent ages of the characters.

Taylor intended to write a separate book about each of her sisters. At the time of her death, she had completed eleven chapters of a book about Henny. If *Ella* had been a hard sell, however, *Henny* would have been almost impossible. Taylor never overcame her tendency to string unconnected episodes together; without the guidance of a committed editor, the lack of an overarching narrative crippled the manuscript. Furthermore, Taylor had run out of stories. The chapters she proposed for the book about Henny were little more than variations on tame encounters with boyfriends and bland descriptions of Jewish holidays.

In her Rosh Hashanah letter of 1977 to Nettie Frishman, Taylor happily announced that Dutton was coming out with *Ella of All-of-a-Kind Family* the following spring and that Doubleday, Doran would include one of her stories in a children's book about New York, also scheduled to appear in 1978.[89] The most astonishing incidence of Taylor's silence about her health was the complete absence of any mention of her cancer to Nettie. In this letter, written six months before her death, Taylor reported that she and Ralph had not gone to Europe the previous spring for various reasons. Those reasons included the rapid expansion of Ralph's business through franchising and the poor health of Ralph's mother ("now about 97 years old, [she] is not well enough for us to be too far away")—and that is all.[90] Nettie's reply in November shows that no one had informed her of the severity of Taylor's condition, and the delay in her response implies that she felt no sense of urgency. Nettie talked about Egyptian-Israeli overtures for peace, the Caswell-Massey franchise in Beverly Hills, her retirement, her volunteer efforts for children in low-income areas, and her grandchildren, but not a word about Taylor's health.[91]

By October 1977, the family expected the worst, even though they kept up a good front. Charlotte dreaded leaving New York for her home in Florida: "I want to go after you've weathered your present impasse. It was comforting to me at least to be able to talk to you almost daily and the weekly visits were such a highlight I'm going to miss them terribly. It really gives me a lift to see how you continue to cope. I well know the inner struggle this involves, and we should all be grateful, the 'five' sisters and others, at your courage and persistence at this time."[92] The letters from family and friends are touching in their helplessness.[93] Charlotte wistfully recalls when she used to live near Gertrude and saw Henny and Taylor several times a week, and she admits to not knowing whether Taylor really wants to read her chatty news about the Himbers' activities in Florida. As for Ralph, Taylor's approaching death rendered him speechless. In October, a three-sentence note from Ralph to Walter Bergmann in England began, "Syd has been very ill with cancer and I just can't write about it."[94]

Even as she received new treatments at Whitestone Hospital in Queens, Taylor's devotion to her fans never flagged. She answered their letters, was honored to participate in a program for young readers to write to their favorite authors, and corrected illustrations for *Ella*. She was gratified to hear from her friends and family about young relatives who loved the books upon being introduced to them by grandmothers, mothers, and aunts. When Ginger sent the notes her young daughters dictated and illustrated, Taylor responded with her customary imagination and gracious charm.

Sydney Taylor died in the hospital on February 14, 1978. Her brother Irving concluded his eulogy for her by saying: "We are very proud and grateful that Sydney Taylor will be remembered by readers of the past as well as those of the future, as the charmingly winsome Sarah, the middle sister in the All-of-a-Kind family."

Afterword

AFTER TAYLOR DIED, Henny moved in with Ralph. His domestic cares having been handled by women all his life, the newly widowed Ralph wanted a housekeeper; alone for some fifteen years and in troubled marriages before that, Henny in her seventies sought financial security and an object for her energetic solicitude. Thus, another proficient housekeeper trained with the German standards of Cilly Brenner took over the running of the Taylor household. After her many years of working in various capacities for Caswell-Massey, Henny shared Ralph's interests in the business, while he stood between her and loneliness. During Taylor's lifetime, Henny's letters from Florida frequently mentioned the sighting of Caswell-Massey products in shop windows and ideas for expansion of the business, along with her persistent sadness about her distance from her family. For the next ten years, until the Taylor brothers finally sold the company in 1988, Caswell-Massey continued to expand across the country and overseas. The pharmacy at Lexington and 48th Street closed in 1990. Ralph and Henny never married, but she remained devoted to him until his death in 1993, at which point she found a home with her daughter Harriet, with whom she lived until her death three years later. Milton died in 1994, and Zelda in 2003. Lucille passed away in Israel in 2007, her husband, Rabbi Abraham, having died in 2000. The flagship store itself finally shuttered its doors on April 3, 2010.

What became of the All-of-a-Kind family? These children of Morris and Cilly Brenner stuck with each other to the end, whether living in Florida or New York. Ella's marriage in 1980 to Albert Schoolman as he lay dying in a hospital room scandalized Cejwin and alienated his daughters. Friends speculated that Ella wanted to "be" someone at last, to have her efforts on behalf of Cejwin finally acknowledged for the accomplishment it was, to be able to situate herself within the Schoolman legacy. Suffering from dementia, Ella died in 1988. Cejwin closed in 1992. Gertie died in 1995, Henny in 1996, followed less than a year later by Charlotte, whose husband Lou also died in 1996. Active to her last days, Charlotte had pursued her various artistic hobbies and literary ambitions, publishing articles in newspapers, as well as a book on coping with deafness.[1] Irving—baby Charlie of the books—and Jerry lived into the twenty-first century.

The All-of-a-Kind sisters also endured through their children. Four of the sisters had one child, all daughters, while Ella, Irving, and Jerry had two children each. Jo Taylor Marshall enjoyed a distinguished career as a dancer and choreographer, a social work administrator, and a faculty lecturer and assistant director of fieldwork at Columbia University. She wed her longtime female partner Mase, and both remain good friends with Steve Marshall. Other cousins and their spouses worked as teachers, counselors, and artists, among other professions. They scattered across the country, far from the Lower East Side of their parents. As for the old neighborhood, it was transformed significantly by Robert Moses and other city planners, and by successive generations of immigrants. Its schools, libraries, and settlement houses are still to be found, often in different buildings and under different auspices, where they continue to honor values of the progressive idealists who offered a gateway to America.

Although the All-of-a-Kind family, with its lively, argumentative gatherings, endless stories, and delicious cakes, died away, it has lived on in Taylor's books, where the promise of America and the traditions of Judaism dwelt harmoniously together. The Brenners stood apart from the teeming millions of immigrants who passed through the Lower East Side because of the middle sister's talent and good fortune. The separate strands of Taylor's life—her creative energies, love of theater, role as a children's author who spoke for middle-class Jews in America, devotion to family, and anxieties about mortality—all came together in her books to grant her family at least a temporary immortality.

Taylor's critical role in introducing Americans to Judaism and in demonstrating that Jews are Americans extends through today. Her books have sold millions of copies over the years. After her death, the Association of Jewish Libraries (AJL) renamed its annual children's book award for her, recognizing books for young readers that both display literary merit and authentically portray the Jewish experience. In yet another act of friendship, Nettie Frishman, a member of the AJL book award committee, encouraged

Ralph to establish the Sydney Taylor Book Award in his wife's memory. Ralph attended the AJL convention in 1979 for the awards ceremony, where he accepted the Sydney Taylor Body-of-Work Award as a posthumous prize for his wife's writing career, in which he had been so instrumental.[2] He also continued to answer the hundreds of fan letters addressed to his wife. Jo now sponsors the award and has expanded it to include a teen category. She attends the ceremonies as often as she can in her mother's honor, and states that despite their strained relationship throughout the years, she is eternally grateful for the wonderful gifts her mother gave to her and to countless others of her "reader children," among them an abiding appreciation of the arts, Jewish culture, and especially the value of good writing.

Taylor may have started out simply to retell the stories of her childhood in a way that treated Jewish culture as interesting yet unexceptional, but she became a pioneer in ethnic literature for children. She and her editor Esther Meeks published a series of books that in their popularity were at the forefront of a burgeoning market in children's books. Whereas the average annual sales of many children's books ran to two or three thousand in the 1950s, Taylor's award-winning *All-of-a-Kind Family* sold some seventy thousand copies in its first four years of publication and went into multiple printings. In her role as author, Taylor became a popular speaker in libraries and schools all across the country. She used the opportunity to put her theatrical expertise to work by presenting programs in which children were encouraged to act out various roles to better understand literature and themselves.

Like any other popular product, the *All-of-a-Kind* series both reflected and shaped consumer demand. The first three books, published in the 1950s, were upbeat and portrayed a world full of promise and adventure, even though it had actually been fraught with poverty, danger, and disease. The books assumed that children are the same no matter their circumstances and that they accept their environment as a matter of course, whatever ills adults perceive. The last two books, written around the same time, brought nuance to that picture, but it took the social upheavals of the 1960s to create a market in which glossing over the starker aspects of childhood and American history was no longer desirable. When the last two books in the series were published in the 1970s, Taylor believed that tastes in children's literature had swung too far, and that merit was assigned to books solely on their inclusion of "difficult" topics. She articulated her purpose in writing for children as leading "the reader in the way of the eternal values which centuries of civilization have taught us. . . . In that sense, a children's writer is actually like a mother—a surrogate parent to countless youngsters of her own generation, and hopefully, other generations to come."[3]

Notes

Introduction

1. Just as Gertrude Berg's successful show *The Goldbergs*—on radio and television from 1929 to 1956, and later on stage and the big screen—brought a Jewish family to life in American homes for the first time, Taylor's *All-of-a-Kind* series brought Jewish characters into the popular culture.
2. Krasner, *The Benderly Boys*, 269 (quoting Isaac Berkson).

Chapter 1. Family Background in the Old Country

1. Much of the information about the background of the Marowitz and Brenner families comes from recordings made in the early 1980s by Ella Kornweitz and Charlotte Himber, two of Taylor's sisters [hereafter cited as Ella Tapes]. Ella is the primary storyteller, and her memory is occasionally jogged or criticized by her younger sister. It was Ella who used the words *horrible* and *funny-looking* to convey the sense of the German sentence in English.
2. Buse, "Urban and National Identity," 523, 529.
3. Kaplan, *Making of the Jewish Middle Class*, 91, 96. With some hesitation, Kaplan relies on a German-Jewish memoirist to conclude that some brothers postponed their own marriages until their sisters' dowries were paid, though she is careful not to make national generalizations based on one comment in a memoir. By the 1920s, the practice began to go out of style.
4. Taback, *Joseph Had a Little Overcoat*; Gilman, *Something from Nothing*.
5. In an undated letter to her grandson Danny Baker, Henny says her grandfather's last name was originally Marovyatska, which he changed to Marowitz when they moved from their little town near Warsaw to Bremen.
6. This seems a roundabout route today, but train lines at the time made the connection in Krakow a reasonable choice.
7. The more common spelling is *Tante*, the German word for aunt, but the Brenners almost always used *Tanta* in their letters when referring to Minnie.
8. Lee, "Urban Labor Markets," 458, 443.
9. Kaplan, *Making of the Jewish Middle Class*, ix: "In the Imperial period, 85 percent of Jews were considered middle-class (25 percent of whom were lower-middle-class)." Jews were legally emancipated in 1869. Peter Pulzer, "Introduction," in *Integration in Dispute*, ed. Meyer, 1. Anti-Semitism was prevalent

in Germany before, after, and during this period of emancipation, but at least on paper, discrimination based on religion was illegal in the years the Marowitz and Brenner families lived in Germany.

10. Kaplan, *Making of the Jewish Middle Class*, 8.

11. Ibid., 9. Mendes-Flohr, *German Jews*, 6, 9, draws attention to the important distinction between the cultural and sociopolitical aspects of *Bildungsbürgertum*.

12. Kaplan, *Jewish Daily Life in Germany*, 203.

13. Henny to Danny Baker, n.d.

14. Ella Tapes.

15. Interview with Jerry Brenner, March 2007. He is also the source for the tombstone and violin stories.

16. For a reproduction and detailed discussion of Morris Brenner's papercut, see Rosengarten and Rosengarten, eds., *A Portion of the People*, 147–48. See also Shadur and Shadur, *Traditional Jewish Papercuts*. The papercut is currently in the possession of Susan Baker, daughter of Charlotte Brenner Himber.

17. Ibid., 148.

18. Kaplan, *Jewish Daily Life*, 92.

19. Pulzer, "Introduction," in *Integration in Dispute*, ed. Meyer, 8.

20. Ella Tapes.

21. Ella Tapes.

22. Cilly to Taylor, December 14, 1951: "As for Tanta I send her a Card also wrote something to her in Ellas Letter tell her what is the sense in writing to her as someone has to read it to her so I allways remember her in yours or Ellas Letter." In the Kerlan Collection is an undated letter from the 1950s from Cilly to Tanta: "Dear Sister, I havent heart from you a long time whenever I write to Sid I ad something for you to als I know it is useles to write you extra as someone has to read it to you."

23. Cilly to Taylor, undated letter from the 1950s: "We are glad Tanta looks better. She probably enjoys the Company of her Neighbor and therefor dont come so often. I am ofthen think of her and realy very sorry that it is so hard to get along with her otherwise we wouldn't mind to have her with us as we have the place and plenty of rooms for on person." January 24, 1952: "Tell Tanta I bring her something from florida. don't blame her she is like a Child who likes to have those little trinkets. I remember last year how sorry I was to have forgotten her." March 20, 1952: "As for Tanta I wrote her a Letter last week jet reminding her when to light the jearzeit lamps for our parents."

24. Taylor includes this aspect of her family's relationship with Tanta in *AKF*, 177.

25. Glanz, *The German Jewish Woman*, 8.

26. Glenn, *Daughters of the Shtetl*, 16. See also Steinberg, *The Ethnic Myth*, chap. 6.

27. Glanz, *The German Jewish Woman*, 20.

28. Ibid., 26.

29. Ella Tapes.

30. Taylor alludes to this bit of family history in *Downtown*, when Tanta dozes off and dreams of being a young girl in Europe: "A beau came courting in a carriage drawn by two magnificent horses. The whole town was standing on the rooftops to witness the sight!" (166).

31. Kaplan, *Making of the Jewish Middle Class*, 31, for the role of furniture in displaying class.

32. Sorin, *Tradition Transformed*, 49.

33. Ella Tapes.

Chapter 2. Sarah's Childhood on the Lower East Side

1. Sorin, *Tradition Transformed*, 54.

2. Ibid., 34. To put these numbers in perspective, 23 million people immigrated to the United States between the years 1880 and 1920.

3. Ibid., 62. By 1892, 75 percent of the city's Jews lived on the Lower East Side. Even as Jews left the neighborhood for other parts of the city (the Lower East Side accounted for 50 percent of New York Jews in 1903 and 23 percent in 1916), the total Jewish population in New York continued to grow. By 1916, there were approximately 1.4 million Jews in New York, which was over one-fourth of the city's population. Heinze, *Adapting to Abundance*, 16.

4. The Timbergs had six children in all—three sons and three daughters. Ella remembered Mr. Timberg as musical and said Herman exhibited a wonderful talent not just for the violin, but for mimicry, too. Herman was touring in vaudeville houses already in 1907, went on to play the Palace, and wrote sketches for the Marx Brothers. His sister Hattie, whose stage name was Hattie Darling, also played the violin, sang, and danced; she performed with the Marx Brothers and later had her own show at the Palace and the Winter Garden. Another son, Sammy (1903–1992), was a pianist who later synchronized the music for Fleischer cartoons (*Popeye, Betty Boop*), and both Ella and Charlotte remember seeing their cousin's name on billboards outside movie theaters. In her taped interview, Ella describes Tanta Timberg as the quintessential pushy stage mother. "Herman Timberg, 60, a Theatrical Figure," *New York Times*, April 17, 1952.

5. During this period, Cilly also made room for her younger brothers and sister as they came over from Germany. Frieda came first, followed by Joe and Herman. Herman had the greatest difficulty adjusting. He went back and forth between Bremen and New York about three times, paying approximately $25 for a steerage ticket, and occasionally leaving without informing his New York relatives. Frieda sometimes boarded with Tanta. Ella Tapes.

6. Rischin, *The Promised City*, 89: " 'Genumen di gez' (took gas) was not an uncommon headline in the Yiddish press."

7. Charlotte said Tanta was more fun than her own mother. In her telling, Tanta was abandoned by her husband shortly after their wedding, went to work as a sewing machine operator for nine hours a day, except the Sabbath, and quit her job when her sister had a new baby, taking periodic breaks to work as a housemaid elsewhere (Himber, "Touched with Fire," 1:22). The story on the Ella Tapes differs significantly. Ella says that when her father found out about the relationship between Tanta and her brother Morris, he insisted that Tanta get married. A match was arranged with someone with the last name Schramm, who was from a good family but suffered from mental illness. Before the marriage, after a failed attempt to live in Palestine, he had returned to New York and found a job in a Talmud Torah, which he was unable to hold down, and so was scraping out a living teaching Hebrew to bar mitzvah boys. Tanta left him three months after their marriage, claiming he was crazy. The family urged her to return to her husband, assuring her that the marriage could be successful as long as they did not have children. Tanta promptly got pregnant, left her husband for good, worked in a pickle factory, and gave birth to Irving (Israel) Schramm in 1908, despite having tried to induce a miscarriage by lifting heavy vats in the factory. She often took in boarders when her son was a baby, including her sister Frieda. Due to various disabilities, Irving was committed to a mental institution, Pilgrim State Hospital, where Taylor took care of his expenses. He died in the spring of 1971 after contracting pneumonia, and Taylor paid for his funeral. Taylor to Pilgrim State Hospital, March 26, 1971, and April 8, 1971.

   Taylor referred to him in one letter as "a distant relative of ours who for many years has been confined to a mental institution. He is not violently ill—just a bit illusory—You should see him—He looks younger than any of us though he is my age. There is not a wrinkle in his face—his eyes look at you clearly. He has all his hair—Nothing to worry about—If you like that sort of nebulous existence." Taylor to Janet Weisenfreund, November 21, 1962.

8. Cilly to Taylor, March 18, 1952. For a discussion of the purchase of goods as an expression of Americanization, see Heinze, *Adapting to Abundance*.

9. After the *All-of-a-Kind* books were published, readers frequently asked Taylor whether the stories were true. Her evasive reply was usually "If you believe it, it is true," or words to that effect. In the case of the lost library book, however, she wrote: "And the chapter in my book describing Sarah's agony over a lost library book is very real for it is exactly like my own agony when just such a thing happened to me." December 1951 speech, New York Public Library.

10. Cilly Brenner's height was a matter of perspective. Her son Jerry said she was five feet two inches tall. Also, in Charlotte's memoir "Touched with Fire," Mama's superiority appears less benign: "Among the women in the neighborhood she was marked as an outsider because she could not converse easily in Yiddish and the women resented her German. . . . The women walking wore large woolen shawls all winter and long woolen skirts that picked up the dirt on the sidewalks.

Mama, on the other hand, was never seen in broad daylight without being corseted. Her sweaters and jackets fitted properly. The women in the neighborhood secretly referred to her as 'die stoltze' (the proud one) because of her straight proud stride. She was slim, with a good figure" (1:24). Yet it is precisely Cilly's facility with German and modeling of German culture that aided the family in leaving the Lower East Side. When Cilly found an apartment in the Bronx, the landlady balked at the number of children in the family, but agreed to rent to the Brenners because "she knew that German people are clean and orderly because she's German too." It is clear that the landlady was also swayed by Cilly's fluency in German: "Mama looked exultant. Down on the East Side the women teased her for having difficulty with their Yiddish. They thought she was pretending, being snobbish" (ibid., 35).

11. Himber, "Touched with Fire," 1:11. Taylor later told Janet Weisenfreund that she hated starch and was allergic to wool. Being an *All-of-a-Kind* girl was physically uncomfortable. Interview with Janet Weisenfreund, December 13, 2017.

12. Himber, "Touched with Fire," 1:16.

13. Ibid., 15.

14. Ibid., 24.

15. In a letter to Nettie Frishman of March 27, 1962, Taylor acknowledges that her mother's German discipline shaped her character. Charlotte says Mama was "the model for [Ella and Sara's] graceful carriage, their taste in clothes, their polished manners. Mama hadn't had to teach them. She marveled at how much they were like the young ladies of her German childhood." Himber, "Touched with Fire," 1:95.

16. Kaplan, *Jewish Daily Life in Germany*, 183.

17. Kaplan, *Making of the Jewish Middle Class*, 30–31.

18. Kaplan, *Jewish Daily Life in Germany*, 184.

19. Ibid., 186. Most middle-class Germans, not just Jews, shared these values. But some of the values overlapped, coming from both German and Jewish culture. Kaplan states that good housekeeping, for instance, was specifically a German as well as a particularly Jewish trait.

20. Kaplan, *Making of the Jewish Middle Class*, 34: "Thus the strong tradition of careful housewifery among Jews—also among those one or two generations removed from serious religious observance—supported, even exacerbated, the German mania for housekeeping."

21. It is clear from Taylor's correspondence in the 1950s with her editor and with librarians that they expected books for children to be wholesome and upbeat and that life's challenges should build character rather than lead to despair. "Problem books" for children were still uncommon (discussed in chapter 10).

22. Ella Tapes.

23. Briefly in *Ella*, in a chapter titled "Follow the Leader" (99–101), Charlie is renamed after Taylor's actual brother Irving. After an accident, the boy's life hangs

in the balance, and Papa is urged by Uncle Hyman to follow Jewish tradition and change the child's name. As he recovers, Taylor has Ella call him "Charles-Irving" once, but for the rest of the book he is simply Charlie.

24. Himber, "Touched with Fire," 1:19.
25. Ibid., 19–20.
26. Berrol, "In Their Image."
27. Himber, "Touched with Fire," 1:81, 86. Both Taylor and Himber mention the four candles. Two is the minimum number, but many women add candles for various reasons.
28. Ibid., 34–37.
29. Ibid., 120.
30. Ibid., 35.
31. Ibid., 34.
32. Ibid.

Chapter 3. Gateways to a Wider World

1. Stephan F. Brumberg, *Going to America, Going to School,* 62.
2. Berrol, "Education and Economic Mobility," 261.
3. In the unpublished manuscript "Henny of All-of-a-Kind Family," Gertie has a second school chapter, "Arithmetic Is a Problem." She struggles in an advanced math class in sixth grade but ultimately succeeds after her mother and teacher encourage her to persevere. The chapter rehashes ideas from the earlier books, but it is noteworthy that Mama does not hesitate to make an appointment to speak with the teacher and is ambitious for her daughter to skip grades.
4. "The Real Manhattan Island," *New York Times,* December 18, 1904.
5. Brumberg, *Going to America, Going to School,* 130.
6. Ibid., 131.
7. Ibid.
8. Himber, "Touched with Fire," 1:16.
9. Ibid., 18. Himber includes a copy of the newspaper photo in her memoir.
10. Ibid., 7.
11. Berrol, "In Their Image," 432.
12. Berrol, *Julia Richman.*
13. Ibid., 65.
14. Brumberg, *Going to America, Going to School,* 106.
15. Himber, "Touched with Fire," 1:61. In "Rainy Day Surprise," peddlers of different nationalities congregate in Papa's basement shop, and every indication is that they are speaking English, however ungrammatical (*AKF* 38–41).
16. Brumberg, *Going to America, Going to School,* 10.
17. Ibid., 136.

18. Berrol, "School Days on the Old East Side," 212. Taylor named the kindly principal for an actual person, Miss Ellen A. G. Phillips. Henny wrote a condolence note on behalf of the Brenner sisters to the Phillips family upon her death and received a reply from the principal's nephew, Donald K. Phillips, who was then superintendent of schools in Syosset, Long Island. He related that she and her two sisters raised him, their brother's son, when he was left an orphan at eighteen months: "I was a small boy when she was Principal of P.S. 2 Manhattan [122 Henry Street]. I visited the school frequently, and knew of her deep love for it, the pupils, and their parents. My 'Aunt Nell' was one of the grandest and noblest women who ever lived. She left her mark on all she knew, for she selflessly served everyone she met." Donald K. Phillips to Henny, April 28, 1961. Taylor wrote to Phillips the following January: "I was out of the country when my sister wrote to you on the occasion of the death of your aunt. . . . In one of my books there is an incident in which I have used the name of Miss Phillips and the character. The incident is not exactly authentic but it could have been. I thought that perhaps you might like to have the book since it does mention your aunt's school and your aunt." Taylor to Donald K. Phillips, January 4, 1962.

19. Berrol, "School Days on the Old East Side," 212.

20. Feld, *Lillian Wald,* 37.

21. Ibid.

22. Ibid., 173.

23. Even if readers do not notice the dates stated in the books, they would be aware that the siblings, including baby Charlie, are older in *Uptown* than they are in *Downtown,* and could easily be puzzled by the books' chronology. Taylor and Bertha Jenkinson, the children's book editor at Follett who oversaw the publication of *Downtown,* discussed the problem of chronology, and Jenkinson actually saw it as potentially boosting sales. Taylor to Bertha Jenkinson, Februrary 1, 1971; Bertha Jenkinson to Taylor, May 11, 1971. In a letter to Nettie Frishman of November 4, 1972, Taylor discusses the opinion of her first editor at Follett during the 1950s, Esther K. Meeks, recalling that Meeks did not think it mattered in a series if the author went "backward and forward in time."

24. Interview in *Judaica Book News* (Fall–Winter 1972). Reprinted as a publicity brochure issued by the Dell, Dutton, and Follett Publishing Companies, undated, but some time after 1980.

25. Wald, *The House on Henry Street,* 4–6.

26. Such errors are highly unusual in the girls' speech, and this slip of the tongue may indicate Ella's discomfiture. Another example of an ungrammatical locution comes when Gertie says, " 'All right, Ella. I won't do it no more' " (*Downtown* 124). Gertie is occasionally given more childish speech as a way of keeping the younger children distinct.

27. Wald, *House on Henry Street,* 65.

28. Taylor's familiarity with settlement houses is made clear in her correspondence with Jenkinson, who encouraged Taylor to use the real name of the settlement house and asked for more detail in the book: "The settlement house is very nebulous now and really deserves to be more developed. They were an essential part of children's activities in that period and neighborhood, weren't they?" Bertha Jenkinson to Taylor, May 11, 1971. In rejecting some of Jenkinson's suggestions about Miss Carey, Taylor speaks authoritatively about the career of a settlement nurse and insists on the importance of the playground to the settlement compound. Taylor to Bertha Jenkinson, June 1, 1971. (Correspondence between Esther Meeks and Taylor about Miss Carey and the settlement house also turns up in chapter 10, below.)

29. Quoted in Feld, *Lillian Wald*, 181.

30. Wald, *House on Henry Street*, 102.

31. Taylor to Meeks, December 22, 1951.

32. Although Taylor purposely makes the librarian who befriends the sisters a non-Jew, from 1908 until 1913 the branch librarian at Hamilton Fish Park was Augusta Markowitz (1881–1963), one of seven Jewish librarians to head a branch of the New York Public Library in the period 1901–50. Herself an immigrant from Hungary who had been employed by the Aguilar Free Library Society, Markowitz largely concerned herself with serving the Hungarian Jewish community in New York and figures neither in the *All-of-a-Kind* books nor in the adult Taylor's many remarks about librarians and the role they played in her childhood. Taylor's editor was acutely sensitive to the balance between Jew and Gentile in *All-of-a-Kind Family*. She saw the Library Lady as representative of refined American culture and encouraged Taylor to minimize any parochialism in her fictional family, which may explain in part why Taylor avoided making her romantic librarian Jewish, whatever her personal experiences may have been.

33. Joselit, "Reading, Writing, and a Library Card," 104–5.

34. December 1951 speech, NYPL.

35. Joselit, "Reading, Writing, and a Library Card," 97.

36. December 1951 speech, NYPL. In the early 1900s, circulating free libraries available to all sectors of society were still relatively new, and collections devoted to children's literature newer still. For the innovation of story hours in the library, see Sayers, *Anne Carroll Moore*, 78–80.

37. Alter Brody's poem "In the Circulating Library: Seward Park" (*The Bookman*, September 1918–February 1919, 29) evokes the romantic possibilities offered by the library to young Jews.

38. "Only the local librarian who saved the latest German books for [Mama] sympathized with her in her hunger for her native tongue. She conversed with Mama frequently, using the school-taught accent of her college days." Himber, "Touched with Fire," 1:35. In a book of memories about her mother, the adult Charlotte recalled that Cilly loved reading romances in German and her favorite

author was William Shakespeare, whose works she had studied in German translation as a young woman in Bremen.

Chapter 4. Sarah Becomes Sydney

1. Ella Tapes.
2. "New York Ready for Big Parade," *New York Times,* May 13, 1916.
3. Ella Tapes.
4. P.S. 20 was located on Fox, Simpson, and 167th Streets. It is now P.S. 150. The current P.S. 20 is the George J. Werdann III School, located at 3050 Webster Avenue. For the years Taylor was at P.S. 188, each grade level was assigned a number, followed by the letter A or B, and a superscript number 1 through 4. Sarah's grade was designated as $7a^3$: the first numeral was the grade, the letter was the level, and the superscript number the section.
5. It started out as a branch of Wadleigh High School, established in 1897 as the first public high school for girls in New York City, and opened in the Irving Place facility in 1913.
6. Luna Park was an amusement park in Coney Island, Brooklyn, which opened in 1903. When it opened, it was lit with over 250,000 electric lights and at its center was the 200-foot Electric Tower. Jeffrey Stanton, "Coney Island-Luna Park," May 1, 1998, www.westland.net/coneyisland/articles/lunapark.htm.
7. Margaret Parsons, "Book Chat," *Evening Gazette* [Worcester, Mass.], December 8, 1951. On hostility to all things German, and specifically German-language materials, see Wiegand, *An Active Instrument for Propaganda.*
8. Her children remembered that Cilly could no longer check out German materials from the local library, which was another incentive for her to learn English. Born in 1919, the youngest Brenner, Jerry, absorbed sufficient German to do some translation during his army service during World War II, but his wife expressed surprised that he knew enough for such duties; he asked his parents to send him a German-English dictionary, which suggests that he knew enough to get by but did not claim proficiency.
9. Himber, "Touched with Fire," 1:53–54, 61.
10. Ella Tapes. The traditional week of mourning for a close relative is shortened when the news is received after such a long time. In *A Papa Like Everyone Else* (Follett, 1966), which is based on Taylor's friend Gertrude Holz's stories about her family in Hungary, the older sister, Szerena, reminds her younger sister eloquently and at length how difficult the war years had been with the army requisitioning food and quartering soldiers in the villagers' homes (18–19).
11. Himber, "Touched with Fire," 1:70ff.
12. This was based on a real event, also involving a fall at construction site, although the circumstances were slightly different. Irving's wife, Ethel, said her husband remained semi-conscious in the hospital for several weeks and lost all memory

from before the accident. A friend asked Taylor: "Has your brother entirely re-covered? He certainly is lucky. I had a sister who was hit on the back of the head with a stick. You know how the boys chalk up a slat or other piece of wood on Hallowe'en and strike everyone with it. That is all that happened to my sister and she died in less than forty-eight hours." Agnes [surname unknown] to Taylor, March 24, 1921.

13. As a grown woman, Charlotte wrote: "How I longed for her to be more demon-strative as I grew older. A kiss on three occasions! But her eyes betrayed her—the 'hug and kiss' lurked there." She wished that her mother had explained why, when Morris grabbed her for a secret hug, "she always whispered 'not before the children.'" Himber, "Mother Memory Book." Jerry said he remembered his mother hugging him twice in his entire life: when he bought himself a suit at age sixteen and when he returned from military service after World War II.

14. Taylor did mention baby Ralph's death to her friend Milton Berger when her brother Jerry was sick in December 1920. From Milton's reply, in a letter of De-cember 20, 1920, it is apparent that she needed reassurance that Jerry would re-ceive good care from his doctors, lest he meet the same fate as Ralph. Her diary of January 16, 1923, describes her bursting into tears when her girlfriends for some inexplicable reason start talking about baby Ralph's death. She is com-forted by another friend, Nat, who tries to get the girls to change the subject.

15. Taylor to Judith Wahl (a fan), April 22, 1955.

16. Taylor to Jerri Lauer, October 12, 1956. This letter is just one of many that ad-dress the gender aspect of Sydney's confusing name.

17. Taylor was fairly consistent also in her choice of notebook: she almost always used thin, small, lined composition books, though occasionally she used other sorts of writing materials, such as a stenographer's pad.

18. Anna Kornweitz to Taylor, August 25, 1919.

19. Hermalyn, *Morris High School*, xxi.

20. Diary, January 19, 1920.

21. Milton Berger to Taylor, December 6, 1920.

22. See Hunter, *How Young Ladies Became Girls,* 223; Sellers, "Tossing the Pink Parasol."

23. *The Morris Annual* (New York: Morris High School, 1920), 96.

24. Ibid., 100.

25. *The Morris Annual* (1921), 67.

26. Her position as head of the Spanish faculty is listed in the *Morris Annual* of 1920.

27. *The Morris Annual* (1920), 91.

28. Peiss, *Cheap Amusements,* 7.

29. Marks, *Bicycles, Bangs, and Bloomers,* 116.

30. Diary, March 12, 1920.

31. Kissing games have existed for centuries and can be traced back as early as an-cient Greece. A crucial difference between earlier versions of those games and

those that Taylor records seems to be the element of supervision. Before the twentieth century, kissing games were played outside in public or in large gatherings that included adults. Historian William Wells Newell explains that kisses did not always have the significance of a romantic or erotic gesture: "The caresses [in older games] can alarm neither modesty nor prudence, since a kiss in honor given and taken before numerous witnesses is often an act of propriety. . . . It must be remembered that in medieval Europe, and in England till the end of the seventeenth century, a kiss was the usual salutation of a lady to a gentlemen whom she wished to honor. . . . Kissing in games was, therefore, a matter of course, in all ranks." Newell, *Games and Songs of American Children,* 6. The traditional game Taylor mentions, "This or That," involved a girl deciding whether to accept a kiss or handshake from a boy or to give him a slap. Sutton-Smith, "Kissing Games of Adolescents in Ohio," in describing this game categorizes it as an ancient form of a forfeit game, the type where chance is involved in who kisses whom and penalties are as much a part of the game as favors.

32. Peiss, *Cheap Amusements,* 6.

Chapter 5. Romance and the New Woman

1. Klapper, *Jewish Girls Coming of Age,* 59.
2. Ibid., 74.
3. Ibid., 79. Under William Maxwell, New York City superintendent of schools from 1898 to 1918, the percentage of high school students grew from less than 2 percent of the total number of registered students in 1897 to 7.8 percent in 1914. Nonetheless, by 1920 in the state of New York, while 94.1 percent of urban children aged seven through thirteen attended school, only 35.7 percent between the ages of fourteen and twenty did so. New York Census Data, 1920.
4. Klapper, *Jewish Girls Coming of Age,* 62.
5. The Brenner sisters were acutely aware of financial vulnerability. When it seemed Jo might not stay in college, Taylor thought her daughter was throwing away her future: "Witness Ella for example. As she said the other day if only she had been a teacher, she'd be sitting on the top of the world. Certainly there is nothing that money cannot take care of—and a well planned career is an asset in securing that money." Taylor to Cilly and Morris, April 12, 1954.
6. Klapper, *Jewish Girls Coming of Age,* 63.
7. Himber, "Touched with Fire," 1:95.
8. Ibid., 2:172.
9. Taylor to Cilly and Morris, April 12, 1952.
10. Klapper, *Jewish Girls Coming of Age,* 91.
11. Wise has been written about elsewhere. What is interesting in relation to Taylor's story is that in 1914 he was a co-founder of the National Association for the Advancement of Colored People (NAACP) and served on the board along with

other national figures such as Jacob Schiff and Lillian Wald. He was also an ardent Zionist. As leader of the Free Synagogue, he spoke regularly at Carnegie Hall.

12. LoMonaco, *Every Week, a Broadway Revue*, 5.

13. Taylor to Ralph, October 11, 1923.

14. Although the telephone had been invented, its use as a tool of sociability was not widespread, so the letter writing is not surprising. Fischer, *America Calling*, 79.

15. Milton Berger to Taylor, April 13, 1922.

16. Milton Berger to Taylor, series of letters at the end of December 1920.

17. Diary, extended entry from December 1921 to January 1922.

18. Klapper, *Jewish Girls Coming of Age*, 29.

19. Diary, September 17, 1922.

20. Diary, November 11, 1922. In addition to books, Taylor received presents of clothing: "A pair of quilted satin boudoir slippers with an adorable orchid satin & net bandeaux to match from Hannah. A few days later came a white, dainty-looking set of crêpe-de-chine vest and bloomers. They are far too wonderful to do anything but look at. These came from Anna S. and Ruth. Anna K. presented me with a pair of black kid gloves." See also Kelley, *Book of Hallowe'en*, 154–71.

21. *La Chauve Souris* was a successful Russian touring revue that came to New York from Europe in 1922. It included "The Parade of the Wooden Soldiers" with Leon Jessel's tune, an act that went on to Radio City Music Hall fame. See also "The Century Roof Opens Its Doors," *New York Times*, January 10, 1917.

22. Ella mentions this in her recollections of her father, saying he wore a yarmulke at night when she was a little girl, but that he eventually stopped.

23. Peiss, *Cheap Amusements*, 113.

24. Ibid., 110.

25. Diary, December 1, 1922. Taylor seems to have used the supercilious Julius as the model for the eccentric Alex Shiner in her unpublished manuscript "Henny of All-of-a-Kind Family," at least for his unshakeable confidence in his aesthetic judgments. In the story, he wants to be a conductor and a composer, declares that Debussy's *Pelléas et Mélisande* is superior to Puccini, and makes loud, critical remarks during a performance at Carnegie Hall.

26. Diary, December 1, 1922.

27. Diary, December 5, 1922.

28. Diary, January 8, 1923.

29. Diary, February 1, 1923.

30. Diary, February 5, 1923.

31. Diary, March 5, 1923.

32. Eddie Goldfarb to Taylor, January 30, 1923.

33. Diary, March 5, 1923.

34. Leo Brenner (approximately 1896–1958) and his brother Rafael Brenner (1898–1973; see chapter 11) were born in Poland and founded Photo-Brenner in

Cologne in 1919. The business grew to include three photographic supply stores and a mail order business. Rafael's wife, Nelly Brenner (1901–1991), helped with the business. After Nazi harassment and a boycott in 1933, Rafael was arrested, forced to sign over the family property, and pressured to leave Germany. He moved his wife and two young sons to Rome, where the family opened another store. Leo moved to Palestine and established a business in Haifa. The Rafael Brenner family immigrated to the United States at the end of 1938 and established a camera business in Washington, D.C. United States Holocaust Memorial Museum, "Rafael and Nelly Brenner family papers," https://collections.ushmm.org/search/catalog/irn76376.

35. Paul Miller to Taylor, April 28, 1923.

Chapter 6. Political Awakening and Contentious Courtship

1. Ben Schlamm to Taylor, May 31, 1923.
2. Diary, July 18, 1923.
3. Sometimes Fannie's maiden name is written as Schlomm. The family changed its surname from Schneider to Taylor between 1931 and 1934. Fannie's death notice gives her maiden name as Schlomin. *New York Times,* April 6, 1978. Ben Schlamm was born in 1902 to Fannie's brother Louis, who was married to a sister of Simon Schneider.
4. In official documents and letters throughout his life, Ralph's name was spelled in various ways: Ruben Schneider (eighth-grade report card and diploma; letters from a friend, Ernie; composition book; Stuyvesant grade report from February 24, 1920); Rubin Schneider (marriage certificate and license from 1925); Ruben Shneider (Columbia College of Pharmacy); Ralph Schneider (YPSL membership card of June 3, 1922, and various documents through 1929). He himself wrote "Reuben Schneider" on the table of contents for his eighth-grade composition book and on an essay, "Loyalty," of June 19, 1918, and that is how his name is listed in the *Spectator,* Stuyvesant's student paper, on April 12, 1920. As of May 31, 1930, Taylor and Ralph were receiving mail addressed to Mr. & Mrs. Schneider.
5. Taylor to Nettie Frishman, January 13, 1965.
6. Marvine Howe, "Ralph Taylor, 89, 50-Year Co-Owner of Pharmacy Chain," *New York Times,* June 26, 1993.
7. By 1932, as a result of the Depression, Caswell-Massey was down to its flagship store, opened in 1926 on Lexington and 48th Street in The Barclay. That was the business Ralph and Milton bought in 1936, the first time the pharmacy changed hands for money. The Taylor brothers chose not to change the name.
8. *The American Hatter* 49 (February 1920). By May 1922, according to a letter from Ben Schlamm to Ralph of May 10, 1922, the American Cap Works was at 3 West Third Street. The company both manufactured and sold hats. *The Millinery Trade Review* 47 (October 1922).

9. Music was an early interest with long-lasting ramifications for Ralph. He sang with a choir directed by Henry Lefkowitz, who among other activities ran the Beethoven Musical Society Orchestra, a community orchestra made up largely of young people from the Lower East Side with which George Gershwin was briefly associated. Taylor to Bertha Jenkinson, October 23, 1971.

10. Milton to Ralph, August 1923.

11. With their political activities, social life, work, school, and letter writing, the young people drove their parents to distraction. "My father has tumbled out of bed—is complaining—so late—am I "meschuga"—he'll wake me up seven o'clock just the same—so he says. So here goes—half-past one and my letter is done." Ben Schlamm to Ralph Schneider, December 18, 1923.

12. The following is from Taylor's diary entry of August 6, 1923.

13. Diary, "Thursday" [August 30, 1923]. According to a letter from Taylor to Ralph on October 11, 1923, Julie soon reconciled with his family and found marriage rather dull.

14. The intermarriage rate "was less than 2 percent in 1910 and did not reach 3 percent until the 1940s." By the 1950s, it was still estimated at only 5 to 10 percent. Joselit, *The Wonders of America,* 54.

15. Ben Schlamm to Ralph Schneider, January 1924.

16. Diary, early September 1923.

17. Algernon Lee to Ralph Schneider, October 17, 1923.

18. Many years later, Taylor wrote: "I had for years thought he used to ask me to walk home with him after the meetings we went to (we belonged to the Yipsels—a Young Peoples Socialist Club!) because I thought he liked me. Only to discover many, many years later that it was because he had only one nickel carfare and this had to be saved for his use when going back to Manhattan where he lived from Bklyn., where I lived and where his cousin who organized the club lived." Taylor to Nettie and Harold Frishman, December 10, 1969.

19. Diary, September 9, 1923.

20. Taylor to Ralph, October 4, 1923.

21. Taylor to Ralph, October 11, 1923.

22. In letters of November 24, 1923, and January 1924, Ben teases Ralph about how his attachment to Taylor distracts him from other matters.

23. Taylor to Ralph, October 26, 1923.

24. Bloomers were originally controversial when women wore them as trousers in public. They came to be known as "reform" or "freedom dress" and were associated with the women's rights movement as far back as the 1850s. In part the scandal arose because women were exposing their legs in public and in part because they were seen as invading male territory. Bloomers were accepted by the 1920s, although generally restricted to athletic activities—Henny would have worn them in gym, but not elsewhere. Here, the cap and jacket were Taylor's 1920s equivalent of those shocking Victorian bloomers.

25. Ben to Ralph, December 3, 1923.

26. Diary, November 7, 1923.

27. Taylor to Ralph, December 7, 1923.

28. Peiss, *Hope in a Jar,* 45.

29. Taylor to Ralph, December 20, 1923.

30. Diary, January 22, 1931.

31. Taylor to Ralph, March 7, 1924.

32. Himber, "Touched with Fire," 2:6. "While 35 percent of female workers were married in 1900, they represented less than 10 percent of all gainfully employed females during the 1920s." Eddy, *Bookwomen,* 107.

33. Diary, April 15, 1924.

34. Diary, April 16, 1924.

35. Himber, "Touched with Fire," 2:148.

36. Ibid., 2:143.

37. LoMonaco, *Every Week, a Broadway Revue,* 2.

38. Ibid., 6.

39. Charlotte to Taylor, July 16, 1924.

40. LoMonaco, *Every Week, a Broadway Revue,* 14.

41. Ibid., 8.

42. Charlotte to Taylor, July 16, 1924.

43. LoMonaco, *Every Week, a Broadway Revue,* 9.

44. *Breakfast Serials* 1, no. 10 (July 15, 1924).

45. LoMonaco, *Every Week, a Broadway Revue,* 14.

46. Ibid., 21.

47. Jason Jablonower, 1925 report, Minutes of the People's Educational Camp Society, PECS MSS. Quoted in LoMonaco, *Every Week, a Broadway Revue,* 21.

48. LoMonaco, *Every Week, a Broadway Revue,* 15.

49. Diary, July 16, 1924.

50. Diary, August 16, 1924.

51. Ben to Taylor, August 23, 1924.

52. Ben to Ralph, July 11, 1924.

53. Ibid.

54. Ibid.

55. Milton to Ralph, n.d., but clearly in the spring of 1925.

56. Milton to Ralph, April 11, 1925.

57. Ralph's IBWA Membership Book, March 8, 1925.

58. James Eads How (1874–1930) attended Harvard, Oxford, and the Columbia College of Physicians and Surgeons and was a grandson of the builder of the first bridge across the Mississippi. " 'The Millionaire Hobo,' " *New York Times,* September 30, 1908. National newspapers ran dozens of articles about How, who was considered newsworthy beginning in 1907, for his politics and later for his scandalous marriage and death from starvation and pneumonia.

59. Ella to Cilly, July 21, 1921.
60. Paul Miller to Taylor, February 19, 1925.
61. Diary, October 13, 1924.

Chapter 7. Performance at Home and on Stage

1. Ben to Ralph, May 10, 1925. By the end of August, Ben himself was desperate to leave San Diego: "I have to punch myself to find out if it's true that I really am leaving this goddam town ... A guy can get meschuga if he stays here long enough." Ben to Ralph, August 27, 1925.
2. Himber, "Touched with Fire," 2:176.
3. Ibid., 2:177.
4. Ibid. See Joselit, *Wonders of America*, 30–31, on lavish weddings.
5. Himber, "Touched with Fire," 2:131.
6. Ibid., 2:178.
7. Ibid., 2:202.
8. In a letter to Sydney of June 22, 1975, Helen Montz mentions the Taylors' fiftieth wedding anniversary celebration, which took place on that day.
9. Jo to Taylor, March 30, 1955.
10. Morris [surname unknown] to Taylor, July 22, 1925.
11. Taylor to Ralph, Sunday evening, July 1925.
12. Taylor to Ralph, July 1926.
13. Taylor to Ralph, September 23, 1926. Years later, commenting on the hardship of Jo and Steve Marshall's having to live apart because of their respective jobs, Cilly says, "Yes, Joan has to learn to stay alone as you did for so many years." Cilly to Taylor, July 17, 1959.
14. Taylor to Janet Weisenfreund, February 10, 1973.
15. Taylor to Nettie and Harold Frishman, December 10, 1969. In July 1926, Ralph was working for Robinson & Co., Chemists, either at their store in the Plaza Hotel on Fifth Avenue or in the Ambassador on Park: July 1926 letter to Taylor on their letterhead.
16. A valentine telegram Ralph sent on February 14, 1927, to Taylor at Sutta and Fuchs is addressed to "Miss Syd Brenner."
17. Diary, undated entry, but most likely early 1927.
18. Eddie Goldfarb to Taylor, March 26, 1926.
19. Himber, "Touched with Fire," 2:142. See also Sochen, *The New Woman*, 8.
20. New York Public Library collection at Lincoln Center.
21. Himber, "Touched with Fire," 2:142.
22. Ibid., 2:196.
23. Ibid., 2:188.
24. On Taylor and Ralph's return to New York from Canada in July 1929, they stopped at Provincetown, Mass., where they attended a performance by the

Wharf Players, which they considered amateurish: "It set me wondering if the L.H.P. impressed their audiences similarly." They met Cheryl Crawford, "one of the Theatre Guild's casting directors who knows Lee Strassberg [*sic*] well. From her we learned that the Guild is establishing an experimental studio this year and immediately I feared that my praise of Strassberg would mean his introduction into that studio and the L.H.P.'s loss." Hitchhiking scrapbook 1928–29.

25. Himber, "Touched with Fire," 2:190.

26. Taylor mentions her involvement with Moreno in an undated biographical sketch written after her success as an author.

27. De Mille, *Martha*, 151.

28. Himber, "Touched with Fire," 2:189. Taylor later gave a brief version of the story: "Nights were devoted to a little theatre group—an important one in its time with Mr. Lee Strassberg [*sic*] the director (then unknown). . . . Mr. Strassberg felt his people should involve themselves in dance exercises for their work and so I was exposed to this medium. Then found myself increasingly drawn to it. When the theatre groups folded up for lack of funds, I went on with the dance eventually becoming a member of the Martha Graham Dance Co." Taylor to Mrs. Lazan, January 23, 1968.

29. Himber, "Touched with Fire," 2:189.

30. Quoted in Horosko, *Martha Graham*, 28.

31. De Mille, *Martha*, 127.

32. Ibid., 133.

33. Ibid., 127.

34. Ibid., 145; Horosko, *Martha Graham*, 16.

35. De Mille, *Martha*, 128.

36. Quoted in ibid., 131.

37. Quoted in ibid., 135.

38. Diary, January 19, 1931.

39. Quoted in de Mille, *Martha*, 42. Esther Nelson, a dance educator in the New York area who attended classes with Taylor in Katya Delakova's studio in the 1940s, also recalled Horst's uncanny ability to seem completely oblivious to the dancers behind his back and yet to have seen every mistake. Phone interview, December 14, 2017.

40. McDonagh, *Martha Graham*, 65.

41. De Mille, *Martha*, 89.

42. Ibid., 181.

43. Ibid., 177–78.

44. The dancers sewed the costumes themselves, keeping Taylor in the family tradition of sewing and making clothes. Graham bought the fabric and notions for under a dollar for each outfit.

45. De Mille, *Martha*, 166.

46. For an in-depth analysis of the influence of progressivism on Taylor's writing, see Cummins, "Leaning Left," 390.

47. Quoted in Horosko, *Martha Graham*, 38.

48. Graff, *Stepping Left*, 13. On the political side of dance during this period, see Foulkes, *Modern Bodies*, 201–17; Franko, *Dancing Modernism*, 59; and Graff, *Stepping Left*, 19. De Mille, *Martha*, 193, claims that Graham refused to join the Communist Party despite pressure from her acquaintances.

49. "Ralph Taylor, chairman of the board of Caswell Massey, reminisced about having studied with Miss Graham in 1935. 'Now I don't dance anymore,' he said. 'I just limp.' " "The Evening Hours," *New York Times*, February 3, 1984.

50. Allen Wallace to Ralph, April 19, 1982.

51. Madden, *You Call Me Louis*, 99. Ralph also addressed himself directly to the offending paper, taking Lincoln Kirstein to task for his dismissive, ill-informed views of American dance and his preference for ballet over modern dance in a letter to the *New York Times*, September 1, 1935.

52. Quoted in ibid., 103.

53. Madden, *You Call Me Louis*, 103.

54. De Mille, *Martha*, 148.

55. Interview with Jo Taylor Marshall, June 2003.

Chapter 8. Progressive Motherhood

1. In true Brenner form, Jo's name was spelled many different ways, often by the same person. Taylor herself wrote Jo Ann at times, and Cilly most commonly wrote Joan, but Joanne, JoAnne, and other variations were used over the years. Cejwin friend Janet Weisenfreund commented that Taylor always called her daughter by her full name.

2. The last pictures in the scrapbook are labeled "Spring 1938 End of first school year."

3. Mickenberg, "The Pedagogy of the Popular Front," 230.

4. Doctor's note, no. 1.

5. Doctor's note, no. 2.

6. Related to the specter of Ralph's death, Charlotte Himber's twelve-year struggle to conceive was attributed by herself and family members in writings and interviews to anxiety caused by that loss.

7. Ravitch, *The Great School Wars*, 233.

8. Quoted in ibid.

9. Fisher and Perryman, "A Brief History."

10. Ibid., 2.

11. Grinberg, *Teaching Like That*, 17.

12. Fisher and Perryman, "A Brief History," 6.

13. Cilly to Taylor, January 29, 1955: "I havent forgotten how you denied yourself of wearing good clothes or going for Vacations in order to send her to the best Shooles."

14. When Jo was involved in her dance group as a teenager and had lots of friends over to the Taylor apartment, Taylor remarked that it was good not only for Jo, but for Taylor, too: "I would have liked a large family—now I've got it. After rehearsals, 16 youngsters pile in here ravenous—and they down refreshments like wolves—and after rehearsing 4 hours or so, spend a couple more jitterbugging." Taylor to Meeks, January 23, 1953.

15. "About New York," *New York Times,* October 26, 1939. The hotel still has a display case today with photographs and toiletry products from the old store.

16. Taylor did not often mention her work at Caswell-Massey, but from passing remarks in letters it is evident that she stepped in during busy periods for decades. She not only undertook clerical tasks for Ralph's wholesale end of the business, but also worked in the store in The Barclay and ran special displays at department stores. Taylor to Rosalee Feldman (a fan), June 28, 1955; Taylor to Sarah Lang, June 19, 1968; Taylor to Nettie Frishman, December 10, 1969.

17. The birth of babies drew several of the women together: Ethel and Irving's second son was born in 1943; Norma and Jerry had a daughter, Laurie, on August 31, 1943; Charlotte and Lou welcomed Susan on December 28, 1943; Gertie lost a pregnancy and then gave birth to Judy on January 6, 1945; Ella's daughter, June, was pregnant through the fall of 1945.

18. Joseph J. "Jerry" Brenner to Norma Brenner, January 24, 1945; Norma to Jerry, February 24, 1945: (AFC 2001/001/1014), Correspondence (MS02), Veterans History Project Collection, American Folklife Center, Library of Congress. In her archive, no contemporary record exists of Taylor's response to her family's closest exposure to the Shoah: Morris's sister Leonie or Laja Brenner (b. 1881) and her husband were on the *St. Louis* and survived the war in Belgium after the ship was refused harbor in the United States. In 1946 they came to New York, where their three sons, who had been sponsored by Morris in the 1930s, lived. They both died soon after arriving, their deaths attributed by the family to the starvation and cold they endured during the war.

19. "East Side Chemists Hark Back to 1752: Caswell-Massey, Listing Many Famous Clients, Carries on with Dignity and Pride," *New York Times,* February 12, 1952.

20. Ibid.

21. " 'Lifetime' Perfume Proves Short-Lived," *New York Times,* November 21, 1944.

22. Mickenberg, "Pedagogy of the Popular Front," 230–31.

23. Gladys Oaks, *War Bulletin,* March 1942, 7. The bulletin assumed its readers were familiar with Fifth Columnists, a term used to describe people who work secretly with outside enemies to subvert their country from within.

24. Henry Wallace (1888–1965) served as secretary of agriculture and later as vice president (1940–44) under Franklin Delano Roosevelt. In 1948 he ran unsuccessfully as nominee of the Progressive Party. He was seen as soft on the Soviet Union.

25. Liebman, *Jews and the Left,* 556.

26. Taylor to Nettie Frishman, December 22, 1962.

27. For Ehre and her poet husband David Schubert, see Lenhart, *The Stamp of Class,* 49–53.

28. Quoted in Monique P. Yazigi, "Calling All Campers," *New York Times,* March 2, 1997.

29. Quoted in Nadine Brozan, "Chronicle," *New York Times,* June 6, 1992.

30. Phone interview, April 6, 2017. See also "Far from Blue Serge," *The Campus* 24, no. 4 (October 21, 1953): 4.

31. Hannah to Taylor, January 4, 1949.

32. Faderman, *Odd Girls and Twilight Lovers,* 23. See also Josephson, *Infidel in the Temple,* 38.

33. Faderman, *Odd Girls,* 65.

34. Ibid., 67, 82.

35. Gershick, *Gay Old Girls,* 101.

36. Ibid., 57.

37. Faderman, *Odd Girls,* 87.

38. All but two states in 1950 classed sodomy as a felony, and statutes were rewritten to include sexual activity between women. See d'Emilio, *Sexual Politics, Sexual Communities,* 14. For homosexuality seen as spread by communists in the 1950s: ibid., 43–44. See Faderman, *Odd Girls,* chapter 6, for McCarthyism's effects on the "problem" of homosexuality.

39. Marcus, *Making Gay History,* 55.

40. Ibid., 59.

41. Jane Stevenson quoted in Gershick, *Gay Old Girls,* 12, talking about the late 1940s.

42. D'Emilio, *Sexual Politics,* 27–28, 101; Marcus, *Making Gay History,* 17.

43. Faderman, *Odd Girls,* 173.

44. Ibid., 65. See p. 101 for sensationalist pulp literature with lesbians. An exception to this negative portrayal of lesbians is *Wasteland* by Jo Sinclair, the pseudonym for Ruth Seid (1913–1995), which won the $10,000 Harper Prize when it was published in 1946. Taking place during World War II, the plot is structured around visits of the main character, a Jewish photographer in New York City, to his psychiatrist. In the course of the novel, thirty-five-year-old Jake Brown addresses his alienation from Judaism, which stems in large part from the dysfunction of his immigrant parents and his siblings, whose crushed hopes and inability to express love have warped his view of reality. The one positive character is Jake's younger sister, Debby, who went to the psychiatrist to understand and accept not only her family, but also her lesbianism. In the course of Jake's treatment, he overcomes his repugnance and shame toward his sister's lifestyle—she is also friendly with "coloreds"—and comes to see his family members as buffeted by forces beyond their control. In the last scene, Jake enlists in the army rather than waiting to be drafted and gathers his family for a meaningful Passover

seder. The book suffers from clunky dialogue and little drama. If Taylor ever read it, she could not have failed to draw a connection between her own family and that in the book, some of whose members are characterized by illiteracy, an obsession with cleanliness, unease with sex, and constant anxiety about money.

45. Gershick, *Gay Old Girls,* 40, 80.

46. Telephone interview with Jo, April 6, 2017.

47. Taylor to Cilly and Morris, April 12, 1952.

48. Ibid.

49. "Taylor Dance Group Is Model for Book," *The Campus* 25, no. 15 (February 9, 1955): 7. Taylor to Meeks, January 23, 1953.

50. Taylor to Cilly and Morris, April 12, 1952.

51. Cilly to Taylor, April 18, 1952. See also Cilly to Taylor, January 24, 1952.

52. Taylor to Meeks, April 19, 1951. Taylor described herself as an active member of the Parents Association at Jo's high school.

53. Taylor to Meeks, January 23, 1953. See also letter of March 22, 1953.

54. Fran Dayan, "Jo Taylor's Dance Group Acclaimed by 'Seventeen,' " *The Campus* 24, no. 13 (January 27, 1954): 1.

55. Taylor to Cilly and Morris, April 12, 1952.

56. Many American women began to shave their legs during World War II, when nylon was scarce. As skirts went shorter and dancing movie stars dominated popular culture on screen and on the newsstand, the trend only increased in the next decade.

57. Cilly to Jo, February 17, 1952.

58. Her efforts to get articles published in New York occupy much of her memoir. See also Charlotte Himber, "Whither, the Jewish College Girl?" *Jewish Tribune,* September 3, 1926. Later in life, she said her greatest victory was the publication of "So He Hates Baseball . . . " in the Sunday magazine of the *New York Times,* August 29, 1965. The article concerns sex-role preferences among children, reassuring fathers that their sons will be masculine even if they do not like sports, as long as they receive affectionate support.

59. Himber, *Famous in Their Twenties.*

60. Norma Brenner to Jerry Brenner, November 10, 1944, and February 14, 1945 (AFC 2001/001/1014), Correspondence (MS02), Veterans History Project Collection, American Folklife Center, Library of Congress.

61. Ruderman, "Greenville Diary." In describing his father's difficulties occupying a pulpit position in the South during the civil rights era, David Ruderman provides an insightful overview of his father's life.

Chapter 9. Camp Cejwin

1. Cilly to Taylor, July 17, 1959.

2. Joselit and Mittelman, *A Worthy Use of Summer,* 11.

3. Schoolman, "Jewish Educational Summer Camp," 9.

4. Joselit and Mittelman, *Worthy Use*, 16.

5. Ibid., 237. For a detailed description of Cejwin's early years, see chapter 10, " 'An Environment of Our Own Making': The Origins of the Jewish Culture Camp."

6. Schoolman, "Jewish Educational Summer Camp," 9 (italics in original).

7. At Cejwin in the summer of 1935, "the entire camp participated in a Saturday-morning bat mitzvah, an event so memorable in the life of the camp that it figured subsequently in a commemorative souvenir album." Joselit, *Wonders of America*, 127. Dropping the more formal educational program was also a financial issue— the required teaching staff was too expensive. Krasner, *Benderly Boys*, 293.

8. Schoolman, "Jewish Educational Summer Camp," 14.

9. Taylor to Miriam [surname unknown], June 9, 1953.

10. Krasner, *Benderly Boys*, 224.

11. Ibid., 225.

12. Schoolman, "Jewish Educational Summer Camp," 13.

13. Taylor to Janet Weisenfreund, December 15, 1962: Taylor hosted a dozen family members and friends from Cejwin in a party that lasted until 1:30 in the morning. Taylor to Nettie Frishman, December 10, 1964: Taylor's preparations include Israeli folk dancing and songs from previous shows.

14. Krasner, *Benderly Boys*, 310.

15. Taylor to Elizabeth Hurtig, July 26, 1957.

16. Ibid., 284.

17. Mike Cohen, Peter Addelston, Dave Warshovsky, and Jeffrey Young, "Cejwin Camps Through the Years," copy of VHS video uploaded by Jeffrey Young, September 24, 2011, https://www.vimeo.com/29544721.

18. Wald, *House on Henry Street*, 186.

19. Taylor to Meeks, April 12, 1953.

20. Krasner, *Benderly Boys*, 310.

21. Schoolman, "Jewish Educational Summer Camp," 15.

22. Taylor to Janet Weisenfreund, April 4, 1973.

23. Taylor to Janice Perlman, September 24, 1957.

24. In the family that was Cejwin, a distinction was made early on between teenage staff members and their older staff counterparts, with the latter being called "Aunt" or "Uncle."

25. Susan Addelston, Responses to survey sent to Cejwin campers, June 2008.

26. Taylor to Janet Weisenfreund, April 1964.

27. Jo to Taylor and Ralph, summer of 1957.

28. Taylor to Janet Weisenfreund, January 12, 1963.

29. Janet Weisenfreund to Taylor, November 9, 1962.

30. Susan Addelston, Survey, June 2008.

31. Ibid.

32. Taylor to Elizabeth Hurtig, June 14, 1955.

33. In the program notes for "The Great Quillow," from 1946: "The actual building of this production is the result of complete group participation. The children's improvisations yielded most of the lines of the script, while suggestions for all engaged in the work, both adult and young, were selected and used by the directors."

34. Taylor to Meeks, April 19, 1951.

35. Taylor to Elizabeth Hurtig, June 26, 1957: "I've planned a very busy season—what with dance pageant and plays. But it should be a lot of fun particularly since I shall have 150 children to work with—ranging in ages from 7 to 10 and ¾. A particularly nice age to work with—old enough to be able to take care of themselves physically and to understand what you want of them and yet young enough not to be too knowing and brash (if you know what I mean)."

36. Meeks to Taylor, June 7, 1956. Taylor to Mrs. Garry Myers at *Highlights for Children,* May 2, 1956: Because of her playwriting, Taylor wanted to know the deadline for a story Myers asked her to write.

37. Taylor to fan, June 28, 1956.

38. Krasner, *Benderly Boys,* 354.

39. Schoolman, "Jewish Educational Summer Camp," 11.

40. Taylor to Janet Weisenfreund, May 6, 1964.

41. Taylor to Grace Sager (teacher in Milwaukee), March 24, 1953.

42. Diary, October 29, 1930.

43. Taylor to Nettie Frishman, December 21, 1972.

44. Cilly to Taylor, August 17, 1958. What is remarkable is that it held true well into the 1970s.

45. There are scripts for "The Shy Princess," (1959), "The Worn-Out Shoes" (a retelling of the "Twelve Dancing Princesses"; 1942), "Enchantment" (about a prince and princess; 1949), "The Princess and the Goatherd" (1953), "The Mute Princess" (1957), and "The Ill-Tempered Princess" (n.d.).

46. Taylor to Dr. Abraham P. Gannes, April 5, 1965. In handwritten notes on the letter, Gannes disapproved of the play's subject matter ("What will children carry away from it?"). He and Taylor also argued about another play she had planned. Gannes gave up trying to change the program, but he insisted that in the future Taylor get his approval before writing the summer plays.

47. This model of children traveling in oneiric or fantasy time to experience tradition was not limited to Taylor. A script titled "We Belong" was published by the Jewish Education Committee of New York during World War II. In the play, the prophet Elijah enables two Jewish children to travel back in time "through Jewish history to discover 'why they belong to America and its democratic tradition, and how the Jews have treasured the ideals for which America stands.' " Krasner, *Benderly Boys,* 347.

48. Survey sent to Cejwin campers, June 2008.

49. Jo to Taylor, August 10, 1955.

Chapter 10. Award-Winning Author

1. Meeks to Taylor, February 21, 1951.
2. In a letter to Joanne Dubinsky dated February 6, 1959, Taylor says she began to write when Jo was about seven years old.
3. Draft of speech for Arkansas Book Fair, Fayetteville, June 1958. A check stub Taylor kept shows that she received $1,000 for the Follett award and $2,000 as an advance royalty for the book. Meeks to Taylor, March 7, 1951: "Amazing! To think that you don't know what you won."
4. Draft of speech for Arkansas Book Fair, Fayetteville, June 1958.
5. Cilly to Taylor, February 18, 1952.
6. Morris to Taylor, February 18, 1952.
7. Taylor to Hinda Ozan, December 4, 1958.
8. Draft of speech to New York Public Library librarians, 1961.
9. Taylor to Barbara Ann Gross, September 27, 1956. See also Taylor to Susan Feit, February 24, 1958.
10. "Arts, Architecture, and Literature in Special Collections," University of Oregon Libraries, https://researchguides.uoregon.edu/scua-arts/childrens_lit.
11. For a thorough discussion of this correspondence, see Cummins, "Becoming an 'All-of-a-Kind' American," 324–43.
12. The use of the name Brenner is noteworthy, and must have come from Ralph's submission of the manuscript.
13. Meeks to Taylor, December 28, 1950.
14. Taylor to Meeks, April 15, 1951.
15. Taylor to Meeks, December 22, 1951: "I know how busy you always are . . . If you find these lengthy reports boring or too much of a trial to go through—just say so and I'll cut them out." A year later, on November 20, 1952, after visits to Boston and Lake Placid, Taylor wrote to Meeks, "Forgive the length. I'm still bubbling over with the excitement."
16. Meeks to Taylor, December 28, 1950.
17. Meeks to Taylor, March 29, 1951. On March 4, 1953, Meeks wrote that she wanted more "reverence and spirituality in the religious passages."
18. Meeks to Taylor, March 2, 1951.
19. Meeks to Taylor, November 21, 1950.
20. Meeks to Taylor, December 28, 1950.
21. Meeks to Taylor, April 11, 1951.
22. Ibid.
23. Taylor to Hinda Ozan, December 4, 1958. Taylor to Susanna Weiner, February 26, 1959: "It's interesting to realize that you liked my book because you are Jewish. And yesterday I received a letter from a child who goes to a Catholic School . . . and she liked the book because she learned so much about Jewish people. I'm so glad my book can appeal to Gentiles as well as Jews. That's a better way, don't you think?"

24. "Josette Frank, 96, Dies; Children's Book Expert," *New York Times,* September 14, 1989.
25. Taylor to Meeks, October 31, 1951; Meeks to Taylor, November 2, 1951.
26. Meeks to Taylor, November 23, 1951.
27. Taylor to Meeks, December 2, 1951.
28. Taylor to Meeks, February 18, 1952.
29. Review of *Carol's Side of the Street* by Lorraine Beim, *Kirkus Reviews,* October 1951, www.kirkusreviews.com/book-reviews/lorraine-belm/carols-side-of-the-street.
30. The preoccupation with maintaining a Jewish identity despite increased exposure to gentile culture does not extend in these books to concern about intermarriage. Much of that can be attributed to the age of the target audience. There are no mixed religious marriages in the *All-of-a-Kind* books, and the girls are too young for dating to be an issue until Jules appears. These are not melting-pot families, but melting-pot schools and social relationships.
31. Characteristics of Jewish girls that became increasingly prevalent in literature of the 1960s appear in the novel. Carol is not what came to be known as a "Jewish American Princess," for she lacks a sense of entitlement, lives in a family that speaks openly about its limited budget, and is not spoiled by her parents. Nonetheless, the preoccupation with grooming and clothes, the consumerism, and the focus on female attributes of domestic helpfulness, which she models on her mother, are reminiscent of those values. The kitchen is praised because it looks like something in magazine advertisements, not because it is homey and traditional. See Cummins, "What Are Jewish Boys and Girls Made Of?"
32. It was not until the late 1960s, for example, that African American authors began to reject the assimilationist ideal and to develop themes of black nationalism. Other ethnic groups soon followed suit, and by the mid-1970s the concept of diversity was articulated. Martin, *Brown Gold.*
33. Undated speech to Jewish Book Council [November 1957].
34. Goldstein, "The Jewish Child in Bookland." Online editions of the *Jewish Book Annual* can be found at http://jba.cjh.org. On Goldstein, see "Fanny Goldstein, Librarian and Founder of Jewish Book Week, Is Born," *Jewish Women's Archive,* https://jwa.org/thisweek/may/15/1895/fanny-goldstein.
35. Sayers, *Anne Carroll Moore,* 269; Frances Clarke Sayers to Taylor, November 28, 1951.
36. Taylor to Anne Carroll Moore, October 26, 1952.
37. Anne Carroll Moore to Taylor, March 22, 1953. Grace Sager, a Jewish elementary school teacher in Milwaukee, had no Jewish children in her public school classroom and, in a letter of March 1953, thanked Taylor for writing a book that portrayed Jews so positively. Interestingly enough, she equated Jews and blacks, for she displayed *All-of-a-Kind Family* and *Bright April* ("about colored life") together in a "shadow box" she made to encourage her students to read. *Bright*

April, by eventual Newbery Award winner Marguerite de Angeli (1889–1987) and published in 1946, was considered ahead of its time for having an African American heroine confront racism.

38. Sulzberger (1892–1990) was a trustee of the *New York Times;* her father acquired the newspaper in 1896, and her husband, son-in-law, and son were all publishers at some point. During her school years (around 1910), she worked in the Henry Street Settlement. "Iphigene Ochs Sulzberger Is Dead; Central Figure in Times's History," *New York Times,* February 27, 1990.

    As for cocktail parties, Taylor mentions several times that she does not drink alcohol, usually in the context of surprising non-Jews. She did have a glass of port back in 1929 in Montreal, but it was clear even then that she did not see alcohol as a social lubricant and would ask for a pot of tea at parties. Frances Clarke Sayers to Taylor, October 29, 1951; "I do not drink at all . . . I find it embarrasses everybody else but me." Taylor to Meeks, December 2, 1951.

39. Taylor to Meeks, October 31, 1951.

40. Meeks to Taylor, October 31, 1952.

41. Taylor to Meeks, December 2, 1951.

42. Dorothy L. McFadden to Taylor, January 26, 1955. Taylor describes the "Reading Is Fun" program in a letter to Nettie Frishman of December 22, 1956: "A large collection of books is sent to the public school most important in one district. The collection remains for a month and other schools in the neighboring area come to visit. In addition, authors and illustrators are invited by The Times for personal appearances. It has been a great joy for me to play an active part in this program."

43. For example, Taylor to F. Block of Windsor Library, Bayside, N.Y., November 24, 1952. The response from Florence Block came on the 28th: "The majority of our readers are Jewish and they would enjoy all anecdotes and stories that you may wish to relate."

44. Abraham M. Danzig to Taylor, December 23, 1953. He was the principal of the religious school of the then flourishing Orthodox synagogue Mosholu Jewish Center in the Bronx, where Irving and Ethel Brenner were active members.

45. Emanuel Neumann, Ely E. Pilchik, Meyer Levin, and Charles Angoff to Taylor, June 28, 1957.

46. Grace Sager to Taylor, April 2, 1953.

47. Taylor to Sarah Lang, January 13, 1965.

48. Jacob Stein to Taylor, February 15, 1957, and April 5, 1957.

49. Meeks to Taylor, September 10, 1952: "How is the new book coming?" Taylor to Meeks, October 5, 1952: "I'm working regularly—and hence feel a whole lot better." Taylor to Meeks, November 3, 1952 (after Meeks had been in New York mid-October): "I've just finished the second round on my manuscript. Would have liked to start the final polishing today but I'm due in Far Rockaway to address a Jewish organizational meeting on the book. So it'll have to wait till tomorrow." Taylor to Miss Bodine, November 25, 1952: "It's amazing—really I merely

wrote a simple story—and look what happened? Yes, I'm writing a sequel, with some misgivings. I'm so afraid my little readers won't think it as good as the first—a first always has the highlights in it, doesn't it?"

50. The quotations in the following are all from an unpublished typescript of "Adventures of a Prize Winner."

51. In a letter to Meeks of January 23, 1953, Taylor goes on at length about Jo's organization of a dance company, which rehearsed in the Taylor apartment and appeared on television, and Jo's contributions to *Dance Magazine:* "All this activity might make a good teen-age book."

52. Taylor to Meeks, March 22, 1953. From the reference to the character of Guido in this letter, it is clear that she is referring in her speech to *Downtown,* not published until 1972: Taylor encloses a library chapter, talks about the reverential tone of the Sukkos chapter, and says she cannot make more revisions until she hears from Meeks. She is still rewriting it in May. On May 2, 1953, she wrote to Meeks: "I am very grateful for all of your help with the book. I know how harassed you are always with forthcoming publications and I can appreciate how difficult it must be to find time for everyone."

53. Taylor to Mary Stevens, November 6, 1954.

54. Fanny Goldstein to Taylor, January 13, 1956.

55. Taylor to Joanne Dubinsky, February 6, 1959.

56. Taylor to Meeks, March 8, 1953.

57. Ibid.

58. Meeks to Taylor, January 20, 1955.

59. Taylor to Meeks, November 18, 1956.

60. *Uptown* manuscript sent: Meeks to Taylor, May 11, 1956; revisions: Taylor to Meeks, October 29, 1956; name choice and signed contract: Taylor to Meeks, January 5, 1957; delay because of Stevens: Meeks to Taylor, May 23, 1957; book on the presses: Taylor to Susan Gelber (a fan), April 18, 1958.

61. Taylor to Meeks, January 30, 1959.

62. Meeks to Taylor, March 9, 1959.

63. Cummins, "Leaning Left." The paragraph below about May Day in *More* is based on this article. See Nel, *Crockett Johnson and Ruth Krauss.*

64. March 3, 1952, radio interview with Patsy Campbell on "The Second Mrs. Burton Family Counselor Spot."

65. "East Side Chemists Hark Back to 1752: Caswell-Massey, Listing Many Famous Clients, Carries on with Dignity and Pride," *New York Times,* February 12, 1952.

66. "Soda Fountain Gushes Champagne, Too, as Drug Store Celebrates Its 200th Year," *New York Times,* March 27, 1952.

67. "100-Year Concerns Get City's Tribute: Oldest Business Groups and Other Institutions Here Hailed for Civic Aid," *New York Times,* May 14, 1952. This luncheon was an annual event: Taylor to Janet Weisenfreund, October 1, 1964.

68. Taylor to Cilly and Morris, April 12, 1952.

69. Obituary, *New York Times,* November 7, 1953. He died in the morning "on the platform of the 177th Street Station at Westchester Avenue of the Lexington Avenue subway while on his way to business." The senior Taylors lived at 1945 McGraw Avenue in the Bronx.

70. Taylor to Meeks, April 21, 1955.

71. Taylor to Evelyn Parks, May 5, 1955.

72. Zelda Taylor to Taylor, August 15, 1955.

73. Jo to parents, n.d. [1955].

74. Meeks to Taylor, October 18, 1955; October 21, 1955; December 5, 1955.

75. Cilly to Taylor, February 2, 1956. Sarah Lang, a Cejwin friend and colleague, also thought the strike was over that winter.

76. Cilly to Taylor, February 21, 1956.

77. Jo to parents, July 11, 1956.

78. "Union Aides Sentenced: 2 Get Suspended Terms for Jamming Drug Store Phones," *New York Times,* December 8, 1956. Calling a business to keep the line busy was a felony, and this was believed to be the first prosecution under the new law, passed in 1951.

79. "Strike-Bound Store Faces City Charge," *New York Times,* February 4, 1956.

80. "Pharmacy Here Exonerated," *New York Times,* July 11, 1959.

81. Taylor to Alison Holziner (fan), January 16, 1978. This was Taylor's stock line for over two decades.

82. "Awards Presented for Men's Designs," *New York Times,* May 16, 1958. Robert L. Green, fashion editor at *Playboy,* organized the awards, which became known as Playboy's Creative Menswear Awards. "Robert Lamont Green, 79, Arbiter of Men's Fashions," *New York Times,* July 24, 1997. Taylor mentions him and his connection to *Playboy* frequently in passing. Taylor provided a brief history of the awards to Nettie Frishman in a letter of October 21, 1964: "Ralph's publicity man and he evolved the idea of instituting a men's fashion award—Being a toiletry house, no one could accuse us of playing favorites with any particular concern—or having any other ax to grind save some advertising for ourselves. It began tentatively, small, and with some skepticism on the part of the men's manufacturers themselves. However the idea has taken hold—each year more and more firms are submitting their finest designs (or way out designs)—a board of judges chooses the best in each category."

83. "Awards Are Given for Men's Designs," *New York Times,* September 30, 1959. "Awards for Men's Fashion," *New York Times,* October 25, 1967: there Ralph is listed as president of the company and the event is called "the Caswell-Massey Fashion Awards for Excellence of Design in Menswear for the Gentleman," the equivalent of the Coty American Fashion Critics Award.

84. Taylor to Sarah Lang, October 23, 1963. Taylor contrasts her feelings to those of Henny "(whom we have invited to act as a ticket taker—in order to get her in— there are no seats available the show's become that popular)," who fussed over several outfits, including shoes, beads, earrings, and purses to match.

85. Taylor to Janet Weisenfreund, October 25, 1962.
86. Taylor to Janet Weisenfreund, October 1, 1964. On November 4, Taylor wrote that her dress did not create quite the same sensation as the previous year's model, although with its fuller skirt it was much more comfortable: "When I wore last year's a month ago I split it when I had to go to the John. I only hope my dressmaker will be able to mend it."
87. Taylor to Meeks, September 30, 1965.
88. Taylor to Cilly and Morris, April 12, 1952.
89. Barbara Kaplan, "Becoming Sarah Lawrence," *Sarah Lawrence Magazine* 2004 (Spring): 4–11.
90. "Jo Taylor Dance Group To Be Featured on TV," *The Campus,* May 19, 1954 (23:25), 3.
91. Quoted in Norma George, "Work in the Field," *The Campus* 26, no. 26 (May 30, 1956): 3.
92. Taylor to Meeks, February 25, 1954.
93. Christened Serge Marti-Volkoff, he was in the process of changing his name to Steven Marshall when they met. See Jo to Taylor, March 30, 1955, in which Jo says it required six months of army red tape to make the change official.
94. Sarah Lang to Taylors, October 4, 1955. On the 10th, Lang thanked Taylor for replying about the situation and wished the young couple "only the best."
95. Taylor to Elizabeth Hurtig, June 26, 1957. Cilly was also proud: Cilly to Taylor, April 18, 1957.
96. Cilly to Taylor, February 1, 1955. In a letter from February 10, she implies that she thinks Jo might still be unmarried. She had been trying to fix Jo up with a relative of a friend: "Perhaps he will call he said he knows that College and has many friends there but then again God knows if Joan is still free lets hope so." On March 20, Cilly wistfully remarks that the young man she had in mind for Jo would have been perfect: "Oh well."
97. Cilly to Taylor, January 1, 1956.
98. Cilly to Taylor, February 12, 1956.
99. Cilly to Taylor, December 12, 1955.
100. Cilly to Taylor, January 19, 1956.
101. Interview with Susan Baker.
102. Taylor to Nettie Frishman, December 17, 1963.
103. Taylor to Meeks, October 1, 1956: "Since coming home [from Cejwin], I've been terribly busy helping Jo set up her own establishment right near my own place."
104. Taylor to Karen (a thirteen-year-old Jewish fan), December 31, 1959.

Chapter 11. Personal Loss and Artistic Anxiety

1. Cilly to Taylor, March 1957.
2. Cilly to Taylor, February 17, 1952.

3. Ralph to Taylor, August 20, 1960.

4. Lucille Ruderman to Taylor, August 1960.

5. Harriet to Taylor, January 9, 1961.

6. Taylor to Janet Weisenfreund, January 12, 1963.

7. Cilly to Taylor, December 28, 1955.

8. Gertrude to Taylor and Ralph, May 2, 1963: "Mom's reaction to this—instead of telling Henny how happy she is for her, was 'So who will visit me?'"

9. Sarah Lang to Taylor, n.d. [late spring 1961]: Taylor had written to her friend that Cilly was not eager to go to the shore without Morris; Cilly to Cejwin sisters, July 3, 1962 (on stationery of Sharf's Royale Hotel in Long Beach, N.Y).

10. The Brenner children financed the winters in Florida in the 1950s. Cilly insisted that she did not want Irving, Ella, Gertrude, and Jerry to contribute funds: Cilly to Taylor April 8, 1957. In 1963, Taylor wrote off care for her mother on her taxes.

11. It was a private facility where Jo had once worked. Taylor to Janet Weisenfreund, February 8, 1963.

12. Taylor to Henny, February 2, 1963.

13. See Charlotte to Taylor and Ralph, May 8, 1963: Anticipating her role as the primary visitor throughout the summer, Charlotte complained, "I DREAD those hot evenings, after work in the Wall St. section, being the only daily visitor." Charlotte was working in Manhattan at the National Council of the Young Men's Christian Associations located at 291 Broadway. Charlotte to Gertrude, July 15, 1963.

14. Taylor to Nettie Frishman, April 12, 1963.

15. Ibid. Taylor says she visits her mother five days a week, and the other sisters indicate a similar schedule. Henny grumbled a bit that Ella was not doing her fair share, even after Ella's daughter June was no longer living with her. Henny to Taylor, February 27, 1963.

16. Charlotte to Taylor and Ralph, April 27, 1963.

17. Gertrude to Taylor and Ralph, May 2, 1963.

18. Henny to Taylor, February 27, 1963; Charlotte to Taylor and Ralph, May 8, 1963.

19. Taylor to Sarah Lang, October 23, 1963; March 7, 1964. Taylor to Janet Weisenfreund, n.d. [fall 1964].

20. Gertrude to Taylor and Ralph, May 2, 1963.

21. Charlotte to Gertrude, July 15, 1963.

22. Taylor to Meeks, April 12, 1963.

23. Taylor to Nettie Frishman, April 12, 1963.

24. Taylor to Janet Weisenfreund, February 10, 1964.

25. Taylor to Sarah Lang, January 24, 1964.

26. Taylor to Meeks, September 30, 1965.

27. Taylor to Jo, September 29, 1965.

28. Ella to Taylor, October 11, 1968. Emphasis on *carriage* in the original.

29. Taylor to Nettie and Harold Frishman, December 10, 1974.

30. Cilly to Taylor, February 2, 1956.

31. Cilly to Taylor, April 8, 1957.

32. Sarah Lang to Taylor, n.d. [late 1957].

33. Taylor to Sarah Lang, October 23, 1963 (in response to Sarah's letter to Taylor of October 21).

34. Taylor to Janet Weisenfreund, December 17, 1963.

35. Taylor to Sarah Lang, January 24, 1964; March 7, 1964. Joe entered a nursing facility when Ella worked at Cejwin. Sarah Lang to Taylor, n.d. [August 1964].

36. Taylor to Janet Weisenfreund, n.d. [fall 1964]. In contrast, Taylor condemned Gertrude Holz's husband for neglecting her while she was dying: "He's not much around—I guess one gets weary of the eternally bed-ridden." Taylor to Sarah Lang, March 7, 1964.

37. Sarah Lang to Taylor, n.d. [winter 1964].

38. Ella to Taylor, October 13, 1965.

39. Taylor to Janet Weisenfreund, April 1, 1964.

40. Interview with Janet Weisenfreund, December 13, 2017.

41. Taylor to Janet Weisenfreund, December 15, 1962.

42. Janet Weisenfreund to Taylor, September 19, 1962; Taylor to Janet Weisenfreund, November 6, 1962, and December 15, 1962.

43. Taylor to Janet Weisenfreund, February 8, 1963.

44. Taylor to Janet Weisenfreund, February 10, 1964; Taylor to Sarah Lang, January 24. 1964.

45. Taylor to Janet Weisenfreund, March 5, 1965.

46. Speech at the Ohio Book Fair, Columbus, Ohio, November 1967.

47. Ibid.

48. Ibid.

49. Taylor to Mr. and Mrs. Martin, February 14, 1960. The Martins were a couple from New Zealand whom Ralph and Taylor had met in England the previous year.

50. Jo to Taylor, August 2, 1960.

51. Jo to parents, April 29, 1961.

52. Foster Hailey, "Streets Cleared in Defense Drill; Test Nation-Wide," *New York Times,* April 29, 1961: "Air raid sirens wailed a warning across the country at 4 o'clock yesterday afternoon in a national drill aimed at dispelling public fatalism and apathy toward a possible nuclear attack. TV screens went blank and regular stations fell silent for half an hour while President Kennedy and other national, state and local officials were heard over two special radio channels. . . . All of New York City's millions—except for a few hundred protestors and for defense aides—were off the streets from 4 P. M . to 4:10. It was like a city of the dead, with above-ground traffic halted."

53. Taylor to Nettie Frishman, March 27, 1962.

54. Taylor to Janet Weisenfreund, November 21, 1962. Also October 25, 1962.

55. Taylor to Janet Weisenfreund, October 25, 1962.

56. Taylor to Janet Weisenfreund, November 6, 1962.

57. Steven Marshall to Taylor and Ralph, May 8, 1963.

58. Taylor to Jo, June 3, 1963. Taylor was quoting Ralph.

59. Steven Marshall to Taylor, August 6, 1963; ellipses in the original.

60. Rae Rosenblum to Taylor, August 11, 1963.

61. Taylor to Steven Marshall, September 30, 1963.

62. Taylor to Paul Woolf, January 24, 1964.

63. Hannah to Taylor, n.d. [early summer 1964].

64. Hannah to Taylor, Tuesday n.d. [late summer 1964].

65. Taylor to Jo, September 29, 1965.

66. Taylor to Nettie Frishman, December 15, 1968.

67. Thanks to Bruce Friedman for this explanation.

68. Meeks to Taylor, May 10, 1960.

69. *Chicago Tribune,* November 12, 1961. The reference is to "There Was an Old Man with a Beard."

70. Taylor to Nettie Frishman, June 21, 1962; Taylor to Meeks, April 12, 1963.

71. Taylor to Nettie Frishman, April 12, 1963.

72. Taylor to Nettie Frishman, March 27, 1963.

73. *Bulletin of the Children's Book Center* [Chicago], January 1964.

74. Taylor to Meeks, March 25, 1962; Meeks to Taylor, March 29, 1962. Taylor to Nettie Frishman, June 21, 1962, referring to her disappointment at the delayed release of *Now That You Are Eight:* "Since I've had some rejections of manuscripts this year, it would have been nice to see something else out approved of."

75. Nettie Frishman to Taylor, November 7, 1961.

76. The truth is unclear. Ella adamantly insisted on the tapes she made after Taylor's death that it was Cilly's ambitions for her daughter's career as a singer that derailed an offer from musicologist Samuel Goldfarb—creator of the song "I Had a Little Dreidl"—of a free education at Columbia University. Her resentment of her mother's pushiness is palpable. The admiration Ella and Charlotte expressed for relatives and friends from the Lower East Side who succeeded as musicians and entertainers belies Meeks's remark that immigrant parents did not see an artistic career as a desirable future for their children.

77. Meeks to Taylor, March 29, 1962.

78. Ibid.

79. Taylor to Nettie Frishman, December 22, 1962.

80. Taylor to Nettie Frishman, February 12, 1962; Taylor to Janet Weisenfreund, December 15, 1962.

81. Caroline Myers to Taylor, November 5, 1963.

82. Taylor to Nettie Frishman, December 16, 1965.

83. Elizabeth M. Riley (Thomas Crowell) to Taylor, December 14, 1961 (asks for more time to assess), and January 23, 1962 (rejects); Frances Schwartz (children's book editor, Abelard-Schuman) to Taylor, February 5, 1963.

84. The book was titled *Ricky/Rickey the Recorder:* Taylor to Thomas Crowell Co., January 22, 1961/Elizabeth M. Riley to Taylor, February 14, 1963; Taylor to Atheneum, February 27, 1963/Jean Karl (editor of children's books, Atheneum) to Taylor, March 26, 1963; Golden Press to "Mr. Taylor," April 5, 1963; Mary-Prue Agius (Blackie & Son) to Taylor, October 8, 1963.

85. Meeks to Taylor, February 8, 1961.

86. Taylor to Meeks, May 24, 1964.

87. Taylor to Meeks, September 30, 1965.

88. *Chicago Tribune,* November 6, 1966; *Bulletin of the Children's Book Center* [Chicago], November 1966; *Sacramento Bee,* November 27, 1966.

89. Taylor to Nettie Frishman, June 1, 1964.

90. *Kirkus Reviews,* October 1, 1966, available at www.kirkusreviews.com/book-reviews/sydney-taylor/papa-everyone-else.

91. Sarah Lang to Taylor, February 1956; Taylor to fan, October 19, 1959.

92. Sarah Lang to Taylor, spring 1961; Taylor to Charlotte, December 14, 1976.

93. Taylor to Janet Weisenfreund, December 1962.

94. Taylor to Sarah Lang, April 1, 1964. See also Taylor to Sarah Lang, January 23, 1965, and June 1, 1968. The constant theme was that the time had come to bow out.

95. Taylor to Nettie Frishman, December 17, 1963.

96. Taylor to Nettie Frishman, June 28, 1965.

97. Ibid.

98. Taylor to Meeks, September 12, 1965.

99. Taylor to Nettie Frishman, July 25, 1964.

100. Janet Weisenfreund to Taylor, 1976.

101. Taylor to Nettie Frishman, September 19, 1968.

102. Taylor to Sarah Lang, March 22, 1969.

103. Janet Weisenfreund to Taylor, December 31, 1962. See also chapter 9, n. 46.

104. Taylor to Janet Weisenfreund, December 26, 1963; January 18, 1964; January 24, 1964; May 6, 1964; January 7, 1965; January 23, 1965; to Nettie Frishman, December 10, 1969.

105. Taylor to Janet Weisenfreund, January 23, 1965.

106. Taylor to Nettie Frishman, December 15, 1968.

107. Taylor to Sarah Lang, March 22, 1969.

108. Sarah Lang to Taylor, February 1956.

109. Taylor to Ruth Sideroff, September 11, 1970; Taylor to Rae Rosenblum, December 19, 1970.

110. Taylor to Nettie Frishman, December 17, 1963.

111. Taylor to Meeks, September 10, 1963; Taylor to Nettie Frishman, September 12, 1965.

112. Taylor to Sarah Lang, March 22, 1969.

113. Ralph occasionally brought little bottles of Caswell-Massey products as gifts for friends and counselors at the end of the summer.

114. Hitchhiking scrapbook, July 9, 1929.

115. Rome in 1960 was for Ralph's business (Taylor to Meeks, March 9, 1960); Paris and Switzerland in 1963 were on the itinerary for business; the trip to Portugal in 1969 was for Ralph's business; the hotel in Bologna, Italy, in 1970 was paid for by the Taylors' hosts, who invited them to a drug and cosmetics fair.

116. Taylor to Follett & Co., July 15, 1959. Linton J. Keith (editor in chief at Follett) to Miss Adam (Blackie), October 9, 1959: clarifies royalty payments, with details about the illustrations, and gives Blackie exclusive distribution in the British Commonwealth, excluding Canada. Taylor to Meeks, March 9, 1960: says Taylor did not know the current state of negotiations and wanted an update so she could "handle the matter intelligently." Linton Keith to Taylor, April 16, 1960: Dwight Follett will be in England in May and will conclude the negotiations.

117. France: Taylor to Dwight Follett, June 7, 1962; Hachette to Taylor, June 28, 1962. Israel: Dr. Lipa Katz to Taylor, September 4, 1960 (regarding unsuccessful efforts to translate *All-of-a-Kind Family* into Hebrew); Taylor to Mr. Barasch in Ramat Gan, May 13, 1974.

118. Taylor to Nettie Frishman, December 13, 1968; Employee to Ralph, May 1, 1962: Murray was clearly in charge.

119. Travel journal, 1963.

120. Taylor to Nettie Frishman, March 27, 1962; June 21, 1962. The trip to California in 1964 also had a musical component: the Taylors visited Erich Katz, another pioneer in the early music movement, who had taught Ralph in New York. Taylor to Janet Weisenfreund, April 28, 1964.

121. On one musical evening, the musicians retired to play after dinner, while Taylor and Greta Bergmann washed the dishes. Taylor found Greta's housekeeping sloppy, but the story of her escape from Germany fascinated her and she transcribed it in detail.

122. The story of the Landau daughters is intertwined with medical and media developments in France over the last seventy years. For information on the Riga branch of the family, see Alix Brijatoff, *Tombes lointaines: Le destin tragique d'une femme dans la "Shoah par balles"* (Paris: Robert Laffont, 2009). For the experiences of Adek and Bluma during World War II focused on the revocation of their citizenship, see Landau-Brijatoff, *Indignes d'être français.*

123. Taylor to Nettie Frishman, June 21, 1962.

124. The Landaus visited the Taylors in New York in the winter of 1964. Taylor to Janet Weisenfreund, February 10, 1964: "My relatives from Paris arrived—with one day's notice—They had been good to us when we were there—the result was we exhausted ourselves returning their many kindnesses. I believe when they left—last night—the books were overly balanced—Certainly we had spent considerably more in time, effort, and money on them than they on us mostly because they are less resourceful than Ralph and I—and secondly though not born in France, have absorbed the French philosophy completely—they are inclined

to be wary of how they spend money. Still we enjoyed it—I saw things I would not have bothered to go to see by myself about our city. I ate out in restaurants so frequently, I've lost the taste for cooking almost."

125. Taylor to Nettie Frishman, March 24, 1973.

126. Cilly to Taylor, January 13, 1956. In a letter to Taylor of January 12, 1952, Cilly called Israel "Palastina." She indicated that the Rafael Brenners were traveling there, as well as to some European countries, including Germany and Italy. During the 1950s, Cilly kept Taylor informed of Leo Brenner's activities—how he always remembered Morris's birthday, worried that Israel had won the war but still had no peace, and hoped to send the younger of his two sons to study in the United States: e.g., Cilly to Taylor, January 4, 1957. Taylor to Janet Weisenfreund, October 1964.

127. Taylor to Sarah Lang, January 13, 1965; Taylor to Nettie Frishman, January 13, 1965; Adek Landau to Taylor, December 3, 1964 (in French).

128. Taylor to Mr. and Mrs. Martin, February 14, 1960.

129. Taylor to Bertha Jenkinson, May 12, 1960.

130. Nettie Frishman to Taylor, February 8, 1962.

131. Taylor to Nettie Frishman, February 12, 1962.

132. Taylor to Sarah Lang, January 13, 1965.

133. Taylor to Nettie Frishman, February 12, 1962.

134. Taylor to Meeks, June 1, 1968.

135. Taylor to David Ruderman, November 27, 1968. Already in 1963, Taylor voiced doubts: "I have no intention of leaving my own country for Israel though perhaps were I young like our children I might consider it—but at least it keeps me in touch with Judaism." Taylor to Nettie Frishman, December 17, 1963.

136. Taylor to Follett, January 29, 1969. Dozens of letters repeated this complaint.

137. Taylor to the Repertory Theatre of Lincoln Center, January 24, 1964.

138. Taylor to Mr. F. J. Mullins of American Airlines, November 19, 1968.

139. Taylor to PanAm, May 30, 1965.

140. Nettie Frishman to Taylor, November 28, 1977.

141. Obituary, *Santa Barbara News-Press,* July 8, 2005. Nettie Frishman to Taylor, September 20, 1962: The Los Angeles Library was literally Nettie's life for many years. The Children's Literature Department of the Los Angeles Public Library continues to hold an annual Nettie Frishman Fundraiser.

142. Nettie Peltzman (Frishman) to Taylor, December 12, 1956.

143. Nettie Frishman to Taylor, August 30, 1961.

144. Taylor to Nettie Frishman, October 19, 1961.

145. Nettie Frishman to Taylor, November 7, 1961.

146. Nettie Frishman to Taylor, December 4, 1961.

147. Ibid.

148. Taylor to Nettie Frishman, November 17, 1961.

149. Nettie Frishman to Taylor, January 31, 1962.

150. Taylor to Nettie Frishman, February 12, 1962.
151. The blackout of November 9, 1965, left about thirty million people in the Northeast and Canada without power for approximately twelve hours.
152. Taylor to Mr. and Mrs. Martin, February 14, 1960.
153. Taylor to Janet Weisenfreund, November 21, 1961.
154. Taylor to Steve Marshall, September 30, 1963.
155. Adek Landau to Taylor and Ralph, December 3, 1964.
156. Taylor to Mrs. Lazan, January 23, 1968.

Chapter 12. Last Years and Legacy

1. Nettie Frishman to Taylor, January 31, 1962.
2. Taylor to Meeks, March 12, 1969.
3. Meeks to Taylor, March 26, 1969. Follett did undergo retrenchment, but Taylor suspected that the talk of funding cuts and downsizing was simply an excuse not to publish her work. Taylor to Nettie Frishman, November 3, 1970. Title 2 of the Elementary and Secondary School Act of 1965 provided generous funding to school libraries, which led to a boom in publishing until the Nixon administration began dismantling its provisions in early 1969. Marcus, *Minders of Make-Believe*, 238, 241, 244.
4. Taylor to Nettie Frishman, September 18, 1969; Meeks to Taylor, February 29, 1968.
5. Samuel French Editorial Department to Taylor, December 4, 1969; Taylor to Danny Schaffer, February 9, 1974.
6. Ralph to Meredith Bernstein, December 5, 1977.
7. In a letter to Taylor of October 1, 1970, Robert Follett gave details about the shake-up at his publishing company, which reorganized as part of Follett Educational Corporation, moved to new offices, and underwent drastic changes in personnel. Meeks and her husband had bought a property in Ireland, where, upon her retirement, they spent several months each year.
8. Taylor to Bertha Jenkinson, February 1, 1971.
9. Taylor to Nettie Frishman, November 4, 1972.
10. Taylor to Bertha Jenkinson, February 1, 1971. The circumstances of Meeks's retirement are not specified in Taylor's correspondence. She told Jenkinson that Meeks had not replied to her last letter: "I suppose she was too disturbed—and too overwhelmed with cleaning up."
11. Bertha Jenkinson to Taylor, May 11, 1971.
12. Taylor to Bertha Jenkinson, March 18, 1972.
13. Taylor to Sandra Greifenstein, March 22, 1972; Taylor to Bertha Jenkinson, March 22, 1972.
14. Taylor to Nettie Frishman, November 4, 1972.
15. Taylor to Sandra Greifenstein, March 30, 1972.

16. Sandra Greifenstein to Taylor, March 31, 1972.

17. Sandra Greifenstein to Taylor, May 3, 1972.

18. Mary Reidy (subsidiary rights manager at Follett) to Taylor, June 17, 1970. That letter relates that Scott, Foresman & Co. had the rights to reprint *The Dog Who Came to Dinner* and *More All-of-a-Kind Family* as part of a classroom library set. It also gives a clear explanation of Dell's paperback rights, the advances it paid, and the selling price of the books. See also Donna Stefan (permissions manager at Follett) to Taylor, May 17, 1972, with a breakdown of sales by Dell and Blackie. Only one hundred copies were sold in England, where *All-of-a-Kind Family* had gone out of print.

19. Taylor to Nettie Frishman, November 4, 1972.

20. The *Kirkus* review can be found at www.kirkusreviews.com/book-reviews/sydney-taylor/all-of-a-kind-family-downtown.

21. Taylor to Janet Weisenfreund, March 25, 1973. The reference is to *Julie of the Wolves* by Jean Craighead George. Taylor's plot summary is inaccurate.

22. Ibid.

23. Sandra Greifenstein to Taylor, December 1972; February 12, 1973.

24. Sandra Greifenstein to Taylor, April 4, 1973.

25. Marci Ridlon Carafoli to Taylor, September 14, 1973.

26. Sandra Greifenstein to Taylor, May 2, 1973.

27. Marci Carafoli to Taylor, April 4, 1973; July 16, 1973.

28. Taylor to Bertha Jenkinson, October 23, 1972.

29. Taylor to Marci Carafoli, January 30, 1974.

30. Ralph to Meredith Bernstein, December 5, 1977. Ralph was trying to get Bernstein to republish the book as *Pieces of Eight.*

31. Marci Carafoli to Taylor, September 3, 1974.

32. Taylor to Janet Weisenfreund, February 10, 1973.

33. Taylor to Charlotte, August 15, 1975.

34. Charlotte to Taylor and Ralph, April 20, 1975: At a family gathering, Irving's wife, Ethel, spoke harshly about Schoolman's refusal to give her a raise: "Poor Ella had to listen to her diatribes against the great God Schoolman—difficult and embarrassing, and I told them all it was really hard for her to hear all these negative things when she personally was having such a good friendship with this man. That slowed them down a little, and perked her up."

35. Taylor to Charlotte, March 19, 1977.

36. Taylor to Charlotte, December 14, 1976; Charlotte to Taylor, March 8, 1977.

37. Taylor to Marci Carafoli, September 12, 1974.

38. Taylor to Sarah Lang, March 5, 1975.

39. Taylor to Charlotte, August 15, 1975. Aviv-Aviva refers to the boys' and girls' division at Cejwin for campers approximately thirteen to fifteen years old.

40. Taylor to Janet Weisenfreund, March 25, 1973.

41. Taylor to Janet Weisenfreund, May 31, 1975. Taylor to Charlotte, August 15, 1975: "I wanted to spare myself physically and spent much more time with creative dramatics."

42. Taylor to Helen Heinrich (Hofstra University), November 4, 1971.

43. Taylor to Nettie Frishman, May 27, 1970.

44. Naomi Jackson, "Katya Delakova," *The Encyclopedia of Jewish Women*, March 1, 2009. https://jwa.org/encyclopedia/article/delakova-katya. Delakova (1914–1991) immigrated to the United States in 1939, was a pioneer in Jewish dance, worked with Louis Horst, among others, and taught at Sarah Lawrence College (1966–75).

45. Taylor to Janet Weisenfreund, October 3, 1972.

46. Taylor to Nettie Frishman, March 24, 1973.

47. Taylor to Janet Weisenfreund, January 31, 1972. In 1953, Rabbi Ruderman had made a solo trip to Israel "in order to satisfy a life-long dream." Lucille Ruderman to Taylor and Ralph, spring 1953 and April 16, 1953.

48. Phyllis Ruderman to Taylor and Ralph, January 14, 1974.

49. Phyllis Ruderman to Taylor and Ralph, February 20, 1974.

50. Taylor to Nettie Frishman, March 25, 1975.

51. Taylor to Nettie Frishman, May 27, 1970.

52. The one instance of anti-Semitism that Taylor cites came during the oil embargo of 1973, and it is what she heard rather than anything directed specifically at her: "Listening to the comments coming over the media—watching one country after another forsake their principles to knuckle under to the piracy of the Arabs, makes one truly disgusted. Comments like 'we don't need the Jews but we do need oil!' come over frequently. We should as Jews be accustomed to anti-semitism but here in America, it has never flared actively into the open." Taylor to Nettie Frishman, December 31, 1973.

53. Taylor to Janet Weisenfreund, March 25, 1973.

54. Taylor to Henny, January 8, 1972: "You see—things come home to roost. All through her years away from me and my care in dietary regulation—she's gone in for all the rich fattening things—that's partly why she's so fat too—and I'm afraid it's caught up with her. As for the hernia, Daddy thinks that's a break down of muscular tissues and I wonder if that too can come from giving up all exercise particularly for one who for so many years worked so hard physically. Of course I don't know—I may be way out about this. But Ella tells me that with her hiatus hernia she has to eliminate all spices (and Jo surely loves ketchup even to spoiling the taste of a shell steak by dousing it with the red goo)."

55. Charlotte to Taylor, December 19, 1976.

56. Henny to Taylor, fall 1973: "It would be nice if Ralph could retire. It's a shame Milton's boys are not interested—Young people are so foolish. To have such a wonderful opportunity for a secure future in an interesting business, what more can one ask." Also Zelda Taylor to Taylor, August 2, 1974.

57. Taylor to David Ruderman, November 27, 1968.

58. Taylor to Nettie Frishman, November 3, 1970.

59. Taylor to Rae Rosenblum, December 19, 1970.

60. Taylor to Nettie Frishman, September 26, 1977.

61. Zelda Taylor to Taylor, August 4, 1975.

62. Charlotte to Taylor, January 24, 1975.

63. Taylor to Nettie Frishman, March 25, 1975.

64. "Businesses in New York over 200 Years Honored," *New York Times,* June 29, 1976.

65. Taylor to the City Rent Commission, September 19, 1971; Taylor to Robert E. Herman (State Rent Commission), September 30, 1971; Taylor to Nelson Rockefeller, September 16, 1971; Taylor to Richard Nixon, September 15, 1971.

66. Taylor to City Rent Commission, September 19, 1971.

67. Taylor to Daniel Patrick Moynihan, February 18, 1977; Daniel Patrick Moynihan to Taylor, March 18, 1977.

68. Taylor to Nettie Frishman, May 27, 1970.

69. Henny to Taylor, February 18, 1970: on hearing about the diagnosis from Taylor, Henny said she "was so shocked about the news of Carol that I feel almost ill. . . . I feel so awful for Ella, it seems she has had more troubles than anyone I know. How she can continue to bear up under it all is amazing."

70. Taylor to Charlotte, January 16, 1974.

71. Taylor to Nettie Frishman, October 30, 1970.

72. Taylor to Nettie Frishman, May [*sic:* this would have been November or December] 3, 1970.

73. Ibid.

74. Taylor to Charlotte, January 28, 1974.

75. Charlotte to Taylor, January 25, 1974.

76. Taylor to Dr. Caldwell Esselstyn, November 21, 1974.

77. Charlotte to Taylor, February 20, 1976.

78. Taylor to Charlotte, December 14, 1976.

79. Lou Himber to Ralph, February 28, 1977.

80. Taylor to Peggy Charren (Action for Childrens' Television), September 1, 1976.

81. Henny to Taylor, n.d. [April 1976].

82. The Brenner sisters' ambitions for one another never faltered. At a family gathering at Ella's, Taylor gushed about her sister's painting: "It is unbelievable what she has accomplished in so short a time. Of course she always had the gift—just never used it after her elementary school work in it. But now she is blossoming out—There's no telling how far she can go." Taylor to Janet Weisenfreund, March 25, 1973. The sisters constantly praised one another for their artistic achievements, occasionally even throwing in a nice word for their brothers' writing skills. Henny's attempts at pottery were a family joke, but even there, Taylor complimented her efforts.

83. Taylor to Marci Carafoli, January 20, 1977.
84. Ann Durell to Taylor, May 18, 1977.
85. Ann Durell to Taylor, June 29, 1977.
86. Taylor to Ann Durell, June 13, 1977.
87. A letter from Durell on July 21, 1977, shows she had not yet agreed to illustrations. On September 6, she informed Taylor that Gail Owens had agreed to illustrate the book in time for a spring 1978 publication.
88. Taylor to Ann Durell, November 20, 1977.
89. Taylor to Nettie Frishman, September 26, 1977. Taylor mentioned the New York project to Charlotte in a March 19, 1977, letter, in which she also said she had sent out "some beginning to read items."
90. Fannie Taylor died in Jerusalem on April 2, 1978, "in her 100th year." Obituary, *New York Times,* April 6, 1978. In 1972, Taylor had called her "blooming" mother-in-law a "tough old bird." Taylor to Sarah Lang, November 2, 1972. In 1975, however, she said Fannie had been sent to Lucille because Milton felt "she's beginning to be a drag in the store—pests the customers—etc." Taylor to Charlotte, August 15, 1975. In another letter to Charlotte of December 14, 1976, Taylor notes that Fannie looks perceptibly older and had begun to call Ralph at all hours of the night for medical concerns.
91. Nettie Frishman to Taylor, November 28, 1977.
92. Charlotte to Taylor, October 10, 1977.
93. Rae Rosenblum to Taylor, November 30, 1977.
94. Ralph to Walter Bergmann, October 13, 1977.

Afterword

1. Himber, *How to Survive Hearing Loss.*
2. Association of Jewish Libraries, "Sydney Taylor Book Award," https://jewishlibraries.org/Sydney_Taylor_Book_Award.
3. Undated speech, after the publication of *Downtown.*

Bibliography

Taped conversation between Ella Kornweitz and Charlotte Himber, letters until 1940, diaries, scrapbooks, travel journals, and drafts of speeches come from the collection of Jo Taylor Marshall.

Book drafts, financial documents, and correspondence after 1950 are from the Kerlan Collection at the University of Minnesota.

Joseph Brenner (AFC 2001/001/1014), Correspondence (MS02), Veterans History Project Collection, American Folklife Center, Library of Congress.

Interviews conducted by June Cummins:

   Susan Baker, January 2003, August 2005.

   Charlie Brenner, June 2005.

   Ethel Brenner, October and November 2003.

   Jerry Brenner, March 2007.

   Laurie Brenner, October 2004.

   Judy Magid, August and October 2003, September 2004.

   Harriet and Sheldon Schaffer, July and August 2004.

   Rhoda Schlamm, August 2006.

   Numerous interviews with Jo Taylor Marshall.

Written surveys of Cejwin alumni (Susan Addelston, Ina Bruskin, Jessica Shapiro Gribetz, Barbara Kirsh, Barbara Ain Lieberman, Judy Prigal, Judith Selsky, Carla Silver), June 2008.

Interviews conducted by Alexandra Dunietz with Susan Addelston, Judy Prigal, Esther Nelson, and Janet Weisenfreund, December 2017.

Armitage, Merle. *Martha Graham, the Early Years.* New York: Da Capo, 1978.

Barkai, Avraham. *Branching Out: German-Jewish Immigration to the United States, 1820–1914.* New York: Holmes & Meier, 1994.

Beck, Evelyn Torton. *Nice Jewish Girls: A Lesbian Anthology.* Boston: Beacon, 1989.

Beck, Nelson. "The Board of Directors of the Aguilar Free Library Society, 1886–1903: A Prosopographical Study." *Libri* 28, no. 1 (2009): 141–64.

Beim, Lorraine. *Carol's Side of the Street.* New York: Harcourt, 1951.

Berrol, Selma Cantor. "Education and Economic Mobility: The Jewish Experience in New York City, 1880–1920." *American Jewish Historical Quarterly* 65, no. 3 (March 1976): 257–71.

———. *Growing Up American: Immigrant Children in America, Then and Now.* London: Twayne, 1995.

———. "In Their Image: German Jews and the Americanization of the *Ost Juden* in New York City." *New York History* 63, no. 4 (October 1982): 417–33.

———. *Julia Richman: A Notable Woman.* Philadelphia: Balch Institute Press, 1993.

———. "School Days on the Old East Side: The Italian and Jewish Experience." *New York History* 57, no. 2 (April 1976): 200–213.

Brodkin, Karen. *How Jews Became White Folks and What That Says About Race in America.* New Brunswick, N.J.: Rutgers University Press, 1998.

Brumberg, Stephan F. *Going to America, Going to School: The Jewish Immigrant Public School Encounter in Turn-of-the-Century New York City.* New York: Praeger, 1986.

Buhle, Mari Jo. *Women and American Socialism, 1870–1920.* The Working Class in American History. Urbana: University of Illinois Press, 1981.

Buse, Dieter K. "Urban and National Identity: Bremen, 1860–1920." *Journal of Social History* 26, no. 3 (1993): 521–37.

Caro, Robert. *The Power Broker: Robert Moses and the Fall of New York.* New York: Alfred A. Knopf, 1974.

Cohen, Sol. *Progressives and Urban School Reform: The Public Education Association, of New York City, 1895–1954.* Teachers College Studies in Education. New York: Bureau of Publications, Teachers College, Columbia University, 1964.

Cremin, Lawrence A. *The Transformation of the School: Progressivism in American Education, 1876–1957.* New York: Alfred A. Knopf, 1961.

Cummins, June. "Becoming an 'All-of-a-Kind' American: Sydney Taylor and the Strategies of Assimilation." *The Lion and the Unicorn* 27, no. 3 (September 2003): 324–43.

———. "Leaning Left: Progressive Politics in Sydney Taylor's All-of-a-Kind Family Series." *Children's Literature Association Quarterly* 30, no. 4 (Winter 2005): 386–408.

———. "What Are Jewish Boys and Girls Made Of? Gender in Contemporary Jewish Teen and 'Tween Fiction." *Children's Literature Association Quarterly* 36, no. 3 (Fall 2011): 296–317.

Davis, Enid. *A Comprehensive Guide to Children's Literature with a Jewish Theme.* New York: Schocken Books, 1981.

de Lima, Agnes. *The Little Red School House.* New York: Macmillan, 1942.

d'Emilio, John. *Sexual Politics, Sexual Communities: The Making of a Homosexual Minority in the United States, 1940–1970.* 2nd ed. Chicago: University of Chicago Press, 1998.

de Mille, Agnes. *Martha: The Life and Work of Martha Graham.* New York: Random House, 1991.

Diner, Hasia R. *Lower East Side Memories: A Jewish Place in America.* Princeton, N.J.: Princeton University Press, 2000.

Eddy, Jacalyn. *Bookwomen: Creating an Empire in Children's Book Publishing, 1919–1939.* Madison: University of Wisconsin Press, 2006.

Ellis, Havelock. *Man and Woman: A Study of Human Secondary Sexual Characteristics.* London: Walter Scott, 1894.

Faderman, Lillian. *Odd Girls and Twilight Lovers: A History of Lesbian Life in Twentieth-Century America.* New York: Columbia University Press, 1991.

Feld, Marjorie N. *Lillian Wald: A Biography.* Chapel Hill: University of North Carolina Press, 2008.

Fischer, Claude S. *America Calling: A Social History of the Telephone to 1940.* Berkeley: University of California Press, 1992.

Fisher, Patricia, and Anne Perryman. "A Brief History: Bank Street College of Education." New York: Bank Street College of Education, 2000. http://educate. bankstreet.edu/books/1.

Foulkes, Julia L. *Modern Bodies: Dance and American Modernism from Martha Graham to Alvin Ailey.* Chapel Hill: University of North Carolina Press, 2002.

Franko, Mark. *Dancing Modernism/Performing Politics.* Bloomington: Indiana University Press, 1995.

Gershick, Zsa Zsa. *Gay Old Girls.* Los Angeles: Alyson Books, 1998.

Gilman, Phoebe. *Something from Nothing.* New York: Scholastic, 1992.

Glanz, Rudolf. *The German Jewish Woman.* Vol. 2 of *The Jewish Woman in America: Two Female Immigrant Generations, 1820–1929.* New York: Ktav, 1977.

Glenn, Susan A. *Daughters of the Shtetl: Life and Labor in the Immigrant Generation.* Ithaca, N.Y.: Cornell University Press, 1990.

Goldstein, Eric L. *The Price of Whiteness: Jews, Race, and American Identity.* Princeton, N.J.: Princeton University Press, 2006.

Goldstein, Fanny. "The Jewish Child in Bookland." *Jewish Book Annual* 5 (1946–47): 84–100.

Gordis, David M., and Yoav Ben-Horin. *Jewish Identity in America.* Los Angeles: Susan and David Wilstein Institute of Jewish Policy Studies, 1991.

Graff, Ellen. *Stepping Left: Dance and Politics in New York City, 1928–1942.* Durham, N.C.: Duke University Press, 1997.

Grinberg, Jaime G. A. *Teaching Like That: The Beginnings of Teacher Education at Bank Street.* New York: P. Lang, 2005.

Hagen, William W. *Germans, Poles, and Jews: The Nationality Conflict in the Prussian East, 1772–1914.* Chicago: University of Chicago Press, 1980.

Hall, Radclyffe. *The Well of Loneliness.* New York: Anchor Books, 1990.

Heinze, Andrew R. *Adapting to Abundance: Jewish Immigrants, Mass Consumption, and the Search for American Identity.* New York: Columbia University Press, 1990.

Hermalyn, Gary. *Morris High School and the Creation of the New York City Public High School System.* Bronx, N.Y.: The Bronx County Historical Society, 1995.

Higham, John. *Send These to Me: Immigrants in Urban America.* Baltimore: Johns Hopkins University Press, 1984.

Himber, Charlotte. *Famous in Their Twenties.* New York: Association Press, 1942.

———. *How to Survive Hearing Loss.* Washington, D.C.: Gallaudet University Press, 1989.

———. "Touched with Fire." Unpublished manuscript in 2 volumes made available by Susan Baker.

Hollinger, David A. *Postethnic America: Beyond Multiculturalism.* New York: Basic-Books, 1995.

Horosko, Marian. *Martha Graham: The Evolution of Her Dance Theory and Training.* Gainesville: University Press of Florida, 2002.

Hunt, Mabel Leigh. *Ladycake Farm.* Philadelphia: J. B. Lippincott, 1952.

Hunter, Jane. *How Young Ladies Became Girls: The Victorian Origins of American Girlhood.* New Haven: Yale University Press, 2002.

Isaacs, Stephen D. *Jews and American Politics.* Garden City, N.Y.: Doubleday, 1974.

Ish-Kishor, Judith. *Joel Is the Youngest.* New York: J. Messner, 1954.

Joselit, Jenna Weissman. *New York's Jewish Jews: The Orthodox Community in the Interwar Years.* Bloomington: Indiana University Press, 1990.

———. "Reading, Writing, and a Library Card: New York Jews and the New York Public Library." *Biblion: The Bulletin of the New York Public Library* 5 (Fall 1996): 97–117.

———. *The Wonders of America: Reinventing Jewish Culture 1880–1950.* New York: Hill & Wang, 1994.

Joselit, Jenna Weissman, and Karen S. Mittelman. *A Worthy Use of Summer: Jewish Summer Camping in America.* Philadelphia: National Museum of American Jewish History, 1993.

Josephson, Matthew. *Infidel in the Temple.* New York: Knopf, 1967.

Kaplan, Marion A. *Jewish Daily Life in Germany, 1618–1945.* New York: Oxford University Press, 2005.

———. *The Making of the Jewish Middle Class: Women, Family, and Identity in Imperial Germany.* New York: Oxford University Press, 1994.

Kelley, Ruth Edna. *The Book of Hallowe'en.* Boston: Lothrop, Lee & Shepard, 1919.

Klapper, Melissa R. *Jewish Girls Coming of Age in America, 1860–1920.* New York: New York University Press, 2005.

Kranson, Rachel. *Ambivalent Embrace: Jewish Upward Mobility in Postwar America.* Chapel Hill: University of North Carolina Press, 2017.

Krasner, Jonathan B. *The Benderly Boys and American Jewish Education.* Brandeis Series in American Jewish History, Culture, and Life. Waltham, Mass.: Brandeis University Press, 2011.

Landau-Brijatoff, Alix. *Indignes d'être français: Dénaturalisés et déchus sous Vichy.* Paris: Buchet/Chastel, 2013.

———. *Tombes lointaines: Le destin tragique d'une femme dans la "Shoah par balles."* Paris: Laffont, 2009.

Lee, Robert. "Urban Labor Markets, In-Migration, and Demographic Growth: Bremen, 1815–1914." *Journal of Interdisciplinary History* 30, no. 3 (2000): 437–73.

Lenhart, Gary. *The Stamp of Class: Reflections on Poetry and Social Class.* Ann Arbor: University of Michigan Press, 2006.

Lewiton, Mina. *Rachel and Herman.* New York: F. Watts, 1957.

Liebman, Arthur. *Jews and the Left.* New York: Wiley, 1979.

LoMonaco, Martha Schmoyer. *Every Week, a Broadway Revue: The Tamiment Playhouse, 1921–1960.* New York: Greenwood, 1992.

Lowery, Ruth McKoy. *Immigrants in Children's Literature.* New York: P. Lang, 2000.

Lutz, Tom. *Cosmopolitan Vistas: American Regionalism and Literary Value.* Ithaca, N.Y.: Cornell University Press, 2004.

Lynd, Helen Merrell. *Field Work in College Education.* Sarah Lawrence College Publications. New York: Columbia University Press, 1945.

Madden, Dorothy Gifford. *You Call Me Louis, Not Mr. Horst.* Amsterdam: Harwood Academic, 1996.

Marcus, Eric. *Making Gay History: The Half-Century Fight for Lesbian and Gay Equal Rights.* New York: Perennial, 2002.

Marcus, Leonard S. *Minders of Make-Believe: Idealists, Entrepreneurs, and the Shaping of American Children's Literature.* Boston: Houghton Mifflin, 2008.

Marks, Patricia. *Bicycles, Bangs, and Bloomers: The New Woman in the Popular Press.* Lexington: University Press of Kentucky, 1990.

Martin, Michelle H. *Brown Gold: Milestones of African-American Children's Picture Books, 1845–2002.* New York: Routledge, 2004.

Mauch, Christof, and Joe Salmons. *German-Jewish Identities in America.* Madison, Wisc.: Max Kade Institute for German-American Studies, 2003.

McDonagh, Don. *Martha Graham: A Biography.* New York: Praeger, 1973.

Mendes-Flohr, Paul R. *German Jews: A Dual Identity.* New Haven: Yale University Press, 1999.

Meyer, Michael A., ed. *German-Jewish History in Modern Times.* Vol. 3: *Integration in Dispute, 1871–1918.* New York: Columbia University Press, 1996.

Mickenberg, Julia. "The Pedagogy of the Popular Front: 'Progressive Parenting' for a New Generation, 1918–1945." In *The American Child: A Cultural Studies Reader,* edited by Caroline Levander and Carol Singley, 226–45. New Brunswick, N.J.: Rutgers University Press, 2003.

Mishler, Paul C. *Raising Reds: The Young Pioneers, Radical Summer Camps, and Communist Political Culture in the United States.* New York: Columbia University Press, 1999.

Moore, Deborah Dash. *GI Jews: How World War II Changed a Generation.* Cambridge: Belknap Press of Harvard University Press, 2004.

Munroe, Ruth Learned. *Teaching the Individual.* New York: Columbia University Press, 1942.

Nel, Philip. *Crockett Johnson and Ruth Krauss: How an Unlikely Couple Found Love, Dodged the FBI, and Transformed Children's Literature.* Jackson: University Press of Mississippi, 2012.

Newell, William Wells. *Games and Songs of American Children, Collected and Compared.* New York: Dover, 1963.

Opalski, Magdalena, and Israel Bartal. *Poles and Jews: A Failed Brotherhood.* The Tauber Institute for the Study of European Jewry Series. Hanover, N.H.: University Press of New England, 1992.

Peiss, Kathy Lee. *Cheap Amusements: Working Women and Leisure in Turn-of-the-Century New York.* Philadelphia: Temple University Press, 1986.

———. *Hope in a Jar: The Making of America's Beauty Culture.* New York: Metropolitan Books, 1998.

Plesur, Milton. *Jewish Life in Twentieth-Century America: Challenge and Accommodation.* Chicago: Nelson-Hall, 1982.

Ravitch, Diane. *The Great School Wars: A History of the New York City Public Schools.* Baltimore: Johns Hopkins University Press, 2000.

Rischin, Moses. *The Promised City: New York's Jews, 1870–1914.* Cambridge: Harvard University Press, 1962.

Rosengarten, Theodore, and Dale Rosengarten, eds. *A Portion of the People: Three Hundred Years of Southern Jewish Life.* Columbia: University of South Carolina Press, in association with McKissick Museum, 2002.

Roskolenko, Harry. *The Time That Was Then: The Lower East Side, 1900–1914—An Intimate Chronicle.* New York: Dial Press, 1971.

Ruderman, David B. "Greenville Diary: A Northern Rabbi Confronts the Deep South, 1966–70." *Jewish Quarterly Review* 94, no. 4 (Fall 2004): 643–65.

Sargeant, Winthrop. *In Spite of Myself: A Personal Memoir.* Garden City, N.Y.: Doubleday, 1970.

Sarna, Jonathan. "The Crucial Decade in American Camping." In *A Place of Our Own: The Rise of Reform Jewish Camping,* edited by Michael Lorge and Gary Zola, 27–51. Tuscaloosa: University of Alabama Press, 2006.

Sayers, Frances Clarke. *Anne Carroll Moore: A Biography.* New York: Atheneum, 1972.

Schmidt, Gary D. *Making Americans: Children's Literature from 1930 to 1960.* Iowa City: University of Iowa Press, 2013.

Schoener, Allon, and Jewish Museum [New York]. *Portal to America: The Lower East Side, 1870–1925.* New York: Henry Holt, 1967.

Schoolman, Albert P. "The Jewish Educational Summer Camp: A Survey of Its Development and Implications." *Jewish Education* 17, no. 3 (June 1946): 6–15.

Sellers, Kelli M. "Tossing the Pink Parasol: *Rebecca of Sunnybrook Farm,* the New Woman, and Progressive Era Reform." *Children's Literature* 40 (2012): 108–30.

Shadur, Joseph, and Yehudit Shadur. *Traditional Jewish Papercuts: An Inner World of Art and Symbol.* Hanover, N.H.: University Press of New England, 2002.

Shpak-Lisak, Rivkah. *Pluralism and Progressives: Hull House and the New Immigrants, 1890–1919.* Chicago: University of Chicago Press, 1989.

Silver, Linda R. *Best Jewish Books for Children and Teens.* Philadelphia: Jewish Publication Society, 2010.

Sinclair, Jo [Ruth Seid]. *Wasteland.* New York: Harper & Brothers, 1946.

Sochen, June. *The New Woman: Feminism in Greenwich Village, 1910–1920.* New York: Quadrangle Books, 1972.

Sollors, Werner. *Beyond Ethnicity: Consent and Descent in American Culture.* New York: Oxford University Press, 1986.

Sorin, Gerald. *Tradition Transformed: The Jewish Experience in America.* Baltimore: Johns Hopkins University Press, 1997.

Spewack, Bella Cohen. *Streets: A Memoir of the Lower East Side.* New York: Feminist Press at the City University of New York, 1995.

Stanislawski, Michael. *Autobiographical Jews: Essays in Jewish Self-Fashioning.* The Samuel & Althea Stroum Lectures in Jewish Studies. Seattle: University of Washington Press, 2004.

Steinberg, Stephen. *The Ethnic Myth: Race, Ethnicity, and Class in America.* 3rd ed. Boston: Beacon, 2001.

Stodelle, Ernestine. *Deep Song: The Dance Story of Martha Graham.* New York: G. Schirmer Books, 1984.

Sutton-Smith, Brian. "The Kissing Games of Adolescents in Ohio." *Midwest Folklore* 9, no. 4 (Winter 1959): 189–211.

Taback, Simms. *Joseph Had a Little Overcoat.* New York: Viking, 1977.

Tessman, Lisa, and Bat-Ami Bar On, eds. *Jewish Locations: Traversing Racialized Landscapes.* Lanham, Md.: Rowman & Littlefield, 2001.

Thompson, Helen Bradford. *The Mental Traits of Sex: An Experimental Investigation of the Normal Mind in Men and Women.* Chicago: University of Chicago Press, 1903.

Thorndike, Edward L. *The Elements of Psychology.* New York: A. G. Seiler, 1905.

Tomko, Linda J. *Dancing Class: Gender, Ethnicity, and Social Divides in American Dance, 1890–1920.* Bloomington: Indiana University Press, 1999.

Van Slyck, Abigail Ayres. *A Manufactured Wilderness: Summer Camps and the Shaping of American Youth, 1890–1960.* Minneapolis: University of Minnesota Press, 2006.

Wald, Lillian D. *The House on Henry Street.* 1915; New York: Dover, 1971.

———. *Windows on Henry Street.* Boston: Little, Brown, 1934.

Walkowitz, Daniel J. *Working with Class: Social Workers and the Politics of Middle-Class Identity.* Chapel Hill: University of North Carolina Press, 1999.

Warren, Constance. *A New Design for Women's Education.* New York: Frederick A. Stokes, 1940.

Wenger, Beth S. *History Lessons: The Creation of American Jewish Heritage.* Princeton, N.J.: Princeton University Press, 2010.

————. *New York Jews and the Great Depression: Uncertain Promise.* New Haven: Yale University Press, 1996.

Wiegand, Wayne A. *"An Active Instrument for Propaganda": The American Public Library During World War I.* New York: Greenwood, 1989.

Zipes, Jack. *The Brothers Grimm: From Enchanted Forests to the Modern World.* New York: Palgrave Macmillan, 2002.

Index